Tcl and the Tk Toolkit

Addison-Wesley Professional Computing Series

Brian W. Kernighan, Consulting Editor

Tcl and the Tk Toolkit

John K. Ousterhout

ADDISON-WESLEY PUBLISHING COMPANY

Reading, Massachusetts   Menlo Park, California   New York
Don Mills, Ontario   Wokingham, England   Amsterdam   Bonn
Sydney   Singapore   Tokyo   Madrid   San Juan
Paris   Seoul   Milan   Mexico City   Taipei

The publisher offers discounts on this book when ordered in quantity for special sales. For more information please contact:

Corporate & Professional Publishing Group
Addison-Wesley Publishing Company
One Jacob Way
Reading, Massachusetts 01867

Library of Congress Cataloging-in-Publication Data

Ousterhout, John K.
     Tcl and the Tk toolkit / John K. Ousterhout.
          p.   cm.
     Includes index.
     ISBN 0-201-63337-X (alk. paper)
     1. Tcl (Computer program language)   2. Tk toolkit.   I. Title.
QA76.73.T44097   1994
005.13'3--dc20   93-49567
                                                                      CIP

Cover art by Michael J. McLennan and Sani R. Nassif

ISBN 0-201-63337-X

Printed on recycled and acid-free paper.
5 6 7 8 9 10 11 -CRW-98979695
Fifth printing, July 1995

To Rita, Kay, and Amy

Contents

Part II: Writing Scripts for Tk

Part III: Writing Tcl Applications in C

Part IV: Tk's C Interfaces

Preface

Tcl was born of frustration. In the early 1980s my students and I developed a number of interactive tools at the University of California at Berkeley, mostly for integrated circuit design, and we found ourselves spending a lot of time building bad command languages. Each tool needed to have a command language of some sort, but our main interest was in the tool rather than its command language. We spent as little time as possible on the command language and always ended up with a language that was weak and quirky. Furthermore, the command language for one tool was never quite right for the next tool, so we ended up building a new bad command language for each tool. This became increasingly frustrating.

In the fall of 1987 it occurred to me that the solution was to build a reusable command language. If a general-purpose scripting language could be built as a C library package, then perhaps it could be reused for many different purposes in many different applications. Of course, the language would need to be extensible so that each application could add its own specific features to the core provided by the library. In the spring of 1988 I decided to implement such a language, and the result was Tcl.

Tk was also born of frustration. The basic idea for Tk arose in response to Apple's announcement of HyperCard in the fall of 1987. HyperCard generated tremendous excitement because of the power of the system and the way in which it allowed many different interactive elements to be scripted and work together. However, I was discouraged. The HyperCard system had obviously taken a large development effort, and it seemed unlikely to me that a small group such as a university research project could ever mount such a massive effort. This suggested that we would not be able to participate in the development of new forms of interactive software in the future.

I concluded that the only hope for us was a component approach. Rather than building a new application as a self-contained monolith with hundreds of thousands of lines of code, we needed to find a way to divide applications into many smaller reusable components. Ideally each component would be small enough to be implemented by a small group, and interesting applications could be created by assembling components. In this environment it should be possible to create an exciting new application by developing one new component and then combining it with existing components.

The component-based approach requires a powerful and flexible "glue" for assembling the components, and it occurred to me that perhaps a shared scripting language could provide that glue. Out of this thinking grew Tk, an X11 toolkit based on Tcl. Tk allows components to be either individual user-interface controls or entire applications; in either case components can be developed independently and Tcl can be used to assemble the components and communicate between them.

I started writing Tcl and Tk as a hobby in my spare time. As other people began to use the systems I found myself spending more and more time on them, to the point where today they occupy almost all of my waking hours and many of my sleeping ones.

Tcl and Tk have succeeded beyond my wildest dreams. The Tcl/Tk developer community now numbers in the tens of thousands and there are thousands of Tcl applications in existence or under development. The application areas for Tcl and Tk cover virtually the entire spectrum of graphical and engineering applications, including computer-aided design, software development, testing, instrument control, scientific visualization, and multimedia. Tcl is used by itself in many applications, and Tcl and Tk are used together in many others. Tcl and Tk are being used by hundreds of companies, large and small, as well as universities and research laboratories.

One benefit that came as a surprise to me is that it is possible to create interesting graphical user interfaces (GUIs) entirely as Tcl scripts. I had always assumed that every Tcl application would contain some new C code that implements new Tcl commands, plus some Tcl scripts that combine the new commands with the built-in facilities provided by Tcl. However, once a simple Tcl/Tk application called `wish` became available, many people began creating user interfaces by writing Tcl scripts for it, without writing any C code at all! It turned out that the Tcl and Tk commands provide a high-level interface to GUI programming that hides many of the details faced by a C programmer. As a result, it is much easier to learn how to use `wish` than a C-based toolkit, and user interfaces can be written with much less code. Most Tcl/Tk users never write any C code at all and most of the Tcl/Tk applications consist solely of Tcl scripts.

This book is intended as an introduction to Tcl and Tk for programmers who plan to write or modify Tcl/Tk applications. I assume that readers have programmed in C and have at least passing familiarity with a shell such as `sh` or `csh` or `ksh`. I also assume that readers have used the X Window System and are familiar with basic ideas such as using the mouse, resizing windows, etc. No prior experience with Tcl or Tk is needed in order to read this book, and you need not have written X applications using other toolkits such as Motif.

The book is organized so that you can learn Tcl without learning Tk if you wish. Also, the discussion of how to write Tcl scripts is separate from the discussion of how to use the C library interfaces provided by Tcl and Tk. The first two parts of the book describe Tcl and Tk at the level of writing scripts, and the last two parts describe the C interfaces for Tcl and Tk; if you are like the majority of Tcl/Tk users who only write scripts, you can stop after reading the first two parts.

In spite of my best efforts, I'm sure that there are errors in this edition of the book. I'm interested in hearing about any problems that you encounter, whether they are typos, formatting errors, sections or ideas that are hard to understand, or bugs in the examples. I'll attempt to correct the problems in future printings of the book. The best way to report problems is with electronic mail sent to `tclbookbugs@cs.berkeley.edu`.

Many people have helped in the creation of this book. First and foremost I would like to thank Brian Kernighan, who reviewed several drafts of the manuscript with almost terrifying thoroughness and uncovered numerous problems both large and small. I am also grateful for the detailed comments provided by the other Addison-Wesley technical reviewers: Richard Blevins, Gerard Holzmann, Curt Horkey, Ron Hutchins, Stephen Johnson, Oliver Jones, David Korn, Bill Leggett, Don Libes, Kent Margraf, Stuart McRobert, David Richardson, Alexei Rodrigues, Gerald Rosenberg, John Slater, and Win Treese. Thanks also to Bob Sproull, who read the next-to-last draft from cover to cover and provided countless bug fixes and suggestions.

I made early drafts of the manuscript available to the Tcl/Tk community via the Internet and received countless comments and suggestions from all over the world in return. I'm afraid that I didn't keep careful enough records to acknowledge all the people who contributed in this way, but the list of contributors includes at least the following people: Marvin Aguero, Miriam Amos Nihart, Jim Anderson, Frederik Anheuser, Jeff Blaine, John Boller, David Boyce, Terry Brannon, Richard Campbell, J. Cazander, Wen Chen, Richard Cheung, Peter Chubb, De Clarke, Peter Collinson, Peter Costantinidis, Alistair Crooks, Peter Davies, Tal Dayan, Akim Demaille, Mark Diekhans, Matthew Dillon, Tuan Doan, Tony Duarte, Paul DuBois, Anton Eliens, Marc R. Ewing, Luis Fernandes, Martin Forssen, Ben Fried, Matteo Frigo, Andrej Gabara, Steve Gaede, Sanjay Ghemawat, Bob Gibson, Michael Halle, Jun Hamano, Stephen Hansen, Brian Harrison, Marti Hearst, Fergus Henderson, Kevin Hendrix, David Herron, Patrick Hertel, Carsten Heyl, Leszek Holenderski, Jamie Honan, Rob W.W. Hooft, Nick Hounsome, Christopher Hylands, Jonathan Jowett, Poul-Henning Kamp, Karen L. Karavanic, Sunil Khatri, Vivek Khera, Jon Knight, Roger Knopf, Ramkumar Krishnan, Dave Kristol, Peter LaBelle, Tor-Erik Larsen, Tom Legrady, Will E. Leland, Kim Lester, Joshua Levy, Don Libes, Oscar Linares, David C.P. Linden, Toumas J. Lukka, Steve Lord, Steve Lumetta, Earlin Lutz, David J. Mackenzie, B.G. Mahesh, John Maline, Graham Mark, Stuart McRobert, George Moon, Michael Morris, Russell Nelson, Dale K. Newby, Richard Newton, Peter Nguyen, David Nichols, Marty Olevitch, Rita Ousterhout, John Pierce, Stephen Pietrowicz, Anna Pluzhnikov, Nico Poppelier, M.V.S. Ramanath, Cary D. Renzema, Mark Roseman, Samir Tiongson Saxena, Jay Schmidgall, Dan M. Serachitopol, Hume Smith, Frank Stajano, Larry Streepy, John E.

Stump, Michael Sullivan, Holger Teutsch, Bennett E. Todd, Glenn Trewitt, D.A. Vaughan-Pope, Richard Vieregge, Larry W. Virden, David Waitzman, Matt Wartell, Glenn Waters, Wally Wedel, Juergen Weigert, Mark Weiser, Brent Welch, Alex Woo, Su-Lin Wu, Kawata Yasuro, Chut Ngeow Yee, Richard Yen, Stephen Ching-Sing Yen, and Mike Young.

Many many people have made significant contributions to the development of Tcl and Tk. Without all of their efforts there would have been nothing of interest to write about in this book. Although I cannot hope to acknowledge all the people who helped to make Tcl and Tk what they are today, I would like to thank the following people specially: Don Libes, for writing the first widely used Tcl application; Mark Diekhans and Karl Lehenbauer, for TclX; Alastair Fyfe, for supporting the early development of Tcl; Mary Ann May-Pumphrey, for developing the original Tcl test suite; George Howlett, Michael McLennan, and Sani Nassif, for the BLT extensions; Kevin Kenny, for showing that Tcl can be used to communicate with almost any imaginable program; Joel Bartlett, for many challenging conversations and for inspiring Tk's canvas widget with his ezd program; Larry Rowe, for developing Tcl-DP and for providing general advice and support; Sven Delmas, for developing the XF application builder based on Tk; and Andrew Payne, for the widget tour and for meritorious Tcl evangelism.

Several companies have provided financial support for the development of Tcl and Tk, including Digital Equipment Corporation, Hewlett-Packard Corporation, Sun Microsystems, and Computerized Processes Unlimited. I am particularly grateful to Digital's Western Research Laboratory and its director, Richard Swan, for providing me with a one-day-per-week hideaway where I could go to gather my thoughts and work on Tcl and Tk.

Terry Lessard-Smith and Bob Miller have provided fabulous administrative support for this and all my other projects. I don't know how I would get anything done without them.

Finally, I owe a special debt to my colleague and friend Dave Patterson, whose humor and sage advice have inspired and shaped much of my professional career, and to my wife Rita and daughters Kay and Amy, who have tolerated my workaholic tendencies with more cheer and affection than I deserve.

Berkeley, California   John Ousterhout
February, 1994

Chapter 1
Introduction

1.1 Introduction

This book is about two software packages called Tcl and Tk. Together they provide a programming system for developing and using graphical user interface (GUI) applications. Tcl is a simple scripting language for controlling and extending applications; its name stands for "tool command language". Tcl provides generic programming facilities, such as variables and loops and procedures, that are useful for a variety of applications. Furthermore, Tcl is *embeddable*. Its interpreter is a library of C procedures that can easily be incorporated into applications, and each application can extend the core Tcl features with additional commands for that application.

One of the most useful extensions to Tcl is Tk, which is a toolkit for the X Window System. Tk extends the core Tcl facilities with commands for building user interfaces, so that you can construct Motif-like user interfaces by writing Tcl scripts instead of C code. Like Tcl, Tk is implemented as a library of C procedures so it can be used in many different applications. Individual applications can also extend the base Tk features with new user-interface widgets and geometry managers written in C.

Together, Tcl and Tk provide four benefits to application developers and users. The first benefit is rapid development. Many interesting GUI applications can be written entirely as Tcl scripts, using a windowing shell called `wish`. This allows you to program at a much higher level than you would in C or C++, and Tk hides many of the details that C programmers must address. Compared to toolkits where you program in C, such as the Motif toolkit, there is much less to learn in order to use Tcl and Tk and much less code to write. New Tcl/Tk users can often create interesting user interfaces after just a few hours of learning, and many people have reported tenfold reductions in code size and development time when they switched from other toolkits to Tcl and Tk.

Another reason for rapid development with Tcl and Tk is that Tcl is an interpreted language. When you use a Tcl application such as wish, you can generate and execute new scripts on the fly without recompiling or restarting the application. This allows you to test out new ideas and fix bugs rapidly. Since Tcl is interpreted, it executes more slowly than compiled C code, of course, but modern workstations are surprisingly fast. For example, you can execute scripts with hundreds of Tcl commands on each movement of the mouse with no perceptible delay. In the rare cases where performance becomes an issue, you can reimplement the performance-critical parts of your Tcl scripts in C.

The second benefit is that Tcl makes it easy for applications to have powerful scripting languages. To create a new application, all you need do is implement a few new Tcl commands that provide the basic features of the application. Then you can link your new commands with the Tcl library to produce a full-function scripting language that includes both the commands provided by Tcl (called the *Tcl core*) and those that you wrote, as in Figure 1.1(a).

For example, an application for reading electronic bulletin boards might contain C code that implements one Tcl command to query a bulletin board for new messages and another Tcl command to retrieve a given message. Once these commands exist, Tcl scripts can be written to cycle through the new messages from all the bulletin boards and display them one at a time, or keep a record in disk files of which messages have been read and which haven't, or search one or more bulletin boards for messages on a particular topic. Users of the application could write additional Tcl scripts to add more functions to the application.

The third benefit of Tcl is that it makes an excellent "glue language." A Tcl application can include many different library packages, each of which provides an interesting set of Tcl commands, as in Figure 1.1(b). Tk is one example of a library package; many other packages have been developed by the Tcl/Tk community, and you can also write your own packages. Tcl scripts for such an application can include commands from any of the packages.

Tcl scripts can also be used as a communication mechanism to allow different applications to work together. For example, any windowing application based on Tk can send a Tcl script to any other Tk application to be executed there. This feature makes multimedia effects much more accessible: once audio and video applications have been built with Tk (and several exist already), any Tk application can issue record and play commands to them. In addition, spreadsheets can update themselves from database applications, user-interface editors can modify the appearance and behavior of live applications as they run, and so on. Tcl's use of a common interpreted language for communication between applications is more powerful and flexible than static approaches such as Microsoft's OLE and Sun Microsystem's ToolTalk.

The fourth benefit of Tcl is user convenience. Once you learn Tcl and Tk, you will be able to write scripts for any Tcl and Tk application merely by learning the few application-

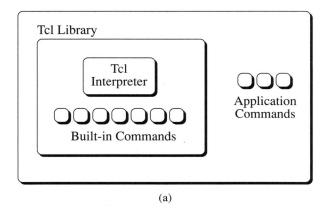

(a)

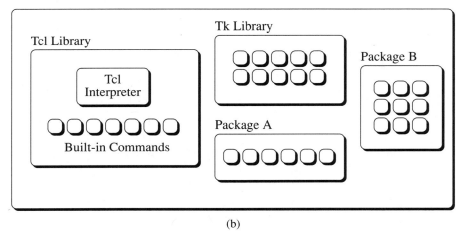

(b)

Figure 1.1. Examples of Tcl applications. A simple application might consist of the Tcl interpreter plus a few application-specific commands, as in (a). A more complex application might include the commands defined by Tk plus additional commands defined by other packages, as in (b).

specific commands for the new application. This should make it possible for more users to personalize and enhance their applications.

1.2 Organization of the book

Chapter 2 uses several simple scripts to provide a quick overview of the most important features of Tcl and Tk. It is intended to give you the flavor of the systems and convince you that they are useful, without explaining anything in detail. The remainder of the book goes through everything again in a more comprehensive fashion. It is divided into four parts:

- **Part I** introduces the Tcl scripting language. After reading this section you will be able to write scripts for Tcl applications. You will need to know at least some of this part in order to write Tk applications.

- **Part II** describes the additional Tcl commands provided by Tk, which allow you to create user-interface widgets such as menus and scrollbars and arrange them in windowing applications. After reading this section you will be able to create new windowing application as `wish` scripts and write scripts to enhance existing Tk applications.

- **Part III** discusses the C procedures in the Tcl library and how to use them to create new Tcl commands. After reading this section you will be able to write new Tcl packages and applications in C. However, you will be able to do a great deal (perhaps everything you need) without this information.

- **Part IV** describes Tk's library procedures. After reading this section you will be able to create new widgets and geometry managers in C. You will probably only need this material if you are writing a major new Tk application that requires new widgets.

Each of these parts contains about 10 short chapters. Each chapter is intended to be a self-contained description of a piece of the system, and you need not necessarily read the chapters in order. I recommend that you start by reading through Chapters 2 through 8 quickly, then skip to Chapters 15 through 19, then read other chapters as you need them.

Not every feature of Tcl and Tk is covered here, and the explanations are organized to provide a smooth introduction rather than a complete reference source. A separate set of reference manual entries is available with the Tcl and Tk distributions. These are much more terse but they cover absolutely every feature of both systems. I will refer to this information as the *reference documentation* for Tcl and Tk. Appendix A describes how to retrieve the Tcl and Tk distributions, including reference documentation, via the Internet.

This book assumes that you are familiar with the C programming language as defined by the ANSI C standard and that you have some experience with UNIX and X. To understand Part IV you will need to understand many of the features provided by the Xlib interface, such as graphics contexts and window attributes; however, these details are not necessary except in Part IV. You need not know anything about either Tcl or Tk before reading this book; both of them will be introduced from scratch.

1.3   **Notation**

Throughout the book I use a `Courier` font for anything that might be typed to a computer, such as Tcl scripts, C code, and names of variables, procedures, and commands. The examples of Tcl scripts use notation like the following:

```
    set a 44
⇒  44
```

Tcl commands, such as `set a 44` in the example, appear in Courier; their results, such as *44* in the example, appear in slanted Courier. The ⇒ symbol before the result indicates that this is a normal return value. If an error occurs in a Tcl command, the error message appears in Courier oblique, preceded by a ∅ symbol to indicate that this is an error rather than a normal return:

```
    set a 44 55
∅  wrong # args: should be "set varName ?newValue?"
```

When describing the syntax of Tcl commands, slanted Courier is used for formal argument names. If an argument or group of arguments is enclosed in question marks it means that the arguments are optional. For example, the syntax of the `set` command is as follows:

```
    set varName ?newValue?
```

This means that the word `set` must be entered verbatim to invoke the command, while *varName* and *newValue* are the names of `set`'s arguments; when invoking the command you type a variable name instead of *varName* and a new value for the variable instead of *newValue*. The *newValue* argument is optional.

1.4   **Pronunciation**

The official pronunciation for Tcl is "tickle", although "tee-see-ell" is also used frequently. Tk is pronounced "tee-kay."

1.5   **Versions**

This book corresponds to Tcl version 7.3 and Tk version 3.6.

Chapter 2
An Overview of Tcl and Tk

This chapter introduces Tcl and Tk with a series of scripts illustrating the main features of the systems. Although you should be able to start writing simple scripts after reading this chapter, the explanations here are not complete. All of the information in this chapter will be revisited in more detail in later chapters, and several important aspects, such as the Tcl and Tk C interfaces, are not discussed at all in this chapter. The purpose of this chapter is to show you the overall structure of Tcl and Tk and the kinds of things they can do, so that when individual features are discussed in detail you'll be able to see why they are useful.

2.1 Getting started

To invoke Tcl scripts, you must run a Tcl application. If Tcl is installed on your system, there should exist a simple Tcl shell application called `tclsh`, which you can use to try out some of the examples in this chapter. If Tcl has not been installed on your system, refer to Appendix A for information on how to obtain and install it. Then type the command

```
tclsh
```

to your shell to invoke `tclsh`. `tclsh` will start up in interactive mode, reading Tcl commands from the keyboard and passing them to the Tcl interpreter for evaluation. For starters, type the following command to `tclsh`:

```
expr 2 + 2
```

`tclsh` will print the result (4) and prompt you for another command.

This example illustrates several features of Tcl. First, Tcl commands are similar in form to shell commands. Each command consists of one or more *words* separated by spaces or tabs. In the example there are four words: expr, 2, +, and 2. The first word of each command is its name: the name selects a C procedure in the application that will carry out the function of the command. The other words are *arguments* that are passed to the C procedure. expr is one of the core commands provided by the Tcl library, so it exists in every Tcl application. It concatenates its arguments into a single string and evaluates the string as an arithmetic expression.

Each Tcl command returns a result string. For the expr command the result is the value of the expression. Results are always returned as strings, so expr converts its numerical result back to a string in order to return it. If a command has no meaningful result, it returns an empty string.

From now on I will use notation such as the following to describe examples:

```
expr 2 + 2
⇒  4
```

The first line is the command you type and the second line is the result returned by the command. The ⇒ symbol indicates that the line contains a return value; the ⇒ will not actually be printed out by tclsh. I will omit return values in cases where they aren't important, such as sequences of commands where only the last command's result matters.

Commands are normally terminated by newlines, so each line that you type to tclsh normally becomes a separate command. Semicolons also act as command separators, in case you wish to enter multiple commands on a single line. It is also possible for a single command to span multiple lines; you'll see how to do this later.

The expr command supports an expression syntax similar to that of expressions in ANSI C, including the same precedence rules and most of the C operators. Here are a few examples that you could type to tclsh:

```
expr 3 << 2
⇒  12
expr 14.1*6
⇒  84.6
expr (3 > 4) || (6 <= 7)
⇒  1
```

The first example illustrates the bitwise left-shift operator <<. The second example shows that expressions can contain real values as well as integer values. The last example shows the use of relational operators > and <= and the logical OR operator ||. As in C, Boolean results are represented numerically with 1 for true and 0 for false.

To leave tclsh, invoke the exit command:

```
exit
```

This command terminates the application and returns you to your shell.

Figure 2.1. The "hello world" application. All of the decorations around the "Hello, world!" button are provided by the mwm window manager. If you use a different window manager, your decorations may be different.

2.2 Hello world with Tk

Although Tcl provides a full set of programming features such as variables, loops, and procedures, it is not usually used by itself. Tcl is intended to be used as part of applications that contain their own Tcl commands in addition to those in the Tcl core. The application-specific extensions provide interesting primitives and Tcl is used to assemble the primitives into useful functions. It is easier to understand Tcl's facilities if you have seen some application-specific commands to use with Tcl.

One of the most interesting extensions to Tcl is the set of windowing commands provided by the Tk toolkit. Most of the examples in the book will use an application called wish ("windowing shell"), which is similar to tclsh except that it also includes the commands defined by Tk. Tk's commands allow you to create graphical user interfaces. If Tcl and Tk have been installed on your system, you can invoke wish from your shell just as you did for tclsh; it will display a small empty window on your screen and then read commands from standard input. Here is a simple wish script:

```
button .b -text "Hello, world!" -command exit
pack .b
```

If you type these two Tcl commands to wish, the window's appearance will change to that shown in Figure 2.1. If you move the pointer over the "Hello, world!" text and click mouse button 1, which is the left-most button in most configurations, the window will disappear and wish will exit.

Several things about this example need explanation. First let us deal with the syntactic issues. The example contains two commands, button and pack, both of which are implemented by Tk. Although these commands do not look like the expr command in the previous section, they have the same basic structure as all Tcl commands: one or more words separated by white space. The button command contains six words and the pack command contains two words.

The fourth word of the button command is enclosed in double quotes. This allows the word to include white space characters; without the quotes, Hello, and world! would be separate words. The double quotes are not part of the word itself; they are removed by the Tcl interpreter before the command is executed.

For the `expr` command the word structure doesn't matter much since `expr` concatenates all its arguments together. However, for the `button` and `pack` commands, and for most Tcl commands, the word structure is important. The `button` command expects its first argument to be the name of a new window to create. The following arguments must come in pairs, where the first argument of each pair is the name of a *configuration option* and the second argument is a value for that option. Thus if the double quotes were omitted, the value of the `-text` option would be `Hello`, and `world!` would be treated as the name of a separate configuration option. Since there is no option defined with the name `world!` the command would return an error.

Now let us move on to the behavior of the commands. The basic building block for a graphical user interface in Tk is a *widget*. A widget is a window with a particular appearance and behavior (the terms "widget" and "window" are used synonymously in Tk). Widgets are divided into classes such as buttons, menus, and scrollbars. All the widgets in the same class have the same general appearance and behavior. For example, all button widgets display a text string or bitmap and execute a Tcl command when they are invoked with the mouse.

Widgets are organized hierarchically in Tk, with names that reflect their positions in the hierarchy. The *main widget*, which appeared on the screen when you started `wish`, has the name ".". The name `.b` refers to a child `b` of the main widget. Widget names in Tk are like file names in UNIX except that they use `.` as a separator character instead of `/`. Thus `.a.b.c` refers to a widget that is a child of widget `.a.b`, which in turn is a child of `.a`, which is a child of the main widget.

Tk provides one command for each class of widgets, called a *class command*, which you invoke to create widgets of that class. For example, the `button` command creates button widgets. All of the class commands have the same form: the first argument is the name of a new widget to create, and additional arguments specify configuration options. Different widget classes support different sets of options. Widgets typically have many options (there are about 20 different options defined for buttons, for example), and default values are provided for the options that you don't specify. When a class command like `button` is invoked, it creates a new widget with the given name and configures it as specified by the options.

The `button` command in the example specifies two options: `-text`, which is a string to display in the button, and `-command`, which is a Tcl script to execute when the user invokes the button. In this example the `-command` option is `exit`. Here are a few other button options that you can experiment with:

`-background`	The background color for the button, such as `blue`.
`-foreground`	The color of the text in the button, such as `black`.
`-font`	The name of the font to use for the button, such as `*-times-medium-r-normal--*-120-*` for a 12-point Times Roman font.

The `pack` command causes the button widget to appear on the screen. Creating a widget does not automatically cause it to be displayed. Independent entities called *geometry managers* are responsible for computing the sizes and locations of widgets and making them appear on the screen. The `pack` command in the example asks a geometry manager called the *packer* to manage `.b`. The command asks that `.b` fill the entire area of its parent window; furthermore, if the parent has more space than needed by its child, as in the example, the parent is shrunk so that it is just large enough to hold the child. Thus when you typed the `pack` command the main window ("`.`") shrank from its original size to the size that appears in Figure 2.1.

2.3 Script files

In the examples so far, you have typed Tcl commands interactively to `tclsh` or `wish`. You can also place commands into script files and invoke the script files just like shell scripts. To do this for the hello world example, place the following text in a file named `hello`:

```
#!/usr/local/bin/wish -f
button .b -text "Hello, world!" -command exit
pack .b
```

This script is the same as the one you typed earlier except for the first line. As far as `wish` is concerned, this line is a comment, but if you make the file executable (type "`chmod +x hello`" to your shell, for example) you can then invoke the file directly by typing `hello` to your shell. When you do this the system will invoke `wish`, passing it the file as a script to interpret. `wish` will display the same window shown in Figure 2.1 and wait for you to interact with it. In this case you will not be able to type commands interactively to `wish`; all you can do is click on the button.

Note: *This script will work only if* `wish` *is installed in* `/usr/local/bin`. *If* `wish` *has been installed somewhere else, you will need to change the first line to reflect its location on your system. Some systems will misbehave in confusing ways if the first line of the script file is longer than 32 characters, so beware if the full path name of the* `wish` *binary is longer than 27 characters.*

In practice, users of Tk applications rarely type Tcl commands; they interact with the applications using the mouse and keyboard in the usual ways you would expect for graphical applications. Tcl works behind the scenes where users don't normally see it. The `hello` script behaves just the same as an application that has been coded in C with a toolkit such as Motif and compiled into a binary executable file.

During debugging, though, it is common for application developers to type Tcl commands interactively. For example, you could test the `hello` script by starting `wish` interactively (type `wish` to your shell instead of `hello`). Then type the following Tcl command:

```
source hello
```

`source` is a Tcl command that takes a file name as an argument. It reads the file and evaluates it as a Tcl script. This will generate the same user interface as if you had invoked `hello` directly from your shell, but you can now type Tcl commands interactively too. For example, you could edit the script file to change the `-command` option to

```
-command "puts Good-bye!; exit"
```

then type the following commands interactively to `wish` without restarting the program:

```
destroy .b
source hello
```

The first command will delete the existing button and the second command will recreate the button with the new `-command` option. Now when you click on the button the `puts` command will print a message on standard output before `wish` exits.

2.4 Variables and substitutions

Tcl allows you to store values in variables and use those values in commands. For example, consider the following script, which you could type to either `tclsh` or `wish`:

```
      set a 44
  ⇒   44
      expr $a*4
  ⇒   176
```

The first command assigns the value 44 to variable a and returns the variable's value. In the second command the $ causes Tcl to perform *variable substitution*: the Tcl interpreter replaces the dollar sign and the variable name following it with the value of the variable, so that the actual argument received by `expr` is `44*4`. Variables need not be declared in Tcl; they are created automatically when set. Variable values are stored as strings and arbitrary string values of any length are allowed. Of course, in this example an error will occur in `expr` if the value of a doesn't make sense as an integer or real number (try other values and see what happens).

Tcl also provides *command substitution*, which allows you to use the result of one command in an argument to another command:

```
      set a 44
      set b [expr $a*4]
  ⇒   176
```

Square brackets invoke command substitution: everything inside the brackets is evaluated as a separate Tcl script, and the result of that script is substituted into the word in place of the bracketed command. In this example the second argument of the second `set` command will be `176`.

The final form of substitution in Tcl is *backslash substitution*, which allows you to use various special characters in a command as in the following example:

```
set x \$a
set newline \n
```

The first command sets variable x to the string $a (the characters \$ are replaced with a dollar sign and no variable substitution occurs). The second command sets variable new-line to hold a string consisting of the newline character (the characters \n are replaced with a newline character).

2.5   Control structures

The next example uses variables and substitutions along with some simple control structures to create a Tcl *procedure* called power, which raises a base to an integer power:

```
proc power {base p} {
    set result 1
    while {$p>0} {
        set result [expr $result*$base]
        set p [expr $p-1]
    }
    return $result
}
```

If you type the preceding lines to wish or tclsh, or if you enter them into a file and then source the file, a new command power will become available. The command takes two arguments, a number and an integer power, and its result is the number raised to the power:

```
    power 2 6
⇒   64
    power 1.15 5
⇒   2.01136
```

This example uses one additional piece of Tcl syntax: braces. Braces are like double quotes in that they can be placed around a word that contains embedded spaces. However, braces are different from double quotes in two respects. First, braces nest. The last word of the proc command starts after the open brace on the first line and contains everything up to the close brace on the last line. The Tcl interpreter removes the outer braces and passes everything between them, including several nested pairs of braces, to proc as an argument. The second difference between braces and double quotes is that no substitutions occur inside braces, whereas they do inside quotes. All of the characters between the braces are passed verbatim to proc without any special processing.

The proc command takes three arguments: the name of a procedure, a list of argument names separated by white space, and the body of the procedure, which is a Tcl script. proc enters the procedure name into the Tcl interpreter as a new command. Whenever the command is invoked, the body of the procedure will be evaluated. While the procedure body is executing, it can access its arguments as variables: base will hold the first argument to power and p will hold the second argument.

The body of the `power` procedure contains three Tcl commands: `set`, `while`, and `return`. The `while` command does most of the work of the procedure. It takes two arguments, an expression $p>0 and a body, which is another Tcl script. The `while` command evaluates its expression argument and if the result is nonzero then it evaluates the body as a Tcl script. It repeats this process over and over until eventually the expression evaluates to zero. In the example, the body of the `while` command multiplies the result value by `base` and then decrements p. When p reaches zero the result contains the desired power of `base`.

The `return` command causes the procedure to exit with the value of variable `result` as the procedure's result. If it is omitted, the return value of the procedure will be the result of the last command in the procedure's body. In the case of `power` this would be the result of `while`, which is always an empty string.

The use of braces in this example is crucial. The single most difficult issue in writing Tcl scripts is managing substitutions: making them happen when you want them and preventing them when you don't. The body of the procedure must be enclosed in braces because we don't want variable and command substitutions to occur at the time the body is passed to `proc` as an argument; we want the substitutions to occur later, when the body is evaluated as a Tcl script. The body of the `while` command is enclosed in braces for the same reason: rather than performing the substitutions once, while parsing the `while` command, we want the substitutions to be performed over and over, each time the body is evaluated. Braces are also needed in the `{$p>0}` argument to `while`. Without them the value of variable p would be substituted when parsing the `while` command; the expression would have a constant value and `while` would loop forever. You can try replacing some of the braces in the example with double quotes to see what happens.

In the examples in this book I use a style where the open brace for an argument that is a Tcl script appears at the end of one line, the script follows on successive lines indented, and the close brace is on a line by itself after the script. Although I think that this makes for readable scripts, Tcl doesn't require this particular syntax. Arguments that are scripts are subject to the same syntax rules as any other arguments; in fact, the Tcl interpreter doesn't even know that an argument is a script at the time it parses it. One consequence is that the open brace must be on the same line as the preceding portion of the command. If the open brace is moved to a line by itself, the newline before the open brace will terminate the command.

The variables in a procedure are normally local to that procedure and will not be visible outside the procedure. In the `power` example the local variables include the arguments `base` and p as well as the variable `result`. A fresh set of local variables is created for each call to a procedure (arguments are passed by copying their values), and when a procedure returns, its local variables are deleted. Variables named outside any procedure are called *global variables*; they last forever unless explicitly deleted. You'll find out later how a procedure can access global variables and the local variables of other active procedures.

2.6   On the Tcl language

As a programming language, Tcl is defined quite differently than most other languages. In most languages there is a grammar that defines the entire language. For example, consider the following statement in C:

```
while (p>0) {
    result *= base;
    p -= 1;
}
```

The grammar for C defines the structure of this statement in terms of a reserved word `while`, an expression, and a substatement to execute repeatedly until the expression evaluates to zero. The C grammar defines both the overall structure of the `while` statement and the internal structure of its expression and substatement.

In Tcl no fixed grammar explains the entire language. Instead, Tcl is defined by an interpreter that parses single Tcl commands, plus a collection of procedures that execute individual commands. The interpreter and its substitution rules are fixed, but new commands can be defined at any time and existing commands can be replaced. Features such as control flow, procedures, and expressions are implemented as commands; they are not understood directly by the Tcl interpreter. For example, consider the Tcl command that is equivalent to the preceding `while` loop:

```
while {$p>0} {
    set result [expr $result*$base]
    set p [expr $p-1]
}
```

When this command is evaluated, the Tcl interpreter knows nothing about the command except that it has three words, the first of which is a command name. The Tcl interpreter has no idea that the first argument to `while` is an expression and the second is a Tcl script. Once the command has been parsed, the Tcl interpreter passes the words of the command to `while`, which treats its first argument as an expression and the second as a Tcl script. If the expression evaluates to nonzero, then `while` passes its second argument back to the Tcl interpreter for evaluation. At this point the interpreter treats the contents of the argument as a script (e.g., it performs command and variable substitutions and invokes the `expr` and `set` commands).

Now consider the following command:

```
set {$p>0} {
    set result [expr $result*$base]
    set p [expr $p-1]
}
```

As far as the Tcl interpreter is concerned, the `set` command is identical to the `while` command except that it has a different command name. The interpreter handles this command in exactly the same way as the `while` command, except that it invokes a different procedure to execute the command. The `set` command treats its first argument as a variable name and its second argument as a new value for that variable, so it will set a variable with the rather unusual name of $p>0.

The most common mistake made by new Tcl users is to try to understand Tcl scripts in terms of a grammar; this leads people to expect much more sophisticated behavior by the interpreter than actually exists. For example, a C programmer using Tcl for the first time might think that the first pair of braces in the `while` command serves a different purpose than the second pair. In reality, there is no difference. In each case the braces are present so that the Tcl interpreter passes the characters between the braces to the command without performing any substitutions.

Thus the entire Tcl "language" consists of about a half-dozen simple rules for parsing arguments and performing substitutions. At the same time, Tcl is powerful enough to allow a rich set of structures such as loops and procedures to be built as ordinary commands. Applications can extend Tcl not just with new commands but also with new control structures.

2.7 Event bindings

The next example provides a graphical front-end for the `power` procedure. In addition to demonstrating two new widget classes it illustrates Tk's *binding* mechanism. A binding causes a particular Tcl script to be evaluated whenever a particular event occurs in a particular window. The `-command` option for buttons is an example of a simple binding implemented by a particular widget class. Tk also includes a more general mechanism that can be used to extend the behavior of widgets in nearly arbitrary ways.

To run the example, copy the following script into a file `power` and invoke the file from your shell.

```
#!/usr/local/bin/wish -f
proc power {base p} {
    set result 1
    while {$p>0} {
        set result [expr $result*$base]
        set p [expr $p-1]
    }
    return $result
}
entry .base -width 6 -relief sunken -textvariable base
label .label1 -text "to the power"
entry .power -width 6 -relief sunken -textvariable power
label .label2 -text "is"
label .result -textvariable result
pack .base .label1 .power .label2 .result -side left \
        -padx 1m -pady 2m
bind .base <Return> {set result [power $base $power]}
bind .power <Return> {set result [power $base $power]}
```

This script will produce a screen display like that in Figure 2.2. There are two entry widgets in which you can click with the mouse and type numbers. If you press the return key

Figure 2.2. A graphical user interface that computes powers of a base.

in either of the entries, the result will appear on the right side of the window. You can compute different results by modifying either the base or the power and then pressing return again.

This application consists of five widgets: two entries and three labels. Entries are widgets that display one-line text strings that you can edit interactively. The two entries, `.base` and `.power`, are used for entering the numbers. Each entry is configured with a `-width` of 6, which means it will be large enough to display about 6 digits, and a `-relief` of `sunken`, which gives the entry a depressed appearance. The `-textvariable` option for each entry specifies the name of a global variable to hold the entry's text — any changes you make in the entry will be reflected in the variable and vice versa.

Two of the labels, `.label1` and `.label2`, hold decorative text and the third, `.result`, holds the result of the power computation. The `-textvariable` option for `.result` causes it to display whatever string is in global variable `result` and to update itself whenever the variable changes. In contrast, `.label1` and `.label2` display constant strings.

The `pack` command arranges the five widgets in a row from left to right. The command occupies two lines in the script; the backslash at the end of the first line is a line-continuation character, which causes the newline to be treated as a space. The `-side` option means that each widget is placed at the left side of the remaining space in the main widget: first `.base` is placed at the left edge of the main widget, then `.label1` is placed at the left side of the space not occupied by `.base`, and so on. The `-padx` and `-pady` options make the display a bit more attractive by arranging for 1 millimeter of extra space on the left and right sides of each widget, plus 2 millimeters of extra space above and below each widget. The m suffix specifies millimeters; you could also use c for centimeters, i for inches, p for points, or no suffix for pixels.

The `bind` commands connect the user interface to the `power` procedure. Each `bind` command has three arguments: the name of a widget, an event specification, and a Tcl script to invoke when the given event occurs in the given widget. `<Return>` specifies an event consisting of the user pressing the return key on the keyboard. Here are a few other event specifiers that you might find useful:

    `<Button-1>`   Mouse button 1 is pressed.

`<1>`	Shorthand for `<Button-1>`.
`<ButtonRelease-1>`	Mouse button 1 is released.
`<Double-Button-1>`	Double-click on mouse button 1.
`<Key-a>`	Key a is pressed.
`<a>` or a	Shorthand for `<Key-a>`.
`<Motion>`	Pointer motion with no buttons or modifier keys pressed.
`<B1-Motion>`	Pointer motion with button 1 pressed.
`<Any-Motion>`	Pointer motion with any (or no) buttons or modifier keys pressed.

The scripts for the bindings invoke power, passing it the values in the two entries, and they store the result in the result variable so that it will be displayed in the .result widget. These bindings extend the generic built-in behavior of the entries (editing text strings) with application-specific behavior (computing a value based on two entries and displaying that value in a third widget).

The script for a binding has access to several pieces of information about the event, such as the location of the pointer when the event occurred. For an example, start up wish interactively and type the following command to it:

```
bind . <Any-Motion> {puts "pointer at %x,%y"}
```

Now move the pointer over the window. Each time the pointer moves a message will be printed on standard output giving its new location. When the pointer motion event occurs, Tk scans the script for % sequences and replaces them with information about the event before passing the script to Tcl for evaluation. %x is replaced with the pointer's x-coordinate and %y is replaced with the pointer's y-coordinate.

2.8 Subprocesses

Normally Tcl executes each command by invoking a C procedure in the application to carry out its function. This is different from a shell program like sh where each command is normally executed in a separate subprocess. However, Tcl also allows you to create subprocesses, using the exec command. Here is a simple example of exec:

```
    exec grep #include tk.h
⇒   #include <tcl.h>
    #include <X11/Xlib.h>
    #include <stddef.h>
```

The exec command treats its arguments much like the words of a shell command line. In this example exec creates a new process to run the grep program and passes it #include and tk.h as arguments, just as if you had typed

```
    grep #include tk.h
```

to your shell. The `grep` program searches file `tk.h` for lines that contain the string `#include` and prints those lines on its standard output. However, `exec` arranges for standard output from the subprocess to be piped back to Tcl. `exec` waits for the process to exit and then it returns all of the standard output as its result. With this mechanism you can execute subprocesses and use their output in Tcl scripts. `exec` also supports input and output redirection using standard shell notation such as <, <<, and >, pipelines with |, and background processes with &.

The following example creates a simple user interface for saving and reinvoking commonly used shell commands. Type the following script into a file named `redo` and invoke it:

```
#!/usr/local/bin/wish -f
set id 0
entry .entry -width 30 -relief sunken -textvariable cmd
pack .entry -padx 1m -pady 1m
bind .entry <Return> {
    set id [expr $id + 1]
    if {$id > 5} {
        destroy .b[expr $id - 5]
    }
    button .b$id -command "exec <@stdin >@stdout $cmd" \
            -text $cmd
    pack .b$id -fill x
    .b$id invoke
    .entry delete 0 end
}
```

Initially the script creates an interface with a single entry widget. You can type a shell command such as `ls` into the entry, as shown in Figure 2.3(a). When you press return, the command gets executed as if you had typed it to the shell from which you invoked `redo`; the <@ and >@ arguments to `exec` cause the standard input and output files for the command to be the same as those for `wish`. Furthermore, the script creates a new button widget that displays the command, as shown in Figure 2.3(b), and you can reinvoke the command later by clicking on the button. As you type more commands, more buttons appear, up to a limit of five remembered commands as in Figure 2.3(c).

Note: *This example suffers from several limitations. For example, you cannot specify wildcards such as * in command lines, and the cd command doesn't behave properly. In Part I you'll read about Tcl facilities that you can use to remove these limitations.*

The most interesting part of the `redo` script is in the `bind` command. The binding for <Return> must execute the command, which is stored in the `cmd` variable, and create a new button widget. First it creates the widget. The button widgets have names like `.b1`, `.b2`, and so on, where the number comes from the variable `id`. `id` starts at zero and increments before each new button is created. The notation `.b$id` generates a widget name by concatenating `.b` with the value of `id`. Before creating a new widget the script checks to see if there are already five saved commands; if so, the oldest existing button is deleted. The notation ".b[expr $id - 5]" produces the name of the oldest button by subtracting five from the number of the new button and concatenating it with `.b`. The

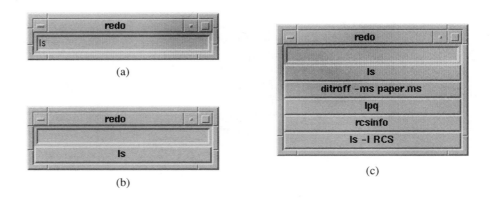

Figure 2.3. The redo application. The user can type a command in the entry widget, as in (a). When the user presses the return key, the command is invoked as a subprocess using exec and a new button is created that can be used to reinvoke the command later, as in (b). Additional commands can be typed to create additional buttons, up to a limit of five buttons as in (c).

-command option for the new button invokes exec and redirects standard input and standard output for the subprocess(es) to wish's standard input and standard output, which are the same as those of the shell from which wish was invoked. This causes output from the subprocesses to appear in the shell's window instead of being returned to wish.

The command "pack .b$id -fill x" makes the new button appear at the bottom of the window. The option -fill x improves the appearance by stretching the button horizontally so that it fills the width of the window even if it doesn't really need that much space for its text. Try omitting the -fill option to see what happens without it.

The last two commands of the binding script are called *widget commands*. Whenever a new widget is created, a new Tcl command is also created with the same name as the widget, and you can invoke this command to communicate with the widget. The first argument to a widget command selects one of several operations and additional arguments are used as parameters for that operation. In the redo script the first widget command causes the button widget to invoke its -command option just as if you had clicked the mouse button on it. The second widget command clears the entry widget in preparation for a new command to be typed.

Each class of widget supports a different set of operations in its widget commands, but many of the operations are similar from widget to widget. For example, every widget class supports a configure widget command that can be used to modify any of the configuration options for the widget. If you run the redo script interactively, you could type the following command to change the background of the entry widget to yellow:

```
.entry configure -background yellow
```

Or you could type:

```
.b1 configure -foreground brown
.b1 flash
```

to change the color of the text in button `.b1` to brown and then cause the button to flash.

One of the most important things about Tcl and Tk is that they make every aspect of an application accessible and modifiable at runtime. For example, the `redo` script modifies its own interface on the fly. In addition, Tk provides commands that you can use to query the structure of the widget hierarchy, and you can use `configure` widget commands to query and modify the configuration options of individual widgets.

2.9 Additional features of Tcl and Tk

The examples in this chapter used every aspect of the Tcl language syntax and they illustrated many of the most important features of Tcl and Tk. However, Tcl and Tk contain many other facilities that are not used in this chapter; all of these will be described later in the book. Here is a sampler of some of the most useful features that haven't been mentioned yet:

Arrays and lists. Tcl provides associative arrays for storing key–value pairs efficiently and lists for managing aggregates of data.

More control structures. Tcl provides several additional commands for controlling the flow of execution, such as `eval`, `for`, `foreach`, and `switch`.

String manipulation. Tcl contains a number of commands for manipulating strings, such as measuring their length, regular expression pattern matching and substitution, and format conversion.

File access. You can read and write files from Tcl scripts and retrieve directory information and file attributes such as length and creation time.

More widgets. Tk contains many widget classes besides those shown here, such as menus, scrollbars, a drawing widget called a *canvas*, and a text widget that makes it easy to achieve hypertext effects.

Access to other X facilities. Tk provides commands for accessing all of the major facilities in the X Window System, such as a command for communicating with the window manager (to set the window's title, for example), a command for retrieving the selection, and a command to manage the input focus.

Interapplication communication. Tk provides a `send` command that can be used to issue arbitrary Tcl/Tk scripts to other Tk-based applications.

C interfaces. Tcl provides C library procedures that you can use to define new Tcl commands in C, and Tk provides a library that you can use to create new widget classes and geometry managers in C.

2.10 Extensions and applications

Tcl and Tk have an active and rapidly growing user community that now numbers in the tens of thousands. Many people have built packages that extend the base functionality of Tcl and Tk and applications based on Tcl and Tk. Several of these packages and applications are publicly available and widely used in the Tcl/Tk community. There isn't space in this book to discuss all of the available Tcl/Tk software in detail, but this section gives a quick overview of five extensions and applications. See Appendix A for information on how you can obtain them and other contributed Tcl/Tk software.

2.10.1 expect

expect is one of the oldest Tcl applications and also one of the most popular. It is a program that "talks" to interactive programs. Following a script, expect knows what output can be expected from a program and what the correct responses should be. It can be used to control automatically programs such as ftp, telnet, rlogin, crypt, fsck, tip, and others that cannot be automated from a shell script because they require interactive input. expect also allows the user to take control and interact directly with the program when desired. For example, the following expect script logs into a remote machine using the rlogin program, sets the working directory and display to that of the originating machine, then turns control over to the user:

```
#!/usr/local/bin/expect
spawn rlogin [lindex $argv 0]
expect -re "(%|#) "
send "cd [pwd]\r"
expect -re "(%|#) "
send "setenv DISPLAY $env(DISPLAY)"
interact
```

The spawn, expect, send, and interact commands are implemented by expect, while lindex and pwd are built-in Tcl commands. The spawn command starts up rlogin, using a command-line argument as the name of the remote machine (lindex extracts the first argument from the command line, which is available in the variable argv). The expect command waits for rlogin to output a prompt (either % or #, followed by a space), then send outputs a command to change the working directory, just as if a user had typed the command interactively. The second expect command waits for a prompt signifying that the cd command has been processed, then send is invoked again to set the DISPLAY environment variable on the remote machine from the corresponding value on the local machine (environment variables are available through the env Tcl variable). Finally, interact causes expect to step out of the way so that the user who invoked the expect script can now type directly to rlogin.

expect can be used for many purposes, such as a scriptable front-end to debuggers, mailers, and other programs that don't have scripting languages of their own. The programs require no changes to be driven by expect. expect is also useful for regression testing of interactive programs. `expect` can be combined with Tk or other Tcl extensions. For example, by using Tk and `expect` together, it is possible to write a graphical front-end for an existing interactive application without changing the application.

`expect` was created by Don Libes of the National Institute of Standards and Technology.

2.10.2 Extended Tcl

Extended Tcl (TclX) is a library package that augments the built-in Tcl commands with many additional commands and procedures oriented toward system programming tasks. It can be used with any Tcl application. Here are a few of the most popular features of TclX:

- Access to many additional POSIX system calls and functions.
- A file scanning facility with functionality much like that of the `awk` program.
- Keyed lists, which provide functionality similar to C structures.
- Commands for manipulating times and dates and converting them to and from ASCII.
- An on-line help facility.
- Facilities for debugging, profiling, and program development.

Many of the best features of TclX are no longer part of TclX: they turned out to be so widely useful that they were incorporated into the Tcl core. Among the Tcl features pioneered by TclX are file input and output, array variables, real arithmetic and transcendental functions, autoloading, XPG-based internationalization, and the `upvar` command.

For example, consider the following script, which uses the `scancontext`, `scanmatch`, and `scanfile` commands from TclX, plus several of the core Tcl commands:

```
set context [scancontext create]
scanmatch $context {^FATAL:|SERIOUS:} {
    puts $matchInfo(line)
}
foreach file $logFiles {
    set id [open $logFile r]
    scanfile $context $id
    close $id
}
scancontext delete $context
```

This script scans a collection of files and prints all of the lines beginning with `FATAL:` or `SERIOUS:`. The first two lines create a "scan context", which consists of patterns and Tcl scripts to invoke whenever the patterns match. The `foreach` loop iterates over a group of files; for each file, the file is opened and then `scanfile` is invoked with the scan context. `scanfile` reads the file, finds all the lines that match patterns in the scan context, and invokes the corresponding script for each match. The last line deletes the scan context, which is no longer needed.

Extended Tcl was created by Karl Lehenbauer of NeoSoft, Inc., and Mark Diekhans of Santa Cruz Operation.

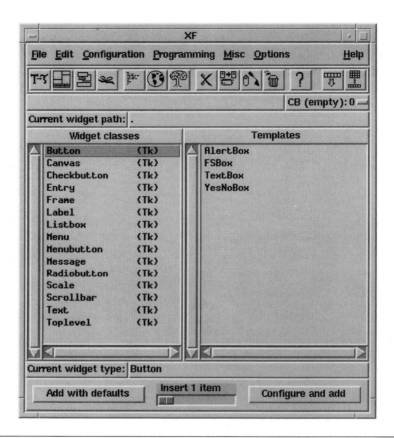

Figure 2.4. A screen dump showing the main window of XF, an interactive application builder for Tcl and Tk.

2.10.3 XF

Tk makes it relatively easy to create graphical user interfaces by writing Tcl scripts, but XF makes it even easier. XF is an interactive interface builder. You design a user interface by manipulating objects on the screen, then XF creates a Tcl script that will generate the interface you have designed (see Figure 2.4). XF provides tools for creating and configuring widgets, arranging them with Tk's geometry managers, creating event bindings, and so on. XF manipulates a live application while it is running, so the full effect of each change in the interface can be seen and tested immediately.

XF supports all of Tk's built-in widget classes and allows you to add new widget classes by writing class-specific Tcl scripts for XF to use to handle the classes. You needn't use XF exclusively — you can design part of a user interface with XF and part by writing Tcl scripts. XF supports most of the currently available extensions to Tcl and Tk, and XF itself is written in Tcl.

XF was created by Sven Delmas of the Technical University of Berlin. It is based on an earlier interface builder for Tk called BYO, which was developed at the Victoria University of Wellington, New Zealand.

2.10.4 Distributed programming

Tcl Distributed Programming (Tcl-DP) is a collection of Tcl commands that simplifies the development of distributed programs. Tcl-DP's most important feature is a *remote procedure call* facility, which allows Tcl applications to communicate by exchanging Tcl scripts. For example, the following script uses Tcl-DP to implement a trivial "id server", which returns unique identifiers in response to GetId requests:

```
set myId 0
proc GetId {} {
    global myId
    set myId [expr $myId+1]
    return $myId
}
MakeRPCServer 4545
```

All of the code in this script except the last line is ordinary Tcl code that defines a global variable myId and a procedure GetId that increments the variable and returns its new value. The MakeRPCServer command is implemented by Tcl-DP; it causes the application to listen for requests on TCP socket 4545.

Other Tcl applications can communicate with this server using scripts that look like the following:

```
set server [MakeRPCClient server.company.com 4545]
RPC $server GetId
```

The first command opens a connection with the server and saves an identifier for that connection. The arguments to MakeRPCClient identify the server's host and the socket on which the server is listening. The RPC command performs a remote procedure call. Its arguments are a connection identifier and an arbitrary Tcl script. RPC forwards the script to the server; the server executes the script and returns its result (a new identifier in this case), which becomes the result of the RPC command. Any script whatsoever could be substituted in place of the GetId command.

Tcl-DP also includes several other features, including asynchronous remote procedure calls, where the client need not wait for the call to complete, a distributed object system in which objects can be replicated in several applications and updates are automatically propagated to all copies, and a simple name service. Tcl-DP has been used for applications such as a video playback system, groupware, and games. Tcl-DP is more flexible than most remote procedure call systems because it is not based on compiled interfaces between clients and servers: it is easy in Tcl-DP to connect an existing client to a new server without recompiling or restarting the client.

Tcl-DP was created at the University of California at Berkeley by Lawrence A. Rowe, Brian Smith, and Steve Yen.

2.10.5 Ak

Ak is an audio extension for Tcl. It is built on top of AudioFile, a network-transparent, device-independent audio system that runs on a variety of platforms. Ak provides Tcl commands for file playback, recording, telephone control, and synchronization. The basic abstractions in Ak are connections to AudioFile servers, device contexts (which encapsulate the state for a particular audio device), and requests such as file playback. For example, here is a script that plays back an audio file on a remote machine:

```
audioserver remote "server.company.com:0"
remote context room -device 1
room create play "announcement-file.au"
```

The first command opens a connection to the audio server on the machine `server.company.com` and gives this connection the name `remote`. It also creates a command named `remote`, which is used to issue commands over the connection. The second command creates a context named `room`, which is associated with audio device 1 on the server, and also creates a command named `room` for communicating with the context. The last command initiates a playback of a particular audio file.

Ak implements an unusual model of time that allows clients to specify precisely when audio samples are going to emerge. It also provides a mechanism to execute arbitrary Tcl scripts at specified audio times; this can be used to achieve a variety of hypermedia effects, such as displaying images or video in sync with an audio playback. When combined with Tk, Ak provides a powerful and flexible scripting system for developing multimedia applications such as tutorials and telephone inquiry systems.

Ak was created by Andrew C. Payne of Digital Equipment Corporation.

Part I:

The Tcl Language

Chapter 3
Tcl Language Syntax

To write Tcl scripts, you must learn two things. First, you must learn the Tcl syntax, which consists of about a half-dozen rules that determine how commands are parsed. The Tcl syntax is the same for every command. Second, you must learn about the individual commands that you use in your scripts. Tcl provides about 60 built-in commands, Tk adds several dozen more, and any application based on Tcl or Tk will add a few more of its own. You'll need to know all of the syntax rules right away, but you can learn about the commands more gradually as you need them.

This chapter describes the Tcl language syntax. The remaining chapters in Part I describe the built-in Tcl commands, and Part II describes Tk's commands.

3.1 Scripts, commands, and words

A Tcl *script* consists of one or more *commands*. Commands are separated by newlines or semicolons. For example,

```
set a 24
set b 15
```

is a script with two commands separated by a newline character. The same script could be written on a single line using a semicolon separator:

```
set a 24; set b 15
```

Each command consists of one or more *words*, where the first word is the name of a command and additional words are arguments to that command. Words are separated by spaces or tabs. Each of the commands in the preceding examples has three words. There

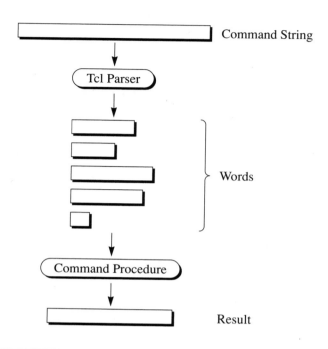

Figure 3.1. Tcl commands are evaluated in two steps. First the Tcl interpreter parses the command string into words, performing substitutions along the way. Then a command procedure executes the command, processing the words to produce a result string. Each command has a separate command procedure.

may be any number of words in a command, and each word may have an arbitrary string value. The white space that separates words is not part of the words, nor are the newlines and semicolons that terminate commands.

3.2 Evaluating a command

Tcl evaluates a command in two steps as shown in Figure 3.1: *parsing* and *execution*. In the parsing step the Tcl interpreter applies the rules described in this chapter to divide the command up into words and perform substitutions. Parsing is done in exactly the same way for every command. During the parsing step, the Tcl interpreter does not apply any meaning to the values of the words. Tcl just performs a set of simple string operations such as replacing the characters $a with the string stored in variable a; Tcl does not know or care whether a or the resulting word is a number or the name of a widget or anything else.

In the execution step, meaning is applied to the words of the command. Tcl treats the first word as a command name, checking to see if the command is defined and locating a *command procedure* to carry out its function. If the command is defined, the Tcl interpreter invokes its command procedure, passing all of the words of the command to the command procedure. The command procedure is free to interpret the words in any way that it pleases, and different commands apply different meanings to their arguments.

Note: *I use the terms "word" and "argument" interchangeably to refer to the values passed to command procedures. The only difference between these two terms is that the first argument is the second word.*

The following commands illustrate some of the meanings that are commonly applied to arguments:

```
set a 122
```
In many cases, such as the `set` command, arguments may take any form whatsoever. The `set` command simply treats the first argument as a variable name and the second argument as a value for the variable. The command "`set 122 a`" is valid too: it creates a variable whose name is 122 and whose value is a.

```
expr 24/3.2
```
The argument to `expr` must be an arithmetic expression that follows the rules described in Chapter 5. Several other commands also take expressions as arguments.

```
eval {set a 122}
```
The argument to `eval` is a Tcl script. `eval` passes it to the Tcl interpreter where another round of parsing and execution occurs for the argument. Other control-flow commands such as `if` and `while` also take scripts as arguments.

```
lindex {red green blue purple} 2
```
The first argument to `lindex` is a *list* consisting of four values separated by spaces. This command will extract element 2 (`blue`) from the list and return it. Tcl's commands for manipulating lists are described in Chapter 6.

```
string length abracadabra
```
Some commands, like `string` and the Tk widget commands, are actually several commands rolled into one. The first argument of the command selects one of several operations to perform and determines the meaning of the remaining arguments. For example `string length` requires one additional argument and computes its length, whereas `string compare` requires two additional arguments.

```
button .b -text Hello -fg red
```
The arguments after `.b` are option-value pairs that allow you to specify the options you care about and use default values for the others.

In writing Tcl scripts one of the most important things to remember is that the Tcl parser doesn't apply any meaning to the words of a command while it parses them. All of the preceding meanings are applied by individual command procedures, not by the Tcl parser. Another way of saying this is that arguments are quoted by default; if you want evaluation you must request it explicitly. This approach is similar to that of most shell languages but different than most programming languages. For example, consider the following C program:

```
x = 4;
y = x+10;
```

In the first statement C stores the integer value 4 in variable x. In the second statement C evaluates the expression x+10, fetching the value of variable x and adding 10, and stores the result in variable y. At the end of execution, y has the integer value 14. If you want to use a literal string in C without evaluation, you must enclose it in quotes. Now consider a similar-looking program written in Tcl:

```
set x 4
set y x+10
```

The first command assigns the *string* 4 to variable x. The value of the variable need not have any particular form. The second command simply takes the string x+10 and stores it as the new value for y. At the end of the script y has the string value x+10, not the integer value 14. In Tcl if you want evaluation you must ask for it explicitly:

```
set x 4
set y [expr $x+10]
```

Evaluation is requested twice in the second command. First, the second word of the command is enclosed in brackets, which tells the Tcl parser to evaluate the characters between the brackets as a Tcl script and use the result as the value of the word. Second, a dollar sign has been placed before x. When Tcl parses the expr command it substitutes the value of variable x for the $x. If the dollar sign were omitted, expr's argument would contain the string x, resulting in a syntax error. At the end of the script y has the string value 14.

3.3 Variable substitution

Tcl provides three forms of *substitution:* variables, commands, and backslashes. Each substitution causes some of the original characters of a word to be replaced with some other value. Substitutions may occur in any word of a command, including the command name, and there may be any number of substitutions within a single word.

The first form of substitution is *variable substitution*. It is triggered by a dollar sign character and it causes the value of a Tcl variable to be inserted into a word. For example, consider the following commands:

```
set kgrams 20
expr $kgrams*2.2046
```
⇒ *44.092*

The first command sets the value of variable `kgrams` to `20`. The second command computes the corresponding weight in pounds by multiplying the value of `kgrams` by 2.2046. It does this using variable substitution: the string `$kgrams` is replaced with the value of variable `kgrams`, so that the actual argument received by the `expr` command procedure is `20*2.2046`.

Variable substitution can occur anywhere within a word and any number of times, as in the following command:

```
expr $result*$base
```

The variable name consists of all of the numbers, letters, and underscores following the dollar sign. Thus the first variable name (`result`) extends up to the `*` and the second variable name (`base`) extends to the end of the word. Variable substitution can be used for many purposes, such as generating new names:

```
foreach num {1 2 3 4 5} {
    button .b$num
}
```

This example will create five button widgets, with names `.b1`, `.b2`, `.b3`, `.b4`, and `.b5`.

These examples show only the simplest form of variable substitution. Two other forms of variable substitution are used for associative array references and to provide more explicit control over the extent of a variable name (e.g., so that there can be a letter or number immediately following the variable name). These other forms are discussed in Chapter 4.

3.4   Command substitution

The second form of substitution provided by Tcl is *command substitution*. Command substitution causes part or all of a word to be replaced with the result of a Tcl command. Command substitution is invoked by enclosing a command in brackets:

```
set kgrams 20
set lbs [expr $kgrams*2.2046]
```
⇒ *44.092*

The characters between the brackets must constitute a valid Tcl script. The script may contain any number of commands separated by newlines or semicolons in the usual fashion. The brackets and all of the characters between them are replaced with the result of the script. Thus in the foregoing example the `expr` command is executed while parsing the words for `set`; its result, the string `44.092`, becomes the second argument to `set`. As with variable substitution, command substitution can occur anywhere in a word and there may be more than one command substitution within a single word.

3.5 Backslash substitution

The final form of substitution in Tcl is *backslash substitution*. It is used to insert special characters such as newlines into words and also to insert characters such as [and $ without them being treated specially by the Tcl parser. For example, consider the following command:

```
set msg Eggs:\ \$2.18/dozen\nGasoline:\ \$1.49/gallon
```
⇒ *Eggs: $2.18/dozen*
   Gasoline: $1.49/gallon

There are two sequences of a backslash followed by a space; each of these sequences is replaced in the word by a single space and the space characters are not treated as word separators. There are also two sequences of a backslash followed by a dollar sign; each of these is replaced in the word with a single dollar sign, and the dollar signs are treated like ordinary characters (they do not trigger variable substitution). The backslash followed by n is replaced with a newline character

Table 3.1 lists all of the backslash sequences supported by Tcl. These include all of the sequences defined for ANSI C, such as \t to insert a tab character and \xd4 to insert the character whose hexadecimal value is 0xd4. If a backslash is followed by any character not listed in the table, as in \$ or \ [, then the backslash is dropped from the word and the following character is included in the word as an ordinary character. This allows you to include any of the Tcl special characters in a word without the character being treated specially by the Tcl parser. The sequence \ \ will insert a single backslash into a word.

The sequence backslash–newline can be used to spread a long command across multiple lines, as in the following example:

```
pack .base .label1 .power .label2 .result \
        -side left -padx 1m -pady 2m
```

The backslash and newline, plus any leading white space on the next line, are replaced by a single space character in the word. Thus the two lines together form a single command.

Note: *Backslash-newline sequences are unusual in that they are replaced in a separate preprocessing step before the Tcl interpreter parses the command. This means, for example, that the space character that replaces backslash-newline will be treated as a word separator unless it is between double quotes or braces.*

3.6 Quoting with double quotes

Tcl provides several ways for you to prevent the parser from giving special interpretation to characters such as $ and semicolon. These techniques are called *quoting*. You have already seen one form of quoting in backslash subsitution. For example, \$ causes a dollar sign to be inserted into a word without triggering variable substitution. In addition to backslash substitution, Tcl provides two other forms of quoting: double quotes and braces.

Backslash Sequence	Replaced By
\a	Audible alert (0x7)
\b	Backspace (0x8)
\f	Form feed (0xc)
\n	Newline (0xa)
\r	Carriage return (0xd)
\t	Tab (0x9)
\v	Vertical tab (0xb)
\ddd	Octal value given by *ddd* (one, two, or three *d*'s)
\xhh	Hex value given by *hh* (any number of *h*'s)
\newline space	A single space character.

Table 3.1. Backslash substitutions supported by Tcl. Each of the sequences in the first column is replaced by the corresponding character from the second column. If a backslash is followed by a character other than those in the first column, the two characters are replaced by the second character.

Double quotes disable word and command separators, while braces disable almost all special characters.

If a word is enclosed in double quotes, then spaces, tabs, newlines, and semicolons are treated as ordinary characters within the word. The example from page 34 can be rewritten more cleanly with double quotes as follows:

```
    set msg "Eggs: \$2.18/dozen\nGasoline: \$1.49/gallon"
⇒   Eggs: $2.18/dozen
    Gasoline: $1.49/gallon
```

Note that the quotes themselves are not part of the word. The \n in the example could also be replaced with an actual newline character, as in

```
    set msg "Eggs: \$2.18/dozen
    Gasoline: \$1.49/gallon"
```

but I think the script is more readable with \n.

Variable substitutions, command substitutions, and backslash substitutions all occur as usual inside double quotes. For example, the following script sets `msg` to a string containing the name of a variable, its value, and the square of its value:

```
set a 2.1
set msg "a is $a; the square of a is [expr $a*$a]"
⇒ a is 2.1; the square of a is 4.41
```

If you would like to include a double quote in a word enclosed in double quotes, use back-lash substitution:

```
set name a.out
set msg "Couldn't open file \"$name\""
⇒ Couldn't open file "a.out"
```

3.7 Quoting with braces

Braces provide a more radical form of quoting where all the special characters lose their meaning. If a word is enclosed in braces, the characters between the braces are the value of the word, verbatim. No substitutions are performed on the word, and spaces, tabs, new-lines, and semicolons are treated as ordinary characters. The example on page 34 can be rewritten with braces as follows:

```
set msg {Eggs: $2.18/dozen
Gasoline: $1.49/gallon}
```

The dollar signs in the word do not trigger variable substitution and the newline does not act as a command separator. In this case \n cannot be used to insert a newline into the word as on page 35, because the \n will be included in the argument as is without trigger-ing backslash substitution:

```
set msg {Eggs: $2.18/dozen\nGasoline: $1.49/gallon}
⇒ Eggs: $2.18/dozen\nGasoline: $1.49/gallon
```

One of the most important uses for braces is to *defer evaluation*. Deferred evaluation means that special characters aren't processed immediately by the Tcl parser. Instead they are passed to the command procedure as part of its argument. The command procedure will then process the special characters itself, often by passing the argument back to the Tcl interpreter for evaluation. For example, consider the following procedure, which counts the number of occurrences of a particular value in a list:

```
proc occur {value list} {
    set count 0
    foreach el $list {
        if $el==$value {
            incr count
        }
    }
    return $count
}
```

The body of the procedure is enclosed in braces so that it is passed verbatim to proc. Thus the value of variable list will not be substituted at the time the proc command is parsed. This is necessary if the procedure is to work correctly: a different value must be substituted for $list each time the procedure is invoked. Note that braces nest, so that the last argument to `proc` extends up to the matching close brace. Figure 3.2 illustrates what happens when the following Tcl script is subsequently evaluated:

```
occur 18 {1 34 18 16 18 72 1994 -3}
```

The braces around the second argument to `occur` cause the entire list of numbers to be passed to `occur` as a single word. The Tcl procedure mechanism then passes the procedure's body to the Tcl interpreter for evaluation. When Tcl parses the `foreach` command in the body, the value of variable `list` is substituted, but the last argument to `foreach` (the loop body) is enclosed in braces so no substitutions are performed on it. The `foreach` command procedure sets variable `el` to each element of the list in turn and calls the Tcl interpeter to evaluate the loop body for each element. As part of this evaluation, Tcl parses the `if` command, substituting the values of variables `el` and `value`. In the snapshot shown in Figure 3.2, the `if` test succeeded so `if` evaluates the `incr` command.

Note: *If a brace is backslashed, it does not count in finding the matching close brace for a word enclosed in braces. The backslash will not be removed when the word is parsed.*

Note: *The only form of substitution that occurs between braces is for backslash-newline. As discussed in Section 3.5, backslash-newline sequences are actually removed in a pre-processing step before the command is parsed.*

3.8 Comments

If the first nonblank character of a command is #, the # and all the characters following it up through the next newline are treated as a comment and discarded. Note that the hashmark must occur in a position where Tcl is expecting the first character of a command. If a hashmark occurs anywhere else, it is treated as an ordinary character that forms part of a command word:

```
# This is a comment
set a 100                # Not a comment
```
∅ *wrong # args: should be "set varName ?newValue?"*
```
set b 101                ;# This is a comment
```
⇒ *101*

The # on the second line is not treated as a comment character because it occurs in the middle of a command. As a result, the first `set` command receives six arguments and generates an error. The last # is treated as a comment character, since it occurs just after a command was terminated with a semicolon.

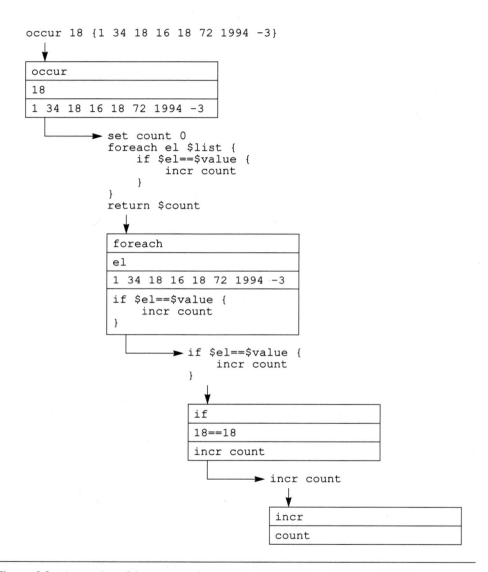

Figure 3.2. A snapshot of the nested scripts being evaluated at a particular point in the `occur` procedure. Each unboxed piece of text is a script being evaluated, and each down-pointing arrow corresponds to a call to the Tcl parser. Each box shows the words passed to a particular command procedure, after substitutions. Each right-pointing arrow corresponds to a recursive call to the Tcl interpreter. For example, the `foreach` command procedure calls the Tcl interpreter to evaluate the body of the loop.

3.9   Normal and exceptional returns

A Tcl command can complete in several different ways. A *normal return* is the most common case; it means that the command completed successfully and the return includes a string result. Tcl also supports *exceptional returns* from commands. The most frequent form of exceptional return is an error. When an error return occurs, it means that the command could not complete its intended function. The command is aborted and any commands that follow it in the script are skipped. An error return includes a string identifying what went wrong; the string is normally displayed by the application. For example, the following `set` command generates an error because it has too many arguments:

```
set state West Virginia
Ø  wrong # args: should be "set varName ?newValue?"
```

Different commands generate errors under different conditions. For example, `expr` accepts any number of arguments but requires the arguments to have a particular syntax; it generates an error if, for example, parentheses aren't matched:

```
expr 3 * (20+4
Ø  unmatched parentheses in expression "3 * (20+4"
```

The complete exceptional return mechanism for Tcl is discussed in Chapter 12. It supports a number of exceptional returns other than errors, provides additional information about errors besides the error message mentioned previously, and allows errors to be "caught" so that effects of the error can be contained within a piece of Tcl code. For now, though, all you need to know is that commands normally return string results but they sometimes return errors that cause Tcl command interpretation to be aborted.

Note: *You may also find the `errorInfo` variable useful. After an error Tcl sets `errorInfo` to hold a stack trace indicating exactly where the error occurred. You can print out this variable with the command "`set errorInfo`".*

3.10   More on substitutions

The most common difficulty for new Tcl users is understanding when substitutions do and do not occur. A typical scenario is for a user to be surprised at the behavior of a script because a substitution didn't occur when the user expected it to happen, or a substitution occurred when it wasn't expected. However, I think that you will find Tcl's substitution mechanism to be simple and predictable if you just remember two related rules:

1. Tcl parses a command and makes substitutions in a single pass from left to right. Each character is scanned exactly once.

2. At most a single layer of substitution occurs for each character; the result of one substitution is not scanned for further substitutions.

Tcl's substitutions are simpler and more regular than you may be used to if you've programmed with UNIX shells (particularly `csh`). When new users run into problems with Tcl substitutions it is often because they have assumed a more complex model than actually exists.

For example, consider the following command:

```
set x [format {Earnings for July: $%.2f} $earnings]
```
⇒ *Earnings for July: $1400.26*

The characters between `[ ]` are scanned exactly once, during command substitution, and the value of the `earnings` variable is substituted at that time. It is *not* the case that Tcl first scans the whole `set` command to substitute variables, then makes another pass to perform command substitution; everything happens in a single scan. The result of the `format` command is passed verbatim to `set` as its second argument without any additional scanning (for example, the dollar sign in `format`'s result does not trigger variable substitution).

One consequence of the substitution rules is that all the word boundaries within a command are immediately evident and are not affected by substitutions. For example, consider the following script:

```
set city "Los Angeles"
set bigCity $city
```

The second `set` command is guaranteed to have exactly three words regardless of the value of variable `city`. In this case `city` contains a space character but the space is *not* treated as a word separator.

In some situations the single-layer-of-substitutions rule can be a hindrance rather than a help. For example, the following script is an erroneous attempt to delete all files with names ending in `.o`:

```
exec rm [glob *.o]
```
∅ *rm: a.o b.o c.o nonexistent*

The `glob` command returns a list of all file names that match the pattern `*.o`, such as "a.o b.o c.o". The `exec` command then attempts to invoke the `rm` program to delete all of these files. However, the entire list of files is passed to `rm` as a single argument; `rm` reports an error because it cannot find a file named "a.o b.o c.o". For `rm` to work correctly, the result of `glob` must be split up into multiple words.

Fortunately, it is easy to add additional layers of parsing if you want them. Remember that Tcl commands are evaluated in two phases: parsing and execution. The substitution rules apply only to the parsing phase. Once Tcl passes the words of a command to a command procedure for execution, the command procedure can do anything it likes with them. Some commands will reparse their words — for example, by passing them back to the Tcl interpreter again. `eval` is an example of such a command, and it can be used to solve the problems with `rm` above:

```
eval exec rm [glob *.o]
```

`eval` concatenates all of its arguments with spaces in between and then evaluates the result as a Tcl script, at which point another round of parsing and evaluation occurs. In this example `eval` receives three arguments: `exec`, `rm`, and "`a.o b.o c.o`". It concatenates them to form the string "`exec rm a.o b.o c.o`". When this string is parsed as a Tcl script, it yields five words. Each of the file names is passed to `exec` and then to the `rm` program as a separate argument, so the files are all removed successfully. See Section 7.5 for more details.

One final note. It is possible to use substitutions in very complex ways, but I urge you not to do so. Substitutions work best when used in very simple ways such as "`set a $b`". If you use too many substitutions in a single command, and particularly if you use many backslashes, your code will be unreadable and unreliable. In situations like these I suggest breaking up the offending command into several commands that build up the arguments in simple stages. Tcl provides several commands, such as `format` and `list`, that should make this easy to do.

Chapter 4
Variables

Tcl supports two kinds of variables: simple variables and associative arrays. This chapter describes the basic Tcl commands for manipulating variables and arrays, and it also provides a more complete description of variable substitution. See Table 4.1 for a summary of the commands discussed in this chapter.

4.1 Simple variables and the set command

A simple Tcl variable has a name and a value. Both the name and the value may be arbitrary strings of characters. For example, it is possible to have a variable named "`xyz !# 22`" or "`March earnings: $100,472`". In practice, variable names usually start with a letter and consist of a combination of letters, digits, and underscores, since that makes it easier to use variable substitution. Variable names, like all names in Tcl, are case sensitive: `numwords` refers to a different variable than `NumWords`.

Variables may be created, read, and modified with the `set` command, which takes either one or two arguments. The first argument is the name of a variable and the second, if present, is a new value for the variable:

```
    set a {Four score and seven years ago}
⇒ Four score and seven years ago
    set a
⇒ Four score and seven years ago
    set a 12.6
⇒ 12.6
```

`append varName value ?value ...?`	
	Appends each of the `value` arguments to variable `varName`, in order. If `varName` doesn't exist, it is created with an empty value before appending. The return value is the new value of `varName`.
`incr varName ?increment?`	
	Adds `increment` to the value of variable `varName`. `increment` and the old value of `varName` must both be integer strings (decimal, hexadecimal, or octal). If `increment` is omitted, it defaults to 1. The new value is stored in `varName` as a decimal string and returned as the result of the command.
`set varName ?value?`	
	If `value` is specified, sets the value of variable `varName` to `value`. In any case the command returns the (new) value of the variable.
`unset varName ?varName varName ...?`	
	Deletes the variables given by the `varName` arguments. Returns an empty string.

Table 4.1. A summary of the basic commands for manipulating variables. Optional arguments are indicated by enclosing them in question marks.

The first command creates a new variable a if it doesn't already exist and sets its value to the character sequence "Four score and seven years ago". The result of the command is the new value of the variable. The second set command has only one argument: a. In this form it simply returns the current value of the variable. The third set command changes the value of a to 12.6 and returns that new value.

Although the final value of a looks like a real number, it is stored as a character string. Tcl variables can be used to represent many things, such as integers, real numbers, names, lists, and Tcl scripts, but they are always stored as strings. This use of a single representation for all values allows different values to be manipulated in the same way and communicated easily. Since variables don't have types, there is no need for declarations. Tcl variables are created automatically when they are assigned values.

4.2 Arrays

In addition to simple variables Tcl also provides *arrays*. An array is a collection of *elements*, each of which is a variable with its own name and value. The name of an array element has two parts: the name of the array and the name of the element within that array. Both array names and element names may be arbitrary strings. For this reason Tcl arrays are sometimes called *associative arrays* to distinguish them from arrays in other languages where the element names must be integers.

Array elements are referenced using notation like `earnings(January)` where the array name (`earnings` in this case) is followed by the element name in parentheses (`January` in this case). Arrays may be used anywhere that simple variables may be used, such as in the `set` command:

```
    set earnings(January) 87966
⇒ 87966
    set earnings(February) 95400
⇒ 95400
    set earnings(January)
⇒ 87966
```

The first command creates an array named `earnings`, if it doesn't already exist. Then it creates an element `January` within the array, if it doesn't already exist, and assigns it the value `87966`. The second command assigns a value to the `February` element of the array, and the third command returns the value of the `January` element.

Note: *For a way to list all of the elements of an array, see Section 13.1.*

4.3   Variable substitution

Chapter 3 introduced the use of $-notation for substituting variable values into Tcl commands. This section describes the mechanism in more detail.

Variable substitution is triggered by the presence of an unquoted $ character in a Tcl command. The characters following the $ are treated as a variable name, and the $ and name are replaced in the word by the value of the variable. Tcl provides three forms of variable substitution. So far you have seen only the simplest form, which is used like this:

```
    expr $a+2
```

In this form the $ is followed by a variable name consisting of letters, digits, and underscores. The first character that is not a letter or digit or underscore (+ in the example) terminates the name.

The second form of variable substitution allows array elements to be substituted. This form is like the first one except that the variable name is followed immediately by an element name enclosed in parentheses. Variable, command, and backslash substitutions are performed on the element name in the same way as a command word in double quotes, and spaces in the element name are treated as part of the name rather than as word separators. For example, consider the following script:

```
set yearTotal 0
foreach month {Jan Feb Mar Apr May Jun Jul Aug Sep \
    Oct Nov Dec} {
  set yearTotal [expr $yearTotal+$earnings($month)]
}
```

In the `expr` command `$earnings($month)` is replaced with the value of an element of the array `earnings`. The element's name is given by the value of the `month` variable, which varies from iteration to iteration.

The last form of substitution is used for simple variables in places where the variable name is followed by a letter or number or underscore. For example, suppose that you wish to pass a value such as `1.5m` to a command as an argument, but the number is in a variable `size` (in Tk you might do this to specify a size in millimeters). If you try to substitute the variable value with a form like `$sizem`, Tcl will treat the `m` as part of the variable name. To get around this problem, you can enclose the variable name in braces as in the following command:

```
.canvas configure -width ${size}m
```

You can also use braces to specify variable names containing characters other than letters or numbers or underscores.

Note: *Braces can be used to delimit only simple variables; there is no way to specify an element of an array with brace notation.*

Tcl's variable substitution mechanism is intended to handle only the most common situations; there exist scenarios where none of the preceding forms of substitution achieves the desired effect. More complicated situations can be handled with a sequence of commands. For example, the `format` command can be used to generate a variable name of almost any imaginable form, `set` can be used to read or write the variable with that name, and command substitution can be used to substitute the value of the variable into other commands.

4.4   Removing variables: unset

The `unset` command destroys variables. It takes any number of arguments, each of which is a variable name, and removes all of the variables. Future attempts to read the variables will result in errors just as if the variables had never been set in the first place. The arguments to `unset` may be either simple variables, elements of arrays, or whole arrays, as in the following example:

```
unset a earnings(January) b
```

In this case the variables a and b are removed entirely and the `January` element of the `earnings` array is removed. The `earnings` array continues to exist after the `unset` command. If a or b is an array, all of the elements of that array are removed along with the array itself.

4.5 **Multidimensional arrays**

Tcl implements only one-dimensional arrays, but multidimensional arrays can be simulated by concatenating multiple indices into a single element name. The program below simulates a two-dimensional array indexed with integers:

```
set matrix(1,1) 140
set matrix(1,2) 218
set matrix(1,3) 84
set i 1
set j 2
set cell $matrix($i,$j)
```
⇒ *218*

Matrix is an array with three elements whose names are 1,1 and 1,2 and 1,3. However, the array behaves just as if it were a two-dimensional array; in particular, variable substitution occurs while scanning the element name in the set command, so that the values of i and j get combined into an appropriate element name.

Note: *Spaces are significant in this example:* matrix(1,1) *refers to a different variable than* matrix(1, 1). *I recommend leaving out the spaces, since they can also cause confusion when parsing commands. For example, the command*

```
set matrix(1, 1) 140
```

is a command with four words, of which the third is "1)". This will result in three arguments to set, *which will then cause an error. The entire variable name would have to be enclosed in double quotes to get around this problem.*

4.6 **The incr and append commands**

incr and append provide simple ways to change the value of a variable. incr takes two arguments, which are the name of a variable and an integer. incr adds the integer to the variable's value, stores the result back into the variable as a decimal string, and returns the variable's new value as result:

```
set x 43
incr x 12
```
⇒ *55*

The number can have either a positive or negative value. It can also be omitted, in which case it defaults to 1:

```
set x 43
incr x
```
⇒ *44*

Both the variable's original value and the increment must be integer strings, either in decimal, octal (indicated by a leading 0), or hexadecimal (indicated by a leading 0x).

The append command adds text to the end of a variable. It takes two arguments, which are the name of the variable and the new text to add to the variable. It appends the new text to the variable and returns the variable's new value. The following example uses append to compute a table of squares:

```
set msg ""
foreach i {1 2 3 4 5} {
    append msg "$i squared is [expr $i*$i]\n"
}
set msg
```
⇒ *1 squared is 1*
   2 squared is 4
   3 squared is 9
   4 squared is 16
   5 squared is 25

Neither incr nor append adds any new functionality to Tcl, since the effects of these commands can be achieved in other ways. However, they provide simple ways to do common operations. In addition, append is implemented in a fashion that avoids character copying. If you need to construct a very large string incrementally from pieces, it will be much more efficient to use a command such as

```
append x $piece
```
instead of

```
set x "$x$piece"
```

4.7 Predefined variables

Several variables are used in standard ways across almost all Tcl applications. For example, when you invoke a tclsh or wish script file, the name of the script file is stored in variable argv0, the command-line arguments are stored in variable argv, and the number of command-line arguments is stored in variable argc. Consider the following tclsh script:

```
#!/usr/local/bin/tclsh
puts "The command name is \"$argv0\""
puts "There were $argc arguments: $argv"
```
If you place this script in a file named printargs, make the file executable, and then invoke it from your shell, it will print out information about its arguments:

```
printargs red green blue
```
⇒ *The command name is "printargs"*
   There were 3 arguments: red green blue

Tcl doesn't require that all applications support argv0, argv, and argc in this way, but most Tcl applications do.

The variable `env` is predefined by Tcl. It is an array variable whose elements are all of the process's environment variables. For example, the following command will print out the user's home directory, as determined by the HOME environment variable:

```
puts "Your home directory is $env(HOME)"
```

4.8 Preview of other variable facilities

Tcl provides a number of other commands for manipulating variables. These commands will be introduced in full after you've learned more about the Tcl language, but this section contains a short preview of some of the facilities.

The `trace` command can be used to monitor a variable so that a Tcl script gets invoked whenever the variable is set, read, or unset. Variable tracing is sometimes useful during debugging, and it allows you to create read-only variables. You can also use traces for *propagation* so that, for example, a database or screen display gets updated whenever a variable changes value. Variable tracing is discussed in Section 13.4.

The `array` command can be used to find the names of all the elements in an array and to step through them one at a time (see Section 13.1). It's possible to find out what variables exist using the `info` command (see Section 13.2).

The `global` and `upvar` commands can be used by a procedure to access variables other than its own local variables. These commands are discussed in Chapter 8.

Chapter 5
Expressions

Expressions combine values (or *operands*) with *operators* to produce new values. For example, the expression 4+2 contains two operands, 4 and 2, and one operator, +; it evaluates to 6. Many Tcl commands expect one or more of their arguments to be expressions. The simplest such command is `expr`, which just evaluates its arguments as an expression and returns the result as a string:

```
expr (8+4) * 6.2
```
⇒ *74.4*

Another example is `if`, which evaluates its first argument as an expression and uses the result to determine whether or not to evaluate its second argument as a Tcl script:

```
if $x<2 {set x 2}
```

This chapter uses the `expr` command for all of its examples, but the same syntax, substitution, and evaluation rules apply to all other uses of expressions too. See Table 5.1 for a summary of the `expr` command.

5.1 Numeric operands

Expression operands are normally integers or real numbers. Integers are usually specified in decimal, but if the first character is 0 (zero), the number is read in octal (base 8), and if the first two characters are 0x, the number is read in hexadecimal (base 16). For example, 335 is a decimal number, 0517 is an octal number with the same value, and 0x14f is a hexadecimal number with the same value. 092 is not a valid integer: the leading 0 causes

> expr *arg* ?*arg arg* ...?
>> Concatenates all the *arg* values together (with spaces between), evaluates
>> the result as an expression, and returns a string corresponding to the
>> expression's value.

Table 5.1. A summary of the `expr` command.

---

the number to be read in octal but 9 is not a valid octal digit. Real operands may be specified using most of the forms defined for ANSI C, including the following examples:

```
2.1
7.91e+16
6E4
3.
```

Note: *These same forms are allowable not just in expressions but anywhere in Tcl that an integer or real value is required.*

Expression operands can also be non-numeric strings. String operands are discussed in Section 5.5.

5.2 Operators and precedence

Table 5.2 lists all of the operators supported in Tcl expressions; they are similar to the operators for expressions in ANSI C. Horizontal lines separate groups of operators with the same precedence, and operators with higher precedence appear in the table above operators with lower precedence. For example, $4*2<7$ evaluates to 0 because the $*$ operator has higher precedence than $<$. Except in the simplest and most obvious cases you should use parentheses to indicate the way operators should be grouped; this will prevent errors by you or by others who modify your programs.

Operators with the same precedence group from left to right. For example, $10-4-3$ is the same as $(10-4)-3$; it evaluates to 3.

5.2.1 Arithmetic operators

Tcl expressions support the arithmetic operators $+$, $-$, $*$, $/$, and $\%$. The $-$ operator may be used either as a binary operator for subtraction, as in $4-2$, or as a unary operator for negation, as in $-(6*\$i)$. The $/$ operator truncates its result to an integer value if both operands are integers. $\%$ is the modulus operator; its result is the remainder when its first operand is divided by the second. Both of the operands for $\%$ must be integers.

Syntax	Result	Operand Types
$-a$	Negative of a	int, real
$!a$	Logical NOT: 1 if a is zero, 0 otherwise	int, real
$\sim a$	Bit-wise complement of a	int
$a*b$	Multiply a and b	int, real
a/b	Divide a by b	int, real
$a\%b$	Remainder after dividing a by b	int
$a+b$	Add a and b	int, real
$a-b$	Subtract b from a	int, real
$a<<b$	Left-shift a by b bits	int
$a>>b$	Arithmetic right-shift a by b bits	int
$a<b$	1 if a is less than b, 0 otherwise	int, real, string
$a>b$	1 if a is greater than b, 0 otherwise	int, real, string
$a<=b$	1 if a is less than or equal to b, 0 otherwise	int, real, string
$a>=b$	1 if a is greater than or equal to b, 0 otherwise	int, real, string
$a==b$	1 if a is equal to b, 0 otherwise	int, real, string
$a!=b$	1 if a is not equal to b, 0 otherwise	int, real, string
$a\&b$	Bit-wise AND of a and b	int
a^b	Bit-wise exclusive OR of a and b	int
$a|b$	Bit-wise OR of a and b	int
$a\&\&b$	Logical AND: 1 if both a and b are non-zero, 0 otherwise	int, real
$a||b$	Logical OR: 1 if either a is non-zero or b is non-zero, 0 otherwise	int, real
$a?b:c$	Choice: if a is non-zero then b, else c	a: int, real

Table 5.2. Summary of the operators allowed in Tcl expressions. These operators have the same behavior as in ANSI C except that some of the operators allow string operands. Groups of operands between horizontal lines have the same precedence; higher groups have higher precedence.

Note: *The / and % operators have a more consistent behavior in Tcl than in ANSI C. In Tcl the remainder is always greater than or equal to zero and it has an absolute value less than the absolute value of the divisor. ANSI C guarantees only the second property. In both ANSI C and Tcl, the quotient will always have the property that $(x/y)*y + x\%y$ is x for all x and y.*

5.2.2 Relational operators

The operators < (less than), <= (less than or equal), >= (greater than or equal), > (greater than), == (equal), and != (not equal) are used for comparing two values. Each operator produces a result of 1 (true) if its operands meet the condition and 0 (false) if they don't.

5.2.3 Logical operators

The logical operators &&, ||, and ! are typically used for combining the results of relational operators, as in the expression

```
($x > 4) && ($x < 10)
```

Each operator produces a 0 or 1 result. && (logical AND) produces a 1 result if both its operands are nonzero, || (logical OR) produces a 1 result if either of its operands is nonzero, and ! (NOT) produces a 1 result if its single operand is zero.

In Tcl, as in ANSI C, a zero value is treated as false and anything other than zero is treated as true. Whenever Tcl generates a true/false value, though, it always uses 1 for true and 0 for false.

As in C, the operands of && and || are evaluated sequentially: if the first operand of && evaluates to 0, or if the first operand of || evaluates to 1, then the second operand is not evaluated.

5.2.4 Bitwise operators

Tcl provides six operators that manipulate the individual bits of integers: &, |, ^, <<, >>, and ~. These operators require their operands to be integers. The &, |, and ^ operators perform bitwise AND, OR, and exclusive OR: each bit of the result is generated by applying the given operation to the corresponding bits of the left and right operands. Note that & and | do not always produce the same result as && and ||:

```
    expr 8&&2
⇒   1
    expr 8&2
⇒   0
```

The operators << and >> use the right operand as a shift count and produce a result consisting of the left operand shifted left or right by that number of bits. During left shifts zeros are shifted into the low-order bits. Right shifting is always "arithmetic right shift", meaning that it shifts in zeros for positive numbers and ones for negative numbers. This behavior is different from right-shifting in ANSI C, which is machine-dependent.

The ~ operand ("ones complement") takes only a single operand and produces a result whose bits are the opposite of those in the operand: zeros replace ones and vice versa.

5.2.5   Choice operator

The ternary operator ?: may be used to select one of two results:

```
expr {($a < $b) ? $a : $b}
```

This expression returns the smaller of $a and $b. The choice operator checks the value of its first operand for truth or falsehood. If it is true (nonzero), the argument following the ? is the result; if the first operand is false (zero), the third operand is the result. Only one of the second and third arguments is evaluated.

5.3   Math functions

Tcl expressions support a number of mathematical functions, such as sin and exp. Math functions are invoked using standard functional notation:

```
expr 2*sin($x)
expr hypot($x, $y) + $z
```

The arguments to math functions may be arbitrary expressions, and multiple arguments are separated by commas. See Table 5.3 for a list of all the built-in functions.

5.4   Substitutions

Substitutions can occur in two ways for expression operands. The first way is through the normal Tcl parser mechanisms, as in the following command:

```
expr 2*sin($x)
```

In this case the Tcl parser substitutes the value of variable x before executing the command, so the first argument to expr will have a value such as 2*sin(0.8). The second way is through the expression evaluator, which performs an additional round of variable and command substitution on the expression while evaluating it. For example, consider the command:

```
expr {2*sin($x)}
```

In this case the braces prevent the Tcl parser from substituting the value of x, so the argument to expr is 2*sin($x). When the expression evaluator encounters the dollar sign it performs variable substitution itself, using the value of variable x as the argument to sin.

Having two layers of substitution doesn't usually make any difference for the expr command, but it is vitally important for other commands such as while that evaluate an expression repeatedly and expect to get different results each time. For example, consider the following script, which finds the smallest power of two greater than a given number:

Function	Result
abs(*x*)	Absolute value of *x*.
acos(*x*)	Arc cosine of *x*, in the range 0 to π.
asin(*x*)	Arc sine of *x*, in the range $-\pi/2$ to $\pi/2$.
atan(*x*)	Arc tangent of *x*, in the range $-\pi/2$ to $\pi/2$.
atan2(*x*, *y*)	Arc tangent of *x*/*y*, in the range $-\pi/2$ to $\pi/2$.
ceil(*x*)	Smallest integer not less than *x*.
cos(*x*)	Cosine of *x* (*x* in radians).
cosh(*x*)	Hyperbolic cosine of *x*.
double(*i*)	Real value equal to integer *i*.
exp(*x*)	*e* raised to the power *x*.
floor(*x*)	Largest integer not greater than *x*.
fmod(*x*, *y*)	Real remainder of *x* divided by *y*.
hypot(*x*, *y*)	Square root of $(x^2 + y^2)$.
int(*x*)	Integer value produced by truncating *x* toward 0.
log(*x*)	Natural logarithm of *x*.
log10(*x*)	Base 10 logarithm of *x*.
pow(*x*, *y*)	*x* raised to the power *y*.
round(*x*)	Integer value produced by rounding *x*.
sin(*x*)	Sine of *x* (*x* in radians).
sinh(*x*)	Hyperbolic sine of *x*.
sqrt(*x*)	Square root of *x*.
tan(*x*)	Tangent of *x* (*x* in radians).
tanh(*x*)	Hyperbolic tangent of *x*.

Table 5.3. The mathematical functions supported in Tcl expressions. In most cases the functions have the same behavior as the ANSI C library procedures with the same names.

```
set pow 1
while {$pow<$num} {
    set pow [expr $pow*2]
}
```

The expression $pow<$num gets evaluated by `while` at the beginning of each iteration to decide whether or not to terminate the loop. It is essential that the expression evaluator use a new value of `pow` each time. If the braces were omitted so that variable substitution is performed while parsing the `while` command, for example, "while $pow<$num ...", then while's argument would be a constant expression such as 1>44; either the loop would never execute or it would execute forever.

Note: *When the expression evaluator performs variable or command substitution, the value substituted must be an integer or real number (or a string, as described next). It cannot be an arbitrary expression.*

5.5 String manipulation

Unlike expressions in ANSI C, Tcl expressions allow string operands for some operators, as in the following command:

```
if {$x == "New York"} {
...
}
```

In this example, the expression evaluator compares the value of variable x to the string New York using string comparison; the body of the if will be executed if they are identical. To specify a string operand, you must either enclose it in quotes or braces or use variable or command substitution. It is important to enclose the expression in the preceding example in braces so that the expression evaluator substitutes the value of x. If the braces are left out, the argument to if will be a string such as

```
Los Angeles == "New York"
```

The expression parser will not be able to parse Los (it isn't a number, it doesn't make sense as a function name, and it can't be interpreted as a string because it doesn't have quotes around it) so a syntax error will occur.

If a string is enclosed in quotes, the expression evaluator performs command, variable, and backslash substitution on the characters between the quotes. If a string is enclosed in braces, then no substitutions are performed. Braces nest for strings in expressions in the same way that they nest for words of a command.

The only operators that allow string operands are <, >, <=, >=, ==, and !=. For all other operators the operands must be numeric. Furthermore, Tcl only uses string operations if one or both of the operands cannot be parsed as a number. For example, consider the following script:

```
set x 0
set y 00
if {$x == $y} {
    ...
}
```

Arithmetic comparison will be used for the if test so the test will evaluate to 1. If you want to force string comparison even for numeric operands, you must use a command such as string compare.

For operators like <, the strings are compared lexicographically using the system's strcmp library function. The sorting order may vary from system to system.

Note: *If the two operands of == are both numbers, then Tcl uses numeric comparison rather*
            than string comparison. If you want to compare two values as strings in a situation where
            they may both look like numbers (e.g., the values are stored in variables so you don't know
            what their values are), then don't use the == operator; use the `string compare`
            command instead.

5.6 Types and conversions

Tcl evaluates expressions numerically whenever possible. String operations are performed
only for the relational operators and only if one or both of the operands doesn't make
sense as a number. Most operators permit either integer or real operands but a few, such as
<< and &, allow only integers.

   If the operands for an operator have different types, Tcl automatically converts one of
them to the type of the other. If one operand is an integer and the other is a real, then the
integer operand is converted to real. If one operand is a non-numeric string and the other is
an integer or real, then the integer or real operand is converted to a string. The result of an
operation always has the same type as the operands except for relational operators such as
<, which always produce 0/1 integer results. You can use the math function `double` to
promote an integer to a real explicitly, and `int` and `round` to convert a real value back to
integer by truncation or rounding.

5.7 Precision

During expression evaluation, Tcl represents integers internally with the C type `int`,
which provides at least 32 bits of precision on most machines. Real numbers are represented with the C type `double`, which is usually represented with 64-bit values (about 15
decimal digits of precision) using the IEEE Floating Point Standard.

   Numbers are kept in internal form throughout the evaluation of an expression and are
only converted back to strings when necessary, such as when `expr` returns its result. Integers are converted to signed decimal strings without any loss of precision. When a real
value is converted to a string, only six significant digits are retained by default:

```
    expr 1.11111111 + 1.11111111
⇒  2.22222
```

If you would like more significant digits to be retained when real values are converted to
strings you can set the `tcl_precision` global variable with the desired number of significant digits:

```
    set tcl_precision 12
    expr 1.11111111 + 1.11111111
⇒  2.22222222
```

The `tcl_precision` variable is used not just for the `expr` command but anywhere that a Tcl application converts a real number to a string.

Note: *If you set `tcl_precision` to 17 on a machine that uses IEEE floating point, you will guarantee that string conversions do not lose information: if an expression result is converted to a string and then later used in a different expression, the internal form after conversion back from the string will be identical to the internal form before converting to the string.*

Chapter 6
Lists

Lists are used in Tcl to deal with collections of things, such as all the users in a group or all the files in a directory or all the options for a widget. Lists allow you to collect together any number of values in one place, pass around the collection as a single entity, and later get the component values back again. A list is an ordered collection of *elements* where each element can have any string value, such as a number, a person's name, the name of a window, or a word of a Tcl command. Lists are represented as strings with a particular structure; this means that you can store lists in variables, type them to commands, and nest them as elements of other lists.

This chapter describes the structure of lists and presents a dozen basic commands for manipulating lists. The commands perform operations like creating lists, inserting and extracting elements, and searching for particular elements (see Table 6.1 for a summary). Later chapters describe additional commands that take lists as arguments or return them as results.

6.1 Basic list structure and the lindex command

In its simplest form a list is a string containing any number of elements separated by spaces or tabs. For example, the string

```
John Anne Mary Jim
```

is a list with four elements. There can be any number of elements in a list, and each element can be an arbitrary string. In this simple form, elements cannot contain spaces, but there is additional list syntax that allows spaces within elements, as discussed later.

`concat ?list list ...?`
> Joins multiple lists into a single list (each element of each `list` becomes an element of the result list) and returns the new list.

`join list ?joinString?`
> Concatenates list elements together with `joinString` as separator and returns the result. `JoinString` defaults to a space.

`lappend varName value ?value ...?`
> Appends each `value` to variable `varName` as a list element and returns the new value of the variable. Creates the variable if it doesn't already exist.

`lindex list index`
> Returns the `index`'th element from `list` (0 refers to the first element).

`linsert list index value ?value ...?`
> Returns a new list formed by inserting all of the `value` arguments as list elements before `index`'th element of `list` (0 refers to the first element).

`list ?value value ...?`
> Returns a list whose elements are the `value` arguments.

`llength list`
> Returns the number of elements in `list`.

`lrange list first last`
> Returns a list consisting of elements `first` through `last` of `list`. If `last` is end, it selects all elements up to the end of the list.

`lreplace list first last ?value value ...?`
> Returns a new list formed by replacing elements `first` through `last` of `list` with zero or more new elements, each formed from one `value` argument.

`lsearch ?-exact? ?-glob? ?-regexp? list pattern`
> Returns the index of the first element in `list` that matches `pattern` or -1 if none. The optional switch selects a pattern-matching technique (default: `-glob`).

Table 6.1. A summary of the list-related commands in Tcl (continued).

```
lsort ?-ascii? ?-integer? ?-real? ?-command command? \
    ?-increasing? ?-decreasing? list
                Returns a new list formed by sorting the elements of list. The switches
                determine the comparison function and sorted order (default: -ascii
                -increasing).
```
```
split string ?splitChars?
                Returns a list formed by splitting string at instances of splitChars and
                turning the characters between these instances into list elements.
```

Table 6.1, continued.

The `lindex` command extracts an element from a list:

```
lindex {John Anne Mary Jim} 1
```
⇒ *Anne*

`lindex` takes two arguments, a list and an index, and returns the selected element of the list. An index of 0 corresponds to the first element of the list, 1 corresponds to the second element, and so on. If the index is outside the range of the list, an empty string is returned.

When a list is entered in a Tcl command, the list is usually enclosed in braces, as in the previous example. The braces are not part of the list; they are needed on the command line to pass the entire list to the command as a single word. When lists are stored in variables or printed out, there are no braces around them:

```
set x {John Anne Mary Jim}
```
⇒ *John Anne Mary Jim*

Braces and backslashes within list elements are handled by the list commands in the same way that the Tcl command parser treats them in words. This means that you can enclose a list element in braces if it contains spaces, and you can use backslash substitution to get special characters such as braces into list elements. Braces are often used to nest lists within lists, as in the following example:

```
lindex {a b {c d e} f} 2
```
⇒ *c d e*

In this case element 2 of the list is itself a list with three elements. There is no intrinsic limit on how deeply lists may be nested.

6.2 Creating lists: concat, list, and llength

Tcl provides two commands that combine strings to produce lists: `concat` and `list`. Each of these commands accepts an arbitrary number of arguments, and each produces a list as a result. However, they differ in the way they combine their arguments. The con-cat command takes any number of lists as arguments and joins all of the elements of the argument lists into a single large list:

```
concat {a b c} {d e} f {g h i}
⇒ a b c d e f g h i
```

concat expects its arguments to have proper list structure; if the arguments are not well-formed lists, the result may not be a well-formed list either. In fact, all that concat does is to concatenate its argument strings into one large string with space characters between the arguments. The same effect as concat can be achieved using double quotes:

```
set x {a b c}
set y {d e}
set z [concat $x $y]
⇒ a b c d e
set z "$x $y"
⇒ a b c d e
```

The list command joins its arguments so that each argument becomes a distinct element of the resulting list:

```
list {a b c} {d e} f {g h i}
⇒ {a b c} {d e} f {g h i}
```

In this case, the result list contains only four elements. The list command will always produce a list with proper structure, regardless of the structure of its arguments (it adds braces or backslashes as needed), and the lindex command can always be used to extract the original elements of a list created with list. The arguments to list need not themselves be well-formed lists.

The llength command returns the number of elements in a list:

```
llength {{a b c} {d e} f {g h i}}
⇒ 4
llength a
⇒ 1
llength {}
⇒ 0
```

As you can see from the examples, a simple string like a is a proper list with one element and an empty string is a proper list with zero elements.

6.3 Modifying lists: linsert, lreplace, lrange, and lappend

The linsert command forms a new list by adding one or more elements to an existing list:

```
    set x {a b {c d} e}
⇒  a b {c d} e
    linsert $x 2 X Y Z
⇒  a b X Y Z {c d} e
    linsert $x 0 {X Y} Z
⇒  {X Y} Z a b {c d} e
```

linsert takes three or more arguments. The first is a list, the second is the index of an element within that list, and the third and additional arguments are new elements to insert into the list. The return value from linsert is a list formed by inserting the new elements just before the element indicated by the index. If the index is zero, the new elements go at the beginning of the list; if it is one, the new elements go after the first element in the old list; and so on. If the index is greater than or equal to the number of elements in the original list, the new elements are inserted at the end of the list.

The lreplace command deletes elements from a list and optionally adds new elements in their place. It takes three or more arguments. The first argument is a list and the second and third arguments give the indices of the first and last elements to be deleted. If only three arguments are specified, the result is a new list produced by deleting the given range of elements from the original list:

```
    lreplace {a b {c d} e} 3 3
⇒  a b {c d}
```

If additional arguments are specified to lreplace as in the following example, they are inserted into the list in place of the elements that were deleted.

```
    lreplace {a b {c d} e} 1 2 {W X} Y Z
⇒  a {W X} Y Z e
```

The lrange command extracts a range of elements from a list. It takes as arguments a list and two indices and it returns a new list consisting of the range of elements that lie between the two indices (inclusive):

```
    set x {a b {c d} e}
⇒  a b {c d} e
    lrange $x 1 3
⇒  b {c d} e
    lrange $x 0 1
⇒  a b
```

The lappend command provides an efficient way to append new elements to a list stored in a variable. It takes as arguments the name of a variable and any number of additional arguments. Each of the additional arguments is appended to the variable's value as a new list element and lappend returns the variable's new value:

```
    set x {a b {c d} e}
⇒  a b {c d} e
```

```
      lappend x XX {YY ZZ}
  ⇒   a b {c d} e XX {YY ZZ}
      set x
  ⇒   a b {c d} e XX {YY ZZ}
```

lappend is similar to append except that it enforces proper list structure. As with
append, it isn't strictly necessary. For example, the command

```
      lappend x $a $b $c
```

could be written instead as

```
      set x "$x [list $a $b $c]"
```

However, as with append, lappend is implemented in a way that avoids string copies.
For large lists, this can make a big difference in performance.

Note: *lappend is different from other list commands such as lreplace in that the list is not
included directly in the command; instead, you specify the name of a variable containing
the list.*

6.4   Searching lists: lsearch

The lsearch command searches a list for an element with a particular value. It takes
two arguments, the first of which is a list and second of which is a pattern:

```
      set x {John Anne Mary Jim}
      lsearch $x Mary
  ⇒   2
      lsearch $x Phil
  ⇒   -1
```

lsearch returns the index of the first element in the list that matches the pattern, or −1 if
there was no matching element.

One of three different pattern matching techniques can be selected by specifying one
of the switches −exact, −glob, and −regexp before the list argument:

```
      lsearch -glob $x A*
  ⇒   1
```

The −glob switch causes matching to occur with the rules of the string match command described in Section 9.2. A −regexp switch causes matching to occur with regular
expression rules as described in Section 9.3, and −exact insists on an exact match only.
If no switch is specified, −glob is assumed by default.

6.5   Sorting lists: lsort

The `lsort` command takes a list as argument and returns a new list with the same elements, but sorted in increasing lexicographic order:

```
    lsort {John Anne Mary Jim}
⇒ Anne Jim John Mary
```

You can precede the list with any of several switches to control the sort. For example, `-decreasing` specifies that the result should have the "largest" element first and `-integer` specifies that the elements should be treated as integers and sorted according to integer value:

```
    lsort -decreasing {John Anne Mary Jim}
⇒ Mary John Jim Anne
    lsort {10 1 2}
⇒ 1 10 2
    lsort -integer {10 1 2}
⇒ 1 2 10
```

You can use the `-command` option to specify your own sorting function (see the reference documentation for details).

6.6   Converting between strings and lists: split and join

The `split` command breaks a string into component pieces so that you can process the pieces independently. It creates a list whose elements are the pieces, so that you can use any of the list commands to process the pieces. For example, suppose a variable contains a UNIX file name with components separated by slashes, and you want to convert it to a list with one element for each component:

```
    set x a/b/c
    set y /usr/include/sys/types.h
    split $x /
⇒ a b c
    split $y /
⇒ {} usr include sys types.h
```

The first argument to `split` is the string to be split up and the second argument contains one or more *split characters*. `split` locates all instances of any of the split characters in the string. It then creates a list whose elements consist of the substrings between the split characters. The ends of the string are also treated as split characters. If there are consecutive split characters, or if the string starts or ends with a split character as in the second example, then empty elements are generated in the results. The split characters themselves are discarded. Several split characters can be specified, as in the following example:

```
    split xbaybz ab
⇒ x {} y z
```

If an empty string is specified for the split characters, each character of the string is made into a separate list element:

```
    split {a b c} {}
⇒ a { } b { } c
```

The join command is approximately the inverse of split. It concatenates list elements together with a given separator string between them:

```
    join {{} usr include sys types.h} /
⇒ /usr/include/sys/types.h
    set x {24 112 5}
    expr [join $x +]
⇒ 141
```

join takes two arguments: a list and a separator string. It extracts all of the elements from the list and concatenates them together with the separator string between each pair of elements. The separator string can contain any number of characters, including zero. In the first example here, a file name is generated by joining the list elements with /. In the second example, a Tcl expression is generated by joining the list elements with +.

One of the most common uses for split and join is for dealing with file names as shown earlier. Another common use is for splitting up text into lines by using newline as the split character.

6.7   Lists and commands

A very important relationship exists between lists and commands in Tcl. Any proper list is also a well-formed Tcl command. If a list is evaluated as a Tcl script, it will consist of a single command whose words are the list elements. In other words, the Tcl parser will perform no substitutions whatsoever. It will simply extract the list elements with each element becoming one word of the command. This property is very important because it allows you to generate Tcl commands that are guaranteed to parse in a particular fashion even if some of the command's words contain special characters such as spaces or $.

For example, suppose you are creating a button widget in Tk, and when the user clicks on the widget you would like to reset a variable to a particular value. You might create such a widget with the following command:

```
    button .b -text Reset -command {set x 0}
```

The Tcl script "set x 0" will be evaluated whenever the user clicks on the button. Now suppose that the value to be stored in the variable is not constant, but instead is computed just before the button command and must be taken from a variable initValue. Furthermore, suppose that `initValue` could contain any string whatsoever. You might rewrite the command as

```
button .b -text Reset -command {set x $initValue}
```

The script "`set x $initValue`" will be evaluated when the user clicks on the button. However, this will use the value of `initValue` at the time the user clicks on the button, which may not be the same as the value when the button was created. For example, the same variable might be used to create several buttons, each with a different intended reset value.

To solve this problem, you must generate a Tcl command that contains the *value* of the `initValue` variable, not its name, and use this as part of the `-command` option for the `button` command. Unfortunately, a simple approach like

```
button .b -text Reset -command "set x $initValue"
```

will not work in general. If the value of `initValue` is something simple like 47, then this will work fine. The resulting command will be "`set x 47`", which will produce the desired result. However, what if `initValue` contains `New York`? In this case the resulting command will be "`set x New York`", which has four words; `set` will generate an error because there are too many arguments. Even worse, what if `initValue` contains special characters such as `$` or `[`? These characters could cause unwanted substitutions to occur when the command is evaluated.

The only solution that is guaranteed to work for any value of `initValue` is to use list commands to generate the command, as in the following example:

```
button .b -text Reset -command [list set x $initValue]
```

The result of the `list` command is a Tcl command whose first word will be `set`, whose second word will be `x`, and whose third word will be the value of `initValue` at the time the button is created (not when it is pressed). For example, suppose that the value of `initValue` is `New York`. The command generated by `list` will be

```
set x {New York}
```

which will parse and execute correctly. Whatever value is present in `initVal` when the `button` command is invoked will be assigned to `x` when the button is pressed, and this is guaranteed to work regardless of the contents of `initVal`. Any of the Tcl special characters will also be handled correctly by `list`:

```
set initValue {Earnings: $1410.13}
list set x $initValue
```
⇒   *set x {Earnings: $1410.13}*
```
set initValue "{ \\"
list set x $initValue
```
⇒   *set x \{\ *

Chapter 7
Control Flow

This chapter describes the Tcl commands for controlling the flow of execution in a script. Tcl's control flow commands are similar to the control flow statements in the C programming language and csh, including if, while, for, foreach, switch, and eval. Table 7.1 summarizes these commands.

7.1 The if command

The if command evaluates an expression, tests its result, and conditionally executes a script based on the result. For example, consider the following command, which sets variable x to zero if it was previously negative:

```
if {$x < 0} {
    set x 0
}
```

In this case if receives two arguments. The first is an expression and the second is a Tcl script. The expression can have any of the forms for expressions described in Chapter 5. The if command evaluates the expression and tests the result; if it is nonzero, if evaluates the Tcl script. If the value is zero, if returns without taking any further action.

If commands can also include one or more elseif clauses with additional tests and scripts, plus a final else clause with a script to evaluate if no test succeeds:

`break`	Terminates the innermost nested looping command.
`continue`	Terminates the current iteration of the innermost looping command and goes on to the next iteration of that command.
`eval arg ?arg arg ...?`	Concatenates all of the `arg`'s with separator spaces, then evaluates the result as a Tcl script and returns its result.
`for init test reinit body`	Executes `init` as a Tcl script. Then evaluates `test` as an expression. If it evaluates to nonzero then executes `body` as a Tcl script, executes `reinit` as a Tcl script, and reevaluates `test` as an expression. Repeats until `test` evaluates to zero. Returns an empty string.
`foreach varName list body`	For each element of `list`, in order, set variable `varName` to that value and execute `body` as a Tcl script. Returns an empty string. `list` must be a valid Tcl list.
`if test1 body1 ?elseif test2 body2 elseif ...? ?else bodyn?`	Evaluates `test1` as an expression. If its value is nonzero, executes `body1` as a Tcl script and returns its value. Otherwise evaluates `test2` as an expression; if its value is nonzero, executes `body2` as a script and returns its value. If no test succeeds, executes `bodyn` as a Tcl script and returns its result.
`source fileName`	Reads the file whose name is `fileName` and evaluates its contents as a Tcl script. Returns the result of the script.
`switch ?options? string pattern body ?pattern body ...?` `switch ?options? string {pattern body ?pattern body ...?}`	Matches `string` against each `pattern` in order until a match is found, then executes the `body` corresponding to the matching `pattern`. If the last pattern is `default`, it matches anything. Returns the result of the `body` executed, or an empty string if no pattern matches. `options` may be `-exact`, `-glob`, `-regexp`, or `--` to indicate the end of options.
`while test body`	Evaluates `test` as an expression. If its value is nonzero, executes `body` as a Tcl script and re-evaluates `test`. Repeats until `test` evaluates to zero. Returns an empty string.

Table 7.1. A summary of the Tcl commands for controlling the flow of execution.

```
if {$x < 0} {
    ...
} elseif {$x == 0} {
    ...
} elseif {$x == 1} {
    ...
} else {
    ...
}
```

This command will execute one of the four scripts indicated by "...", depending on the value of x. The result of the command will be the result of whichever script is executed. If an if command has no else clause and none of its tests succeeds, then it returns an empty string.

Remember that the expressions and scripts for if and other control flow commands are parsed using the same approach as all arguments to all Tcl commands. It is almost always a good idea to enclose the expressions and scripts in braces so that substitutions are deferred until the command is executed. Furthermore, each open brace must be on the same line as the preceding word or else the newline will be treated as a command separator. The following script is parsed as two commands, which probably isn't the desired result:

```
if {$x < 0}
{
    set x 0
}
```

7.2   Looping commands: while, for, and foreach

Tcl provides three commands for looping: while, for, and foreach. While and for are similar to the corresponding C statements and foreach is similar to the corresponding feature of the csh shell. Each of these commands executes a script over and over again; they differ in the kinds of setup they do before each iteration and in the ways they decide to terminate the loop.

The while command takes two arguments: an expression and a Tcl script. It evaluates the expression and if the result is nonzero then it executes the Tcl script. This process repeats over and over until the expression evaluates to zero, at which point the while command terminates and returns an empty string. For example, the script below copies a list from variable a to variable b, reversing the order of the elements along the way:

```
set b ""
set i [expr [llength $a] -1]
while {$i >= 0} {
    lappend b [lindex $a $i]
    incr i -1
}
```

The `for` command is similar to `while` except that it provides more explicit loop control. The program to reverse the elements of a list can be rewritten using `for` as follows:

```
set b ""
for {set i [expr [llength $a]-1]} {$i >= 0} {incr i -1} {
    lappend b [lindex $a $i]
}
```

The first argument to `for` is an initialization script, the second is an expression that determines when to terminate the loop, the third is a reinitialization script, which is evaluated after each execution of the loop body before evaluating the test again, and the fourth argument is a script that forms the body of the loop. `For` executes its first argument (the initialization script) as a Tcl command, then evaluates the expression. If the expression evaluates to nonzero, then `for` executes the body followed by the reinitialization script and reevaluates the expression. It repeats this sequence over and over again until the expression evaluates to zero. If the expression evaluates to zero on the first test, neither the body script nor the reinitialization script is ever executed. Like `while`, `for` returns an empty string as the result.

For and `while` are equivalent in that anything you can write using one command you can also write using the other command. However, `for` has the advantage of placing all of the loop control information in one place where it is easy to see. Typically the initialization, test, and reinitialization arguments are used to select a set of elements to operate on (integer indices in the preceding example), and the body of the loop carries out the operations on the chosen elements. This clean separation between element selection and action makes `for` loops easier to understand and debug. Of course, some situations exist in which a clean separation between selection and action is not possible, and in these cases a `while` loop may make more sense.

The `foreach` command iterates over all of the elements of a list. For example, the following script provides yet another implementation of list reversal:

```
set b ""
foreach i $a {
    set b [linsert $b 0 $i]
}
```

Foreach takes three arguments. The first is the name of a variable, the second is a list, and the third is a Tcl script that forms the body of the loop. `foreach` will execute the body script once for each element of the list, in order. Before executing the body in each iteration, `foreach` sets the variable to hold the next element of the list. Thus if variable a has the value "`first second third`" in the preceding example, the body will be executed three times. In the first iteration i will have the value `first`, in the second iteration it will have the value `second`, and in the third iteration it will have the value `third`. At the end of the loop, b will have the value "`third second first`" and i will have the value `third`. As with the other looping commands, `foreach` always returns an empty string.

7.3 Loop control: break and continue

Tcl provides two commands that can be used to abort part or all of a looping command: break and continue. These commands have the same behavior as the corresponding statements in C. Neither takes any arguments. The break command causes the innermost enclosing looping command to terminate immediately. For example, suppose that in the list reversal example in the last section we want to stop as soon as an element equal to ZZZ is found in the source list. In other words, the result list should consist of a reversal of only those source elements up to (but not including) a ZZZ element. This can be accomplished with break as follows:

```
set b ""
foreach i $a {
    if {$i == "ZZZ"} break
    set b [linsert $b 0 $i]
}
```

The continue command causes only the current iteration of the innermost loop to be terminated; the loop continues with its next iteration. In the case of while, this means skipping out of the body and reevaluating the expression that determines when the loop terminates; in for loops, the reinitialization script is executed before reevaluating the termination condition. For example, the following program is another variant of the list reversal example, where ZZZ elements are simply skipped without copying them to the result list:

```
set b ""
foreach i $a {
    if {$i == "ZZZ"} continue
    set b [linsert $b 0 $i]
}
```

7.4 The switch command

The switch command tests a value against a number of patterns and executes one of several Tcl scripts depending on which pattern matched. The same effect as switch can be achieved with an if command that has lots of elseif clauses, but switch provides a more compact encoding. Tcl's switch command has two forms; here is an example of the first:

```
switch $x {a {incr t1} b {incr t2} c {incr t3}}
```

The first argument to switch is the value to be tested (the contents of variable x in the example). The second argument is a list containing one or more pairs of elements. The first argument in each pair is a pattern to compare against the value, and the second is a script to execute if the pattern matches. The switch command steps through these pairs in order, comparing the pattern against the value. As soon as it finds a match, it executes the corresponding script and returns the value of that script as its value. If no pattern matches, no script is executed and switch returns an empty string. This particular command increments variable t1 if x has the value a, t2 if x has the value b, t3 if x has the value c, and does nothing otherwise.

The second form spreads the patterns and scripts out into separate arguments rather than combining them all into one list:

```
switch $x a {incr t1} b {incr t2} c {incr t3}
```

This form has the advantage that you can invoke substitutions on the pattern arguments more easily, but most people prefer the first form because you can easily spread the patterns and scripts across multiple lines like this:

```
switch $x {
    a {incr t1}
    b {incr t2}
    c {incr t3}
}
```

The outer braces keep the newlines from being treated as command separators. With the second form you would have to use backslash-newlines like this:

```
switch $x \
    a {incr t1} \
    b {incr t2} \
    c {incr t3}
```

The switch command supports three forms of pattern matching. You can precede the value to test with a switch that selects the form you want: −exact selects exact comparison, −glob selects pattern matching as in the string match command (see Section 9.2 for details) and −regexp selects regular-expression matching as described in Section 9.3. The default is −glob.

If the last pattern in a switch command is default, it matches any value. Its script will thus be executed if no other patterns match. For example, the following script will examine a list and produce three counters. The first, t1, counts the number of elements in the list that contain an a. The second, t2, counts the number of elements that are unsigned decimal integers. The third, t3, counts all of the other elements:

```
set t1 0
set t2 0
set t3 0
foreach i $x {
    switch -regexp $i {
        a              {incr t1}
        ^[0-9]+$       {incr t2}
        default        {incr t3}
    }
}
```

If a script in a `switch` command is -, `switch` uses the script for the next pattern instead. This makes it easy to have several patterns that all execute the same script, as in the following example:

```
switch $x {
    a -
    b -
    c {incr t1}
    d {incr t2}
}
```

This script increments variable `t1` if x is a, b, or c, and it increments `t2` if x is d.

7.5 The eval command

`eval` is a general-purpose building block for creating and executing Tcl scripts. It accepts any number of arguments, concatenates them with separator spaces, and then executes the result as a Tcl script. One use of `eval` is for generating commands, saving them in variables, and then later evaluating the variables as Tcl scripts. For example, the script

```
set cmd "set a 0"
...
eval $cmd
```

clears variable a to 0 when the `eval` command is invoked.

Perhaps the most important use for `eval` is to force another level of parsing. The Tcl parser performs only one level of parsing and substitution when parsing a command; the results of one substitution are not reparsed for other substitutions. However, there are times when another level of parsing is necessary, and `eval` provides the mechanism to achieve this. For example, suppose that a variable `vars` contains a list of variables and that you wish to unset each of these variables. One solution is to use the following script:

```
set vars {a b c d}
foreach i $vars {
    unset $i
}
```

This script will work just fine, but the `unset` command takes any number of arguments so it should be possible to unset all of the variables with a single command. Unfortunately the following script will not work:

```
set vars {a b c d}
unset $vars
```

The problem with this script is that all of the variable names are passed to `unset` as a single argument, rather than using a separate argument for each name. Thus `unset` tries to unset a variable named "a b c d". The solution is to use `eval`, as with the following command:

```
set vars {a b c d}
eval unset $vars
```

eval concatenates its arguments to form a new command "unset a b c d", which it then passes to Tcl for evaluation. The command string gets reparsed so each variable name ends up in a different argument to unset.

Note: *This approach works even if some of the variable names contain spaces or special characters such as $. As described in Section 6.7, the only safe way to generate Tcl commands is using list operations such as* list *and* concat. *The command*

```
eval unset $vars
```

is identical to the command

```
eval [concat unset $vars]
```

In either case, the script evaluated by eval *is a proper list whose first element is* unset *and whose other elements are the elements of* vars.

7.6   Executing from files: source

The source command is similar to the command by the same name in the csh shell. It reads a file and executes the contents of the file as a Tcl script. source takes a single argument that specifies the name of the file. For example, the command

```
source init.tcl
```

will execute the contents of the file init.tcl. The return value from source will be the value returned when the file contents are executed, which is the return value from the last command in the file. In addition, source allows the return command to be used in the file's script to terminate the processing of the file. See Section 8.1 for more information on return.

Chapter 8
Procedures

A Tcl procedure is a command that is implemented with a Tcl script rather than C code. You can define new procedures at any time with the `proc` command described in this chapter. Procedures make it easy for you to package solutions to problems so that they can be reused easily. Procedures also provide a simple way for you to prototype new features in an application. Once you've tested the procedures, you can reimplement them in C for higher performance; the C implementations can be used in scripts just like the original procedures, so none of the scripts that invoke them will have to change.

Tcl provides special commands for dealing with variable scopes. Among other things, these commands allow you to pass arguments by reference instead of by value and to implement new Tcl control structures as procedures. Table 8.1 summarizes the Tcl commands related to procedures.

8.1 Procedure basics: proc and return

Procedures are created with the `proc` command, as in the following example:

```
proc plus {a b} {expr $a+$b}
```

The first argument to `proc` is the name of the procedure to be created, `plus` in this case. The second argument is a list of names of arguments to the procedure (`a` and `b` in the example). The third argument to `proc` is a Tcl script that forms the body of the new procedure. After the `proc` command completes, a new command, `plus`, will exist, which can be invoked just like any other Tcl command. When `plus` is invoked, Tcl will arrange for the procedure's body to be evaluated with variables `a` and `b` set to the values of the

---

global *name1* ?*name2* ...?
> Binds variable names *name1*, *name2*, etc. to global variables. References to these names will refer to global variables instead of local variables for the duration of the current procedure. Returns an empty string.

---

proc *name argList body*
> Defines a procedure whose name is *name*, replacing any existing command by that name. *argList* is a list with one element for each of the procedure's arguments, and *body* contains a Tcl script that is the procedure's body. Returns an empty string.

---

return ?*options*? ?*value*?
> Returns from the innermost nested procedure or source command with *value* as the result of the procedure. *value* defaults to an empty string. Additional options may be used to trigger an exceptional return (see Section 12.4).

---

uplevel ?*level*? *arg* ?*arg arg* ...?
> Concatenates all of the *arg*'s with spaces as separators, then executes the resulting Tcl script in the variable context of stack level *level*. *level* consists of a number or a number preceded by #, and defaults to 1. Returns the result of the script.

---

upvar ?*level*? *otherVar1 myVar1* ?*otherVar2 myVar2* ...?
> Binds the local variable name *myVar1* to the variable at stack level *level* whose name is *otherVar1*. For the duration of the current procedure, variable references to *myVar1* will be directed to *otherVar1* instead. Additional bindings may be specified with *otherVar2* and *myVar2*, etc. *level* has the same syntax and meaning as for uplevel and defaults to 1. Returns an empty string.

Table 8.1. A summary of the Tcl commands related to procedures and variable scoping.

---

arguments. plus must always be invoked with exactly two arguments. The return value for the plus command is the value returned by the last command in plus's body. Here are some correct and incorrect invocations of plus:

```
    plus 3 4
⇒   7
    plus 3 -1
⇒   2
    plus 1
∅   no value given for parameter "b" to "plus"
```

It is important to realize that proc is just an ordinary Tcl command. It is not a declaration with special syntax, like you might see in other languages such as C. The arguments to proc are processed in the same way as for any other Tcl command. For example, the braces in the argument {a b} are not a special syntactic construct for this command; they are just used in the normal fashion to pass both of plus's argument names to proc as a single word. If a procedure has only a single argument, then the braces aren't needed around its name. Similarly, the braces around proc's last argument are used to pass the entire body to proc as a single argument without performing substitutions on its contents.

If you would like a procedure to return early without executing its entire script, you can invoke the return command: it causes the enclosing procedure to return immediately and the argument to return will be the result of the procedure. Here is an implementation of factorial that uses return:

```
proc fac x {
    if {$x <= 1} {
        return 1
    }
    expr $x * [fac [expr $x-1]]
}
fac 4
⇒ 24
fac 0
⇒ 1
```

If the argument to fac is less than or equal to one, fac invokes return to return immediately. Otherwise it executes the expr command. The expr command is the last one in the procedure's body, so its result is returned as the result of the procedure.

8.2 Local and global variables

When the body of a Tcl procedure is evaluated, it uses a different set of variables from its caller. These variables are called *local variables*, since they are accessible only within the procedure and are deleted when the procedure returns. Variables referenced outside any procedure are called *global variables*. It is possible to have a local variable with the same name as a global variable or a local variable in another active procedure, but these will be different variables: changes to one will not affect any of the others. If a procedure is invoked recursively, each recursive invocation will have a distinct set of local variables.

The arguments to a procedure are just local variables whose values are set from the words of the command that invoked the procedure. When execution begins in a procedure, the only local variables with values are those corresponding to arguments. Other local variables are created automatically when they are set.

A procedure can reference global variables with the global command. For example, the following command makes the global variables x and y accessible inside a procedure:

```
global x y
```

The global command treats each of its arguments as the name of a global variable and sets up bindings so that references to those names within the procedure will be directed to global variables instead of local ones. global can be invoked at any time during a procedure; once it has been invoked, the bindings will remain in effect until the procedure returns.

Note: *Tcl does not provide a form of variable equivalent to static variables in C, which are limited in scope to a given procedure but have values that persist across calls to the procedure. In Tcl you must use global variables for purposes like this. To avoid name conflicts with other such variables, you should include the name of the procedure or the name of its enclosing package in the variable name, for example* Hypertext_numLinks.

8.3   Defaults and variable numbers of arguments

In the examples so far, the second argument to proc (which describes the arguments to the procedure) has taken a simple form consisting of the names of the arguments. Three additional features are available for specifying arguments. First, the argument list may be specified as an empty string. In this case the procedure takes no arguments. For example, the following command defines a procedure that prints out two global variables:

```
proc printVars {} {
    global a b
    puts "a is $a, b is $b"
}
```

The second additional feature is that defaults may be specified for some or all of the arguments. The argument list is actually a list of lists, with each sublist corresponding to a single argument. If a sublist has only a single element (which has been the case in the previous examples) that element is the name of the argument. If a sublist has two arguments, the first is the argument's name and the second is a default value for it. For example, here is a procedure that increments a given value by a given amount, with the amount defaulting to 1:

```
proc inc {value {increment 1}} {
    expr $value+$increment
}
```

The first element in the argument list, value, specifies a name with no default value. The second element specifies an argument with name increment and a default value of 1. This means that inc can be invoked with either one or two arguments:

```
    inc 42 3
⇒   45
    inc 42
⇒   43
```

If a default isn't specified for an argument in the proc command, the argument must be supplied whenever the procedure is invoked. The defaulted arguments, if any, must be the last arguments for the procedure. This is true both in the proc command and when invoking a procedure. If a default is specified for a particular argument, then defaults must be provided for all the arguments following that one; similarly, if an argument is omitted when the procedure is invoked, all the arguments after it must also be omitted.

The third special feature in argument lists is support for variable numbers of arguments. If the last argument in the argument list has the special name args, the procedure may be called with varying numbers of arguments. Arguments before args in the argument list are handled as before, but any number of additional arguments may be specified. The procedure's local variable args will be set to a list whose elements are all of the extra arguments. If there are no extra arguments, args will be set to an empty string. For example, the following procedure takes any number of arguments and returns their sum:

```
proc sum args {
    set s 0
    foreach i $args {
        incr s $i
    }
    return $s
}
sum 1 2 3 4 5
```
⇒ *15*
```
sum
```
⇒ *0*

If a procedure's argument list contains additional arguments before args, then they may be defaulted as just described. Of course, if this happens there will be no extra arguments so args will be set to an empty string. No default value may be specified for args — the empty string is its default.

8.4 Call by reference: upvar

The upvar command provides a general mechanism for accessing variables outside the context of a procedure. It can be used to access either global variables or local variables in some other active procedure. Most often it is used to implement call-by-reference argument passing for arrays. If a is an array, you cannot pass it to a procedure myproc with a command like "myproc $a", because there is no value for an array as a whole; there are only values for the individual elements. Instead, you pass the name of the array to the procedure, as in "myproc a", and use the upvar command to access the array's elements from the procedure.

Here is a simple example of upvar in a procedure that prints out the contents of an array:

```
proc parray name {
    upvar $name a
    foreach el [lsort [array names a]] {
        puts "$el = $a($el)"
    }
}
set info(age) 37
set info(position) "Vice President"
parray info
```
⇒ *age = 37*
   position = Vice President

When parray is invoked it is given the name of an array as an argument. The upvar command then makes this array accessible through local variable a in the procedure. The first argument to upvar is the name of a variable accessible to the procedure's caller. This may be either a global variable, as in the example, or a local variable in a calling procedure. The second argument is the name of a local variable. upvar arranges things so that accesses to local variable a will actually refer to the variable in the caller whose name is given by variable name. In the example this means that when parray reads elements of a, it is actually reading elements of the info global variable. If parray were to write a, it would modify info. parray uses the array names command to retrieve a list of all the elements in the array. Then it sorts them with lsort and prints each the elements in order.

Note: *In the example it appears as if the output is returned as the procedure's result; in fact, it is printed by the procedure directly to standard output and the result of the procedure is an empty string.*

The first variable name in an upvar command normally refers to the context of the current procedure's caller. However, it is also possible to access variables from any level on the call stack, including the global level. For example,

```
upvar #0 other x
```

makes global variable other accessible via local variable x (the #0 argument specifies that other should be interpreted as a global variable, regardless of how many nested procedure calls are active), and

```
upvar 2 other x
```

makes variable other in the caller of the caller of the current procedure accessible as local variable x (2 specifies that the context of other is two levels up the call stack). See the reference documentation for more information on specifying a level in upvar.

8.5 Creating new control structures: uplevel

The uplevel command is a cross between eval and upvar. It evaluates its argument(s) as a script, just like eval, but the script is evaluated in the variable context of a

different stack level, like upvar. With uplevel you can define new control structures as
Tcl procedures. For example, here is a new control flow command called do:

```
proc do {varName first last body} {
    upvar $varName v
    for {set v $first} {$v <= $last} {incr v} {
        uplevel $body
    }
}
```

The first argument to do is the name of a variable. do sets that variable to consecutive
integer values in the range between its second and third arguments, and executes the
fourth argument as a Tcl command once for each setting. Given this definition of do, the
following script creates a list of squares of the first five integers:

```
set squares {}
do i 1 5 {
    lappend squares [expr $i*$i]
}
set squares
⇒  1 4 9 16 25
```

The do procedure uses upvar to access the loop variable (i in the example) as its local
variable v. Then do uses the for command to increment the loop variable through the
desired range. For each value, it invokes uplevel to execute the loop body in the variable context of the caller; this causes references to variables squares and i in the body
of the loop to refer to variables in do's caller. If eval were used instead of uplevel,
squares and i would be treated as local variables in do, which would not produce the
desired effect.

Note: *This implementation of do does not handle exceptional conditions properly. For example,
if the body of the loop contains a return command, it will only cause the do procedure
to return, which is more like the behavior of break. If a return occurs in the body of a
built-in control-flow command such as for or while, it causes the procedure that
invoked the command to return. In Chapter 12 you will see how to implement this
behavior for do.*

As with upvar, uplevel takes an optional initial argument that specifies an
explicit stack level. See the reference documentation for details.

Chapter 9
String Manipulation

This chapter describes Tcl's facilities for manipulating strings. The string manipulation commands provide pattern matching in two different forms — one that mimics the rules used by shells for file name expansion and another that uses regular expressions as patterns. Tcl also has commands for formatted input and output in a style similar to the C procedures `scanf` and `printf`. Finally, there are several utility commands for computing the length of a string, extracting characters from a string, case conversion, etc. Table 9.1 summarizes the Tcl commands for string processing.

9.1 Character set issues

Tcl is "8-bit clean" in that it allows the use of arbitrary 8-bit characters in strings, not just the ASCII 7-bit subset. For example, any of the characters in the ISO 8859-1 character set can be represented in Tcl strings. This applies uniformly to all uses of strings in Tcl, including scripts, words in commands, results of commands, and variable values. Tcl itself does not apply any interpretation to characters outside the ASCII subset, nor does it generate characters outside the ASCII subset on its own (for example, all of Tcl's error messages use printing ASCII characters only).

Tcl stores strings using a null (zero) character for termination, so it is not possible to store zero characters in strings. If you want to represent binary data in Tcl, you must convert it to a form that includes no zero characters, for example by translating bytes to their corresponding hexadecimal values.

```
format formatString ?value value ...?
                Returns a result equal to formatString except that the value arguments
                have been substituted in place of % sequences in formatString.
```

```
regexp ?-indices? ?-nocase? ?--? exp string ?matchVar? \
    ?subVar subVar ...?
                Determines whether the regular expression exp matches part or all of
                string and returns 1 if it does, 0 if it doesn't. If there is a match,
                information about matching range(s) is placed in the variables named by
                matchVar and the subVar's, if they are specified.
```

```
regsub ?-all? ?-nocase? ?--? exp string subSpec varName
                Matches exp against string as for regexp and returns 1 if there is a
                match, 0 if there is none. Also copies string to the variable named by
                varName, making substitutions for the matching portion(s) as specified by
                subSpec.
```

```
scan string format varName ?varName varName ...?
                Parses fields from string as specified by format and places the values
                that match % sequences into variables named by the varName arguments.
                Returns the number of fields successfully parsed.
```

```
string compare string1 string2
                Returns −1, 0, or 1 if string1 is lexicographically less than, equal to, or
                greater than string2.
string first string1 string2
                Returns the index in string2 of the first character in the leftmost
                substring that exactly matches string1, or −1 if there is no match.
string index string charIndex
                Returns the charIndex'th character of string, or an empty string if there
                is no such character. The first character in string has index 0.
string last string1 string2
                Returns the index in string2 of the first character in the rightmost
                substring that exactly matches string1, or −1 if there is no match.
string length string
                Returns the number of characters in string.
string match pattern string
                Returns 1 if pattern matches string using glob-style matching rules (*,
                ?, [], and \) and 0 if it doesn't.
string range string first last
                Returns the substring of string that lies between the indices given by
                first and last, inclusive. An index of 0 refers to the first character in
                the string, and last may be end to refer to the last character of the string.
```

Table 9.1. A summary of the Tcl commands for string manipulation (continued).

```
string tolower string
            Returns a value identical to string except that all uppercase characters
            have been converted to lowercase.
string toupper string
            Returns a value identical to string except that all lowercase characters
            have been converted to uppercase.
string trim string ?chars?
            Returns a value identical to string except that any leading or trailing
            characters that appear in chars are removed. chars defaults to the white
            space characters (space, tab, newline, and carriage return).
string trimleft string ?chars?
            Same as string trim except that only leading characters are removed.
string trimright string ?chars?
            Same as string trim except that only trailing characters are removed.
```

Table 9.1, continued.

9.2 Glob-style pattern matching

The simplest of Tcl's two forms of pattern matching is called "glob" style. It is named after the mechanism for file name expansion in UNIX shells, which is called "globbing". Glob-style matching is easier to learn and use than the regular expressions described in the next two sections, but it works well only for simple cases. For more complex pattern matching you will probably need to use regular expressions.

The command string match implements glob-style pattern matching. For example, the following script extracts all of the elements of a list that begin with Tcl:

```
set new {}
foreach el $list {
    if [string match Tcl* $el] {
        lappend new $el
    }
}
```

The string command is actually a dozen string-manipulation commands rolled into one. If the first argument is match, the command performs glob-style pattern matching and there must be two additional arguments, a pattern and a string. The command returns 1 if the pattern matches the string, 0 if it doesn't. For the pattern to match the string, each character of the pattern must be the same as the corresponding character of the string, except that a few pattern characters are interpreted specially. For example, a * in the pattern matches a substring of any length, so Tcl* matches any string whose first three characters are Tcl. Here is a list of all the special characters supported in glob-style matching:

*	Matches any sequence of zero or more characters.
?	Matches any single character.

[*chars*]	Matches any single character in *chars*. If *chars* contains a sequence of the form *a-b,* any character between *a* and *b*, inclusive, will match.
x	Matches the single character *x*. This provides a way to avoid special interpretation for any of the characters * ? [ ] \\ in the pattern.

Many simple things can be done easily with glob-style patterns. For example, *. [ch] matches all strings that end with either .c or .h. However, many interesting forms of pattern matching cannot be expressed at all with glob-style patterns. For example, there is no way to use a glob-style pattern to test whether a string consists entirely of digits: the pattern [0-9] tests for a single digit, but there is no way to specify that there may be more than one digit.

9.3 Pattern matching with regular expressions

Tcl's second form of pattern matching uses regular expressions like those for the egrep program. Regular expressions are more complex than glob-style patterns but more powerful. Tcl's regular expressions are based on Henry Spencer's publicly available implementation, and parts of the following description are copied from Spencer's documentation.

A regular expression pattern can have several layers of structure. The basic building blocks are called *atoms*, and the simplest form of regular expression consists of one or more atoms. For a regular expression to match an input string, there must be a substring of the input where each of the regular expression's atoms (or other components, as you'll see later) matches the corresponding part of the substring. In most cases atoms are single characters, each of which matches itself. Thus the regular expression abc matches any string containing abc, such as abcdef or xabcy.

A number of characters have special meanings in regular expressions; they are summarized in Table 9.2. The characters ^ and $ are atoms that match the beginning and end of the input string, respectively; thus ^abc matches any string that starts with abc, abc$ matches any string that ends in abc, and ^abc$ matches abc and nothing else. The atom . matches any single character, and the atom *x*, where *x* is any single character, matches *x*. For example, the regular expression . \\$ matches any string that contains a dollar sign, as long as the dollar sign isn't the first character, while \\. $ matches any string that ends with a period.

Besides the atoms already described, there are two other forms for atoms in regular expressions. The first form consists of any regular expression enclosed in parentheses, such as (a.b). Parentheses are used for grouping. They allow operators such as * to be applied to entire regular expressions as well as atoms. They are also used to identify pieces of the matching substring for special processing. Both of these uses are described in more detail later.

The final form for an atom is a *range*, which is a collection of characters between square brackets. A range matches any single character that is one of the ones between the

Character(s)	Meaning
.	Matches any single character.
^	Matches the null string at the start of the input string.
$	Matches the null string at the end of the input string.
\x	Matches the character x.
[chars]	Matches any single character from chars. If the first character of chars is ^, the pattern matches any single character not in the remainder of chars. A sequence of the form a-b in chars is treated as shorthand for all of the ASCII characters between a and b, inclusive. If the first character in chars (possibly following a ^) is], it is treated literally (as part of chars instead of a terminator). If a – appears first or last in chars, it is treated literally.
(regexp)	Matches anything that matches the regular expression regexp. Used for grouping and for identifying pieces of the matching substring.
*	Matches a sequence of 0 or more matches of the preceding atom.
+	Matches a sequence of 1 or more matches of the preceding atom.
?	Matches either a null string or a match of the preceding atom.
regexp1 | regexp2	Matches anything that matches either regexp1 or regexp2.

Table 9.2. The special characters permitted in regular expression patterns.

brackets. Furthermore, if there is a sequence of the form a-b among the characters, all of the ASCII characters between a and b are treated as acceptable. Thus the regular expression [0-9a-fA-F] matches any string that contains a hexadecimal digit. If the character after the [is a ^, the sense of the range is reversed: it only matches characters *not* among those specified between the ^ and the].

The three operators *, +, and ? may follow an atom to specify repetition. If an atom is followed by *, it matches a sequence of zero or more matches of that atom. If an atom is followed by +, it matches a sequence of one or more matches of the atom. If an atom is followed by ?, it matches either an empty string or a match of the atom. For example, ^(0x)?[0-9a-fA-F]+$ matches strings that are proper hexadecimal numbers, i.e., those consisting of an optional 0x followed by one or more hexadecimal digits.

Finally, regular expressions may be joined together with the | operator. The resulting regular expression matches anything that matches either of the regular expresssions that surround the |. For example, the following pattern matches any string that is either a hexadecimal number or a decimal number:

```
^((0x)?[0-9a-fA-F]+|[0-9]+)$
```

Note that the information between parentheses may be any regular expression, including additional regular expressions in parentheses, so it is possible to build quite complex structures.

The `regexp` command invokes regular expression matching. In its simplest form it takes two arguments: the regular expression pattern and an input string. It returns 0 or 1 to indicate whether or not the pattern matched the input string:

```
regexp {^[0-9]+$} 510
```
⇒ *1*
```
regexp {^[0-9]+$} -510
```
⇒ *0*

Note: *The pattern must be enclosed in braces so that the characters $, [, and] are passed through to the* regexp *command instead of triggering variable and command substitution. It is almost always a good idea to enclose regular expression patterns in braces.*

If `regexp` is invoked with additional arguments after the input string, each additional argument is treated as the name of a variable. The first variable is filled in with the substring that matched the entire regular expression. The second variable is filled in with the portion of the substring that matched the leftmost parenthesized subexpression within the pattern; the third variable is filled in with the match for the next parenthesized subexpression, and so on. If there are more variable names than parenthesized subexpressions, the extra variables are set to empty strings. For example, after executing the command

```
regexp {([0-9]+) *([a-z]+)} "Walk 10 km" a b c
```
variable a will have the value "10 km", b will have the value 10, and c will have the value km. This ability to extract portions of the matching substring allows `regexp` to be used for parsing.

It is also possible to specify two extra switches to `regexp` before the regular expression argument. A −nocase switch specifies that alphabetic atoms in the pattern should match either uppercase or lowercase letters in the string. For example:

```
regexp {[a-z]} A
```
⇒ *0*
```
regexp -nocase {[a-z]} A
```
⇒ *1*

The −indices switch specifies that the additional variables should not be filled in with the values of matching substrings. Instead, each should be filled in with a list giving the first and last indices of the substring's range within the input string. After the command

```
regexp -indices {([0-9]+) *([a-z]+)} "Walk 10 km" \
     a b c
```
variable a will have the value "5 9", b will have the value "5 6", and c will have the value "8 9".

9.4 Using regular expressions for substitutions

Regular expressions can also be used to perform substitutions using the regsub command. Consider the following example:

```
regsub there "They live there lives" their x
```
⇒ *1*

The first argument to regsub is a regular expression pattern, and the second argument is an input string, just as for regexp. Also, like regexp, regsub returns 1 if the pattern matches the string, 0 if it doesn't. However, regsub does more than just check for a match: it creates a new string by substituting a replacement value for the matching substring. The replacement value is contained in the third argument to regsub, and the new string is stored in the variable named by the final argument to regsub. Thus, after the above command completes, x will have the value "They live their lives". If the pattern had not matched the string, 0 would have been returned and x would have the value "They live there lives" (the variable is set whether or not substitution took place).

Two special switches may appear as arguments to regsub before the regular expression. The first is −nocase, which causes case differences between the pattern and the string to be ignored just as for regexp. The second possible switch is −all. Normally regsub makes only a single substitution, for the first match found in the input string. However, if −all is specified, regsub continues searching for additional matches and makes substitutions for all of the matches found. For example, after the command

```
regsub -all a ababa zz x
```

x will have the value zzbzzbzz. If −all had been omitted, x would have been set to zzbaba.

In the preceding examples, the replacement string is a simple literal value. However, if the replacement string contains a & or \0, the & or \0 is replaced in the substitution with the substring that matched the regular expression. If a sequence of the form \n appears in the replacement string, where *n* is a decimal number, then the substring that matched the *n*'th parenthesized subexpression is substituted instead of the \n. For example, the command

```
regsub -all a|b axaab && x
```

doubles all of the a's and b's in the input string. In this case it sets x to aaxaaaabb. Alternatively, the command

```
regsub -all (a+)(ba*) aabaabxab {z\2} x
```

replaces sequences of a's with a single z if they precede a b but don't also follow a b. In this case x is set to zbaabxzb. Backslashes may be used in the replacement string to allow &, \0, \n, or backslash characters to be substituted verbatim without any special interpretation.

Note: *It's usually a good idea to enclose complex replacement strings in braces as in the preceding example; otherwise the Tcl parser will process backslash sequences and the replacement string received by* regsub *may not contain backslashes that are needed.*

9.5 Generating strings with format

Tcl's format command provides facilities like those of the sprintf procedure from the ANSI C library. For example, consider the following command:

```
format "The square root of 10 is %.3f" [expr sqrt(10)]
```
⇒ *The square root of 10 is 3.162*

The first argument to format is a format string, which may contain any number of conversion specifiers such as %.3f. For each conversion specifier format generates a replacement string by reformatting the next argument according to the conversion specifier. The result of the format command consists of the format string with each conversion specifier replaced by the corresponding replacement string. In the preceding example, %.3f specifies that the next argument (the result of the expr command) is to be formatted as a real number with three digits after the decimal point. format supports almost all of the conversion specifiers defined for ANSI C sprintf, such as %d for a decimal integer, %x for a hexadecimal integer, and %e for real numbers in mantissa-exponent form.

The format command plays a less significant role in Tcl than printf and sprintf play in C. Many of the uses of printf and sprintf are simply for conversion from binary to string format or for string substitution. Binary-to-string conversion isn't needed in Tcl because values are already stored as strings, and substitution is already available through the Tcl parser. For example, the command

```
set msg [format "%s is %d years old" $name $age]
```
can be written more simply as

```
set msg "$name is $age years old"
```
The %d conversion specifier in the format command could be written just as well as %s; with %d, format converts the value of age to a binary integer, then it converts the integer back to a string again.

format is typically used in Tcl to reformat a value to improve its appearance, or to convert from one representation to another (for example, from decimal to hexadecimal). As an example of reformatting, here is a script that prints the first ten powers of *e* in a table:

```
puts "Number  Exponential"
for {set i 1} {$i <= 10} {incr i} {
    puts [format "%4d %12.3f" $i [expr exp($i)]]
}
```

This script generates the following output on standard output:

```
Number   Exponential
     1         2.718
     2         7.389
     3        20.085
     4        54.598
     5       148.413
     6       403.429
     7      1096.630
     8      2980.960
     9      8103.080
    10     22026.500
```

The conversion specifier %4d causes the integers in the first column of the table to be printed right-justified in a field four digits wide, so that they line up under their column header. The conversion specifier %12.3f causes each of the real values to be printed right-justified in a field 12 digits wide, so that the values line up; it also sets the precision at 3 digits to the right of the decimal point.

The second main use for format, changing the representation of a value, is illustrated by the following script, which prints a table showing the ASCII characters that correspond to particular integer values:

```
puts "Integer   ASCII"
for {set i 95} {$i <= 101} {incr i} {
    puts [format "%4d          %c" $i $i]
}
```

This script generates the following output on standard output:

```
Integer   ASCII
    95          _
    96          `
    97          a
    98          b
    99          c
   100          d
   101          e
```

The value of i is used twice in the format command, once with %4d and once with %c. The %c specifier takes an integer argument and generates a replacement string consisting of the ASCII character represented by the integer.

9.6 Parsing strings with scan

The scan command provides almost exactly the same facilities as the sscanf procedure from the ANSI C library. scan is roughly the inverse of format. It starts with a formatted string, parses the string under the control of a format string, extracts fields corresponding to % conversion specifiers in the format string, and places the extracted values in Tcl variables. For example, after the following command is executed, variable a will have the value 16 and variable b will have the value 24.2:

```
scan "16 units, 24.2% margin" "%d units, %f" a b
```
⇒ *2*

The first argument to scan is the string to parse, the second is a format string that controls the parsing, and any additional arguments are names of variables to fill in with converted values. The return value of 2 indicates that two conversions were completed successfully.

scan operates by scanning the string and the format together. Each character in the format must match the corresponding character in the string, except for blanks and tabs, which are ignored, and % characters. When a % is encountered in the format, it indicates the start of a conversion specifier: scan converts the next input characters according to the conversion specifier and stores the result in the variable given by the next argument to scan. White space in the string is skipped except in the case of a few conversion specifiers such as %c.

One common use for scan is for simple string parsing, as in the preceding example. Another common use is for converting ASCII characters to their integer values, which is done with the %c specifier. The following procedure uses this feature to return the character that follows a given character in lexicographic ordering:

```
proc next c {
    scan $c %c i
    format %c [expr $i+1]
}
next a
```
⇒ *b*
```
next 9
```
⇒ *:*

The scan command converts the value of the c argument from an ASCII character to the integer used to represent that character, then the integer is incremented and converted back to an ASCII character with the format command.

9.7 Extracting characters: string index and string range

The remaining string manipulation commands are all implemented as options of the string command. For example, string index extracts a character from a string:

```
string index "Sample string" 3
```
⇒ *p*

The argument after index is a string, and the last argument gives the index of the desired character in the string. An index of 0 selects the first character.

The string range command is similar to string index except that it takes two indices and returns all the characters from the first index to the second, inclusive:

```
string range "Sample string" 3 7
```
⇒ *ple s*

The second index may have the value end to select all the characters up to the end of the string:

```
string range "Sample string" 3 end
```
⇒ *ple string*

9.8 Searching and comparison

The command string first takes two additional string arguments as in the following example:

```
string first th "There is the tub where I bathed today"
```
⇒ *9*

It searches the second string to see if there is a substring that is identical to the first string. If so, it returns the index of the first character in the leftmost matching substring; if not, it returns −1. The command string last is similar except it returns the starting index of the rightmost matching substring:

```
string last th "There is the tub where I bathed today"
```
⇒ *27*

The command string compare takes two additional arguments and compares them in their entirety. It returns 0 if the strings are identical, −1 if the first string sorts before the second, and 1 if the first string is after the second in sorting order:

```
string compare Michigan Minnesota
```
⇒ *−1*

```
string compare Michigan Michigan
```
⇒ *0*

9.9 Length, case conversion, and trimming

The string length command counts the number of characters in a string and returns that number:

```
string length "sample string"
```
⇒ *13*

The string toupper command converts all lowercase characters in a string to uppercase, and the string tolower command converts all uppercase characters in its argument to lowercase:

```
string toupper "Watch out!"
```
⇒ *WATCH OUT!*
```
string tolower "15 Charing Cross Road"
```
⇒ *15 charing cross road*

The `string` command provides three options for trimming: `trim`, `trimleft`, and `trimright`. Each option takes two additional arguments: a string to trim and an optional set of trim characters. The `string trim` command removes all instances of the trim characters from both the beginning and end of its argument string, returning the trimmed string as result:

```
string trim aaxxxbab abc
```
⇒ *xxx*

The `trimleft` and `trimright` options work in the same way, except that they only remove the trim characters from the beginning or end of the string, respectively. The trim commands are most commonly used to remove excess white space; if no trim characters are specified, they default to the white space characters (space, tab, newline, carriage return, and form feed).

Chapter 10
Accessing Files

This chapter describes Tcl's commands for dealing with files. The commands allow you to read and write files sequentially or in a random-access fashion. They also allow you to retrieve information kept by the system about files, such as the time of last access. Lastly, they can be used to manipulate file names; for example, you can remove the extension from a file name or find the names of all files that match a particular pattern. See Table 10.1 for a summary of the file-related commands.

Note: *The commands described in this chapter are available only on systems that support the kernel calls defined in the POSIX standard, such as most UNIX workstations. If you are using Tcl on another system, such as a Macintosh or a PC, the file commands may not be present and there may be other commands that provide similar functionality for your system.*

10.1 File names

File names are specified to Tcl using the normal UNIX syntax. For example, the file name x/y/z refers to a file named z that is located in a directory named y, which in turn is located in a directory named x, which must be in the current working directory. The file name /top refers to a file top in the root directory. You can also use tilde notation to specify a file name relative to a particular user's home directory. For example, the name ~ouster/mbox refers to a file named mbox in the home directory of user ouster, and ~/mbox refers to a file named mbox in the home directory of the user running the Tcl script. These conventions (and the availability of tilde notation in particular) apply to all Tcl commands that take file names as arguments.

`cd ?dirName?`	Changes the current working directory to *dirName*, or to the home directory (as given by the HOME environment variable) if *dirName* isn't given. Returns an empty string.
`close fileId`	Closes the file given by *fileId*. Returns an empty string.
`eof fileId`	Returns 1 if an end-of-file condition has occurred on *fileId*, 0 otherwise.
`file option name ?arg arg ...?`	Performs one of several operations on the file name given by *name* or on the file to which it refers, depending on *option*. See Table 10.2 for details.
`flush fileId`	Writes out any buffered output that has been generated for *fileId*. Returns an empty string.
`gets fileId ?varName?`	Reads the next line from *fileId* and discards its terminating newline. If *varName* is specified, places the line in that variable and returns a count of characters in the line (or −1 for end of file). If *varName* isn't specified, returns line as result (or an empty string for end of file).
`glob ?-nocomplain? ?--? pattern ?pattern ...?`	Returns a list of the names of all files that match any of the *pattern* arguments (special characters ?, *, [ ], { }, and \). If -nocomplain isn't specified, an error occurs if the return list would be empty.
`open name ?access?`	Opens file *name* in the mode given by *access*. Access may be r, r+, w, w+, a, or a+ or a list of flags such as RDONLY; it defaults to r. Returns a file identifier for use in other commands like gets and close. If the first character of *name* is |, a command pipeline is invoked instead of opening a file (see Section 11.2 for more information).
`puts ?-nonewline? ?fileId? string`	Writes *string* to *fileId*, appending a newline character unless -nonewline is specified. *fileId* defaults to stdout. Returns an empty string.
`pwd`	Returns the full path name of the current working directory.

Table 10.1. A summary of the Tcl commands for manipulating files (continued).

```
read ?-nonewline? fileId
            Reads and returns all of the bytes remaining in fileId. If -nonewline is
            specified, the final newline, if any, is dropped.
read fileId numBytes
            Reads and returns the next numBytes bytes from fileId (or up to the end
            of the file, if fewer than numBytes bytes are left).

seek fileId offset ?origin?
            Position fileId so that the next access starts at offset bytes from
            origin. Origin may be start, current, or end, and defaults to
            start. Returns an empty string.

tell fileId
            Returns the current access position for fileId.
```

Table 10.1, continued.

10.2   Basic file I/O

The Tcl commands for file I/O are similar to the procedures in the C standard I/O library, both in their names and in their behavior. Here is a script called tgrep that illustrates most of the basic features of file I/O:

```
#!/usr/local/bin/tclsh
if {$argc != 2} {
    error "Usage: tgrep pattern fileName"
}
set f [open [lindex $argv 1] r]
set pat [lindex $argv 0]
while {[gets $f line] >= 0} {
    if [regexp $pat $line] {
        puts $line
    }
}
close $f
```

This script behaves much like the UNIX grep program. You can invoke it from your shell with two arguments, a regular expression pattern and a file name, and it will print out all of the lines in the file that match the pattern.

When tclsh evaluates the script, it makes the command-line arguments available as a list in variable argv, with the length of that list in variable argc (this is slightly different from the normal UNIX conventions for argv, in that the command name itself isn't included in argv; it is in a separate variable argv0). After making sure that it received enough arguments, the script invokes the open command on the file to search, which is the second argument. Open takes two arguments: the name of a file and an access mode.

The access mode provides information such as whether you'll be reading the file or writing it, and whether you want to append to the file or access it from the beginning. The access mode may have one of the following values:

r	Open for reading only. The file must already exist. This is the default if the access mode isn't specified.
r+	Open for reading and writing; the file must already exist.
w	Open for writing only. Truncate the file if it already exists, otherwise create a new empty file.
w+	Open for reading and writing. Truncate the file if it already exists, otherwise create a new empty file.
a	Open for writing only and set the initial access position to the end of the file. If the file doesn't exist, create a new empty file.
a+	Open the file for reading and writing and set the initial access position to the end of the file. If the file doesn't exist, create a new empty file.

The access mode may also be specified as a list of POSIX flags like RDONLY, CREAT, and TRUNC. See the reference documentation for more information about these flags.

The open command returns a string such as file3 that identifies the open file. This *file identifier* is used when invoking other commands to manipulate the open file, such as gets, puts, and close. Normally you will save the file identifier in a variable when you open a file and then use that variable to refer to the open file. You should not expect the identifiers returned by open to have any particular format.

Three file identifiers have well-defined names and are always available to you, even if you haven't explicitly opened any files. These are stdin, stdout, and stderr; they refer to the standard input, output, and error channels for the process in which the Tcl script is executing.

After opening the file to search, the tgrep script reads the file one line at a time with the gets command. gets normally takes two arguments: a file identifier and the name of a variable. It reads the next line from the open file, discards the terminating newline character, stores the line in the named variable, and returns a count of the number of characters stored into the variable. If the end of the file is reached before reading any characters, gets stores an empty string in the variable and returns −1.

Note: *Tcl also provides a second form of* gets *where the line is returned as the result of the command, and a command* read *for non-line-oriented input.*

For each line in the file the tgrep script matches the line against the pattern and prints it with puts if it matches. The puts command takes two arguments, which are a file identifier and a string to print. puts adds a newline character to the string and outputs the line on the given file. The script uses stdout as the file identifier so the line is printed on standard output.

When tgrep reaches the end of the file, gets will return −1, which ends the while loop. The script then closes the file with the close command; this releases the resources associated with the open file. In most systems there is a limit on how many files may be open at one time in an application, so it is important to close files as soon as you are finished reading or writing them. In this example the close is unnecessary, since the file will be closed automatically when the application exits.

10.3 Output buffering

The puts command uses the buffering scheme of the C standard I/O library. This means that information passed to puts may not appear immediately in the target file. In many cases (particularly if the file isn't a terminal device) output will be saved in the application's memory until a large amount of data has accumulated for the file, at which point all of the data will be written out in a single operation. If you need data to appear in a file immediately, you should invoke the flush command:

```
flush $f
```

The flush command takes a file identifier as its argument and forces any buffered output data for that file to be written to the file. flush doesn't return until the data have been written. Buffered data are also flushed when a file is closed.

10.4 Random access to files

File I/O is sequential by default — each gets or read command returns the next bytes after the previous gets or read command, and each puts command writes its data immediately following the data written by the previous puts command. However, you can use the seek, tell, and eof commands to access files nonsequentially.

Each open file has an *access position*, which is the location in the file where the next read or write will occur. When a file is opened the access position is set to the beginning or end of the file, depending on the access mode you specified to open. After each read or write operation the access position increments by the number of bytes transferred. The seek command may be used to change the current access position. In its simplest form seek takes two arguments, which are a file identifier and an integer offset within the file. For example, the command

```
seek $f 2000
```

changes the access position for the file so that the next read or write will start at byte number 2000 in the file.

Seek can also take a third argument that specifies an origin for the offset. The third argument must be either start, current, or end. start produces the same effect as if the argument is omitted: the offset is measured relative to the start of the file. current means that the offset is measured relative to the file's current access position, and end means that the offset is measured relative to the end of the file. For example, the following command sets the access position to 100 bytes before the end of the file:

```
      seek $f -100 end
```
If the origin is `current` or `end`, the offset may be either positive or negative; for `start` the offset must be positive.

Note: *It is possible to seek past the current end of the file, in which case the file may contain a hole. Check the documentation for your operating system for more information on what this means.*

The `tell` command returns the current access position for a particular file identifier:

```
      tell $f
```
⇒   *186*

This allows you to record a position and return to it later.

The `eof` command takes a file identifier as argument and returns 0 or 1 to indicate whether the most recent `gets` or `read` command for the file attempted to read past the end of the file:

```
      eof $f
```
⇒   *0*

10.5   The current working directory

Tcl provides two commands that help to manage the current working directory: `pwd` and `cd`. `pwd` takes no arguments and returns the full path name of the current working directory. `cd` takes a single argument and changes the current working directory to the value of that argument. If `cd` is invoked with no arguments, it changes the current working directory to the home directory of the user running the Tcl script (`cd` uses the value of the `HOME` environment variable as the path name of the home directory).

10.6   Manipulating file names: glob and file

Tcl has two commands for manipulating file *names* as opposed to file contents: `glob` and `file`. The `glob` command takes one or more patterns as arguments and returns a list of all the file names that match the pattern(s):

```
      glob *.c *.h
```
⇒   *main.c hash.c hash.h*

`glob` uses the matching rules of the `string match` command (see Section 9.2). In the preceding example `glob` returns the names of all files in the current directory that end in `.c` or `.h`. `glob` also allows patterns to contain comma-separated lists of alternatives between braces, as in the following example:

```
      glob {{src,backup}/*.[ch]}
```
⇒   *src/main.c src/hash.c src/hash.h backup/hash.c*

`glob` treats this pattern as if it were actually multiple patterns, one containing each of the strings, as in the following example:

```
glob {src/*.[ch]} {backup/*.[ch]}
```

Note: *The extra braces around the patterns in these examples are needed to keep the brackets inside the patterns from triggering command substitution. They are removed by the Tcl parser in the usual fashion before invoking the command procedure for* `glob`*.*

If a `glob` pattern ends in a slash, then it matches only directory names. For example, the command

```
glob */
```

will return a list of all the subdirectories of the current directory.

If the list of file names to be returned by `glob` is empty, it normally generates an error. However, if the first argument to `glob`, before any patterns, is `-nocomplain`, `glob` will not generate an error if its result is an empty list.

The second command for manipulating file names is `file`. `file` is a general-purpose command with many options that can be used both to manipulate file names and to retrieve information about files. See Table 10.2 for a summary of the options to `file`. This section discusses the name-related options and Section 10.7 describes the other options. The commands in this section operate purely on file names. They make no system calls and do not check to see if the names actually correspond to files.

`file dirname` removes the last component from a file name, which ostensibly produces the name of the directory containing the file:

```
    file dirname /a/b/c
⇒ /a/b
    file dirname main.c
⇒ .
```

However, the `file` command does not check to be sure that there really is a file or directory corresponding to the name.

`file extension` returns the extension for a file name (all the characters starting with the last `.` in the name), or an empty string if the name contains no extension:

```
    file extension src/main.c
⇒ .c
```

`file rootname` returns everything in a file name except the extension:

```
    file rootname src/main.c
⇒ src/main
    file rootname foo
⇒ foo
```

Last, `file tail` returns the last component of a file name (i.e., the name of the file within its directory):

`file atime` *name*	Returns a decimal string giving the time at which file *name* was last accessed, measured in seconds from 12:00 A.M. on January 1, 1970.
`file dirname` *name*	Returns all of the characters in *name* up to but not including the last / character. Returns . if *name* contains no slashes, / if the last slash in *name* is its first character.
`file executable` *name*	Returns 1 if *name* is executable by the current user, 0 otherwise.
`file exists` *name*	Returns 1 if *name* exists and the current user has search privilege for the directories leading to it, 0 otherwise.
`file extension` *name*	Returns all of the characters in *name* after and including the last dot. Returns an empty string if there is no dot in *name* or no dot after the last slash in *name*.
`file isdirectory` *name*	Returns 1 if *name* is a directory, 0 otherwise.
`file isfile` *name*	Returns 1 if *name* is an ordinary file, 0 otherwise.
`file lstat` *name* *arrayName*	Invokes the `lstat` system call on *name* and sets elements of *arrayName* to hold information returned by `lstat`. This option is identical to the `stat` option unless *name* refers to a symbolic link, in which case this command returns information about the link instead of the file to which it points.
`file mtime` *name*	Returns a decimal string giving the time at which file *name* was last modified, measured in seconds from 12:00 A.M. on January 1, 1970.
`file owned` *name*	Returns 1 if *name* is owned by the current user, 0 otherwise.
`file readable` *name*	Returns 1 if *name* is readable by the current user, 0 otherwise.
`file readlink` *name*	Returns the value of the symbolic link given by *name* (the name of the file to which it points).

Table 10.2. A summary of the options for the `file` command (continued).

`file rootname` *name*
Returns all of the characters in *name* up to but not including the last . character. Returns *name* if it doesn't contain any dots or if it doesn't contain any dots after the last slash.
`file size` *name*
Returns a decimal string giving the size of file *name* in bytes.
`file stat` *name* *arrayName*
Invokes `stat` system call on *name* and sets elements of *arrayName* to hold information returned by `stat`. The following elements are set, each as a decimal string: `atime`, `ctime`, `dev`, `gid`, `ino`, `mode`, `mtime`, `nlink`, `size`, and `uid`.
`file tail` *name*
Returns all of the characters in *name* after the last / character. Returns *name* if it contains no slashes.
`file type` *name*
Returns a string giving the type of file *name*. The return value will be one of `file`, `directory`, `characterSpecial`, `blockSpecial`, `fifo`, `link`, or `socket`.
`file writable` *name*
Returns 1 if *name* is writable by the current user, 0 otherwise.

Table 10.2, continued.

```
        file tail /a/b/c
    ⇒   c
        file tail foo
    ⇒   foo
```

10.7 File information commands

In addition to the options already discussed in Section 10.6, the `file` command provides many other options that can be used to retrieve information about files. Each of these options except `stat` and `lstat` has the form:

    file *option* *name*

where *option* specifies the information desired, such as `exists` or `readable` or `size`, and *name* is the name of the file. Table 10.2 summarizes the options for the `file` command.

The `exists, isfile, isdirectory,` and `type` options return information about the nature of a file. `file exists` returns 1 if there exists a file by the given name and 0 if there is no such file or the current user doesn't have search permission for the directories leading to it. `file isfile` returns 1 if the file is an ordinary disk file and 0 if it is something else, such as a directory or device file. `file isdirectory` returns 1 if the file is a directory and 0 otherwise. `file type` returns a string such as `file, directory,` or `socket` that identifies the file type.

The `readable, writable,` and `executable` options return 0 or 1 to indicate whether the current user is permitted to carry out the indicated action on the file. The `owned` option returns 1 if the current user is the file's owner and 0 otherwise.

The `size` option returns a decimal string giving the size of the file in bytes. `file mtime` returns the time when the file was last modified. The time value is returned in the standard POSIX form for times, namely an integer that counts the number of seconds since 12:00 A.M. on January 1, 1970. The `atime` option is similar to `mtime` except that it returns the time when the file was last accessed.

The `stat` option provides a simple way to get many pieces of information about a file at one time. This can be significantly faster than invoking `file` many times to get the pieces of information individually. `file stat` also provides additional information that isn't accessible with any other file options. It takes two additional arguments, which are the name of a file and the name of a variable, as in the following example:

```
file stat main.c info
```

In this case the name of the file is `main.c` and the variable name is `info`. The variable will be treated as an array and the following elements will be set, each as a decimal string:

`atime`	Time of last access.
`ctime`	Time of last status change.
`dev`	Identifier for device containing file.
`gid`	Identifier for the file's group.
`ino`	Serial number for the file within its device.
`mode`	Mode bits for file.
`mtime`	Time of last modification.
`nlink`	Number of links to file.
`size`	Size of file, in bytes.
`uid`	Identifier for the user that owns the file.

The `atime, mtime,` and `size` elements have the same values as produced by the corresponding `file` options discussed earlier. For more information on the other elements, refer to your system documentation for the `stat` system call; each of the elements is taken directly from the corresponding field of the structure returned by `stat`.

The `lstat` and `readlink` options are useful when dealing with symbolic links, and they can be used only on systems that support symbolic links. `file lstat` is identical to `file stat` for ordinary files, but when it is applied to a symbolic link it returns information about the symbolic link itself, whereas `file stat` will return information about the file to which the link points. `file readlink` returns the contents of a symbolic link, i.e., the name of the file to which it refers; it may be used only on symbolic links. For all of the other `file` commands, if the name refers to a symbolic link, the command operates on the target of the link, not the link itself.

10.8 Errors in system calls

Most of the commands described in this chapter invoke calls on the operating system, and in many cases the system calls can return errors. This can happen, for example, if you invoke `open` or `file stat` on a file that doesn't exist, or if an I/O error occurs in reading a file. The Tcl commands detect these system call errors and in most cases the Tcl commands will return errors themselves. The error message will identify the error that occurred:

```
    open bogus
  ∅ couldn't open "bogus": no such file or directory
```

When an error occurs in a system call, Tcl also sets the `errorCode` variable to provide additional information as described in Section 12.1.

Chapter 11
Processes

Tcl provides several commands for dealing with processes. You can create new processes with the exec command, or you can create new processes with open and then use file I/O commands to communicate with them. You can access process identifiers with the pid command. You can read and write environment variables using the env variable and you can terminate the current process with the exit command. Like the file commands in Chapter 10, these commands are available only on systems that support POSIX kernel calls. Table 11.1 summarizes the commands related to process management.

11.1 Invoking subprocesses with exec

The exec command creates one or more subprocesses and waits until they complete before returning. For example,

```
exec rm main.o
```

executes rm as a subprocess, passes it the argument main.o, and returns after rm completes. The arguments to exec are similar to what you would type as a command line to a shell program such as sh or csh. The first argument to exec is the name of a program to execute, and each additional argument forms one argument to that subprocess.

To execute a subprocess, exec looks for an executable file with a name equal to exec's first argument. If the name contains a / or starts with ~, exec checks the single file indicated by the name. Otherwise exec checks each of the directories in the PATH environment variable to see if the command name refers to an executable file in that directory. exec uses the first executable that it finds.

`exec ?-keepnewline? ?--? arg ?arg ...?` Executes command pipeline specified by *args* using one or more subprocesses, and returns the pipeline's standard output or an empty string if output is redirected (the trailing newline, if any, is dropped unless `-keepnewline` is specified). I/O redirection may be specified with <, <<, >, >>, and several other forms. Pipes may be specified with │ . If the last *arg* is &, the pipeline is executed in background and the return value is a list of its process ids.
`exit ?code?` Terminates process, returning *code* to parent as exit status. *code* must be an integer. *Code* defaults to 0.
`open │command ?access?` Treats *command* as a list with the same structure as arguments to exec and creates subprocess(es) to execute command(s). Depending on *access*, creates pipes for writing input to pipeline and reading output from it. Returns a file identifier for communicating with the subprocesses.
`pid ?fileId?` If *fileId* is omitted, returns the process identifier for the current process. Otherwise returns a list of all the process ids in the pipeline associated with *fileId* (which must have been opened using │).

Table 11.1. A summary of Tcl commands for manipulating processes.

exec collects all of the information written to standard output by the subprocess and returns that information as its result, as in the following example:

```
      exec wc /usr/include/stdio.h
⇒        71      230     1732 /usr/include/stdio.h
```

If the last character of output is a newline, exec removes the newline. This behavior may seem strange but it makes exec consistent with other Tcl commands, which don't normally terminate the last line of the result; you can retain the newline by specifying `-keepnewline` as the first argument to exec.

exec supports I/O redirection in a fashion similar to the UNIX shells. For example, if one of the arguments to exec is >foo, output from the process is placed in file foo instead of returning to Tcl as exec's result. In this case exec's result will be an empty string. Many other forms of input and output redirection are supported as well, including the following:

`>> file`	Appends standard output to *file* instead of replacing *file*.
`>@fileId`	Redirects standard output to the open file whose identifier (returned by open) is *fileId*.
`>&file`	Redirects both standard output and standard error to *file*.

`2>`*file*	Redirects standard error to *file*.
`<`*file*	Causes standard input to be taken from *file*.
`<<`*value*	Passes *value* (an immediate value) to the subprocess as its standard input.
`<@`*fileId*	Causes standard input to be taken from the open file whose identifier is *fileId*.

In each of these cases, *file* or *value* or *fileId* may follow the redirection symbol in a single argument or it may be in a separate argument. As an example of using redirection, consider the following command:

```
exec cat << "test data" > foo
```

This command overwrites file `foo` with the string "`test data`". The string is passed to `cat` as its standard input; `cat` copies the string to its standard ouput, which has been redirected to file `foo`. If no input redirection is specified, the subprocess inherits the standard input channel from the Tcl application; if no output redirection is specified, the standard output from the subprocess is returned as `exec`'s result.

You can also invoke a pipeline of processes instead of a single process, as in the following example:

```
exec grep #include tclInt.h | wc
⇒           8      25      212
```

The `grep` program extracts all the lines containing the string `#include` from the file `tclInt.h`. These lines are then piped to the `wc` program, which computes the number of lines, words, and characters in the `grep` output and prints this information on its standard output. The `wc` output is returned as the result of `exec`.

If the last argument to `exec` is `&`, the subprocess(es) will be executed in background. `exec` will return immediately, without waiting for the subprocesses to complete. Its return value will be a list containing the process identifiers for all of the processes in the pipeline; standard output from the subprocesses will go to the standard output of the Tcl application unless redirected. No errors will be reported for abnormal exits or standard error output, and standard error for the subprocesses will be directed to the standard error channel of the Tcl application.

If a subprocess is suspended or exits abnormally (i.e., it is killed or returns a nonzero exit status), or if it generates output on its standard error channel and standard error was not redirected, then `exec` returns an error. The error message will consist of the output generated by the last subprocess (unless it was redirected with `>`), followed by an error message for each process that exited abnormally, followed by the information generated on standard error by the processes, if any. In addition, `exec` will set the `errorCode` variable to hold information about the last process that terminated abnormally, if any (see Section 12.1 and the reference documentation for details).

Note: *Many UNIX programs are careless about the exit status that they return. If you invoke such a program with* exec *and it accidentally returns a nonzero status, the* exec *command will generate a false error. To prevent these errors from aborting your scripts, invoke* exec *inside a* catch *command as described in Chapter 12.*

Although exec's features are similar to those of the UNIX shells, there is one important difference: exec does not perform any file name expansion. For example, suppose you invoke the following command with the goal of removing all .o files in the current directory:

```
exec rm *.o
Ø  rm: *.o nonexistent
```

rm receives *.o as its argument and exits with an error when it cannot find a file by this name. If you want file name expansion to occur you can use the glob command to get it, but not in the obvious way. For example, the following command will not work:

```
exec rm [glob *.o]
Ø  rm: a.o b.o nonexistent
```

This fails because the list of file names that glob returns is passed to rm as a single argument. If, for example, there exist two .o files, a.o and b.o, rm's argument will be "a.o b.o"; since there is no file by that name rm will return an error. The solution to this problem is the one described in Section 7.5: use eval to reparse the glob output so that it gets divided into multiple words. For example, the following command will do the trick:

```
eval exec rm [glob *.o]
```

In this case eval concatenates its arguments to produce the string

```
exec rm a.o b.o
```

which it then evaluates as a Tcl script. The names a.o and b.o are passed to rm as separate arguments and the files are deleted as expected.

Note: *The same effect can also be achieved with the command*

```
exec sh -c rm *.o
```

*In this case the command "*rm *.o*" isn't executed directly but is instead passed to the* sh *shell.* sh *expands the pattern* *.o *and then invokes* rm.

11.2   I/O to and from a command pipeline

You can also create subprocesses using the open command; once you've done this, you can use commands like gets and puts to interact with the pipeline. Here are two simple examples:

```
set f1 [open {|tbl | ditroff -ms} w]
set f2 [open |prog r+]
```

If the first character of the "file name" passed to open is the pipe symbol |, the argument isn't really a file name at all. Instead, it specifies a command pipeline. The remainder of the argument after the | is treated as a list whose elements have exactly the same meaning as the arguments to the `exec` command. `open` will create a pipeline of subprocesses just as for `exec` and it will return an identifier that you can use to transfer data to and from the pipeline. In the first example the pipeline is opened for writing, so a pipe is used for standard input to the `tbl` process and you can invoke `puts` to write data on that pipe; the output from `tbl` goes to `ditroff`, and the output from `ditroff` goes to the standard output of the Tcl application. The second example opens a pipeline for both reading and writing so separate pipes are created for `prog`'s standard input and standard output. Commands like `puts` can be used to write data to `prog` and commands like `gets` can be used to read the output from `prog`.

Note: *When writing data to a pipeline, don't forget that output is buffered. It probably will not be sent to the child process until you invoke the `flush` command to force the buffered data to be written.*

When you close a file identifier that corresponds to a command pipeline, the `close` command flushes any buffered output to the pipeline, closes the pipes leading to and from the pipeline, if any, and waits for all of the processes in the pipeline to exit. If any of the processes exits abnormally, `close` returns an error in the same way as `exec`.

11.3 Process ids

Tcl provides three ways that you can access process identifiers. First, if you invoke a pipeline in background using `exec`, `exec` returns a list containing the process identifiers for all of the subprocesses in the pipeline. You can use these identifiers, for example, if you wish to kill the processes. Second, you can invoke the `pid` command with no arguments and it will return the process identifier for the current process. Third, you can invoke `pid` with a file identifier as an argument, as in the following example:

```
set f [open {| tbl | ditroff -ms} w]
pid $f
⇒ 7189 7190
```

If there is a pipeline corresponding to the open file, as in the example, the `pid` command will return a list of identifiers for the processes in the pipeline.

11.4 Environment variables

Environment variables can be read and written using the standard Tcl variable mechanism. The array variable `env` contains all of the environment variables as elements, with the name of the element in `env` corresponding to the name of the environment variable. If you modify the `env` array, the changes will be reflected in the process's environment variables and the new values will also be passed to any child process created with `exec` or `open`.

11.5   Terminating the Tcl process with exit

If you invoke the `exit` command, it will terminate the process in which the command was executed. `exit` takes an optional integer argument. If this argument is provided, it is used as the exit status to return to the parent process. 0 indicates a normal exit and nonzero values correspond to abnormal exits; values other than 0 and 1 are rare. If no argument is given to `exit`, it exits with a status of 0. Since `exit` terminates the process, it doesn't have any return value.

Chapter 12
Errors and Exceptions

As you have seen in previous chapters, many things can result in errors in Tcl commands. Errors can occur because a command doesn't exist, or because it doesn't receive the right number of arguments, or because the arguments have the wrong form, or because some other problem occurs in executing the command, such as an error in a system call for file I/O. In most cases errors represent severe problems that make it impossible for the application to complete the script it is processing. Tcl's error facilities are intended to make it easy for the application to unwind the work in progress and display an error message to the user that indicates what went wrong. Presumably the user will fix the problem and retry the operation.

Errors are just one example of a more general phenomenon called *exceptions*. Exceptions are events that cause scripts to be aborted; they include the break, continue, and return commands as well as errors. Tcl allows exceptions to be "caught" by scripts so that only part of the work in progress is unwound. After catching an exception the script can ignore it or take steps to recover from it. If the script can't recover, it can reissue the exception. Table 12.1 summarizes the Tcl commands related to exceptions.

12.1 What happens after an error?

When a Tcl error occurs, the current command is aborted. If that command is part of a larger script, the script is also aborted. If the error occurs while executing a Tcl procedure, the procedure is aborted, along with the procedure that called it, and so on until all the active procedures have aborted. After all Tcl activity has been unwound in this way, control eventually returns to C code in the application, along with an indication that an error

`catch` *command* ?*varName*? Evaluates *command* as a Tcl script and returns an integer code that identifies the completion status of the command. If *varName* is specified, it gives the name of a variable that will be modified to hold the return value or error message generated by *command*.
`error` *message* ?*info*? ?*code*? Generates an error with *message* as the error message. If *info* is specified and is not an empty string, it is used to initialize the `errorInfo` variable. If *code* is specified, it is stored in the `errorCode` variable.
`return` ?`-code` *code*? ?`-errorinfo` *info*? ?`-errorcode` *code*? ?*string*? Causes the current procedure to return an exceptional condition. *Code* specifies the condition and must be `ok`, `error`, `return`, `break`, `continue`, or an integer. The `-errorinfo` option may be used to specify a starting value for the `errorInfo` variable, and `-errorcode` may be used to specify a value for the `errorCode` variable. *string* gives the return value or error message associated with the return; it defaults to an empty string.

Table 12.1. A summary of the Tcl commands related to exceptions.

occurred and a message describing the error. It is up to the application to decide how to handle this situation, but most interactive applications will display the error message for the user and continue processing user input. In a batch-oriented application where there is no user to see the error message, the application might print the error message into a log and abort.

For example, consider the following script, which is intended to sum the elements of a list:

```
set list {44 16 123 98 57}
set sum 0
foreach el $list {
    set sum [expr $sum+$element]
}
```
Ø `can't read "element": no such variable`

This script is incorrect because there is no variable `element`: the variable name `element` in the `expr` command should have been `el` to match the loop variable for the `foreach` command. When the script is executed an error will occur as Tcl parses the `expr` command: Tcl will attempt to substitute the value of variable `element` but will not be able to find a variable by that name, so it will signal an error. This error indication will be returned to the `foreach` command, which had invoked the Tcl interpreter to evaluate the loop body. When `foreach` sees that an error has occurred, it will abort its loop and return the same error indication as its own result. This in turn will cause the overall script to be aborted. The error message

```
can't read "element": no such variable
```

will be returned along with the error and will probably be displayed for the user.

In many cases the error message will provide enough information for you to fix the problem. However, if the error occurred in a deeply nested set of procedure calls, you may not be able to figure out where the error occurred from the message alone. To help pinpoint the location of the error, Tcl creates a stack trace as it unwinds the commands that were in progress, and it stores the stack trace in the global variable errorInfo. The stack trace describes each of the nested calls to the Tcl interpreter. For example, after the preceding error, errorInfo will have the following value:

```
can't read "element": no such variable
    while executing
"expr $sum+$element"
    invoked from within
"set sum [expr $sum+$element]..."
    ("foreach" body line 2)
    invoked from within
"foreach el $list {
    set sum [expr $sum+$element]
} "
```

Tcl provides one other piece of information after errors, in the global variable errorCode. errorCode has a format that is easy to process with Tcl scripts; it is most commonly used in Tcl scripts that attempt to recover from errors using the catch command described later. The errorCode variable consists of a list with one or more elements. The first element identifies a general class of errors and the remaining elements provide more information in a class-dependent fashion. For example, if the first element of errorCode is POSIX, it means that an error occurred in a POSIX system call. error-Code will contain two additional elements giving the POSIX name for the error, such as ENOENT, and a human-readable message describing the error. See the reference documentation for a complete description of all the forms errorCode can take.

In the current version of Tcl the errorCode variable is set by only a few commands, most of which deal with file access and child processes. If a command generates an error without setting errorCode, Tcl fills it in with the value NONE.

12.2 Generating errors from Tcl scripts

Most Tcl errors are generated by the C code that implements the Tcl interpreter and the built-in commands. However, it is also possible to generate an error by executing the error Tcl command as in the following example:

```
if {($x < 0) || ($x > 100)} {
    error "x is out of range ($x)"
}
```

The `error` command generates an error and uses its argument as the error message.

As a matter of programming style, you should use the `error` command only in situations where the correct action is to abort the script being executed. If you think that an error is likely to be recovered from without aborting the entire script, it is probably better to use the normal return value mechanism to indicate success or failure (e.g., return one value from a command if it succeeded and another if it failed, or set variables to indicate success or failure). Although it is possible to recover from errors (you'll see how in Section 12.3) the recovery mechanism is more complicated than the normal return value mechanism. Thus you should only generate errors when recovery is unlikely.

12.3 Trapping errors with catch

Errors generally cause all active Tcl commands to be aborted, but there are some situations where it is useful to continue executing a script after an error has occurred. For example, suppose that you want to unset variable x if it exists, but it may not exist at the time of the unset command. If you invoke `unset` on a variable that doesn't exist, `unset` generates an error:

```
unset x
```
∅ *can't unset "x": no such variable*

You can use the `catch` command to ignore the error in this situation:

```
catch {unset x}
```
⇒ *1*

The argument to `catch` is a Tcl script, which `catch` evaluates. If the script completes normally, `catch` returns 0. If an error occurs in the script, `catch` traps the error (so that the `catch` command itself is not aborted by the error) and returns 1 to indicate that an error occurred. This example ignores any errors in `unset`, so x is unset if it existed and the script has no effect if x didn't previously exist.

The `catch` command can also take a second argument. If the argument is provided, it is the name of a variable and `catch` modifies the variable to hold either the script's return value (if it returns normally) or the error message (if the script generates an error):

```
catch {unset x} msg
```
⇒ *1*

```
set msg
```
⇒ *can't unset "x": no such variable*

In this case the `unset` command generates an error, so msg is set to contain the error message. If variable x had existed, `unset` would have returned successfully, so the return value from `catch` would have been 0 and `msg` would have contained the return value from the `unset` command, which is an empty string. This longer form of `catch` is useful if you need access to the return value when the script completes successfully. It's also useful if you need to do something with the error message after an error, such as logging it to a file.

12.4 Exceptions in general

Errors are not the only things in Tcl that cause work in progress to be aborted. Errors are just one example of a set of events called *exceptions*. In addition to errors there are three other kinds of exceptions in Tcl, which are generated by the `break`, `continue`, and `return` commands. All exceptions cause active scripts to be aborted in the same way, except for two differences. First, the `errorInfo` and `errorCode` variables are set only during error exceptions. Second, the exceptions other than errors are almost always caught by an enclosing command, whereas errors usually unwind all the work in progress. For example, `break` and `continue` commands are normally invoked inside a looping command such as `foreach`; `foreach` will catch break and continue exceptions and terminate the loop or skip to the next iteration. Similarly, `return` is normally invoked only inside a procedure or a file being `source`'d. Both the procedure implementation and the `source` command catch return exceptions.

Note: *If a `break` or `continue` command is invoked outside any loop, active scripts are unwound until the outermost script for a procedure is reached or all scripts in progress have been unwound. At this point Tcl turns the break or continue exception into an error with an appropriate message.*

All exceptions are accompanied by a string value. In the case of an error, the string is the error message. In the case of `return`, the string is the return value for the procedure or script. In the case of `break` and `continue` the string is always empty.

The `catch` command actually catches all exceptions, not just errors. The return value from `catch` indicates what kind of exception occurred and the variable specified in `catch`'s second argument is set to hold the string associated with the exception (see Table 12.2). For example,

```
catch {return "all done"} string
```
⇒ *2*
```
set string
```
⇒ *all done*

Whereas `catch` provides a general mechanism for catching exceptions of all types, `return` provides a general mechanism for generating exceptions of all types. If its first argument consists of the keyword `-code`, as in:

```
return -code return 42
```

Return value from catch	Description	Caught by
0	Normal return. String gives return value.	Not applicable
1	Error. String gives message describing the problem.	catch
2	The return command was invoked. String gives return value for procedure or source command.	catch, source, procedures
3	The break command was invoked. String is empty.	catch,for,foreach,while,procedures
4	The continue command was invoked. String is empty.	catch,for,foreach,while,procedures
anything else	Defined by user or application.	catch

Table 12.2. A summary of Tcl exceptions. The first column indicates the value returned by catch in each instance. The second column describes when the exception occurs and the meaning of the string associated with the exception. The last column lists the commands that catch exceptions of that type ("procedures" means that the exception is caught by a Tcl procedure when its entire body has been aborted). The top row refers to normal returns where there is no exception.

then its second argument is the name of an exception (return in this case) and the third argument is the string associated with the exception. The enclosing procedure will return immediately, but instead of a normal return it will return with the exception described by the return command's arguments. In the preceding example, the procedure will generate a return exception, which will then cause the calling procedure to return as well.

In Section 8.5 you saw how a new looping command do could be implemented as a Tcl procedure using upvar and uplevel. However, the example in Section 8.5 did not properly handle exceptions within the loop body. Here is a new implementation of do that uses catch and return to deal with exceptions properly:

```
proc do {varName first last body} {
    global errorInfo errorCode
    upvar $varName v
    for {set v $first} {$v <= $last} {incr v} {
        set code [catch {uplevel $body} string]
        if {$code == 1} {
            return -code error -errorinfo $errorInfo \
                    -errorcode $errorCode $string
        } elseif {$code == 2} {
            return -code return $string
        } elseif {$code == 3} {
            return
        } elseif {$code > 4} {
            return -code $code $string
        }
    }
}
```

This new implementation handles exceptions in the same way as built-in looping commands such as foreach and while. It evaluates the loop body inside a catch command and then checks to see how the body terminates. If no exception occurs (code is 0) or if the exception is a continue (code is 4), do goes on to the next iteration. If an error or return occurs (code is 1 or 2), do uses the return command to reflect the exception upward to the caller. If a break exception occurs (code is 3), do returns to its caller normally, ending the loop. If any other completion code occurs, do simply reflects that exception back to its caller.

When do reflects an error upward, it uses the -errorinfo option to return to make sure that a proper stack trace is available after the error. If that option were omitted, a fresh stack trace would be generated starting with do's error return; the stack trace would not indicate where in body the error occurred. The context within body is available in the errorInfo variable at the time catch returns, and the -errorinfo option causes this value to be used as the initial contents of the stack trace when do returns an error. As additional unwinding occurs, more information gets added to the initial value, so that the final stack trace includes both the context within body and the context of the call to do. The -errorcode option serves a similar purpose for the errorCode variable, retaining the errorCode value from the original error as the errorCode value when do propagates the error. Without the -errorcode option the errorCode variable will always end up with the value NONE.

Chapter 13
Managing Tcl Internals

This chapter describes a collection of commands that allows you to query and manipulate the internal state of the Tcl interpreter. For example, you can use these commands to see if a variable exists, to find out what entries are defined in an array, to monitor all accesses to a variable, to rename or delete a command, or to handle references to undefined commands. Table 13.1 summarizes the commands.

13.1 Querying the elements of an array

The `array` command provides information about the elements currently defined for an array variable. It provides this information in several different ways, depending on the first argument passed to it. The command `array size` returns a decimal string indicating how many elements are defined for a given array variable and the command `array names` returns a list whose entries are the names of the elements of a given array variable:

```
    set currency(France) franc
    set "currency(Great Britain)" pound
    set currency(Germany) mark
    array size currency
⇒  3
    array names currency
⇒  {Great Britain} France Germany
```

For each of these commands, the final argument must be the name of an array variable. The list returned by `array names` does not have any particular order.

```
array anymore name searchId
            Returns 1 if there are any more elements to process in search searchId
            of array name, 0 if all elements have already been returned.
array donesearch name searchId
            Terminates search searchId of array name and discards any state
            associated with the search. Returns an empty string.
array names name
            Returns a list containing the names of all the elements of array name.
array nextelement name searchId
            Returns the name of the next element in search searchId of array name,
            or an empty string if all elements have already been returned in this search.
array size name
            Returns a decimal string giving the number of elements in array name.
array startsearch name
            Initializes a search through all of the elements of array name. Returns a
            search identifier that may be passed to array nextelement, array
            anymore, or array donesearch.
```

```
auto_mkindex dir pattern
            Scans all of the files in directory dir whose names match pattern (using
            the glob-style rules of string match) and generates a file tclIndex in
            dir that allows the files to be autoloaded.
```

```
info args procName
            Returns a list whose elements are the names of the arguments to procedure
            procName, in order.
info body procName
            Returns the body of procedure procName.
info cmdcount
            Returns a count of the total number of Tcl commands that have been
            executed in this interpreter.
info commands ?pattern?
            Returns a list of all the commands defined for this interpreter, including
            built-in commands, application-defined commands, and procedures. If
            pattern is specified, only the command names matching pattern are
            returned (string match's rules are used for matching).
info default procName argName varName
            Checks to see if argument argName to procedure procName has a default
            value. If so, stores the default value in variable varName and returns 1.
            Otherwise, returns 0 without modifying varName.
info exists varName
            Returns 1 if there exists a variable named varName in the current context,
            0 if no such variable is currently accessible.
```

Table 13.1. A summary of commands for manipulating Tcl's internal state (continued).

```
info globals ?pattern?
              Returns a list of all the global variables currently defined. If pattern is
              specified, only the global variable names matching pattern are returned
              (string match's rules are used for matching).
info level ?number?
              If number isn't specified, returns a number giving the current stack level
              (0 corresponds to top-level, 1 to the first level of procedure call, and so
              on). If number is specified, returns a list whose elements are the name and
              arguments for the procedure call at level number.
info library
              Returns the full path name of the library directory in which standard Tcl
              scripts are stored.
info locals ?pattern?
              Returns a list of all the local variables defined for the current procedure, or
              an empty string if no procedure is active. If pattern is specified, only the
              local variable names matching pattern are returned (string match's
              rules are used for matching).
info procs ?pattern?
              Returns a list of the names of all procedures currently defined. If pattern
              is specified, only the procedure names matching pattern are returned
              (string match's rules are used for matching).
info script
              If a script file is currently being evaluated, returns the name of that file.
              Otherwise returns an empty string.
info tclversion
              Returns the version number for the Tcl interpreter in the form
              major.minor, where major and minor are each decimal integers.
              Increments in minor correspond to bug fixes, new features, and backwards-
              compatible changes. major increments only when incompatible changes
              occur.
info vars ?pattern?
              Returns a list of all the names of all variables that are currently accessible.
              If pattern is specified, only the variable names matching pattern are
              returned (string match's rules are used for matching).
```

```
rename old new
              Renames command old to new, or deletes old if new is an empty string.
              Returns an empty string.
```

```
time script ?count?
              Executes script count times and returns a string giving the average
              elapsed time per execution, in microseconds. Count defaults to 1.
```

Table 13.2, continued.

```
trace variable name ops command
            Establishes a trace on variable name such that command is invoked
            whenever one of the operations given by ops is performd on name. Ops
            must consist of one or more of the characters r, w, or u. Returns an empty
            string.
trace vdelete name ops command
            If there exists a trace for variable name that has the operations and
            command given by ops and command, removes that trace so that its
            command will not be executed anymore. Returns an empty string.
trace vinfo name
            Returns a list with one element for each trace currently set on variable
            name. Each element is a sublist with two elements, which are the ops and
            command associated with that trace.

unknown cmd ?arg arg ...?
            This command is invoked by the Tcl interpreter whenever an unknown
            command name is encountered. cmd will be the unknown command name
            and the arg's will be the fully substituted arguments to the command. The
            result returned by unknown will be returned as the result of the unknown
            command.
```

Table 13.2, continued.

The `array names` command can be used in conjunction with `foreach` to iterate through the elements of an array. For example, this code deletes all elements of an array with values that are 0 or empty:

```
foreach i [array names a] {
    if {($a($i) == "") || ($a($i) == 0)} {
        unset a($i)
    }
}
```

Note: *The* `array` *command also provides a second way to search through the elements of an array, using the* `startsearch,` `anymore,` `nextelement,` *and* `donesearch` *options. This approach is more general than the* `foreach` *approach just given, and in some cases it is more efficient, but it is more verbose than the* `foreach` *approach and isn't needed very often. See the reference documentation for details.*

13.2 The info command

The `info` command provides information about the state of the interpreter. It has more than a dozen options, which are discussed in the following subsections.

13.2.1 Information about variables

Several of the `info` options provide information about variables. `info exists` returns a 0 or 1 value indicating whether or not there exists a variable with a given name:

```
set x 24
info exists x
```
⇒ *1*
```
unset x
info exists x
```
⇒ *0*

The options `vars`, `globals`, and `locals` return lists of variable names that meet certain criteria. `info vars` returns the names of all variables accessible at the current level of procedure call; `info globals` returns the names of all global variables, regardless of whether or not they are accessible; and `info locals` returns the names of local variables, including arguments to the current procedure, if any, but not global variables. In each of these commands an additional pattern argument may be supplied. If the pattern is supplied, only variable names matching that pattern (using the rules of `string match`) will be returned.

For example, suppose that global variables `global1` and `global2` have been defined and that the following procedure is being executed:

```
proc test {arg1 arg2} {
    global global1
    set local1 1
    set local2 2
    ...
}
```

Then the following commands might be executed in the procedure:

```
info vars
```
⇒ *global1 arg1 arg2 local2 local1*
```
info globals
```
⇒ *global2 global1*
```
info locals
```
⇒ *arg1 arg2 local2 local1*
```
info vars *al*
```
⇒ *global1 local2 local1*

13.2.2 Information about procedures

Another group of `info` options provides information about procedures. The command `info procs` returns a list of all the Tcl procedures that are currently defined. Like `info vars`, it takes an optional pattern argument that restricts the names returned to those that match a given pattern. `info body`, `info args`, and `info default` return information about the definition of a procedure:

```
proc maybePrint {a b {c 24}} {
    if {$a < $b} {
        puts stdout "c is $c"
    }
}
info body maybePrint
```
⇒
```
    if {$a < $b} {
        puts stdout "c is $c"
    }
```
```
info args maybePrint
```
⇒ *a b c*
```
info default maybePrint a x
```
⇒ *0*
```
info default maybePrint c x
```
⇒ *1*
```
set x
```
⇒ *24*

`info body` returns the procedure's body exactly as it was specified to the `proc` command. `info args` returns a list of the procedure's argument names, in the same order they were specified to `proc`. `info default` returns information about an argument's default value. It takes three arguments: the name of a procedure, the name of an argument to that procedure, and the name of a variable. If the given argument has no default value (for example, `a` in the preceding example), `info default` returns 0. If the argument has a default value (c in the preceding example), `info default` returns 1 and sets the variable to hold the default value for the argument.

As an example of how you might use the commands from the previous paragraph, here is a Tcl procedure that writes a Tcl script file. The script will contain Tcl code in the form of `proc` commands that recreate all of the procedures in the interpreter. The file can then be `source`'d in some other interpreter to duplicate the procedure state of the original interpreter. The procedure takes a single argument, which is the name of the file to write:

```
proc printProcs file {
    set f [open $file w]
    foreach proc [info procs] {
        set argList {}
        foreach arg [info args $proc] {
            if [info default $proc $arg default] {
                lappend argList [list $arg $default]
            } else {
                lappend argList $arg
            }
        }
        puts $f [list proc $proc $argList \
            [info body $proc]]
    }
    close $f
}
```

info provides one other option related to procedures: info level. If
info level is invoked with no additional arguments, it returns the current procedure
invocation level: 0 if no procedure is currently active, 1 if the current procedure was
called from top level, and so on. If info level is given an additional argument, the
argument indicates a procedure level and info level returns a list whose elements are
the name and actual arguments for the procedure at that level. For example, the following
procedure prints out the current call stack, showing the name and arguments for each
active procedure:

```
proc printStack {} {
    set level [info level]
    for {set i 1} {$i < $level} {incr i} {
        puts "Level $i: [info level $i]"
    }
}
```

13.2.3 Information about commands

info commands is similar to info procs except that it returns information about all
existing commands, not just procedures. If invoked with no arguments, it returns a list of
the names of all commands; if an argument is provided, it is a pattern in the sense of
string match, and only command names matching that pattern will be returned.

The command info cmdcount returns a decimal string indicating how many commands have been executed in this Tcl interpreter. It may be useful during peformance tun-
ing to see how many Tcl commands are being executed to carry out various functions.

The command info script indicates whether or not a script file is currently being
processed. If so, the command returns the name of the innermost nested script file that is
active. If there is no active script file, info script returns an empty string. This command is used for relatively obscure purposes such as disallowing command abbreviations
in script files.

13.2.4 Tclversion and library

info tclversion returns the version number for the Tcl interpreter in the form *major.minor.* Each of *major* and *minor* is a decimal string. If a new release of Tcl contains only backwards-compatible changes such as bug fixes and new features, its minor version number increments and the major version number stays the same. If a new release contains changes that are not backwards-compatible, so that existing Tcl scripts or C code that invokes Tcl's library procedures will have to be modified, the major version number increments and the minor version number resets to 0.

The command info library returns the full path name of the Tcl library directory. This directory is used to hold standard scripts used by Tcl, such as a default definition for the unknown procedure described in Section 13.6.

13.3 Timing command execution

The time command is used to measure the performance of Tcl scripts. It takes two arguments, a script and a repetition count:

```
    time {set a xyz} 10000
⇒  92 microseconds per iteration
```

time will execute the given script the number of times given by the repetition count, divide the total elapsed time by the repetition count, and print out a message similar to the preceding example giving the average number of microseconds per iteration. The reason for the repetition count is that the clock resolution on most workstations is many milliseconds. Thus anything that takes less than tens or hundreds of milliseconds cannot be timed accurately. To make accurate timing measurements, I suggest experimenting with the repetition count until the total time for the time command is a few seconds.

13.4 Tracing operations on variables

The trace command allows you to monitor the usage of one or more Tcl variables. Such monitoring is called *tracing.* If a trace has been established on a variable, a Tcl command will be invoked whenever the variable is read or written or unset. Traces can be used for a variety of purposes:

- monitoring the variable's usage (e.g., by printing a message for each read or write operation)
- propagating changes in the variable to other parts of the system (for example, to ensure that a particular widget always displays the picture of a person named in a given variable)

- restricting usage of the variable by rejecting certain operations (for example, generate an error on any attempt to change the variable's value to anything other than a decimal string) or by overriding certain operations (for example, recreate the variable whenever it is unset).

Here is a simple example that causes a message to be printed when either of two variables is modified:

```
trace variable color w pvar
trace variable a(length) w pvar
proc pvar {name element op} {
    if {$element != ""} {
        set name ${name}($element)
    }
    upvar $name x
    puts "Variable $name set to $x"
}
```

The first `trace` command arranges for procedure `pvar` to be invoked whenever variable `color` is written: `variable` specifies that a variable trace is being created, `color` gives the name of the variable, `w` specifies a set of operations to trace (any combination of r for read, w for write, and u for unset), and the last argument is a command to invoke. The second trace command sets up a trace for element `length` of array `a`.

Whenever `color` or `a(length)` is modified, Tcl will invoke `pvar` with three additional arguments, which are the variable's name, the variable's element name (if it is an array element, or an empty string otherwise), and an argument indicating what operation was actually invoked (r for read, w for write, or u for unset). For example, if the command "`set color purple`" is executed, Tcl will evaluate the command "`pvar color {} w`" because of the trace. If "`set a(length) 108`" is invoked, the trace command "`pvar a length w`" will be evaluated.

The `pvar` procedure does three things. First, if the traced variable is an array element, `pvar` generates a complete name for the variable by combining the array name and the element name. Second, the procedure uses `upvar` to make the variable's value accessible inside the procedure as local variable x. Finally, it prints out the variable's name and value on standard output. For the two accesses in the previous paragraph the following messages will be printed:

```
Variable color set to purple
Variable a(length) set to 108
```

The preceding example sets traces on individual variables. It's also possible to set a trace on an entire array, as with the command

```
trace variable a w pvar
```

where a is the name of an array variable. In this case `pvar` will be invoked whenever any element of a is modified.

Write traces are invoked after the variable's value has been modified but before returning the new value as the result of the write. The trace command can write a new value into the variable to override the value specified in the original write, and this value will be returned as the result of the traced write operation. Read traces are invoked just before the variable's result is read. The trace command can modify the variable to affect the result returned by the read operation. Tracing is temporarily disabled for a variable during the execution of read and write trace commands. This means that a trace command can access the variable without causing traces to be invoked recursively.

If a read or write trace returns an error of any sort, the traced operation is aborted. This can be used to implement read-only variables, for example. Here is a script that forces a variable to have a positive integer value and rejects any attempts to set the variable to a noninteger value:

```
trace variable size w forceInt
proc forceInt {name element op} {
    upvar $name x ${name}_old x_old
    if ![regexp {^[0-9]*$} $x] {
        set x $x_old
        error "value must be a positive integer"
    }
    set x_old $x
}
```

By the time the trace command is invoked the variable has already been modified, so if forceInt wants to reject a write it must restore the old value of the variable. To do this, it keeps a shadow variable with a suffix _old to hold the previous value of the variable. If an illegal value is stored in the variable, forceInt restores the variable to its old value and generates an error:

```
    set size 47
⇒  47
    set size red
Ø  can't set "size": value must be a positive integer
    set size
⇒  47
```

Note: *The forceInt procedure works only for simple variables, but it could be extended to handle array elements as well.*

It is legal to set a trace on a nonexistent variable; the variable will continue to appear to be unset even though the trace exists. For example, you can set a read trace on an array and then use it to create new array elements automatically the first time they are read. Unsetting a variable will remove the variable and any traces associated with the variable, then invoke any unset traces for the variable. It is legal, and not unusual, for an unset trace to immediately reestablish itself on the same variable so that it can monitor the variable if it should be recreated in the future.

To delete a trace, invoke trace vdelete with the same arguments passed to trace variable. For example, the trace created on color earlier can be deleted with the following command:

```
trace vdelete color w pvar
```

If the arguments to `trace vdelete` don't match the information for any existing trace exactly, the command has no effect.

The command `trace vinfo` returns information about the traces currently set for a variable. It is invoked with an argument consisting of a variable name, as in the following example:

```
trace vinfo color
```
⇒ *{w pvar}*

The return value from `trace vinfo` is a list, each of whose elements describes one trace on the variable. Each element is itself a list with two elements, which give the operations traced and the command for the trace. The traces appear in the result list in the order in which they will be invoked. If the variable specified to `trace vinfo` is an element of an array, only traces on that element will be returned; traces on the array as a whole will not be returned.

13.5 Renaming and deleting commands

The `rename` command can be used to change the command structure of an application. It takes two arguments:

```
rename old new
```

`rename` does just what its name implies: it renames the command that used to have the name *old* so that it now has the name *new*. *new* must not already exist as a command when `rename` is invoked.

`rename` can also be used to delete a command by invoking it with an empty string as the *new* name. For example, the following script disables file I/O from an application by deleting the relevant commands:

```
foreach cmd {open close read gets puts} {
    rename $cmd {}
}
```

Any Tcl command may be renamed or deleted, including the built-in commands as well as procedures and commands defined by an application. Renaming or deleting a built-in command is probably a bad idea in general, since it will break scripts that depend on the command, but in some situations it can be useful. For example, the `exit` command as defined by Tcl exits the process immediately (see Section 11.5). If an application wants to have a chance to clean up its internal state before exiting, it can create a "wrapper" around `exit` by redefining it:

```
rename exit exit.old
proc exit status {
    application-specific cleanup
    ...
    exit.old $status
}
```

In this example the `exit` command is renamed to `exit.old` and a new `exit` procedure is defined, which performs the cleanup required by the application and then calls the
renamed command to exit the process. This allows existing scripts that call `exit` to be
used without change, while still giving the application an opportunity to clean up its state.

13.6   Unknown commands

The Tcl interpreter provides a special mechanism for dealing with unknown commands. If
the interpreter discovers that the command name specified in a Tcl command doesn't exist,
it checks for the existence of a command named `unknown`. If there is such a command,
the interpreter invokes `unknown` instead of the original command, passing the name and
arguments for the nonexistent command to `unknown`. For example, suppose that you type
the following commands:

```
set x 24
createDatabase library $x
```

If there is no command named `createDatabase`, the following command is invoked:

```
unknown createDatabase library 24
```

Notice that substitutions are performed on the arguments to the original command before
`unknown` is invoked. Each argument to `unknown` will consist of one fully substituted
word from the original command.

The `unknown` procedure can do anything it likes to carry out the actions of the command, and whatever it returns will be returned as the result of the original command. For
example, the following procedure checks to see if the command name is an unambiguous
abbreviation for an existing command; if so, it invokes the corresponding command:

```
proc unknown {name args} {
    set cmds [info commands $name*]
    if {[llength $cmds] != 1} {
        error "unknown command \"$name\""
    }
    uplevel $cmds $args
}
```

Note that when the command is reinvoked with an expanded name, it must be invoked
using `uplevel` so that the command executes in the same variable context as the original
command.

The Tcl script library includes a default version of `unknown` that performs the following functions, in order:

1. If the command is a procedure that is defined in a library file, `source` the file to define the procedure, then reinvoke the command. This is called *autoloading* and is described in the next section.

2. If a program exists with the name of the command, use the `exec` command to invoke the program. This feature is called *autoexec*. For example, you can type `ls` as a command and `unknown` will invoke `exec ls` to list the contents of the current directory. If the command doesn't specify redirection, autoexec will arrange for the command's standard input, standard output, and standard error to be redirected to the corresponding channels of the Tcl application. This is different from the normal behavior of `exec`, but it allows interactive programs such as `more` and `vi` to be invoked directly from a Tcl application.

3. If the command name has one of several special forms such as ` ! !`, compute a new command using history substitution and invoke it. If, for example, the command is ` ! !`, the previous command is reinvoked. See Chapter 14 for more information on history substitution.

4. If the command name is a unique abbreviation for an existing command, the abbreviated command name is expanded and the command is reinvoked.

The last three actions are intended as conveniences for interactive use, and they occur only if the command was invoked interactively. You should not depend on these features when writing scripts. For example, you should not try to use autoexec in scripts; always use the `exec` command explicitly.

If you don't like the default behavior of the `unknown` procedure, you can write your own version or modify the library version to provide additional functions. If you don't want any special actions to be taken for unknown commands, you can just delete the `unknown` procedure, in which case errors will occur whenever unknown commands are invoked.

13.7 Autoloading

One of the most useful functions performed by the `unknown` procedure is *autoloading*. Autoloading allows you to write collections of Tcl procedures and place them in script files in library directories. You can then use these procedures in your Tcl applications without having to `source` the files that define them explicitly. You simply invoke the procedures. The first time that you invoke a library procedure it won't exist, so `unknown` will be called. `unknown` will find the file that defines the procedure, `source` the file to define the procedure, and then reinvoke the original command. The next time the procedure is invoked it will exist, so the autoloading mechanism won't be triggered.

Autoloading provides two benefits. First, it makes it easy to build large libraries of useful procedures and use them in Tcl scripts. You need not know exactly which files to `source` to define which procedures, since the autoloader takes care of that for you. The second benefit of autoloading is efficiency. Without autoloading an application must `source` all of its script files when it starts. Autoloading allows an application to start up without loading any script files at all; the files will be loaded later when their procedures are needed, and some files may never be loaded at all. Thus autoloading reduces startup time and saves memory.

The autoloader is straightforward to use. First, create a library as a set of script files in a single directory. Normally these files have names that end in `.tcl`, for example `db.tcl` or `stretch.tcl`. Each file can contain any number of procedure definitions. I recommend keeping the files relatively small, with just a few related procedures in each file. In order for the autoloader to handle the files properly, the `proc` command for each procedure definition must be at the beginning of a line with no leading space, and it must be followed immediately by white space and the procedure's name on the same line. Other than this, the format of the script files doesn't matter as long as they are valid Tcl scripts.

The second step in using the autoloader is to build an index. To do this, start up a Tcl application such as `tclsh` and invoke the `auto_mkindex` command as in the following example:

```
auto_mkindex . *.tcl
```

`auto_mkindex` isn't a built-in command, but rather a procedure in Tcl's script library. Its first argument is a directory name and the second argument is a glob-style pattern that selects one or more script files in the directory. `auto_mkindex` scans all of the files whose names match the pattern and builds an index that indicates which procedures are defined in which files. It stores the index in a file called `tclIndex` in the directory. If you modify the files to add or delete procedures, you should regenerate the index.

The final step is to set the variable `auto_path` in the applications that wish to use the library. The `auto_path` variable contains a list of directory names. When the auto-loader is invoked it searches the directories in `auto_path` in order, looking in their `tclIndex` files for the desired procedure. If the same procedure is defined in several libraries, the autoloader will use the one from the earliest directory in `auto_path`. Typically, `auto_path` will be set as part of an application's startup script. For example, if an application uses a library in directory `/usr/local/lib/shapes`, it might include the following command in its startup script:

```
set auto_path \
        [linsert $auto_path 0 /usr/local/lib/shapes]
```

This will add `/usr/local/lib/shapes` to the beginning of the path, retaining all the existing directories in the path such as those for the Tcl and Tk script libraries but giving higher priority to procedures defined in `/usr/local/lib/shapes`. Once a directory has been properly indexed and added to `auto_path`, all of its procedures become available through autoloading.

Chapter 14
History

This chapter describes Tcl's history mechanism. In applications where you type commands interactively, the history mechanism keeps track of recent commands and makes it easy for you to reexecute them without having to retype them from scratch. You can also create new commands that are slight variations on old commands without having to completely retype the old commands — to fix typographical errors, for example. Tcl's history mechanism provides many of the features available in csh, but not with the same syntax in all cases. History is implemented by the history command, which is summarized in Table 14.1. Only a few of the most commonly used history features are described in this chapter; see the reference documentation for more complete information.

14.1 The history list

Each command that you type interactively is entered into a *history list*. Each entry in the history list is called an *event*; it contains the text of a command plus a serial number identifying the command. The command text consists of exactly the characters you typed, before the Tcl parser peforms substitutions for $, [], etc. The serial number starts out at 1 for the first command you type and is incremented for each successive command.

Suppose you type the following sequence of commands to an interactive Tcl program:

```
set x 24
set y [expr $x*2.6]
incr x
```

At this point, the history list will contain three events. You can examine the contents of the history list by invoking history with no arguments:

history	Returns a string giving the event number and command for each event on the history list.
history keep *count*	Changes the size of the history list so that the *count* most recent events will be retained. The initial size of the list is 20 events.
history nextid	Returns the number of the next event that will be recorded in the history list.
history redo *?event?*	Reexecutes the command recorded for *event* and returns its result.
history substitute *old new ?event?*	Retrieves the command recorded for *event*, replaces any occurrences of *old* by *new* in it, executes the resulting command, and returns its result. Both *old* and *new* are simple strings. The substitution uses simple equality checks; no wildcards or regular expression features are supported.

Table 14.1. A summary of some of the options for the history command. Several options have been omitted; see the reference documentation for details.

```
      history
⇒         1 set x 24
          2 set y [expr $x*2.6]
          3 incr x
          4 history
```

The value returned by history is a human-readable string describing what's on the history list, which also includes the history command. The result of history is intended to be printed out, not to be processed in Tcl scripts; if you want to write scripts that process the history list, you'll probably find it more convenient to use other history options described in the reference documentation, such as history event.

The history list has a fixed size, which is initially 20. If more commands than that have been typed, only the most recent commands will be retained. The size of the history list can be changed with the history keep command:

```
      history keep 100
```

This command changes the size of the history list so that in the future the 100 most recent commands will be retained.

14.2   Specifying events

Several of the options of the `history` command require you to select an event from the history list; the symbol *event* is used for such arguments in Table 14.1. Events are specified as strings with one of the following forms:

Positive number: Selects the event with that serial number.

Negative number: Selects an event relative to the current event. −1 refers to the last command, −2 refers to the one before that, and so on.

Anything else: Selects the most recent event that matches the string. The string matches an event either if it is the same as the first characters of the event's command, or if it matches the event's command using the matching rules for `string match`.

Suppose that you had just typed the three commands from page 139. The command "incr x" can be referred to as event −1 or 3 or inc, and "set y [expr $x*2.6]" can be referred to as event −2 or 2 or *2*. If an event specifier is omitted, it defaults to −1.

14.3   Reexecuting commands from the history list

The `redo` and `substitute` options to `history` will replay commands from the history list. `history redo` retrieves a command and reexecutes it just as if you had retyped the entire command. For example, after typing the three commands from page 139, the command

        history redo

replays the most recent command, which is `incr x`; it will increment the value of variable x and return its new value (26). If an additional argument is provided for `history redo`, it selects an event as described in Section 14.2; for example,

        history redo 1
    ⇒ 24

replays the first command, `set x 24`.

    The `history substitute` command is similar to `history redo` except that it modifies the old command before replaying it. It is most commonly used to correct typographical errors:

        set x "200 illimeters"
    ⇒ 200 illimeters
        history substitute ill mill -1
    ⇒ 200 millimeters

The `history substitute` command takes three arguments: an old string, a new string, and an event specifier (the event specifier can be defaulted, in which case it defaults to -1). It retrieves the command indicated by the event specifier and replaces all instances of the old string in that command with the new string. The replacement is done using simple textual comparison with no wildcards or pattern matching. Then the resulting command is executed and its result is returned.

14.4 Shortcuts implemented by unknown

The `history redo` and `history substitute` commands are quite bulky; in the previous examples, it took more keystrokes to type the `history` commands than to retype the commands being replayed. Fortunately there are several shortcuts that allow the same functions to be implemented with fewer keystrokes:

`!!`	Replays the last command: same as "`history redo`".
`!event`	Replays the command given by *event*; same as "`history redo event`".
`^old^new`	Replays the last command, substituting new for old; same as "`history substitute old new`".

All of these shortcuts are implemented by the `unknown` procedure described in Section 13.6. `unknown` detects commands that have the forms described here and invokes the corresponding `history` commands to carry them out.

Note: *If your system doesn't use the default version of* unknown *provided by Tcl, these shortcuts may not be available.*

14.5 Current event number: history nextid

The command `history nextid` returns the number of the next event to be entered into the history list:

```
history nextid
⇒ 3
```

It is most commonly used for generating prompts that contain the event number. Many interactive applications allow you to specify a Tcl script to generate the prompt; in these applications you can include a `history nextid` command in the script so that your prompt includes the event number of the command you are about to type.

Part II:

Writing Scripts for Tk

Chapter 15
An Introduction to Tk

Tk is a toolkit that allows you to create graphical user interfaces for the X Window System by writing Tcl scripts. Tk extends the built-in Tcl command set described in Part I with additional commands for creating user interface elements called *widgets*, arranging them into interesting layouts on the screen using *geometry managers*, and connecting them with each other, with the enclosing application, and with other applications. This part of the book describes Tk's Tcl commands.

Like Tcl, Tk is implemented as a C library package that can be included in C applications, and it provides a collection of functions that can be invoked from an application to implement new widgets and geometry managers in C. The library functions are discussed in Part IV of the book.

This chapter introduces the basic structures used for creating user interfaces with Tk, including the hierarchical arrangements of widgets that make up interfaces and the main groups of Tcl commands provided by Tk. Later chapters will go over the individual facilities in more detail. All of the examples in this part can be run with wish, the windowing shell that was introduced in Chapter 2.

15.1 A brief introduction to X

The X Window System provides facilities for manipulating *windows* on *displays*. Figure 15.1 shows the hardware for a display, which consists of one or more *screens*, a single *keyboard*, and a *mouse*. The mouse is used to move a pointer around on the screens, and it also contains one or more buttons for invoking actions. Each screen displays a hierarchical collection of rectangular windows, starting with a *root window* that covers the entire area

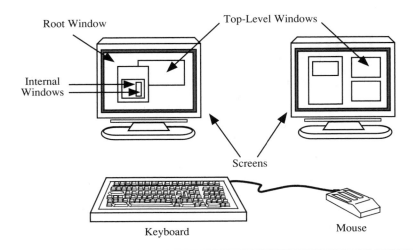

Figure 15.1. A display consists of one or more screens, a keyboard, and a mouse with one or more buttons. Each screen contains a hierarchical collection of overlapping windows.

of the screen. The root window may have any number of child windows, each of which is called a *top-level window*. An X application typically manages several top-level windows, one for each of the application's major panels and dialogs. Top-level windows may have children of their own, which may also have children, and so on. The descendants of top-level windows are called *internal windows*, and they may be nested to any depth. Internal windows are used for individual controls such as buttons, scrollbars, or text entries, and for grouping controls together.

Coordinates in X are measured in pixels relative to some window. The origin of a window's coordinate system is at its upper-left corner; x increases as you move to the right and y increases as you move down.

X allows applications to create and delete windows, move and resize them within their parents, and draw graphics on them such as text, lines, and bitmaps. If two windows overlap, one of them is considered to be "on top of" the other; graphics drawn in the higher window will appear on the screen while graphics drawn in the lower window will be *clipped* so that they are not drawn in the area of overlap. Children are always considered to be on top of their parents, while a modifiable *stacking order* determines the relationships between siblings. Each window is also clipped by its parent: if the window extends outside the parent, X displays only the part that overlaps the parent.

X sends *events* to notify applications of user actions such as key presses, pointer motion, and button presses. Each event identifies what occurred (for example, the pointer just passed into a window) and provides additional information about the event such as the window where the event occurred, the time when it occurred, the position of the pointer, and the state of the mouse buttons. X also generates events for structural changes such as window resizes and deletions, and it uses events to notify applications that they must redraw windows, for example, when one window moves so that it no longer obscures another window.

X does not require windows to have any particular appearance or behavior. An application can draw anything it likes in any window, and it can respond to events in any way that it pleases. Thus it is possible to implement many different variations with X. X provides no support for any particular look and feel, nor does it provide built-in controls such as buttons or menus. It is up to application-level toolkits to provide these features. For example, the Open Software Foundation has defined a standard look and feel called Motif, and OSF provides a toolkit (also called Motif) that implements the Motif look and feel. The Tk toolkit also implements the Motif look and feel, although Tk's implementation is totally different from the Motif toolkit.

An X environment contains three kinds of processes: X servers, applications, and window managers. For each display there is an *X server* process that manages the display's hardware and window hierarchy, draws graphics, and generates events. Applications are the processes such as editors and spreadsheets that provide interesting services to users. Applications communicate with X servers using network protocols such as TCP/IP; this means that an application can draw on displays attached to any host in its network (subject to various access controls) and a single application can create windows on multiple displays.

The third kind of process in an X environment is a *window manager*, one for each display. The window manager allows the user to manipulate top-level windows in a uniform way for all applications. It displays a decorative frame around each top-level window and provides controls within the frame so that users can interactively move, resize, iconify, and deiconify windows. The decorative frame also displays a title for the top-level window. Many different window managers exist, with different decorations and controls, but only one window manager exists for a given display at a given time. The examples in this book use mwm (the Motif window manager).

An X application must communicate with both the X server and the window manager. The application communicates with the X server to create windows, draw on them, and receive events. It communicates with the window manager to specify titles, preferred dimensions, and other information for its top-level windows.

For additional information on the X Window System I recommend *The X Window System*, 3rd Edition, by R. W. Scheifler and J. Gettys, Digital Press, 1992. I will refer to this book both in this part and again in Part IV when discussing widget implementation details.

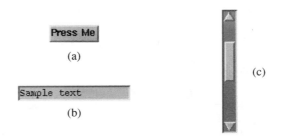

Figure 15.2. Examples of widgets in Tk: (a) a button widget displays a text string and invokes a given Tcl script when a mouse button is clicked over it; (b) an entry widget displays a one-line text string, which can be edited with the mouse and keyboard and retrieved by the application; (c) a scrollbar widget displays a slider and two arrows, which can be manipulated with the mouse to adjust the view in some other widget.

15.2 Widgets

Tk uses X to implement a ready-made set of controls with the Motif look and feel. These controls are called *widgets*. Figure 15.2 shows examples of button, entry, and scrollbar widgets. Each widget is a member of a *class* that determines its appearance and behavior. For example, widgets in the button class display a text string or bitmap as shown in Figure 15.2(a). Different buttons may display their strings or bitmaps in different ways (for example, with different fonts and colors), but each one displays a single string or bitmap. Each button also has a Tcl script associated with it, which is invoked if mouse button 1 (the left button on a three-button mouse) is pressed when the pointer is over the widget. Different button widgets may have different scripts associated with them but each one has an associated script. When you create a widget you select its class and provide additional class-specific *options*, such as a string or bitmap to display or a script to invoke.

Each Tk widget is implemented using one X window, and the terms "window" and "widget" are used interchangeably in this book. As with windows, widgets are nested in hierarchical structures like the one shown in Figure 15.3. A widget can contain any number of children and the widget tree can have any depth. Widgets such as buttons that have meaningful behavior for the user are usually at the leaves of the widget tree; the nonleaf widgets are usually just containers for organizing and arranging the leaf widgets.

Each widget/window has a textual name such as .a.b.c. Widget names are similar to the hierarchical path names for Unix files, except that . is used as the separator character instead of /. The name . refers to the topmost widget in the hierarchy, which is called the *main widget*. The name .a.b.c refers to a widget c that is a child of widget .a.b, which in turn is a child of .a, which is a child of the main widget.

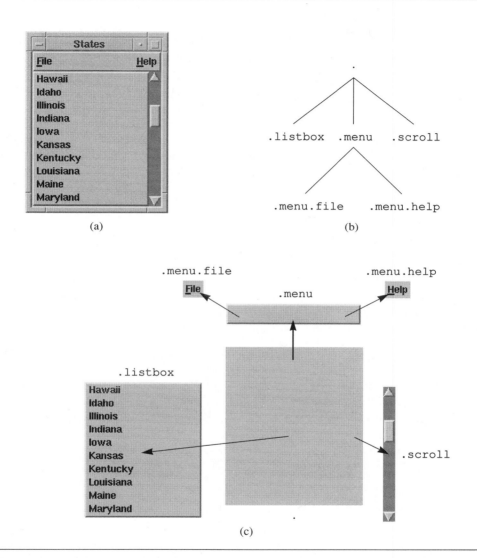

Figure 15.3. Widgets are arranged hierarchically. A collection of widgets is shown in (a) as it appears on the screen, with decorations provided by the mwm window manager. The hierarchical structure of the widgets is shown in (b). An exploded view of the screen is shown in (c) to clarify the widget structure. The topmost widget in the hierarchy (.) contains three children: a menu bar across the top, a scrollbar along the right side, and a listbox filling the remainder. The menu bar contains two children of its own, a File menu button on the left and a Help menu button on the right. Each widget has a name that reflects its position in the hierarchy, such as .menu.help for the Help menu button.

15.3   Applications, top-level widgets, and screens

In Tk the term *application* refers to a single widget hierarchy (a main widget and its descendants), a single Tcl interpreter associated with the widget hierarchy, plus all the commands provided by that interpreter. Each application has its own widget hierarchy so the name . refers to a different widget in each application. Normally there is a separate process for each application, but Tk also allows a single process to manage several applications with separate widget hierarchies and Tcl interpreters. Tk does not provide any particular support for multithreading (using a collection of processes to manage a single application); it is conceivable that Tk could be used in a multithreaded environment but it would not be trivial and I know of no working examples.

The main widget for each application occupies a top-level X window, so it will be decorated and managed by the window manager. Most of the other widgets of an application use internal windows; these widgets are called *internal widgets*. A few widget classes such as `toplevel` use top-level windows so that they can be manipulated independently by the window manager; widgets in these classes are called *top-level widgets*. A top-level widget differs from an internal widget in that its window is a child of the root window for its screen, whereas the window for an internal widget is a child of the window for the widget's parent in the Tk hierarchy. Top-level widgets are typically used as containers for panels and dialogs (see Figure 15.4 for an example).

It is not necessary for all of the widgets of an application to appear on the same screen or even the same display. When you create a top-level widget you can specify a screen. The screen defaults to the screen of the widget's parent in the Tk hierarchy, but you can specify any screen whose X server will accept a connection from the application. For example, it is possible to create a Tk application that broadcasts an announcement to a number of workstations by opening a top-level window on each of their screens.

Once a widget has been created it cannot be moved to another screen. This is a limitation imposed by the X Window System. However, you can achieve a similar effect by deleting the widget and recreating it on a different screen.

15.4   Scripts and events

A Tk application is controlled by two kinds of Tcl scripts: an *initialization script* and *event handlers*. The initialization script is executed when the application starts. It creates the application's user interface, loads the application's data structures, and performs any other initialization needed by the application. Once initialization is complete the application enters an *event loop* to wait for user interactions. Whenever an interesting event occurs, such as the user invoking a menu entry or moving the mouse, a Tcl script is invoked to process that event. These scripts are called event handlers; they can invoke application-specific Tcl commands to enter an item into a database, modify the user interface (for example, by posting a dialog box), or do many other things. Some event handlers are cre-

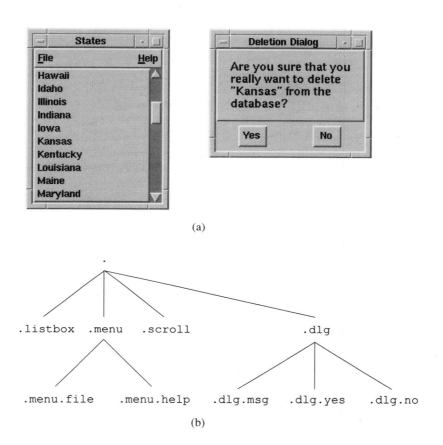

(a)

(b)

Figure 15.4. Top-level widgets appear in the Tk widget hierarchy just like internal widgets, but they are positioned on the screen independently from their parents in the hierarchy. In this example the dialog box .dlg is a top-level widget, as is the main widget. Figure (a) shows how the widgets appear on the screen and (b) shows Tk's widget hierarchy for the application.

ated by the initialization script, but event handlers can also be created and modified by other event handlers (for example, an event handler for a menu might create a new dialog box along with new event handlers for the dialog).

Most of the Tcl code for a Tk application is in the event handlers. Complex applications may contain hundreds of event handlers, and the handlers may create other panels and dialogs that have additional event handlers. Tk applications are thus *event-driven*. There is no well-defined flow of control within the application's scripts, since there is no single task for the application to perform. The application presents a user interface with many features and the user decides what to do next. All the application does is respond to the user's actions. The event handlers implement the responses; event handlers tend to be short and they are mostly independent of each other.

15.5 Creating and destroying widgets

Tk provides four main groups of Tcl commands, for (1) creating and destroying widgets, (2) arranging widgets on the screen, (3) communicating with existing widgets, and (4) interconnecting widgets within and between applications. This section and the three following sections introduce the groups of commands to give you a general feel for Tk's features. All of the commands are discussed in more detail in later chapters.

To create a widget, you invoke a command named after the widget's class: `button` for button widgets, `scrollbar` for scrollbar widgets, and so on. These commands are called *class commands*. For example, the following command creates a button that displays the text "`Press me`" in red:

```
button .b -text "Press me" -foreground red
```

All class commands have a form similar to this. The command's name is the name of a widget class. The first argument is the path name for the new widget, `.b` in this case. The command will create the widget and its corresponding X window. The widget name is followed by any number of pairs of arguments, where the first argument of each pair specifies the name of a *configuration option* for the widget, such as `-text` or `-foreground`, and the second argument specifies a value for that option, such as "`Press me`" or `red`. Each widget class supports a different set of configuration options, but many options, such as `-foreground`, are used in the same way by different classes. Values need not be specified for every option supported by a widget; defaults will be chosen for the unspecified options. For example, buttons support about 20 different options but only 2 were specified in the preceding example. Chapter 16 describes many of the most common configuration options.

To delete a widget, you invoke the `destroy` command:

```
destroy .menubar
```

This command will destroy the widget named `.menubar` and all of its descendants, if there are any.

15.6 Geometry managers

Widgets don't determine their own sizes and locations on the screen. This function is carried out by *geometry managers*. Each geometry manager implements a particular style of layout. Given a collection of widgets to manage and some controlling information about how to arrange them, a geometry manager assigns a size and location to each widget. For

```
button .top -text "Top button"
pack .top
button .bottom -text "Bottom button"
pack .bottom
```

(a)

(b)

Figure 15.5. The script in (a) creates two button widgets and arranges them in a vertical column with the first widget above the second. The application's appearance on the screen is shown in (b).

example, you might tell a geometry manager to arrange a set of widgets in a vertical column. The geometry manager will then position the widgets so that they abut but do not overlap. If a widget should suddenly need more space (for example, because its font was changed to a larger one) the widget will notify the geometry manager and the geometry manager will move other widgets down to preserve the column structure.

The second of the four main groups of Tk commands consists of those for communicating with geometry managers. Tk currently contains three geometry managers. The main geometry manager for Tk is the *packer*, which works by packing a series of widgets sequentially around the edges of a cavity. The packer can be used to generate rows, columns, and many other arrangements. Chapter 17 describes the packer in detail. The other geometry managers in Tk consist of the *placer*, which provides simple fixed placements, plus an internal geometry manager within the canvas widget, which can be used to mix widgets with structured graphics. Refer to the reference documentation for information on the placer and canvas geometry managers.

When you invoke a class command like button the new widget will not immediately appear on the screen. It will be displayed only after you have asked a geometry manager to manage it. If you want to experiment with widgets before reading the full discussion of geometry managers, you can make a widget appear by invoking the pack command with the widget's name as its argument. This will size the widget's parent so that it is just large enough to hold the widget and arrange the widget so that it fills the space of its parent. If you create other widgets and pack them in a similar fashion, the packer will arrange them in a column inside the parent, making the parent just large enough to accommodate them all. See Figure 15.5 for an example.

15.7 Widget commands

Whenever a new widget is created Tk also creates a new Tcl command whose name is the same as the widget's name. This command is called a *widget command*, and the set of all widget commands (one for each widget in the application) constitutes the third major group of Tk commands. After the button command was executed in Section 15.5, a widget command whose name is .b appeared in the application's interpreter. This command will exist as long as the widget exists; when the widget is deleted the command is deleted too.

Widget commands are used to communicate with existing widgets. Here are some commands that could be invoked after the button command from Section 15.5:

```
.b configure -foreground blue
.b flash
.b invoke
```

The first command changes the color of the button's text to blue, the second command causes the button to flash briefly, and the third command invokes the button just as if the user had clicked mouse button 1 on it. In widget commands the command name is the name of the widget and the first argument specifies an *action* to invoke on the widget, such as configure. Some actions, like configure, take additional arguments; the nature of these arguments depends on the specific action.

Note: *I will use the terms "action" and "widget command" interchangeably. For example, the phrase "the configure widget command" really means "the configure action for the widget command".*

The set of widget commands supported by a given widget is determined by its class. All widgets in the same class support the same set of widget commands, but different classes have different command sets. Some common actions are supported by multiple classes. For example, every widget class supports a configure widget command, which can be used to query and change the widget's configuration options.

15.8 Commands for interconnection

The fourth group of Tk commands is used for interconnection. These commands are used to make widgets work together, to make them work cooperatively with the objects defined in the application, and to allow different applications sharing the same display to work together in interesting ways.

Some of the interconnection commands are implemented as event handlers. For example, each button has a -command option that specifies a Tcl script to invoke whenever mouse button 1 is clicked over the widget. Scrollbars provide another example of interconnection via event handlers. Each scrollbar is used to control the view in some other widget. When you click in the scrollbar or drag its slider, the view in the associated widget should change. This connection between widgets is implemented by specifying a Tcl command for the scrollbar to invoke whenever the slider is dragged. The command invokes a widget command for the associated widget to change its view. In addition to

event handlers that are defined by widgets, you can create custom event handlers using the
`bind` command described in Chapter 18.

Tk supports five other forms of interconnection in addition to event handlers: the
selection, the input focus, the window manager, the `send` command, and grabs. The
selection is a highlighted piece of information on the screen, such as a range of text or a
graphic. X provides a protocol that applications can use to claim ownership of the selection and retrieve the contents of the selection from whichever application owns it. Chapter
20 discusses the selection in more detail and describes Tk's `selection` command,
which is used to manipulate the selection.

At any given time the keystrokes typed for an application are directed to a particular
widget, regardless of the mouse cursor's location. This widget is referred to as the *focus
widget* or *input focus*. Chapter 21 describes the `focus` command, which is used to move
the focus among the widgets of an application.

Chapter 22 describes Tk's `wm` command, which is used for communicating with the
window manager. The window manager acts as a geometry manager for main windows
and top-level windows, and the `wm` command can be used to make specific geometry
requests from the window manager, such as "don't let the user make this window smaller
than 20 pixels across". In addition, `wm` can be used to specify a title to appear in the window's decorative border, a title and/or icon to display when the window is iconified, and
many other things.

Chapter 23 describes the `send` command, which provides a general-purpose means
of communication between applications. You can use `send` to issue an arbitrary Tcl command to any Tk application on the display. The command will be transmitted to the target
application, executed there, and the result will be returned to the original application.
`send` allows any application to control any other application in powerful ways. For example, a debugger can send commands to an editor to highlight the current line of execution,
or a spreadsheet can send commands to a database application to retrieve new values for
cells in the spreadsheet, or a mail reader can send commands to a video application to play
a video clip identifying the sender of a message.

The last form of interconnection is *grabs*, which are described in Chapter 24. A grab
restricts keyboard and mouse events so that they are processed only in a subtree of the
widget hierarchy; windows outside the grab subtree become lifeless until the grab is
released. Grabs are used to disable parts of an application and force the user to deal immediately with a high-priority window such as a dialog box.

Chapter 16
A Tour of the Tk Widgets

This chapter introduces most of the widget classes implemented by Tk. Each widget class is defined by three things: its *configuration options*, its *widget commands*, and its *default bindings*. Configuration options represent most of the state of most widgets; they include things such as the colors, font, and text to display in a button widget and the Tcl script to invoke when the user clicks on the widget. All of the widgets in a class support the same configuration options. Different classes may have different options, but there are many options such as -foreground and -font that are supported by many different classes. The configuration options for a widget may be specified when the widget is created and modified later with the configure widget command, and default values can be specified using the option database (see Chapter 25).

The second thing that defines a widget class is its widget command. As described in Section 15.7, one widget command exists for each widget in an application, and it is used to invoke actions in the widget. The actions provided by a widget command vary from class to class, but some actions are supported by several classes. For example, every class supports a configure action for changing the widget's configuration options. For more complex widgets such as menus and listboxes, the widget's internal state is too complex to represent entirely with configuration options, so additional actions are provided to manipulate the state. For example, the widget command for menus provides actions to create and delete entries and to modify existing entries.

The third thing that defines a widget class is its default bindings. The default bindings give widgets their behavior by causing Tcl scripts to be evaluated in response to user actions. Tk creates the default bindings by evaluating an initialization script stored in file tk.tcl in the Tk library directory; the script invokes the bind command described in Chapter 18. This means that the behaviors are not hard-coded into the widgets: you can modify the behavior of individual widgets or entire classes using the bind command. The descriptions in this chapter correspond to the default behaviors.

Tk currently defines 15 widget classes. This chapter gives an overview of 13 of the classes along with the most commonly used configuration options; text and canvas widgets are described separately in Chapter 19. This chapter does not explain every feature of every widget; for that you should refer to the reference documentation for the individual widget classes. If you wish to see additional examples of widget usage besides those in this chapter, I recommend that you run the demonstration scripts in the Tk source distribution. In particular, the script widget contains examples of various widgets. Chapter 27 describes two additional examples, which illustrate several of the widgets plus many other features of Tk.

Note: *The examples in this chapter use the* pack *command to arrange widgets. Geometry management will be discussed in detail in Chapter 17, so I will not attempt to explain the usage of* pack *in this chapter. You should not need to understand the operation of the* pack *commands in order to understand the examples.*

16.1 Frames

Frames are the simplest widgets; they appear as colored rectangular regions and might have 3D borders. As you will see later, frames are typically used as containers for grouping other widgets. Most of the nonleaf widgets in an application are frames, and you'll see in Chapter 17 that frames are particularly important for building nested layouts with geometry managers; when used in this way, frames are often invisible to the user. Frames are also used to generate decorations such as a block of color or a raised or sunken border around a group of widgets. Frames have no default behavior: they do not normally respond to the mouse or keyboard.

16.1.1 Relief options

Frames support only a few configuration options, and most of these are supported by all widget classes. For example, the -relief and -borderwidth options can be used to specify a 3D border. The -relief option determines the 3D appearance of the border and must have one of the values raised, sunken, flat, groove, or ridge. Figure 16.1 shows the effect produced by each value. Tk draws widget borders with light and dark shadows to produce the different effects. For example, if a widget's relief is raised, Tk draws the top and left borders in a lighter color than the widget's background and it draws the lower and right borders in a darker color. This makes the widget appear to protrude from the screen.

```
foreach relief {raised sunken flat groove ridge} {
    frame .$relief -width 15m -height 10m -relief $relief \
            -borderwidth 4
    pack .$relief -side left -padx 2m -pady 2m
}
.flat configure -background black
```

Figure 16.1. Five frames with different reliefs, and the wish script that generates them. From left to right the −relief values are raised, sunken, flat, groove, and ridge. The flat frame has a black background color (otherwise it would be invisible, since the default background color is the same as that of its parent).

16.1.2 Screen distance options

Several commonly used configuration options take *screen distances* as values. For example, the −borderwidth option determines the width of a widget's border, −width and −height options can be used to specify the dimensions of a frame, and widgets such as texts provide an −insertwidth option for specifying the size of the insertion cursor. Screen distances can be specified either in pixels or in absolute units independent of the screen resolution. A distance consists of an integer or floating-point value followed optionally by a single character giving the units. If no unit specifier is given, the units are pixels. Otherwise the unit specifier must be one of the following characters:

c	centimeters
i	inches
m	millimeters
p	printer's points (1/72 inch)

For example, a distance specified as 2.2c will be rounded to the number of pixels that most closely approximates 2.2 centimeters; the number of pixels may vary from screen to screen. Figure 16.1 contains examples of screen distance options specified in millimeters and pixels.

Screen distances are also used for other purposes in Tk besides widget configuration options. One example is the −padx and −pady options to the pack command, which are used in Figure 16.1 to leave extra space around each of the frame widgets.

16.1.3 Color options

The −background option determines the background color of a widget and also the shadow colors used in its border. The value of the −background option may be specified either symbolically or numerically. A symbolic color value is a name such as white or red or SeaGreen2. The valid color names are defined in a file named rgb.txt in your X library directory; common names such as black and white and red exist in virtually every X environment, but names like SeaGreen2 might not be available everywhere. Color names are not case sensitive: black is the same as Black or bLaCk.

Colors can also be specified numerically in terms of their red, green, and blue components. Four forms are available, in which the components are specified with 4-bit, 8-bit, 12-bit, or 16-bit values:

```
#RGB
#RRGGBB
#RRRGGGBBB
#RRRRGGGGBBBB
```

Each R, G, or B in these examples represents one hexadecimal digit of red, green, or blue intensity, respectively. The first character of the specification must be #, and the same number of digits must be provided for each component. If fewer than four digits are given for each component, they represent the most significant bits of the values. For example, #3a7 is equivalent to #3000a0007000. A value of all 1's represents "full on" for that color, and a value of 0 represents "off." Thus #000 is black, #f00 is red, #ff0 is yellow, and #fff is white.

Note: *If you specify a color other than black or white for a monochrome display, Tk will use black or white instead, depending on the overall intensity of the color you requested. Furthermore, if you are using a color display and all of the entries in its color map are in use (e.g., because you're displaying a complex image on the screen), Tk will treat the display as if it were monochrome. See Section 26.6 for more information.*

Virtually every widget class supports a −background option and most widget classes support additional color options. For example, most widget classes provide a −foreground option that determines the color of the text or graphics displayed in the widget

16.1.4 Synonyms

Tk provides special short forms for a few of the most commonly used options. For example, −bd is a synonym for −borderwidth, −bg is a synonym for −background, and −fg is a synonym for −foreground.

```
label .bitmap -bitmap @$tk_library/demos/bitmaps/flagdown
label .label -text "No new mail"
pack .bitmap .label
```

Figure 16.2. Two labels, one displaying a bitmap and one displaying a text string, and the wish script that generates them.

16.2 Toplevels

Toplevel widgets are identical to frames except that they occupy top-level windows whereas frames occupy internal windows. Toplevels are typically used as the outermost containers for an application's panels and dialog boxes. The main widget for an application is also a toplevel. When creating a new toplevel widget you can use the -screen option to specify the screen on which it is to appear. For example, the command

```
toplevel .t -screen unix:0.1
```

will create a new toplevel widget on screen 1 of display unix:0. If no -screen option is given, the new toplevel appears on the same screen as its parent in the Tk widget hierarchy.

16.3 Labels

A label widget is similar to a frame except that it also displays a text string or bitmap. Labels provide several additional configuration options for specifying what to display in the widget; see Figure 16.2 for an example of text and bitmap labels.

16.3.1 Text options

Most widgets that display simple text strings, like labels, provide two options for specifying the string. If a -text option is specified, as for .label in Figure 16.2, its value is the string to display in the widget. If instead you specify a -textvariable option, the option's value is the name of a global variable and the widget will display the contents of

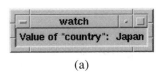
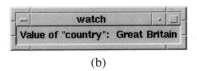

(a)   (b)

Figure 16.3. The watch procedure can be used to display the value of a variable as in (a). If the variable's value changes, so does the display, as in (b).

the variable; whenever the variable changes the widget will resize and/or redisplay itself to reflect the new value. Here is a simple example that uses −textvariable:

```
proc watch name {
    toplevel .watch
    label .watch.label -text "Value of \"$name\": "
    label .watch.value -textvariable $name
    pack .watch.label .watch.value -side left
}
```

This procedure will create a new toplevel widget and pack two labels inside it to display the name of a global variable and its value. For example, the following script can be invoked to create the panel shown in Figure 16.3(a) :

```
set country Japan
watch country
```

Figure 16.3(b) shows how the display changes if the following command is invoked to change the variable's value:

```
set country "Great Britain"
```

16.3.2 Font options

The −font option specifies a font to use when displaying text in a widget. Tk uses standard X font names, which are illustrated in Figure 16.4. The name of a font consists of 14 fields separated by hyphens. The fields have the following meanings:

foundry	The type foundry that supplied the font data.
family	Identifies a group of fonts with a similar typeface design.
weight	Typographic weight of font, such as medium or bold.
slant	Posture of font, such as r for roman or upright, i for italic, or o for oblique.
set width	Proportionate width of font, such as normal, condensed, or narrow.
style	Additional style information, such as serif. This field is empty for most fonts.

pixels	Size of font in pixels.
points	Size of font in tenths of points, assuming screen has *x-res* and *y-res* specified for font.
x-res	Horizontal resolution of screen for which font was designed, in dots per inch.
y-res	Vertical resolution of screen for which font was designed, in dots per inch.
spacing	Escapement class of font, such as m for monospace (fixed-width) or p for proportional (variable-width).
width	Average width of characters in font, in tenths of pixels.
registry	Registration authority that defines the character set encoding for the font.
encoding	Selects one particular encoding from all those defined by the registry.

You can use * and ? wildcards in font names to avoid specifying every field: ? matches any single character in a font name, and * matches any group of characters. For example, the font name

```
*-times-medium-r-normal--*-100-*-*-*-*-*-*
```

requests a 10-point Times Roman font in a medium (normal) weight and normal width. It specifies "don't care" for the foundry, the pixel size, and all fields after the point size. If multiple fonts match this pattern, the X server will pick the first one that matches. I recommend specifying the point size for fonts but not the pixel size, so that characters will be the same absolute size regardless of the display resolution.

You can use the program xlsfonts to find out exactly which fonts are available in your environment. If you invoke xlsfonts from your shell with no arguments, it will print out a list of all available fonts. Or, you can invoke xlsfonts with a pattern as argument, and it will print out the names of all fonts that match the pattern. For example, the following command prints out the names of all available Courier fonts.

```
xlsfonts '*Courier*'
```

You must enclose the pattern in quotes so that your shell passes the * characters through to xlsfonts rather than expanding them itself with file-name matching.

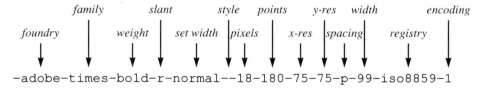

Figure 16.4. The fields of an X font name.

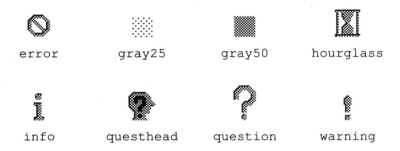

Figure 16.5. Bitmaps defined internally by Tk.

16.3.3 Bitmap options

Labels and many other widgets can display *bitmaps* instead of text. A bitmap is an image with two colors, foreground and background. Bitmaps are specified using the `-bitmap` option, whose values may have two forms. If the first character of the value is `@`, the remainder of the value is the name of a file containing a bitmap in X bitmap file format. These files are generated by programs like `bitmap`. Thus "`-bitmap @face.bit`" specifies a bitmap contained in the file `face.bit`. The example in Figure 16.2 specifies a bitmap as `@$tk_library/demos/bitmaps/flagdown`. This refers to one of the bitmaps in the library of demonstrations that is included with the Tk distribution (the variable `tk_library` holds the name of the directory containing Tk's library files).

If the first character of the value isn't `@`, the value must be the name of a bitmap defined internally. Tk defines several internal bitmaps itself (see Figure 16.5) and individual applications may define additional ones.

The `-bitmap` option determines only the pattern of 1's and 0's that make up the bitmap. The foreground and background colors used to display the bitmap are determined by the `-foreground` and `-background` options for the widget. This means that the same bitmap can appear in different colors at different places in an application, and the colors of a given bitmap may be changed by modifying the `-foreground` and `-background` options.

16.4 Buttons, checkbuttons, and radiobuttons

Buttons, checkbuttons, and radiobuttons make up a family of widget classes with similar characteristics. These classes have all of the features of labels plus they also respond to the mouse. When the pointer moves over a button, the button lights up to indicate that something will happen if a mouse button is pressed; a button in this state is said to be *active*. It

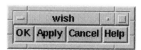

```
button .ok -text OK -command ok
button .apply -text Apply -command apply
button .cancel -text Cancel -command cancel
button .help -text Help -command help
pack .ok .apply .cancel .help -side left
```

Figure 16.6. Four button widgets and the wish script that generates them. The procedures ok, apply, cancel, and help are invoked when the user clicks on one of the buttons with the mouse; the code for these procedures is not provided here. In this example the -command options are all single words, but in general they can be arbitrary scripts.

is a general property of Tk widgets that they light up if the pointer passes over them when they are prepared to respond to button presses. Buttons become inactive when the pointer leaves them.

If mouse button 1 is pressed when a button widget is active, the widget's appearance changes to make it look sunken, as if a real button had been pressed. When the mouse button is released, the widget's original appearance is restored. Furthermore, when the mouse button is released the widget evaluates its -command option as a Tcl script. See Figure 16.6 for an example.

Checkbuttons are used for making binary choices such as enabling or disabling underlining or grid alignment; see Figure 16.7 for an example. Checkbuttons are similar to buttons except for two things. First, when you click mouse button 1 over a checkbutton a global variable toggles in value between 0 and 1. The variable name is specified to the widget with the -variable option. Second, the checkbutton displays a rectangular *selector* to the left of its text or bitmap. When the variable's value is 1 the selector is displayed in a dark color and the checkbutton is said to be *selected*; otherwise the selector box appears empty. Each checkbutton monitors the value of its associated variable and if the variable's value changes (e.g., because of a set command) the checkbutton updates the selector display. Checkbuttons provide additional configuration options for specifying the color of the selector and for specifying "off" and "on" values other than 0 and 1.

Radiobutton widgets provide a way to select one of several mutually exclusive options, much like the radio buttons in cars are used to select one of several stations. Several radiobuttons work together to control a single global variable. Each radiobutton provides a -variable option to name the variable and a -value option to specify a value for the variable; when you click on the widget it sets the variable to the given value. For example, Figure 16.8 shows a collection of radiobuttons that are used to select a font family from among several alternatives. Each radiobutton displays a diamond-shaped selector

```
checkbutton .bold -text Bold -variable bold -anchor w
checkbutton .italic -text Italic -variable italic -anchor w
checkbutton .underline -text Underline -variable underline \
        -anchor w
pack .bold .italic .underline -side top -fill x
```

Figure 16.7. Three checkbuttons and the wish script that generates them. Each checkbutton toggles a particular variable between 0 and 1 and its selector square indicates the current value of the variable (the variables bold and underline are currently 1, italic is 0). The -anchor options cause the buttons to left-justify their text and selectors as described in Section 16.11.2.

```
radiobutton .times -text Times -variable font \
        -value times -anchor w
radiobutton .helvetica -text Helvetica -variable font \
        -value helvetica -anchor w
radiobutton .courier -text Courier -variable font \
        -value courier -anchor w
radiobutton .symbol -text Symbol -variable font \
        -value symbol -anchor w
pack .times .helvetica .courier .symbol -side top -fill x
```

Figure 16.8. Four radiobuttons and the wish script that generates them. The user can select one of four values for the global variable font by clicking on a button. The selector diamond for the .courier widget is illuminated to indicate that it is selected (the variable currently has the value courier).

```
message .msg -width 8c -justify left -relief raised -bd 2 \
        -font -Adobe-Helvetica-Medium-R-Normal--*-180-* \
        -text "You have made changes to this document\
        since the last time it was saved. Is it OK to\
        discard the changes?"
pack .msg
```

Figure 16.9. A sample message widget, and the script that generates it.

to the left of its text or bitmap and lights up the selector when it is selected (i.e., whenever the variable's value matches its -value option). Each radiobutton monitors the variable and turns its selector diamond on or off when the variable value changes.

16.5 Messages

Message widgets are similar to labels except that they display multiline strings. A message automatically breaks long strings up into lines and provides options for controlling the line length and justification. Figure 16.9 shows an example. Message widgets support the following additional options:

-width   A screen distance indicating how long lines should be; if the string is too long to fit on a single line the message widget breaks it up at word boundaries.

-aspect   Used instead of -width; the widget will compute a line length that approximates the specified width/height ratio for the window.

-justify Specifies the justification of lines within the widget; must be left, center, or right.

The text in a message widget cannot be edited by the user. Messages are typically used to display simple unformatted text in dialogs and other panels. For more control over formatting, or to edit multiline text, use text widgets as described in Chapter 19.

```
listbox .colors
pack .colors
set f [open /usr/lib/X11/rgb.txt]
while {[gets $f line] >= 0} {
    .colors insert end [lrange $line 3 end]
}
close $f
bind .colors <Double-Button-1> {
    .colors configure -background [selection get]
}
```

Figure 16.10. A listbox that displays all of the colors named in the system's `rgb.txt` file. The script fills the listbox by scanning through the file one line at a time, stripping off the first three fields of the line and entering the remainder (which is the color name) into the listbox. For example, the `rgb.txt` line for `PeachPuff3` is "205 175 149 PeachPuff3". The user has clicked on the `PeachPuff3` entry to select it. A double-click will cause the listbox's background color to change to the selected color.

16.6 Listboxes

A listbox is a widget that displays a collection of strings and allows the user to select one or more of them. For example, the listbox in Figure 16.10 displays the names in the system's database of colors. If a listbox contains too many entries to display at once, as in Figure 16.10, it displays as many as will fit in the window. The user can control what is displayed by pressing mouse button 2 over the widget and dragging up or down. This is called *scanning*: it has the effect of dragging the listbox contents underneath the window at high speed. All of the Tk widgets with adjustable views support scanning. Scrollbars can also be associated with listboxes as described in Section 16.7, and listboxes can be scanned and scrolled horizontally if their entries are too wide for their windows.

The entries in a listbox are not represented as configuration options. Instead, the listbox widget command provides several actions for manipulating entries, such as `insert` for adding new entries, `delete` for deleting entries, and `get` for retrieving entries. The script in Figure 16.10 uses the `insert` action to fill the listbox using information read from a file.

Listboxes are usually configured so that the user can select an entry by clicking on it with mouse button 1. In some cases the user can also select a range of entries by pressing and dragging with button 1. Selected entries appear in a different color and usually have a raised 3D effect. Once the desired entries have been selected, the user will typically use those entries by invoking another widget, such as a button or menu. For example, the user might select a color name from the listbox in Figure 16.10 and then click on a button widget to apply that color to some object; the Tcl script associated with the button can read out the selected listbox entry. It's also common for a double-click on a listbox entry to invoke an operation on the selected entry. For example, Figure 16.10 creates a binding for double-clicks that sets the background color of the listbox from the selected color.

16.7 Scrollbars

Scrollbars control the views in other widgets. Each scrollbar widget is associated with some other widget such as a listbox or entry. For example, Figure 16.11 shows a scrollbar next to a listbox that displays the names of all the files in a directory. The scrollbar displays an arrow at each end and a rectangular *slider* in the middle. The size and position of the slider indicate which of the listbox's entries are currently visible in its window. In Figure 16.11 the slider covers the bottom 20% of the area between the arrows; this means that the listbox is currently displaying the last 20% of its entries. The user can adjust the view by clicking mouse button 1 on the arrows, which moves the view a small amount in the direction of the arrow, or by clicking in the empty space on either side of the slider, which moves the view by one screenful in that direction. The view can also be changed by pressing on the slider and dragging it.

A scrollbar interacts with its associated widget using Tcl scripts. For example, consider the script in Figure 16.11. The listbox is configured with a `-yscrollcommand` option whose value is ".`scroll set`". Whenever the view in the listbox changes the listbox appends four numbers to the `-yscrollcommand` value to generate a command such as

```
.scroll set 51 10 41 50
```

The numbers give the total number of entries in the listbox, the number of entries that fit in the window at any one time, and the indices of the first and last entries currently visible in the window. The preceding command corresponds to the view in Figure 16.11. Then the listbox evaluates the command. In this case the command happens to be the widget command for the scrollbar, and it invokes the `set` action, which expects four arguments in just the form provided by the listbox. The `set` widget command causes the scrollbar to redraw its slider to correspond to the information in the arguments.

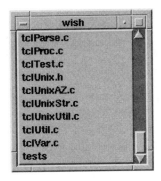

```
listbox .files -relief raised -borderwidth 2 \
        -yscrollcommand ".scroll set"
pack .files -side left
scrollbar .scroll -command ".files yview"
pack .scroll -side right -fill y
foreach i [lsort [glob *]] {
    .files insert end $i
}
```

Figure 16.11. A scrollbar and a listbox working together. The listbox displays the file names in a directory and the scrollbar is used to change the view in the listbox. The scrollbar uses its −command option to notify the listbox when the user invokes scrolling operations, and the listbox uses its −yscrollcommand option to notify the scrollbar when it changes its view.

When the user clicks on the scrollbar to change the view in the listbox, the scrollbar uses its −command option to notify the listbox. For example, suppose that the user clicks on the up arrow in Figure 16.11. The scrollbar computes the index of the entry that should now be at the top of the listbox (40) and generates a Tcl command by appending this number to the value of its −command option:

```
.files yview 40
```

Then the scrollbar evaluates the command. The widget command for the listbox has an action that takes exactly this form, and it causes the listbox to adjust its view so that entry 40 is displayed on the top line. After adjusting its view the listbox invokes its −yscrollcommand option to notify the scrollbar of the new view, and the scrollbar then redraws its slider.

This same approach works for all widgets that support scrolling, and it could support different implementations of scrollbars too. All that a widget must do to be scrollable is to provide a yview action for its widget command and a −yscrollcommand option. Scrollbars are not hard-wired to work with any particular widget or widget class; this information is provided by setting the scrollbar's −command option. It is possible to build new kinds of scrollbar widgets and have them work with any of the existing widgets as long as they provide a `-command` option and a `set` action for their widget commands.

Tk supports horizontal scrolling as well as vertical scrolling. Scrollbars have a vertical orientation by default, but they can be oriented horizontally by specifying the option "`-orient horizontal`". Listboxes have a separate `-xscrollcommand` option and an `xview` action for their widget commands to support horizontal scrolling.

16.8 Scales

A scale is a widget that displays an integer value and allows the user to edit the value by dragging a slider. Figure 16.12 shows an example where three scales are used to edit the red, green, and blue intensities for a swatch of color. The `-label` option for each widget specifies a string to appear next to the scale, and the `-from` and `-to` options specify the the range of values for the scale. The `-length` option indicates how large the scale should be on the screen and the `-orient` option selects a vertical or horizontal orientation in the same way as for scrollbars. It is also possible to display tickmarks next to a scale using a `-tickinterval` option, but the example in Figure 16.12 does not use this feature.

The user can change the value of a scale by clicking mouse button 1 in the scale or by dragging the slider with mouse button 1. Each time the scale's value changes, the scale evaluates a Tcl command consisting of the scale's `-command` option followed by the scale's new value. In Figure 16.12 all three scales invoke the `newColor` procedure. `newColor` ignores its argument, which is the new value of the scale that changed; instead, it fetches the values of all three scales using their widget commands, then it formats a numerical color value and uses it as the background color for the frame widget `.sample`.

16.9 Entries

An entry is a widget that allows the user to type in and edit a one-line text string. For example, if a document is being saved to disk for the first time, the user will have to provide a file name to use; Figure 16.13 shows an entry widget that might be used for entering the file name. To enter text into an entry the user clicks mouse button 1 in the entry. This makes a blinking vertical bar appear, called the *insertion cursor*. The user can then type characters and they will be inserted at the point of the insertion cursor. The insertion cursor can be moved by clicking anywhere in the entry's text. Text in an entry can be selected by pressing and dragging with mouse button 1, and it can be edited with a variety of keyboard actions, such as Delete or Control-h to delete the character just before the insertion cursor; see the reference documentation for details. The widget command for entries provides actions such as `insert` for inserting text, `delete` for deleting text, `icursor` for

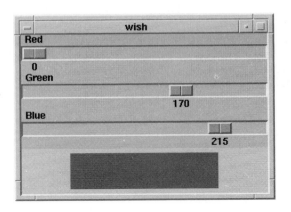

```
scale .red -label Red -from 0 -to 255 -length 10c \
        -orient horizontal -command newColor
scale .green -label Green -from 0 -to 255 -length 10c \
        -orient horizontal -command newColor
scale .blue -label Blue -from 0 -to 255 -length 10c \
        -orient horizontal -command newColor
frame .sample -height 1.5c -width 6c
pack .red .green .blue -side top
pack .sample -side bottom -pady 2m
proc newColor value {
    set color [format #%02x%02x%02x [.red get] [.green get] \
            [.blue get]]
    .sample configure -background $color
}
```

Figure 16.12. Three scale widgets for editing a color, and the wish script that generates them.

positioning the insertion cursor, and index for finding the character displayed at a particular position in the window.

The example in Figure 16.13 specifies a -width option for the entry, which indicates how wide the window should be in characters. If the text becomes too long to fit in this much space, only a portion of it is displayed and the view can be adjusted using an associated scrollbar widget or by scanning with mouse button 2. The example in Figure 16.13 also specifies a -textvariable option, which ties the text in the entry to the contents of global variable name. Whenever the text in the entry is modified name is updated, and vice versa.

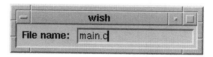

```
label .label -text "File name:"
entry .entry -width 20 -relief sunken -bd 2 -textvariable name
pack .label .entry -side left -padx 1m -pady 2m
```

Figure 16.13. An entry widget with an identifying label, and the wish script that generates them. The vertical bar is an insertion cursor that indicates where new text will be inserted.

16.10   Menus and menubuttons

Tk's menu widget is a building block that can be used to implement several varieties of menus, such as pull-down menus, cascading menus, and pop-up menus. A menu is a top-level widget that contains a collection of *entries* arranged in a column as shown in Figure 16.14. Menu entries are not distinct widgets but they behave much like buttons, checkbuttons, and radiobuttons. The following types of entries may be used in menus:

command	Similar to a button widget. Displays a string or bitmap and invokes a Tcl script when mouse button 1 is released over it.
checkbutton	Similar to a checkbutton widget. Displays a string or bitmap and toggles a variable between 0 and 1 when button 1 is released over the entry. Also displays a square selector like a checkbutton widget.
radiobutton	Similar to a radiobutton widget. Displays a string or bitmap and sets a variable to a particular value associated when button 1 is released over it. Also displays a diamond-shaped selector in the same way as a radiobutton widget.
cascade	Similar to a menubutton widget. Posts a cascaded sub-menu when the mouse passes over it. See below for more details.
separator	Displays a horizontal line for decoration. Does not respond to the mouse.

Menu entries are created with the add widget command for the menu and they have configuration options that are similar to those for buttons, checkbuttons, and radiobuttons.

Menus appear on the screen only for brief periods of time. They spend most of their time in an invisible state called *unposted*. To invoke a menu, it must first be *posted*. This is done with the post action for its widget command; for example, the menu in Figure 16.14 could be posted with the command ".m post 100 100". Once a menu is posted the user can move the pointer over one of the menu's entries and release button 1 to invoke the entry. After the menu has been invoked it is usually unposted until it is needed again.

```
menu .m
.m add checkbutton -label Bold -variable bold
.m add checkbutton -label Italic -variable italic
.m add checkbutton -label Underline -variable underline
.m add separator
.m add radiobutton -label Times -variable font -value times
.m add radiobutton -label Helvetica -variable font \
        -value helvetica
.m add radiobutton -label Courier -variable font \
        -value courier
.m add separator
.m add command -label "Insert Bullet" -command "insertBullet"
.m add command -label "Margins and Tabs..." \
        -command "mkMarginPanel"
```

Figure 16.14. A menu and the wish script that generates it. The add action for the menu's widget command is invoked to create the individual entries in the menu.

Menus can be posted and unposted in various ways to achieve different effects. The sections below describe pull-down menus and cascaded menus, where posting and unposting are handled automatically for you. Other approaches such as pop-up menus and option menus are also possible.

16.10.1   Pull-down menus

Menus are most commonly used in a *pull-down* style. In this style the application displays a *menu bar* near the top of its main window as shown in Figure 16.15. A menu bar is a frame widget that contains several menubutton widgets, each of which is associated with a menu. When a user presses mouse button 1 over a menubutton the associated menu is posted underneath the menubutton (for example, the Text menu is posted in Figure 16.15). Then the user slides the pointer down over the menu with the mouse button still pressed and releases the mouse button over the desired entry. When the button is released

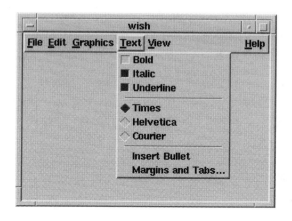

```
frame .mbar -relief raised -bd 2
frame .dummy -width 10c -height 5c
pack .mbar .dummy -side top -fill x
menubutton .mbar.file -text File -underline 0 \
        -menu .mbar.file.menu
menubutton .mbar.edit -text Edit -underline 0 \
        -menu .mbar.edit.menu
menubutton .mbar.graphics -text Graphics -underline 0 \
        -menu .mbar.graphics.menu
menubutton .mbar.text -text Text -underline 0 \
        -menu .mbar.text.menu
menubutton .mbar.view -text View -underline 0 \
        -menu .mbar.view.menu
menubutton .mbar.help -text Help -underline 0 \
        -menu .mbar.help.menu
pack .mbar.file .mbar.edit .mbar.graphics .mbar.text \
        .mbar.view -side left
pack .mbar.help -side right
menu .mbar.text.menu
.mbar.text.menu add checkbutton -label Bold -variable bold
.mbar.text.menu add checkbutton -label Italic -variable italic
...
tk_menuBar .mbar .mbar.file .mbar.edit .mbar.graphics \
        .mbar.text .mbar.view .mbar.help
focus .mbar
```

Figure 16.15. An example of pull-down menus with one menu posted. The menu bar frame (.mbar) has six children, each of which is a menubutton, and each of the menubuttons has a single child consisting of the associated menu. The definition of the menus is incomplete: only part of the definition for a single menu is shown.

the menu entry is invoked and the menu is unposted. The user can release the mouse button outside the menu to unpost it without invoking an entry.

If the user presses button 1 over a menubutton and then moves the pointer over another menubutton, the old menubutton unposts its menu and the new menubutton posts its menu. This allows the user to scan all of the menus by sliding the pointer across the menu bar.

If the user releases the mouse button over a menubutton, the menu stays posted and the user will not be able to do anything else with the application until the menu is unposted by invoking one of its entries or clicking outside of the menu to unpost it without invoking any entry. Situations like this where a user must respond to a particular part of an application and cannot do anything with the rest of the application until responding are called *modal* user interface elements. Menus and dialog boxes are examples of modal interface elements. Modal interface elements are implemented using the grab mechanism described in Chapter 24.

In the script in Figure 16.15 -menu and -underline options are specified for each menubutton in addition to its text string. The -menu option identifies the menu associated with the button. The -underline option gives the index of a character to underline when displaying the text in the menubutton. This character is used for keyboard traversal as described in Section 16.10.3. The last two statements in the script are also needed for keyboard traversal and are explained in Section 16.10.3.

16.10.2 Cascaded menus

A *cascaded menu* is a menu that is subservient to another menu. It is associated with a cascade menu entry in its parent menu, much like a pull-down menu is associated with a menubutton. When the pointer passes over a cascade entry in a menu, the associated menu is posted just to the right of the cascade entry as shown in Figure 16.16. The user can then slide the pointer to the right onto the cascaded menu and invoke an entry in it. After an entry has been invoked in a cascaded menu, both it and its parent are unposted. All that is needed to create a cascaded menu is to define the cascaded menu and create a cascade entry in its parent, using the -menu option in the cascade entry to specify the name of the cascaded menu. Menus can be cascaded to any depth.

16.10.3 Keyboard traversal and shortcuts

Pull-down menus can be posted and invoked without the mouse using a technique called *keyboard traversal*. One of the letters in each menubutton is selected as the traversal character for that menubutton using the -underline option; it is underlined in the menubutton's window. If that letter is typed while holding the Alt key down, the menubutton's menu will be posted. Or, you can type F10 to post the leftmost menu in the menu bar. Once a menu has been posted the arrow keys can be used to move among the menus and their entries. The left and right arrow keys move left or right among the menubuttons,

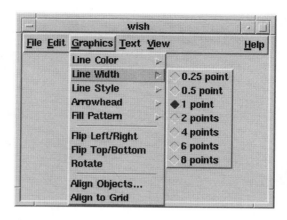

```
frame .mbar -relief raised -bd 2
...
menubutton .mbar.graphics -text Graphics -underline 0 \
        -menu .mbar.graphics.menu
menu .mbar.graphics.menu
.mbar.graphics.menu add cascade -label "Line Color" \
        -menu .mbar.graphics.menu.color
.mbar.graphics.menu add cascade -label "Line Width" \
        -menu .mbar.graphics.menu.width
...
menu .mbar.graphics.menu.width
.mbar.graphics.menu.width add radiobutton -label "0.25 point" \
        -variable lineWidth -value 0.25
...
```

Figure 16.16. A cascaded menu and excerpts from the wish script that generates it.

unposting the menu for the previous menubutton and posting the menu for the new one. The up and down keys move among the entries in a menu, activating the next higher or lower entry. You can type Return to invoke the active menu entry or Escape to abort the menu traversal without invoking anything. Traversal characters can also be defined for individual menu entries using the -underline option as shown in Figure 16.17. The traversal character is underlined when the menu entry is displayed, and if it or its lower-case equivalent is typed at a time when the menu is posted, then the entry is invoked.

In many cases it is possible to invoke the function of a menu entry without even posting the menu by typing *keyboard shortcuts*. If there is a shortcut for a menu entry, the key-stroke for the shortcut will be displayed at the right side of the menu entry (for example, Ctrl+z is displayed in the Undo menu entry in Figure 16.17). This key combination

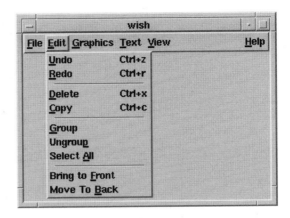

```
. . .
menu .mbar.edit.menu
.mbar.edit.menu add command -label "Undo" -underline 0 \
        -accelerator "Ctrl+z" -command undo
.mbar.edit.menu add command -label "Redo" -underline 0 \
        -accelerator "Ctrl+r" -command redo
. . .
.mbar.edit.menu add command -label "Select All" -underline 7 \
        -command allSelect
. . .
```

Figure 16.17. A menu with underlined traversal characters and shortcut strings for some of its entries.

may be typed in the application to invoke the same function as the menu entry (e.g., type z while holding the Control key down to invoke the Undo operation without going through the menu). The -accelerator option for a menu entry specifies a string to display at the right side of the entry.

Note: *Setting the* -accelerator *option does not automatically define the shortcut; it just causes a string to be displayed. You must also create a binding for the shortcut using the mechanism described in Chapter 18.*

The last two commands in Figure 16.15, tk_menuBar and focus, are needed in order to enable keyboard traversal of menus. The tk_menuBar command identifies the menus associated with a particular menu bar and specifies the order of the menus for use when the left- and right-arrow keys are typed. Its first argument is the name of the frame containing all of the menu buttons and the remaining arguments are the names of the menu buttons in order from left to right. In order for keyboard traversal to work, the input focus must be in a widget that has bindings for the traversal characters such as F10. All of the

Tk widgets that support text type-in, such as entries and texts, have these bindings, and
`tk_menuBar` also creates bindings for the menu bar window. The `focus` command in
Figure 16.15 sets the input focus to the menu bar; without that command there will be no
initial input focus so keystrokes will be ignored and keyboard traversal won't work.

16.11   Other common options

The widget descriptions discussed here introduced most of the common kinds of options,
such as colors and fonts. This section describes two other options, `-cursor` and
`-anchor`, that are supported by many widgets.

16.11.1   Cursor options

Every widget class in Tk supports a `-cursor` option that determines the image to display
for the pointer when it is over that widget. If the `-cursor` option isn't specified or if its
value is an empty string, the widget uses its parent's cursor. Otherwise the value of the
`-cursor` option must be a proper Tcl list with one of the following forms:

```
name fgColor bgColor
name fgColor
name
@sourceFile maskFile fgColor bgColor
@sourceFile fgColor
```

In the first three forms *name* refers to one of the cursors in the standard X cursor font. You
can find a complete list of all the legal names in the X include file `cursorfont.h`. The
names in that file all start with XC_, such as XC_arrow or XC_hand2; when using one
of these names in a `-cursor` option, omit the XC_, for example `arrow` or `hand2`. The
Scheifler and Gettys book contains an appendix that shows the names and images of all
the cursors in the X cursor font. You can also invoke the shell command

```
xfd -fn cursor -center
```

to display the cursor images on your screen, but `xfd` will not give you the textual names
for the cursors.

If *name* is followed by two additional list elements as in the command

```
.f config -cursor {arrow red white}
```

the second and third elements give the foreground and background colors to use for the
cursor; as with all color values, they may have any of the forms described in Section
16.1.3. If only one color value is supplied, it gives the foreground color for the cursor and
the background will be transparent. If no color values are given, black will be used for the
foreground and white for the background.

If the first character in the −cursor value is @, the image(s) for the cursor are taken from files in bitmap format rather than the X cursor font. If two file names and two colors are specified for the value, as in the following widget command:

```
.f config -cursor {@cursors/bits cursors/mask red white}
```

the first file is a bitmap that contains the cursor's pattern (1's represent foreground and 0's background) and the second file is a mask bitmap. The cursor will be transparent everywhere that the mask bitmap has a 0 value; it will display the foreground or background wherever the mask is 1. If only one file name and one color are specified, the cursor will have a transparent background.

16.11.2   Anchor options

An *anchor position* indicates how to attach one object to another. For example, if the window for a button widget is larger than needed for the widget's text, an −anchor option may be specified to indicate where the text should be positioned in the window. Anchor positions are also used for other purposes, such as telling a canvas widget where to position a bitmap relative to a point associated with the item or telling the packer geometry manager where to position a window in its frame.

Anchor positions are specified using one of the following points of the compass:

n	Center of object's top side.
ne	Top right corner of object.
e	Center of object's right side.
se	Lower right corner of object.
s	Center of object's bottom side.
sw	Lower left corner of object.
w	Center of object's left side.
nw	Top left corner of object.
center	Center of object.

The anchor position specifies the point on the object by which it is to be attached, as if a push-pin were stuck through the object at that point and then used to pin the object someplace. For example, if an −anchor option of w is specified for a button, it means that the button's text or bitmap is to be attached by the center of its left side, and that point will be positioned over the corresponding point in the window. Thus w means that the text or bitmap will be centered vertically and aligned with the left edge of the window. For bitmap items in canvas widgets, the −anchor option indicates where the bitmap should be positioned relative to a point associated with the item; in this case, w means that the center of the bitmap's left side should be positioned over the point, so that the bitmap actually lies to the east of the point. Figure 16.18 illustrates these uses of anchor positions.

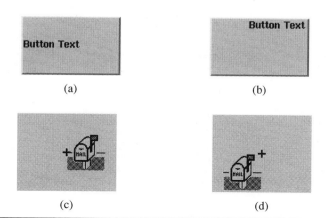

Figure 16.18. Examples of anchor positions used for button widgets and for bitmap items within canvases. Figure (a) shows a button widget with text anchored w, and (b) shows the same widget with an anchor position of ne. Figure(c) shows a canvas containing a bitmap with an anchor position of w relative to its point (the point appears as a cross, even though it wouldn't appear in an actual canvas). Figure (d) shows the same bitmap item with an anchor point of ne.

Chapter 17
Geometry Managers: the Packer

Geometry managers determine the sizes and locations of widgets. Tk is similar to other X toolkits in that it does not allow widgets to determine their own geometries. A widget will not even appear on the screen unless it is managed by a geometry manager. This separation of geometry management from internal widget behavior allows multiple geometry managers to exist simultaneously and permits any widget to be used with any geometry manager. If widgets controlled their own geometry, then this flexibility would be lost: every existing widget would need to be modified to introduce a new style of layout.

This chapter describes the overall structure for geometry management and then presents the packer, which is the most commonly used geometry manager in Tk. The packer makes it easy to generate layouts such as rows or columns of widgets; it can also be used for more complex effects such as "put the menu bar across the top of the window, then the scrollbar across the right side, then fill the remaining space with a text widget." The `pack` command is used to communicate with the packer; see Tables 17.1 and 17.2 for a summary of its features.

17.1 An overview of geometry management

A geometry manager's job is to arrange one or more *slave* widgets relative to a *master* widget. For example, it might arrange three slaves in a row from left to right across the area of the master, or it might arrange two slaves so that they split the space of the master with one slave occupying the top half and the other occupying the bottom half. Different geometry managers embody different styles of layout. The master is usually the parent of

```
pack slave ?slave ...? option value ?option value ...?
                Same as the pack configure command described next.
pack configure slave ?slave ...? option value ?option value ...?
                Arrange for the packer to manage the geometry of the widgets named by
                the slave arguments. The option and value arguments provide
                information that determines the dimensions and positions of the slaves. See
                Table 17.2 for details.
pack forget slave
                Causes the packer to stop managing slave and unmap it from the screen.
                Has no effect if slave isn't currently managed by the packer.
pack info slave
                Returns a list giving the current configuration of slave. The list consists of
                option-value pairs in exactly the same form as might be specified to the
                pack configure command. Returns an empty string if slave isn't
                currently managed by the packer. In Tk releases before 4.0 this action has
                the name newinfo instead of info.
pack propagate master ?boolean?
                boolean specifies whether the packer should set the requested size for
                master based on the needs of its slaves. If boolean is omitted, returns 0
                or 1 to indicate whether geometry propagation is currently enabled for
                master.
pack slaves master
                Returns a list of the slaves on master's packing list, in order.
```

Table 17.1. A summary of the pack command.

the slave but there are times when it's convenient to use other windows as masters (you will see examples of this later). Masters are usually frame widgets.

A geometry manager receives three pieces of information for use in computing a layout (see Figure 17.1). First, each slave widget requests a particular width and height. These are usually the minimum dimensions needed by the widget to display its information. For example, a button widget requests a size just large enough to display its text or bitmap. Although geometry managers aren't obliged to satisfy the requests made by their slave widgets, they usually do.

The second kind of input for a geometry manager comes from the application designer and is used to control the layout algorithm. The nature of this information varies from geometry manager to geometry manager. For example, with the packer an application designer can name three slaves and request that they be arranged in a row from left to right within the master; the packer checks the requested sizes of the slaves and positions them so that they abut in a row, with each slave given just as much space as it needs.

The third piece of information used by geometry managers is the geometry of the master window. For example, the geometry manager might position a slave at the lower left corner of its master, or it might divide the space of the master among one or more

`-after` *window*	Use *window*'s master as the master for the slave and insert the slave into the packing list just after *window*.
`-anchor` *position*	If the slave's parcel is larger than its requested size, this option determines where in the parcel the slave will be positioned. Defaults to `center`.
`-before` *window*	Use *window*'s master as the master for the slave and insert the slave into the packing list just before *window*.
`-expand` *boolean*	If *boolean* is a true value, the slave's parcel will grow to absorb any extra space left over in the master. Defaults to false.
`-fill` *style*	Specifies whether (and how) to grow the slave if its parcel is larger than the slave's requested size. *style* must be either `none`, `x`, `y`, or `both`. Defaults to `none`.
`-in` *master*	Use *master* as the master for the slave. *master* must be the slave's parent or a descendant of the slave's parent. If this option is not specified, the master defaults to the slave's parent.
`-ipadx` *distance*	*distance* specifies internal padding for the slave, which is extra horizontal space to allow inside the slave on each side, in addition to what the slave requests. Defaults to 0.
`-ipady` *distance*	*distance* specifies internal padding for the slave, which is extra vertical space to allow inside the slave on each side, in addition to what the slave requests. Defaults to 0.
`-padx` *distance*	*distance* specifies external padding for the slave (extra horizontal space outside the slave but inside its parcel on each side). Defaults to 0.
`-pady` *distance*	*distance* specifies external padding for the slave (extra vertical space outside the slave but inside its parcel on each side). Defaults to 0.
`-side` *side*	*side* specifies which side of the master the slave should be packed against. Must be `top`, `bottom`, `left`, or `right`. Defaults to `top`.

Table 17.2. A summary of the configuration options supported by the packer.

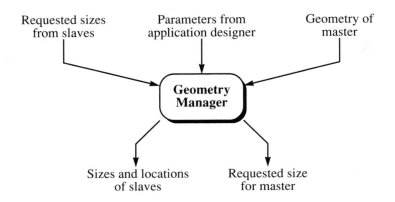

Figure 17.1. A geometry manager receives three kinds of inputs: a requested size for each slave (which usually reflects the information to be displayed in the slave), commands from the application designer (such as "arrange these three windows in a row"), and the actual geometry of the master window. The geometry manager then assigns a size and location to each slave. It may also set the requested size for the master window, which can be used by a higher level geometry manager to manage the master.

slaves, or it might refuse to display a slave altogether if it doesn't fit within the area of its master.

After it has received all of the preceding information, the geometry manager executes a layout algorithm to determine the width, height, and position of each of its slaves. If the geometry manager assigns a slave a size different from what it requested, the widget must make do in the best way it can. Geometry managers usually try to give widgets the space they requested, but they may produce more attractive layouts by giving widgets extra space in some situations. If there isn't enough space in a master for all of its slaves, some of the slaves may get less space than they requested. In extreme cases the geometry manager may choose not to display some slaves at all.

The controlling information for geometry management may change while an application runs. For example, a button might be reconfigured with a different font or bitmap, in which case it will change its requested dimensions. In addition, the geometry manager might be told to use a different approach (for example, arrange a collection of windows from top to bottom instead of left to right), some of the slave windows might be deleted, or the user might interactively resize the master window. When any of these things happens, the geometry manager recomputes the layout.

Some geometry managers will set the requested size for the master window. For example, the packer computes how much space is needed in the master to accommodate all of its slaves in the fashion requested by the application designer. It then sets the requested size for the master to these dimensions, overriding any request made by the master widget itself. This approach allows for hierarchical geometry management, where each master is itself the slave of another higher level master. Size requests pass up through the hierarchy from each slave to its master, resulting ultimately in a size request for a top-level window, which is passed to the window manager. Then actual geometry information passes down through the hierarchy, with the geometry manager at each level using the geometry of a master to compute the geometry of one or more slaves. As a result, the entire hierarchy sizes itself to meet the needs of the lowest level slaves (the master widgets "shrink-wrap" around their slaves).

Each widget can be managed by at most one geometry manager at a time, although it is possible to switch geometry managers during the life of a slave. A widget can act as master to any number of slaves, and it is even possible for different geometry managers to control different groups of slaves within the same master. A single geometry manager can simultaneously manage different groups of slaves associated with different masters.

Only internal widgets may be slaves for geometry management. The techniques described here do not apply to top-level widgets since they are managed by the window manager for the display. See Chapter 22 for information on how to control the geometry of top-level widgets.

17.2 **Packer basics**

The packer is the most commonly used geometry manager in Tk. It arranges the slaves for a master by positioning them one at a time in the master's window, working from the edges toward the center. With the packer you can generate rows, columns, and many other arrangements.

The packer maintains a list of slaves for a given master window, called the *packing list*. The packer arranges the slaves by processing the packing list in order, packing one slave in each step. At the time a particular slave is processed, part of the area of the master window has already been allocated to earlier slaves on the list, leaving a rectangular unallocated area for all the remaining slaves, as shown in Figure 17.2(a). The current slave is positioned in three steps: allocate a parcel, stretch the slave, and position it in the parcel.

In the first step a rectangular region called a *parcel* is allocated from the available space. This is done by "slicing" off a piece along one side of the available space. For example, in Figure 17.2(b) a parcel is sliced from the right side of the available space. One dimension of the parcel is determined by the size of the available space and the other dimension is controllable. The controllable dimension is normally taken from the slave's requested size in that dimension, but the packer allows you to request additional space if you wish. In Figure 17.2(b) the width is the controllable dimension; if the parcel had been sliced from the top or bottom, the parcel's height would have been controllable instead of its width.

In the second step the packer chooses the dimensions of the slave. By default the slave will get the size it requested, but you can specify instead that it should be stretched

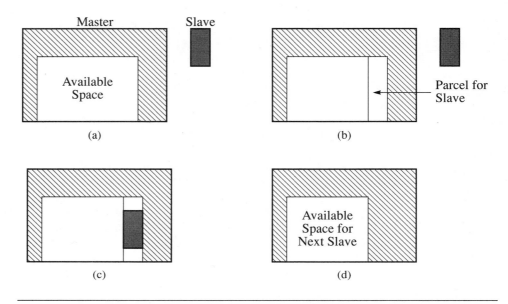

Figure 17.2. The steps taken to pack a single slave. Figure (a) shows the situation before packing a slave. Part of the master's area has already been allocated for previous slaves, and a rectangular region is left for the remaining slaves. The current slave is shown in its requested size. The packer allocates a parcel for the slave along one side of the available space, as shown in (b). The packer may stretch the slave to partially or completely fill the parcel, then it positions the slave over the parcel as in (c). This leaves a smaller rectangular region for the next slave to use, as shown in (d).

in one or both dimensions to fill the space of the parcel. If the slave's requested size is larger than the parcel, it is reduced to fit the size of the parcel.

The third step is to position the slave inside its parcel. If the slave is smaller than the parcel, you can specify an anchor position for the slave such as n, s, or center. In Figure 17.2(c) the slave has been positioned in the center of the parcel, which is the default.

Once the slave has been positioned, a smaller rectangular region is left for the next slave to use, as shown in Figure 17.2(d). If a slave doesn't use all of the space in its parcel, as in Figure 17.2, the leftover space will not be used for later slaves. Thus each step in the packing starts with a rectangular region of available space and ends up with a smaller rectangular region.

17.3 **The pack command and -side options**

The pack command is used to communicate with the packer. In its simplest form it takes one or more widget names as arguments, followed by one or more pairs of additional arguments that indicate how to manage the widgets. For example, consider the following script, which creates three buttons and arranges them in a row:

```
button .ok -text OK
button .cancel -text Cancel
button .help -text Help
pack .ok .cancel .help -side left
```

The pack command asks the packer to manage .ok, .cancel, and .help as slaves and to pack them in that order. The master for the slaves defaults to their parent, which is the main widget. The option -side left applies to all three of the widgets; it indicates that the parcel for each slave should be allocated on the left side of the available space. Because no other options are specified, the parcel for each slave is allocated just large enough for the slave. This causes the slaves to be arranged in a row from left to right across the master. Furthermore, the packer computes the minimum size needed by the master to accommodate all of its slaves and it sets the master's requested size to these dimensions. The window manager sets the main widget's size as requested, so the master ends up shrink-wrapped around the slaves as shown in Figure 17.3(a).

The packer recomputes the layout whenever any of the relevant information changes. For example, if you type the command

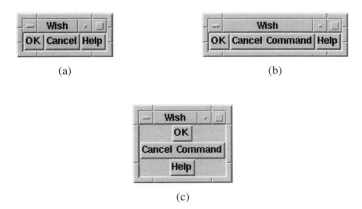

(a)   (b)

(c)

Figure 17.3. Simple packer examples. Figure (a) shows the layout produced by the command "pack .ok .cancel .help -side left". If the space needed by a slave changes, the layout changes to match, as in (b). If the information controlling the layout changes (e.g. the -side option is changed to top for each slave), the layout also changes to match, as in (c).

```
.cancel configure -text "Cancel Command"
```
to change the text in the middle button, then the button changes its requested size and the packer changes the layout to make more space for the button, as in Figure 17.3(b). If you then type the command
```
pack .ok .cancel .help -side top
```
the layout will change so that each slave is allocated at the top of the remaining space, producing the columnar arrangement shown in Figure 17.3(c). In this case the master's width is chosen to accommodate the largest of the slaves (.cancel). Each of the other slaves receives a parcel wider than it needs and the slave is centered in its parcel.

17.4 Padding

The packer provides four options for requesting extra space for a slave. The extra space is called *padding* and it comes in two forms: *external padding* and *internal padding*. External padding is requested with the -padx and -pady options; it causes the packer to allocate a parcel larger than requested by the slave and leave extra space around the outside of the slave. For example, the widgets in Figure 17.4(a) are packed with the options
```
-padx 2m -pady 1m
```
These options specify that there should be 2 millimeters of extra space on each side of each of the widgets and 1 millimeter of extra space above and below each widget. Internal padding is requested with the -ipadx and -ipady options; it also causes a parcel to be larger than the slave requested, but in this case the slave window is enlarged to incorporate the extra space as in Figure 17.4(b). External and internal padding can be used together as in Figure 17.4(c), and different slaves can have different amounts of padding.

17.5 Filling

If a parcel ends up larger than its slave requested, you can use the -fill option to stretch the slave so that it fills the parcel in one or both directions. For example, consider the column of widgets in Figure 17.3(c): each widget is given its requested size, which results in a somewhat ragged look because the buttons are all different sizes. The -fill option can be used to make all the buttons the same size:
```
pack .ok .cancel .help -side top -fill x
```
Figure 17.5 shows the effect produced by this command: each of the slaves is stretched horizontally to fill its parcel, and since the parcels are as wide as the master window all of the slaves end up with the same width.

Figure 17.6 shows another simple example of filling. The three windows are configured differently so a separate pack command is used for each one. The order of the pack commands determines the order of the windows in the packing list. The .label widget

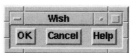

```
pack .ok .cancel .help -side left -padx 2m -pady 1m
```

(a)

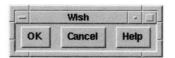

```
pack .ok .cancel .help -side left -ipadx 2m -ipady 1m
```

(b)

```
pack .ok .cancel .help -side left -padx 2m -pady 1m \
     -ipadx 2m -ipady 1m
```

(c)

Figure 17.4. Examples of padding. Each figure shows the results produced by a particular pack command, using the same widgets as in Figure 17.3(a). Figure (a) uses external padding, (b) uses internal padding, and (c) uses both external and internal padding.

Figure 17.5. The effect of filling. This example is the same as the one in Figure 17.3(c) except that the windows are packed with the additional option -fill x.

is packed first, and it occupies the top part of the master window. The -fill x option specifies that the window should be stretched horizontally so that it fills its parcel. The

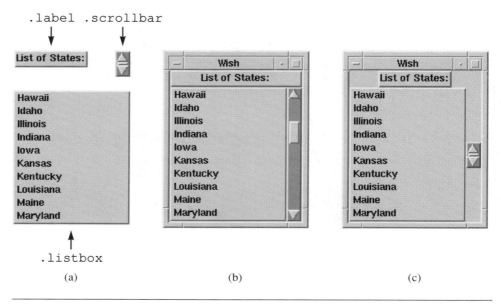

Figure 17.6. Another packer example. Figure (a) shows the requested sizes for three slaves. Figure (b) shows the result of packing the slaves with the script
```
pack .label -side top -fill x
pack .scrollbar -side right -fill y
pack .listbox
```
Figure (c) shows what would have happened without the -fill options.

scrollbar widget is packed next, in a similar fashion except that it is arranged against the right side of the window and stretched vertically. The widget .listbox is packed last. No options need to be specified for it: it will end up in the same place regardless of which side it is packed against.

17.6 Expansion

Sometimes a master window will have more space than needed by its slaves. This can occur, for example, if a user interactively stretches a window. When this happens the default behavior of the packer is to leave the extra space unused as in Figure 17.7(a). However, you can use the -expand option to tell the packer to give any extra space to a particular slave (for example, expand a text widget to fill all the extra space), or to divide the extra space uniformly among a collection of slaves (for example, distribute a collection of buttons uniformly across the available space). The -expand option makes it pos-

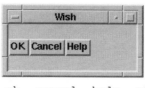

```
pack .ok .cancel .help -side left
```

(a)

```
pack .ok .cancel -side left
pack .help -side left -expand 1 \
    -fill x
```
(b)

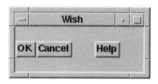

```
pack .ok .cancel -side left
pack .help -side left -expand 1
```
(c)

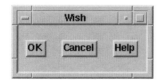

```
pack .ok .cancel .help \
    -side left -expand 1
```
(d)

```
pack .ok .cancel .help -side left \
    -expand 1 -fill both
```
(e)

Figure 17.7. The −expand option. In (a) the −expand option isn't used; in (b) and (c) it is used for a single window, and in (d) and (e) it is used for all of the windows so that extra space is shared. In each of these examples the size of the main widget was fixed with the command "wm geometry . 160x60" to simulate what would happen if the user had interactively resized it.

sible to produce layouts that are attractive regardless of how the user resizes the window, so that the user can choose the size he or she prefers.

Figure 17.7 shows how −expand works. If you specify −expand for a slave, as with .help in Figure 17.7(b), the slave's parcel expands to include any extra space in the master. In Figure 17.7(b) "−fill x" has also been specified for .help so the slave window is stretched to cover the entire width of the parcel. Figure 17.7(c) is similar to Figure 17.7(b) except that no filling is specified, so .help is simply centered in its parcel.

If you specify -expand for multiple slaves, their parcels share the extra space equally. Figure 17.7(d) shows what happens if all of the windows are packed with -expand but no filling, and Figure 17.7(e) shows what happens when the slaves are also filled in both dimensions.

Note: *The options* -expand *and* -fill *are often confused because of the similarity of their names. The* -expand *option determines whether a parcel absorbs extra space in the master and* -fill *determines whether a slave's window absorbs extra space in its parcel. The options are often used together so that a slave's window absorbs all the extra space in its master.*

17.7 Anchors

If a parcel has more space that its slave requested (for example, because you specified -expand for it) and if you choose not to stretch the slave with the -fill option, the packer will normally center the slave in its parcel. The -anchor option allows you to request a different position: its value specifies where the slave should be positioned in the parcel, using one of the forms listed in Section 16.11.2. For example, "-anchor nw" specifies that the slave should be positioned in the upper-left corner of its parcel. Figure 17.8(a) shows how -anchor can be used to left-justify a collection of buttons.

The -fill and -anchor options preserve external padding requested with -padx and -pady. For example, Figure 17.8(b) is the same as Figure 17.8(a) except that external padding has been requested. In this case the buttons aren't positioned at the left edges of their parcels, but instead they are inset by the -padx distance.

17.8 Packing order

The -before and -after options allow you to control a slave's position in the packing list for its master. If you don't specify one of these options, each new slave goes at the end of the packing list. If you specify -before or -after, its value must be the name of a window that is already packed and the new slave(s) will be positioned just before or after the given slave.

17.9 Hierarchical packing

The packer is often used in hierarchical arrangements where slave windows are also masters for other slaves. Figure 17.9 shows an example of hierarchical packing. The resulting layout contains a column of radiobuttons on the left and a column of checkbuttons on the right, with each group of buttons centered vertically in its column. To achieve this effect two extra frame widgets, .left and .right, are packed side by side in the main win-

pack .ok .cancel .help -side top -anchor w

(a)

pack .ok .cancel .help -side top -anchor w -padx 2m -pady 1m

(b)

Figure 17.8. Examples of the -anchor option. Figure (a) shows how -anchor can be used to left-justify a collection of buttons; compare to Figure 17.3(c), which is the same except for the absence of the -anchor option. Figure (b) shows how -anchor preserves external padding.

dow, then the buttons are packed inside them. The packer sets the requested sizes for .left and .right to provide enough space for the buttons, then uses this information to set the requested size for the main widget. The main widget's geometry will be set to the requested size by the window manager, then the packer will arrange .left and .right inside it, and finally it will arrange the buttons inside .left and .right.

Figure 17.9 also illustrates a situation where a slave's master is different from its parent (the -in option is used to specify a master). It would have been possible to create the button windows as children of .left and .right (for example, .left.pts8 instead of .pts8) but it is cleaner to create them as children of . and then pack them inside .left and .right. The windows .left and .right serve no purpose in the application except to help in geometry management; they have the same background color as the main widget, so they are not even visible on the screen. If the buttons were children of their geometry masters, changes to the geometry management (such as adding more levels in the packing hierarchy) might require the button windows to be renamed and would break any code that used the old names (such as entries in .Xdefaults files). It is better to give windows names that reflect their logical purpose in the application, build separate frame hierarchies where needed for geometry management, and then pack the functional windows into the frames.

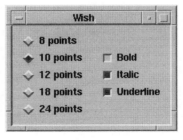

```
frame .left
frame .right
foreach size {8 10 12 18 24} {
    radiobutton .pts$size -text "$size points" -relief flat \
        -variable pts -value $size
}
checkbutton .bold -text Bold -relief flat -variable bold
checkbutton .italic -text Italic -relief flat -variable italic
checkbutton .underline -text Underline -relief flat \
        -variable underline
pack .left -side left -padx 3m -pady 3m
pack .right -side right -padx 3m -pady 3m
pack .pts8 .pts10 .pts12 .pts18 .pts24 -in .left -side \
        top -anchor w
pack .bold .italic .underline -in .right -side top -anchor w
```

Figure 17.9. An example of hierarchical packing. Two frame widgets, `.left` and `.right`, are used to achieve the column effect.

Note: *In the example in Figure 17.9, the frames `.left` and `.right` must be created before the buttons so that the buttons are stacked on top of the frames. The most recently created widget is highest in the stacking order; if `.left` is created after `.pts8` then it will be on top of `.pts8`, so `.pts8` will not be visible. Alternatively, the `raise` and `lower` commands can be used to adjust the stacking order (see Section 26.5).*

A slave's master must be either its parent or a descendant of its parent. The reason for this restriction has to do with X's clipping rules. Each window is clipped to the boundaries of its parent, so no portion of a child that lies outside of its parent will be displayed. Tk's restriction on master windows guarantees that a slave will be visible and unclipped if its master is visible and unclipped. Suppose that the restriction were not enforced, so that window `.x.y` could have `.a` as its master. Suppose also that `.a` and `.x` do not overlap at all. If you asked the packer to position `.x.y` in `.a`, the packer would set `.x.y`'s position as requested, but this would cause `.x.y` to be outside the area of `.x` so X would not display it even though `.a` is fully visible. This behavior would be confusing to application designers so Tk restricts mastership to keep the behavior from occurring. The restriction applies to all of Tk's geometry managers.

17.10 Other options to the pack command

So far the `pack` command has been discussed in its most common form, where the first arguments are the names of slave windows and the last arguments specify configuration options. Table 17.1 shows several other forms for the `pack` command, where the first argument selects one of several operations. The "`pack configure`" command has the same effect as the short form that's been used up until now; the remaining arguments specify windows and configuration options. If "`pack configure`" (or the short form with no command option) is applied to a window that is already managed by the packer, the slave's configuration is modified; configuration options not specified in the `pack` command retain their old values.

The command "`pack slaves`" returns a list of all of the slaves for a given master window. The order of the slaves reflects their order in the packing list:

```
     pack slaves .left
⇒  .pts8 .pts10 .pts12 .pts18 .pts24
```

The command "`pack info`" returns all of the configuration options for a given slave:

```
     pack info .pts8
⇒  -in .left -anchor w -expand 0 -fill none -ipadx 0
     -ipady 0 -padx 0 -pady 0 -side top
```

The return value is a list consisting of names and values for configuration options in exactly the form you would specify them to `pack configure`. This command can be used to save the state of a slave so that it can be restored later.

The command "`pack forget`" causes the packer to stop managing one or more slaves and forget all of its configuration state for them. It also unmaps the windows so that they no longer appear on the screen. This command can be used to transfer control of a window from one geometry manager to another, or simply to remove a window from the screen for a while. If a forgotten window is itself a master for other slaves, the information about those slaves is retained but the slaves won't be displayed on the screen until the master window becomes managed again.

The command "`pack propagate`" allows you to control whether or not the packer sets the requested size for a master window. Normally the packer sets the requested size for each master window to just accommodate the needs of its slaves, and it updates the requested size as the needs of the slaves change. This feature is called *geometry propagation* and it overrides any size that the master might have requested for itself. You can disable propagation with the command

```
     pack propagate master 0
```

where *master* is the name of the master window. This instructs Tk not to set the requested size for *master*, so that the size requested by the master widget itself will be used.

17.11 Other geometry managers in Tk

Although the packer is the most commonly used geometry manager in Tk, there are two other geometry managers that you may also find useful. The first of these is the *placer*. The placer is a simple fixed-placement geometry manger that allows you to position each slave at a fixed absolute or relative position in its master. For example, an absolute position might be "one centimeter down from the top edge of the master and two centimeters over from the left edge" and a relative position might be "halfway across the master and two-thirds of the way down". You can also specify an absolute or relative size for the slave ("one centimeter across" or "half as wide as the master"), or leave the slave with the size it requested internally. See the reference documentation for complete details. The placer considers each slave independently so it's hard to achieve arrangements like rows or columns with the placer, and layouts made with the placer may not be as flexible as those with the packer (for example, if you stretch a window the layout may not stretch to match). For these reasons the placer is used only for a few special purposes.

The third geometry manager in Tk is part of the canvas widget: it allows you to mix embedded widgets with other graphical element such as lines and text. Canvas widgets are described in more detail in Chapter 19.

Chapter 18
Bindings

You have already seen that Tcl scripts can be associated with widgets such as buttons or menus so that the scripts are invoked when certain events occur, such as clicking a mouse button over the widget. These mechanisms are provided as specific features of specific widget classes. Tk also provides a more general mechanism called *bindings*, which allows you to create handlers for any X event in any window. A binding "binds" a Tcl script to an X event or sequence of X events in one or more windows so that the script is evaluated whenever the given event sequence occurs in any of the windows. You can use bindings to extend the basic functions of a widget, for example, by defining shortcut keys for common actions. You can also override or modify the default behaviors of widgets, since they are implemented with bindings. Bindings are manipulated with the `bind` command. Table 18.1 summarizes its syntax.

18.1 X events

An *event* is a record generated by X to notify an application of a potentially interesting occurrence. Each event has a *type* that indicates the general sort of thing that occurred. The event types that are most commonly used in bindings are those for user actions such as key presses or changes in the pointer position:

`Key` or `KeyPress`	A key was pressed.
`KeyRelease`	A key was released.
`Button` or `ButtonPress`	A mouse button was pressed.
`ButtonRelease`	A mouse button was released.

```
bind windowSpec sequence script
```
     Arranges for *script* to be evaluated each time the event sequence given
     by *sequence* occurs in the window(s) given by *windowSpec*. If a binding
     already exists for *windowSpec* and *sequence*, then it is replaced. If
     script is an empty string, the binding for *windowSpec* and *sequence* is
     removed, if there is one.

```
bind windowSpec sequence +script
```
     If there is already a binding for *windowSpec* and *sequence*, appends
     script to the script for the current binding; otherwise creates a new
     binding.

```
bind windowSpec sequence
```
     If there is a binding for *windowSpec* and *sequence*, returns its script.
     Otherwise returns an empty string.

```
bind windowSpec
```
     Returns a list of the sequences for which *windowSpec* has bindings.

```
tkerror message
```
     Invoked by Tk when it encounters a Tcl error in an event handler such as a
     binding. *message* is the error message returned by Tcl.

Table 18.1. A summary of the bind and tkerror commands.

Enter	The pointer moved into a window (it is now over a visible portion of the window).
Leave	The pointer moved out of a window.
Motion	The pointer moved from one point to another within a single window.

There are many other event types besides those listed, which are generated when windows
change size, when windows are destroyed, when windows need to be redisplayed, and so
on. See the reference documentation for the bind command for details.

In addition to its type each event also contains several other fields. One of them specifies a window and two others give the x and y coordinates of the pointer within the window. For Enter and Leave events, the window is the one just entered or left. For
ButtonPress, ButtonRelease, and Motion events, the window is the one currently under the pointer. For KeyPress and KeyRelease events, the window is the one
that has the application's *input focus* (see Chapter 21 for details on the input focus).

Button and key events also contain a field called the *detail*, which indicates the particular button or key that was pressed. For ButtonPress and ButtonRelease events,
the detail is a button number, where 1 usually refers to the leftmost button on the mouse.
For KeyPress and KeyRelease events the detail is a *keysym*, which is a textual name
describing a particular key on the keyboard. The keysym for an alphanumeric ASCII character such as a or A or 2 is just the character itself. Some other examples of keysyms are
Return for the carriage-return key, BackSpace for the backspace key, Delete for the

delete key, and `Help` for the help key. The keysym for a function key such as F1 is normally the same as the name that appears on the key. Section 18.5 contains a script that you can use to find out the keysyms for the keys on your keyboard.

Certain keys are defined as special *modifier keys*; these include the Shift keys, the Control key, plus other keys such as Meta and Alt. The exact set of modifier keys is user-programmable and can be changed with the `xmodmap` program. Up to five modifiers may be defined at any one time in addition to Shift and Control. The events just listed contain a *state* field that identifies which of the modifier keys were pressed at the time of the event, plus which mouse buttons were pressed. The state field is useful, for example, to trigger a script when the pointer moves with button 1 down, or when Control-a is typed on the keyboard.

Events also contain other fields besides the ones described; the exact set of fields varies from event to event. Refer to the Scheifler and Gettys book for details.

18.2   An overview of the bind command

The `bind` command is used to create, modify, query, and remove bindings. This section illustrates the basic features of `bind`, and later sections go over the features in more detail.

Bindings are created with commands like this one:

```
bind .entry <Control-d> {.entry delete insert}
```

The first argument to the command specifies the path name of the window to which the binding applies. It can also be a widget class name such as `Entry`, in which case the binding applies to all widgets of that class (such bindings are called *class bindings*), or it can be `all`, in which case the binding applies to all widgets. The second argument specifies a sequence of one or more X events. The example specifies a single event, which is a keypress of the d character while the `Control` modifier key is down. The third argument may be any Tcl script. The script in the example invokes `.entry`'s widget command to delete the character just after the insertion cursor. The script will be invoked if Control-d is typed when the application's input focus is in `.entry`. The binding can trigger any number of times. It remains in effect until `.entry` is deleted or the binding is explicitly removed by invoking `bind` with an empty script:

```
bind .entry <Control-d> {}
```

The `bind` command can also be used to retrieve information about bindings. If `bind` is invoked with an event sequence but no script, it returns the script for the given event sequence:

```
bind .entry <Control-d>
```
⇒   *.entry delete insert*

If `bind` is invoked with a single argument, it returns a list of all the bound event sequences for that window or class:

```
          bind .entry
⇒    <Control-Key-d>
          bind Button
⇒    <ButtonRelease-1> <Button-1> <Any-Leave> <Any-Enter>
```

The first example returned the bound sequences for .entry, and the second example
returned information about all of the class bindings for button widgets. The class bindings
were created by Tk's initialization script (file tk.tcl in the Tk library directory) to
establish the default behavior for button widgets.

18.3 Event patterns

Event sequences are constructed out of basic units called *event patterns*, which Tk
matches against the stream of X events received by the application. An event sequence can
contain any number of patterns, but most sequences have only a single pattern.

   The most general form for a pattern consists of one or more fields between angle
brackets, with the following syntax:

```
          <modifier-modifier...-modifier-type-detail>
```

White space may be used instead of dashes to separate the various fields, and most of the
fields are optional. The *type* field identifies the particular X event type, such as
KeyPress or Enter. For example, the following script causes a button widget .b to
become active whenever the mouse passes over it and to return to its normal state when
the button passes out of the widget again.

```
          bind .b <Enter> {.b config -state active}
          bind .b <Leave> {.b config -state normal}
```

   For key and button events the event type may be followed by a *detail* field that specifies a particular button or keysym. If no detail field is provided, as in <KeyPress>, the
pattern matches any event of the given type. If a detail field is provided, as in
<KeyPress-Escape> or <ButtonPress-2>, the pattern matches only events for
the specific key or button. If a detail is specified, you can omit the event type: <Escape>
is equivalent to <KeyPress-Escape>.

Note: *The pattern <1> is equivalent to <Button-1>, not <KeyPress-1>.*

   The event type may be preceded by any number of modifiers, each of which must be
one of the values given in Table 18.2. If modifiers are specified, the pattern matches only
events that occur when the specified modifiers are present. For example, the pattern
<Meta-Control-d> requires that both the Meta and Control keys be held down when
d is typed, and <B1-Motion> requires that the pointer move when mouse button 1 is
down. If no modifiers are specified, then none must be present: <KeyPress-a> does not
match an event if the Control key is down.

```
Control       Button4, B4       Mod2, M2, Alt
Shift         Button5, B5       Mod3, M3
Lock          Any               Mod4, M4
Button1, B1   Double            Mod5, M5
Button2, B2   Triple
Button3, B3   Mod1, M1, Meta, M
```

Table 18.2. Modifier names for event patterns. Multiple names are available for some modifiers; for example, Mod1, M1, Meta, and M are all synonyms for the same modifier.

Some of the names in Table 18.2 aren't really modifiers; they are used to achieve a few special effects. The Any "modifier" means that the state of unspecified modifiers should be ignored. For example, <Any-a> matches a press of the a key even if button 1 is down or the Meta key is pressed. <Any-B1-Motion> matches any mouse motion event as long as button 1 is pressed; other modifiers are ignored.

The "modifiers" Double and Triple are used for specifying double and triple mouse clicks. They match a sequence of two or three events, each of which matches the remainder of the pattern. For example, <Double-1> matches a double-click of mouse button 1 with no modifiers down, and <Any-Triple-2> matches any triple click of button 2 regardless of modifiers.

A special shortcut form is available for patterns that specify key presses of printing ASCII characters such as a or @. You can specify a pattern for these events using just the single character. For example,

```
bind .entry a {.entry insert insert a}
```

arranges for the character a to be inserted into .entry at the point of the insertion cursor if it is typed when .entry has the keyboard focus. This command is identical to the command

```
bind .entry <KeyPress-a> {.entry insert insert a}
```

18.4 Sequences of events

An event sequence consists of one or more event patterns optionally separated by white space. For example, the sequence <Escape>a contains two patterns. It triggers when the Escape key is pressed and then the a key is pressed.

A sequence need not necessarily match consecutive events. For example, the sequence <Escape>a matches an event sequence consisting of a KeyPress on Escape, a KeyRelease of Escape, and then a press of a; the release of Escape is ignored in determining the match. Tk generally ignores conflicting events in the input event stream unless they have the same type as the desired event. Thus if some other key is pressed between the Escape and the a, then the sequence will not match. Refer to the reference documentation for complete information on when conflicting events are and are not ignored.

18.5 Substitutions in scripts

The script that handles an event often needs to use some of the fields in the event, such as the pointer coordinates or the particular keysym that was pressed. Tk provides this access by substituting fields from the event wherever there are % characters in the script, in a fashion much like the C procedure printf. Before evaluating the script for a binding, Tk generates a new script from the original one by replacing each % and the character following it with information about the X event. The character following the % selects a specific substitution to make. Here are a few of the most commonly used substitutions:

%x	Substitute the x-coordinate from the event.
%y	Substitute the y-coordinate from the event.
%W	Substitute the path name of the event window.
%K	Substitute the keysym from the event (KeyPress and KeyRelease events only).
%A	Substitute the 8-bit ISO character value that corresponds to a KeyPress or KeyRelease event, or an empty string if the event is for a key like Shift that doesn't have an ISO equivalent.
%%	Substitute the character %.

There are about 30 substitutions defined in all and they provide access to all the fields of events; see the reference documentation for details.

As an example of using substitutions, the following script implements a simple mouse tracker:

```
bind all <Enter> {puts "Entering %W at (%x,%y)"}
bind all <Leave> {puts "Leaving %W"}
bind all <Motion> {puts "Pointer at (%x,%y)"}
```

If you type these commands to wish, messages will be printed as you move the pointer over the windows of the application. Or, you can you use the following script to determine the keysyms for the keys on your keyboard:

```
bind . <Any-KeyPress> {puts "The keysym is %K"}
focus .
```

If you type these two commands to wish, the name of the keysym will be printed for any key that you type. Try typing some normal keys like a, A, and 1, plus special keys like F1, Return, or Shift.

Note: *When Tk makes % substitutions it treats the script as an ordinary string without any special properties. The normal quoting rules for Tcl commands are not considered, so %*

sequences will be substituted even if embedded in braces or preceded by backslashes. The only way to prevent a % substitution is to double the % character.

18.6 Conflict resolution

It is possible for several bindings to match a single X event. For example, suppose there are bindings for `<Button-1>` and `<Double-Button-1>` and button 1 is clicked three times. The first button press event matches only the `<Button-1>` binding but the second and third presses match both bindings. The way conflicts are handled depends on how the bindings were declared and the version of Tk that you are using.

If the same *windowSpec* was used for all the matching bindings as in

```
bind .b <Button-1> ...
bind .b <Double-Button-1> ...
```

then exactly one binding will trigger and it will be the most specific of all the matching bindings. `<Double-Button-1>` is more specific than `<Button-1>`, so its script is executed on the second and third presses. Similarly, `<Escape>a` is more specific than `<a>`, `<Control-d>` is more specific than `<Any-d>` or `<d>`, and `<d>` is more specific than `<KeyPress>`.

Now suppose that there are matching bindings with different *windowSpec*s, as in the following example:

```
bind all <Return> ...
bind .b <Any-KeyPress> ...
```

If the return key is pressed, both of these bindings will match. The behavior in this case is different for different versions of Tk. In Tk versions earlier than 4.0, only one of the bindings will trigger: a window-specific binding receives highest priority, followed by a class binding and lastly an `all` binding. In this case the second binding will trigger even though the first binding is more specific. If multiple window-specific bindings had matched, the most specific of them would have triggered.

In Tk versions 4.0 and later the different *windowSpec*s are handled independently so that one binding can trigger for each kind of *windowSpec*. If any window-specific bindings match the event, the most specific of these will trigger; then the most specific class binding will trigger, followed last of all by the most specific `all` binding. In the previous example both bindings will trigger when return is typed; the widget-specific binding will trigger first, followed by the `all` binding.

The handling of different *windowSpec*s in pre-4.0 versions of Tk causes problems if you try to extend the class bindings for a single widget. For example, suppose that when the pointer enters a button widget you wish to display a status message indicating what will happen when the mouse button is pressed over the widget. You might attempt to use the following script to achieve this effect:

```
bind .exit <Enter> {.status config -text "Exit application"}
```

Unfortunately this binding will interfere with the class bindings for buttons. The default behavior for buttons includes the following binding:

```
bind Button <Any-Enter> {tk_butEnter %W}
```

The tk_butEnter procedure activates the button and performs various other bookkeeping functions. Unfortunately, once the widget-specific binding has been created for Enter the class binding will no longer be invoked on Enter events, so these functions will not be performed. The message will be displayed in .status, but the button will not activate or invoke properly. What we need to do is trigger both bindings: to do this in pre-4.0 versions of Tk, you must look up the class binding (either by reading the Tk initialization script or by using the bind command to query the class bindings), then include the text of the class binding into your widget-specific binding:

```
bind .exit <Enter> {
    tk_butEnter %W
    .status config -text "Exit application"
}
```

This makes it more tedious to create such bindings, and you will have to change your widget-specific bindings if the class bindings change, but it's the only way to extend the default behaviors for widgets in Tk versions older than 4.0.

In Tk 4.0 and later versions, the first bind command above will work just fine: both the widget-specific binding and the class binding will be invoked. In the rare cases where you really want to override a class binding, you can invoke the break command inside the widget-specific binding: this will abort the processing of the event without considering class bindings or all bindings. Tk 4.0 also allows you to change the order in which the various bindings are triggered (for example, trigger the all binding first) and define additional classes of bindings using a tagging mechanism. See the reference documentation for details.

18.7 When are events processed?

Tk only processes events at a few well-defined times. After a Tk application completes its initialization it enters an *event loop* to wait for X events and other events such as timer and file events. When an event occurs the event loop executes C or Tcl code to respond to that event. Once the response has completed, control returns to the event loop to wait for the next interesting event. Almost all events are processed from the top-level event loop. New events will not be considered while responding to the current event, so there is no danger of one binding triggering in the middle of the script for another binding. This approach applies to all event handlers, including those for bindings, those for the script options associated with widgets, and others yet to be discussed, such as window manager protocol handlers.

A few special commands such as `tkwait` and `update` reinvoke the event loop recursively, so bindings may trigger during the execution of these commands. You should invoke these commands only at times when it is safe for bindings to trigger. Commands that invoke the event loop are specially noted in their reference documentation; all other commands complete immediately without reentering the event loop.

Event handlers are always invoked at global level (as if the command "`uplevel #0`" were used), even if the event loop was invoked from a `tkwait` or `update` command inside a procedure. This means that you should use only global variables in binding scripts. The context in which a handler is evaluated is not the same as the context in which the handler was defined. For example, suppose that you invoke `bind` from within a procedure. When the script in the binding eventually triggers, it will not have access to the local variables of the procedure; in most cases the procedure will have returned before the binding is invoked, so the local variables don't even exist anymore.

18.8   Background errors: tkerror

It is possible for a Tcl error to occur while executing the script for a binding. These errors are called *background errors*; when one occurs, the default action is for Tk to display a dialog box containing the error message. However, this behavior is not hard-wired into Tk. It is implemented by a procedure named `tkerror`, and an application can redefine `tkerror` to handle background errors in a different way. When a background error occurs Tk invokes `tkerror` with a single argument consisting of the error message. The `tkerror` procedure can then report the error in a way that makes sense for that application. If `tkerror` returns normally, Tk will assume that `tkerror` has dealt with the error and Tk won't do anything itself. If `tkerror` returns an error, Tk will print the original error message on standard output.

The `tkerror` procedure is invoked not just for errors in bindings, but for all other errors that are returned to Tk at times when it has no one else to return the errors to. For example, menus and buttons call `tkerror` if an error is returned by the script for a menu entry or button; scrollbars call `tkerror` if a Tcl error occurs while communicating with the associated widget; and the window-manager interface calls `tkerror` if an error is returned by the script associated with a window manager protocol.

18.9   Other uses of bindings

The binding mechanism described in this chapter applies to widgets. However, similar mechanisms are available internally within some widgets. For example, canvas widgets allow bindings to be associated with graphical items such as rectangles or polygons, and text widgets allow bindings to be associated with ranges of characters. These bindings are created using the same syntax for event sequences and %-substitutions, but they are created with the widget command for the widget and refer to the widget's internal objects instead of to windows. See Chapter 19 for details.

Chapter 19
Canvas and Text Widgets

This chapter describes Tk's canvas and text widgets. Canvases allow you to display and manipulate a variety of graphical objects such as rectangles, lines, bitmaps, and text strings. Texts are used to display and edit large multiline pieces of text such as files. Both widgets are unusual in that they allow you to tag objects and manipulate all the objects with a given tag. For example, you can move or recolor all of the items with a given tag. You can also create event bindings for tags so that a Tcl script is invoked whenever the pointer passes over a tagged rectangle in a canvas, whenever button 3 is pressed over a word in a text widget, and so on. The tagging and binding mechanisms make it easy to "activate" text and graphics so that they respond to the mouse. This chapter provides an introduction to canvases and texts and shows some examples of how to use them. It doesn't cover every detail, however; for that you should refer to the reference documentation.

19.1 Canvas basics: items and types

A canvas is a widget that displays a drawing surface on which you can place *items* of various *types*. Tk currently supports the following types:

Rectangles, drawn as an outline or a filled area or both; you can specify the outline color, outline width, fill color, and fill stipple pattern.

Circles and ellipses, with the same attributes as rectangles.

Lines, consisting of one or more connected segments, a width, a color, a stipple pattern, and several other attributes such as whether to miter or round the corners between segments and whether or not to draw arrowheads at the ends of the line.

Bézier curves: these are just lines with an additional attribute specifying that Bézier cubic splines should be drawn instead of straight segments.

Polygons, consisting of three or more points, a fill color, and a stipple pattern. You can also specify that the outline of the polygon should be a Bézier curve instead of a collection of straight segments.

Arcs, drawn in any of several styles such as a pie-wedge or a section of a circle. You can specify attributes such as the arc's angular range, outline width, outline color, fill color, and fill stipple.

Text, consisting of one more lines drawn in a single font. You can select a font, color, stipple pattern, justification mode, and line length.

Bitmaps, consisting of a bitmap name, background color, and foreground color.

Widgets: you can embed widgets of any kind as items in a canvas, in which case the canvas acts as a geometry manager for the widgets.

The `create` action for canvas widget commands creates new items. For example, here is a script that creates a canvas `.c` and then creates a new rectangle item in it:

```
canvas .c
pack .c
.c create rectangle 1c 2c 4c 4c -width 2m \
        -outline blue -fill yellow
```

All item types are created in the same way: the first argument after the `create` action gives the type of the item, the next arguments consist of pairs of coordinates, and the coordinates are followed by pairs of arguments specifying configuration options. For rectangles there must be exactly four coordinates giving the locations of the upper-left and lower-right corners of the rectangle; other item types requre different numbers of coordinates with different meanings. The configuration options are specified in the same free-form style as for widgets and they may be defaulted. In this example the outline width, outline color, and fill color are specified but no fill stipple is specified (it defaults to a solid fill).

Note: *Canvas widgets use the same coordinate system that X does: x increases as you move right and y increases as you move down.*

Here is a script that uses line and text items to create a simple ruler:

Figure 19.1. The canvas generated by the `ruler` script.

```
# ruler: draw a ruler on a canvas
canvas .c -width 12c -height 1.5c
pack .c
.c create line 1c 0.5c 1c 1c 11c 1c 11c 0.5c
for {set i 0} {$i < 10} {incr i} {
    set x [expr $i+1]
    .c create line ${x}c 1c ${x}c 0.6c
    .c create line $x.25c 1c $x.25c 0.8c
    .c create line $x.5c 1c $x.5c 0.7c
    .c create line $x.75c 1c $x.75c 0.8c
    .c create text $x.15c .75c -text $i -anchor sw
}
```

Figure 19.1 shows the canvas created by this script. Coordinates are specified using the screen distance notation described in Section 16.1.2; for example, 0.5c means one-half centimeter. For each centimeter of length, four tickmarks are drawn with varying heights, along with a text item that displays the number of centimeters. No options are specified for the line items, since the default values are fine. The option -anchor sw for the text items causes their lower-left corners to be positioned at the specified coordinates.

19.2 Manipulating items with identifiers and tags

Each canvas item has a unique integer identifier. The identifier for an item is returned by the widget command that creates it, and it can be used in other widget commands to refer to the item. For example, you might invoke the command

```
set circle [.c create oval 1c 1c 2c 2c -fill black \
        -outline {}]
```
⇒ *12*

to create a solid black circle and save its identifier (12) in variable `circle`. Later on you could delete the item with the command

```
.c delete $circle
```

The widget command for canvases provides several actions to manipulate items:

- You can move and scale items (but not rotate them yet, alas).

- You can query and change the coordinates and configuration options for items.
- You can find the item nearest to a given point, or all the items in a given rectangular region, or all the items with a given tag.
- For text items you can insert and delete text, display an insertion cursor, set the focus, and select a range of characters.

Canvases also provide a second way of referring to items, called *tags*. A tag is merely a textual string associated with an item. A single item may have any number of tags and a single tag may be applied to any number of items. You can use the −tags option to tag an item when you create it, as in the following command:

```
.c create oval 1c 1c 2c 2c -fill black -outline {} \
        -tags circle
```

You can also add new tags to an item or remove existing tags at any time. Once an item has been tagged you can use any of its tags to refer to it:

```
.c delete circle
```

In this example all of the items with the circle tag will be deleted.

Tags serve three purposes in canvases. First, they allow you to use human-readable names for items so that you don't have to save item identifiers in variables. Second, they provide a grouping mechanism so that you can manipulate related items together. For example, consider the following commands:

```
.c itemconfigure circle -fill red
.c move circle 0 1c
```

The first command changes the fill color to red for all items with the circle tag, and the second command moves all the circle items down one centimeter. In general you can use a tag name anywhere that you can use an item identifier. The third use for tags is for composing behaviors. As you will see later, bindings can be associated with tags, you can apply multiple tags to an item to combine several behaviors, and you can add and remove tags to change an item's behavior dynamically.

19.3 Bindings

When you create a canvas widget you can create bindings in the normal way using the bind command; these bindings apply to the widget as a whole. In addition you can create bindings for individual items within a canvas using the bind widget command. This command has the following form:

```
.c bind itemOrTag sequence script
```

The *itemOrTag* argument gives either the identifier of a single item, in which case the binding applies to that one item, or a tag name, in which case it applies to all items with the tag. *Sequence* and *script* specify an event sequence and script just as for the bind command. The event sequence may use only Enter and Leave events (which trigger when the pointer moves into or out of an item), mouse motion events, button presses and releases, and key presses and releases.

As an example of bindings, the following script allows you to create ball-and-stick graphs interactively on a canvas:

```
# graph: simple interactive graph editor

canvas .c
pack .c

proc mkNode {x y} {                 ;# Create new node at (x,y)
    global nodeX nodeY edgeFirst edgeSecond
    set new [.c create oval [expr $x-10] [expr $y-10] \
            [expr $x+10] [expr $y+10] -outline black \
            -fill white -tags node]
    set nodeX($new) $x
    set nodeY($new) $y
    set edgeFirst($new) {}
    set edgeSecond($new) {}
}

proc mkEdge {first second} {     ;# Create edge between nodes
    global nodeX nodeY edgeFirst edgeSecond
    set edge [.c create line $nodeX($first) $nodeY($first) \
            $nodeX($second) $nodeY($second)]
    .c lower $edge
    lappend edgeFirst($first) $edge
    lappend edgeSecond($second) $edge
}

bind .c <Button-1> {mkNode %x %y}
.c bind node <Any-Enter> {
    .c itemconfigure current -fill black
}
.c bind node <Any-Leave> {
    .c itemconfigure current -fill white
}
bind .c 1 {set firstNode [.c find withtag current]}
bind .c 2 {
    set curNode [.c find withtag current]
    if {($firstNode != "") && ($curNode != "")} {
        mkEdge $firstNode $curNode
    }
}
focus .c
```

If you source this script into wish, you can create nodes by clicking on the canvas with button 1. You can create edges by moving the pointer over a node, typing 1, then moving the pointer over a different node and typing 2. See Figure 19.2 for an example of a graph created with this script.

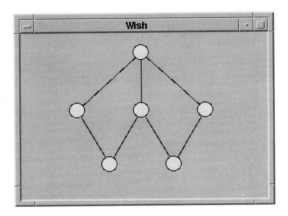

Figure 19.2. A graph created interactively using the `graph` script.

The script consists of two procedures for creating nodes and edges, plus five bindings. The script uses six global variables to hold information about the graph:

- `nodeX` and `nodeY` are associative arrays where the index is the item identifier for a node and the value is the x- or y-coordinate of the node's center. This information could be extracted from the canvas when needed but it's simpler in this case to keep it in a Tcl array.
- `edgeFirst` and `edgeSecond` are associative arrays where the index is the identifier for a node and the value is a list of item identifiers for edges connecting to the node. `edgeFirst` holds the identifiers of all edges for which a node is the starting point, and `edgeSecond` identifies the edges for which a node is the ending point. This information will be used below to drag nodes interactively.
- `firstNode` holds the identifier of the node that was under the pointer when 1 was typed last, or an empty string if 1 was typed when the pointer wasn't over a node.
- `curNode` holds the identifier of the node under the pointer or an empty string if the pointer isn't over a node.

The `mkNode` and `mkEdge` procedures just create new items in the canvas and record information about them in the global variables. The `lower` widget command in `mkEdge` causes edges to be placed at the bottom of the display list for the canvas so that the nodes appear on top of them.

The first binding is set for the entire canvas using the `bind` command; it causes a new node to be created at the position of the pointer whenever button 1 is pressed. The `Enter` and `Leave` bindings apply to all the nodes in the canvas; they cause nodes to change color when the mouse passes over them. The last two bindings are used to create edges; they trigger whenever 1 or 2 is typed in the canvas. Both of these bindings make use of the special tag current, which is managed by Tk. When the mouse moves over an item, Tk adds current to the item's tags, and when the mouse moves out of an item Tk removes the current tag. The binding for 1 invokes the command

```
.c find withtag current
```

which returns a list of identifiers for the items that have the tag current (in this case the result will be either a list with one element or an empty list), and saves the result in firstNode. The binding for 2 retrieves the current item and also creates a new edge.

The script below extends graph to allow nodes to be dragged interactively with mouse button 2:

```
proc moveNode {node xDist yDist} {
    global nodeX nodeY edgeFirst edgeSecond
    .c move $node $xDist $yDist
    incr nodeX($node) $xDist
    incr nodeY($node) $yDist
    foreach edge $edgeFirst($node) {
        .c coords $edge $nodeX($node) $nodeY($node) \
                [lindex [.c coords $edge] 2] \
                [lindex [.c coords $edge] 3]
    }
    foreach edge $edgeSecond($node) {
        .c coords $edge [lindex [.c coords $edge] 0] \
                [lindex [.c coords $edge] 1] \
                $nodeX($node) $nodeY($node)
    }
}

.c bind node <Button-2> {
    set curX %x
    set curY %y
}
.c bind node <B2-Motion> {
    moveNode [.c find withtag current] [expr %x-$curX] \
            [expr %y-$curY]
    set curX %x
    set curY %y
}
```

The procedure moveNode does all the work of moving a node: it uses the move action to move the node item, then it updates all of the edges for which this node is an endpoint. For each edge moveNode uses the coords action to read out the edge's current coordinates and replace either the first two or last two coordinates to reflect the node's new location.

The two new bindings apply to all items with the tag node. When button 2 is pressed the pointer coordinates are stored in variables curX and curY. When the mouse is dragged with button 2 down, the current item is moved by the amount the mouse has moved and new pointer coordinates are recorded.

19.4 Other canvas features

Canvases provide several other features besides those already described. Here is a summary of some of the most useful ones:

Scrolling: canvases support vertical and horizontal scrolling in the standard fashion for Tk widgets. If a canvas is scrolled, the coordinates in the canvas window are not the same as the coordinates on the logical surface of the canvas; to handle this situation canvases provide additional widget command actions for translating from screen to canvas coordinates.

Gridding: canvases provide support for gridded coordinate systems so that you can round off pointer positions to the nearest grid point.

PostScript: canvases can generate Encapsulated PostScript descriptions of their contents, for printing and insertion into other documents.

19.5 Text widgets

A text widget displays one or more lines of text and allows you to edit the text. For example, the following script creates a text widget with an associated scrollbar and reads a file into the text widget:

```
# text: read a file into a text widget

text .text -relief raised -bd 2 \
        -yscrollcommand ".scroll set"
scrollbar .scroll -command ".text yview"
pack .scroll -side right -fill y
pack .text -side left

proc loadFile file {
    .text delete 1.0 end
    set f [open $file]
    while {![eof $f]} {
        .text insert end [read $f 1000]
    }
    close $f
}
loadFile README
```

The first group of lines in the script creates a text widget and a scrollbar, packs them side by side in the main widget, and sets up connections between the text and the scrollbar. The

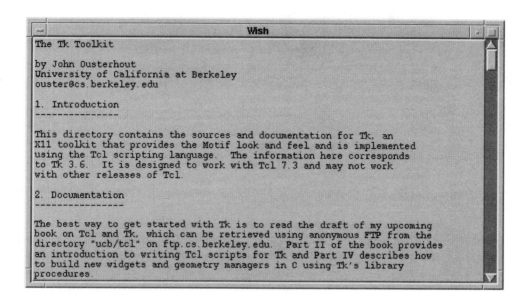

Figure 19.3. A text widget and associated scrollbar.

next part of the script defines and calls the procedure `loadFile`, which opens a file and reads it in 1000 bytes at a time, inserting each block of file data at the end of the text widget. The command `.text delete` in `loadFile`, which deletes all of the text in the widget, isn't necessary in this example since the new widget is already empty. However, it allows `loadFile` to be invoked again later to replace the contents of the widget with a new file.

After the script has completed the screen should look like Figure 19.3 (assuming that you ran the script in Tk's source directory, which contains the README file displayed in the figure). The default bindings for text widgets allow you to manipulate the text in a number of ways:

- You can scroll the text with the scrollbar or by scanning with mouse button 2 in the text.
- You can edit the text; for example, click with mouse button 1 to set the insertion cursor, then type new characters.
- You can select information by dragging with mouse button 1 and then copy the selection into other applications.

See the reference documentation for text widgets for complete information on the default bindings.

19.6 Text indices and marks

Many of the text widget commands require you to name particular places in the text. For example, the `insert` action in the script from Section 19.5 specified `end` as the place to insert each additional block of data. A position specifier in a text widget is called an *index*; it can take any of several forms. The simplest form for an index is two numbers separated by a dot, such as `2.3`. The first number gives a line number and the second number gives a character index within a line (for various historical reasons the first line of the file is 1 but the first character of a line is 0). If an index is specified as `end` it refers to the end of the file, and if it is specified as `@x,y` where *x* and *y* are numbers, it refers to the character closest to the pixel at location *x,y* in the window.

You can also use symbolic names for positions in a text; these symbolic names are called *marks*. For example, the command

    .text mark set first 2.3

sets a mark named `first` to refer to the gap between character 3 of line 2 and the character just before it. In the future you can refer to the character after the mark as `first` instead of `2.3`. The mark will continue to refer to the same logical position even if characters are added to or deleted from the text. For example, if you delete the first character of line 2, `first` becomes synonymous with index `2.2` instead of `2.3`.

Two marks have special meaning in texts. The `insert` mark identifies the location of the insertion cursor; if you modify `insert`, Tk will display the insertion cursor at the new location. The second special mark is `current`, which Tk updates continuously to identify the character underneath the pointer.

Indices can also take more complex forms consisting of a base followed by one or more modifiers. For example, consider the following command:

    .text delete insert "insert + 2 chars"

The `delete` action takes two indices as arguments and deletes the characters between them. Both of the indices use `insert` as base but the second index also has a modifier "`+ 2 chars`", which advances the index by 2 characters over its base value. Thus the command deletes the two characters just to the right of the insertion cursor. Some other examples of modifier usage are "`first lineend`", which refers to the newline at the end of the line containing the mark `first`, and "`insert wordstart`", which refers to the first character of the word containing the insertion cursor.

Here is a procedure that uses marks and other indices to provide a general-purpose searching facility for text widgets:

```
proc forAllMatches {w pattern script} {
    scan [$w index end] %d numLines
    for {set i 1} {$i < $numLines} {incr i} {
        $w mark set last $i.0
        while {[regexp -indices $pattern \
                [$w get last "last lineend"] indices]} {
            $w mark set first \
                    "last + [lindex $indices 0] chars"
            $w mark set last "last + 1 chars \
                    + [lindex $indices 1] chars"
            uplevel $script
        }
    }
}
```

The forAllMatches procedure takes three arguments: the name of a text widget, a regular expression pattern, and a script. It finds all of the ranges of characters that match the regular expression (each range must be on a single line). For each matching range forAllMatches sets the marks first and last to the beginning and end of the range, then it invokes the script. For example, the following script prints out the locations of all instances of the word Tcl in the text:

```
forAllMatches .text Tcl {
    puts "[.text index first] --> [.text index last]"
}
```
⇒ *12.10 --> 12.13*
   14.0 --> 14.3
   . . .

For each matching range the index widget command is invoked for the first and last marks; it returns numerical indices corresponding to the marks, which puts prints on standard output. As another example, you could clean up redundant the words in a text with the following script:

```
forAllMatches .text "the the" {
    .text delete first "first + 4 chars"
}
```

In this script the action taken for each range is to delete the first four characters of the range, which eliminates the redundant the (this example works only if both the's are on the same line).

The forAllMatches procedure computes how many lines there are in the text and then scans over them one line at a time. Within this loop there is an inner loop that handles all the matching ranges within a line. At the beginning of each iteration of the inner loop, the mark last points to the first character of the part of the line still to be searched. forAllMatches extracts the remainder of the line and uses the regexp command to see if any part of it matches the pattern. If there is a match, regexp stores the indices of the first and last matching character as a list in indices; forAllMatches uses this information to set the marks `first` and `last`, then it evaluates its `script` argument and goes on to the next iteration.

19.7 Text tags

Text tags provide a tagging mechanism similar to that of canvases except that text tags apply to ranges of characters instead of graphical items. A tag name can have any string value and it can be applied to arbitrary ranges within the text. A single character may have multiple tags and a single tag may be associated with many ranges of characters. For example, the command

```
.text tag add x 1.0 1.end
```

applies tag x to the first line of the text; the command

```
.text tag remove x "insert wordstart" "insert wordend"
```

removes tag x from all the characters in the word around the insertion cursor; and

```
.text tag ranges x
```
⇒ *1.0 1.3 1.8 1.13*

returns a list of indices for the beginning and end of each range of characters tagged with x. In the preceding example the tag x is present on the characters at indices 1.0 through 1.2 and 1.8 through 1.12.

Tags serve two special purposes in text widgets. First, you can associate display attributes with tags so that the tagged characters are displayed differently from other characters. For example, the following script might be invoked after starting up the `text` script and defining the `forAllMatches` procedure:

```
forAllMatches .text Tcl {
    .text tag add big first last
}
.text tag configure big -background Bisque3 -borderwidth 2 \
        -font -Adobe-Helvetica-Medium-R-Normal--*-240-* \
        -relief raised
```

This will result in the display in Figure 19.4, where all instances of the word Tcl are drawn with a larger font, a darker background color, and a raised relief.

The second special feature of tags is that you can associate bindings with them just as with canvas tags. You can use bindings to make portions of text "active" so that they respond to the mouse or keyboard. Among other things, this allows hypertext effects to be implemented. For example, the following bindings will cause all the Tcl words to turn green whenever the mouse passes over any one of them:

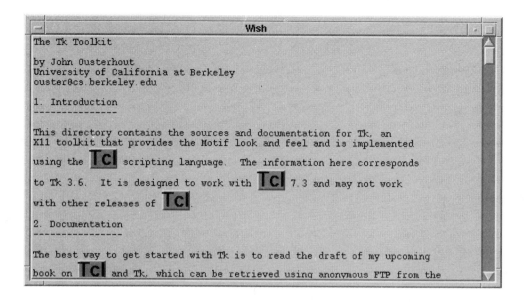

Figure 19.4. The same example as Figure 19.3, except that all instances of the word Tcl have been tagged with big and special display attributes have been associated with big.

```
.text tag bind big <Enter> {
    .text tag configure big -background SeaGreen2
}
.text tag bind big <Leave> {
    .text tag configure big -background Bisque3
}
```

Or, the following binding causes the text widget to reload itself with Tcl's README file when the user clicks button 3 on any of the Tcl words:

```
.text tag bind big <Button-3> {
    .text delete 1.0 end
    loadFile /usr/local/src/tcl/tcl7.0/README
}
```

Chapter 20
The Selection

The *selection* is a mechanism for passing information between widgets and applications. The user first selects one or more objects in a widget, for example, by dragging the mouse across a range of text or clicking on a graphical object. Once a selection has been made, the user can invoke commands in other widgets to retrieve information about the selection, such as the characters in the selected range or the name of the file containing the selection. The widget containing the selection and the widget requesting it can be in the same or different applications. The selection is most commonly used to copy information from one place to another, but it can be used for other purposes as well, such as setting a breakpoint at a selected line or opening a new window on a selected file.

X defines a standard mechanism for supplying and retrieving the selection and Tk provides access to this mechanism with the `selection` command. Table 20.1 summarizes the `selection` command. The rest of this chapter describes its features in more detail. For complete information on the X selection protocol, refer to the Inter-Client Communication Conventions Manual (ICCCM) in the Scheifler and Gettys book.

20.1 Selections, retrievals, and targets

X's selection mechanism allows for multiple selections to exist at once, with names like "primary selection", "secondary selection", and so on. However, Tk supports only the primary selection; Tk applications cannot retrieve or supply selections other than the primary one and the term "selection" always refers to the primary selection in this book. At most one widget has the primary selection at any given time on a given display. When a user selects information in one widget, any selected information in any other widget is auto-

```
selection clear window
          If there is a selection anywhere on window's display, deselect it so that no
          window owns the selection anymore.
selection get ?target?
          Retrieve the value of the primary selection using target as the form in
          which to retrieve it, and return the selection's value as result. target
          defaults to STRING.
selection handle window script ?target? ?format?
          Creates a handler for selection requests: script will be evaluated
          whenever the primary selection is owned by window and someone attempts
          to retrieve it in the form given by target. target defaults to STRING.
          format specifies a representation for transmitting the selection to the
          requester; it defaults to STRING. When script is invoked, two additional
          numbers are appended to it, consisting of the starting offset and maximum
          number of bytes to retrieve. script should return the requested range of
          the selection; if it returns an error, the selection retrieval will be rejected.
selection own ?window? ?script?
          Claims ownership of the selection for window; if some other window
          previously owned the selection, it is deselected. If script is specified, it
          will be evaluated when window is deselected. If neither window nor
          script is specified, the command returns the path name of the window
          that currently owns the selection, or an empty string if no window in this
          application owns the selection.
```

Table 20.1. A summary of the `selection` command.

matically deselected. It is possible for multiple disjoint objects to be selected simultaneously within a widget (for example, three different items in a listbox or several different polygons in a drawing window), but usually the selection consists of a single object or a range of adjacent objects.

    When you retrieve the selection you can ask for several different kinds of information. The different kinds of information are referred to as retrieval *targets*. The most common target is STRING. In this case the contents of the selection are returned as a string. For example, if text is selected, a retrieval with target STRING returns the contents of the selected text; if graphics are selected, a retrieval with target STRING returns some string representation for the selected graphics. If the selection is retrieved with target FILE_NAME, the return value is the name of the file associated with the selection. If target LINE is used, the return value is the number of the selected line within its file. There are many targets with well-defined meanings; refer to the X ICCCM for more information.

    The command `selection get` retrieves the selection. The target may be specified explicitly or it may be left unspecified, in which case it defaults to STRING. For example, the following commands might be invoked when the selection consists of a few words on one line of a file containing the text of Shakespeare's *Romeo and Juliet*:

```
        selection get
⇒   star-crossed lovers
        selection get FILE_NAME
⇒   romeoJuliet
        selection get LINE
⇒   6
```

These commands could be issued in any Tk application on the display containing the selection; they need not be issued in the application containing the selection.

Not every widget supports every possible selection target. For example, if the information in a widget isn't associated with a file, the FILE_NAME target will not be supported. If you try to retrieve the selection with an unsupported target, an error is returned. Fortunately, every widget is supposed to support retrievals with target TARGETS; such retrievals return a list of all the target forms supported by the current selection owner. You can use the result of a TARGETS retrieval to pick the most convenient available target. For example, the following procedure retrieves the selection as PostScript if possible and as an unformatted string otherwise:

```
proc getSelection {} {
    set targets [selection get TARGETS]
    if {[lsearch -exact $targets POSTSCRIPT] >= 0} {
        return [selection get POSTSCRIPT]
    } else {
        return [selection get STRING]
    }
}
```

20.2   Locating and clearing the selection

Tk provides two mechanisms for finding out who owns the selection. The command selection own (with no additional arguments) checks whether the selection is owned by a widget in the invoking application. If so it returns the path name of that widget; if there is no selection or it is owned by some other application, selection own returns an empty string.

The second way to locate the selection is with the retrieval targets APPLICATION and WINDOW_NAME. These targets are both implemented by Tk and are available whenever the selection is in a Tk application. The command

    selection get APPLICATION

returns the name of the Tk application that owns the selection (in a form suitable for use with the send command, for example) and

    selection get WINDOW_NAME

returns the path name of the window that owns the selection. If the application that owns the selection isn't based on Tk, it does not support the APPLICATION and WIN-

DOW_NAME targets and the `selection get` command returns an error. These commands also return errors if there is no selection.

The command

```
selection clear .
```

clears out any selection on the display of the application's main window. It works regardless of whether the selection is in the invoking application or some other application on the same display. The following script clears out the selection only if it is in the invoking application:

```
if {[selection own] != ""} {
    selection clear [selection own]
}
```

20.3 Supplying the selection with Tcl scripts

Earlier sections described Tk's facilities for retrieving the selection; this section describes how to supply the selection. The standard widgets such as entries and texts already contain C code that supplies the selection so you don't usually have to worry about it when writing Tcl scripts. However, it is possible to write Tcl scripts that supply the selection and this section describes how to do it. This feature of Tk is seldom used so you may wish to skip over this material until you need it.

The protocol for supplying the selection has three parts:

1. A widget must claim ownership of the selection. This deselects any previous selection and typically redisplays the selected material in a highlighted fashion.

2. The selection owner must respond to retrieval requests by other widgets and applications.

3. The owner may request that it be notified when it is deselected. Widgets typically respond to deselection by eliminating the highlights on the display.

The next paragraphs describe two scenarios. The first scenario just adds a new target to a widget that already has selection support, so it deals only with the second part of the protocol. The second scenario implements complete selection support for a group of widgets that didn't previously have any; it deals with all three parts of the protocol.

Suppose that you wish to add a new target to those supported for a particular widget. For example, text widgets contain built-in support for the STRING target but they don't automatically support the FILE_NAME target. You could add support for FILE_NAME retrievals with the following script:

```
selection handle .t getFile FILE_NAME
proc getFile {offset maxBytes} {
    global fileName
    set last [expr $offset+$maxBytes-1]
    string range $fileName $offset $last
}
```

This code assumes that the text widget is named .t and that the name of its associated file is stored in a global variable named fileName. The selection handle command tells Tk to invoke getFile whenever .t owns the selection and someone attempts to retrieve it with target FILE_NAME. When such a retrieval occurs, Tk takes the specified command (getFile in this case), appends two additional numerical arguments, and invokes the resulting string as a Tcl command. In this example a command such as

```
getFile 0 4000
```

results. The additional arguments identify a subrange of the selection by its first byte and maximum length, and the command must return this portion of the selection. If the requested range extends beyond the end of the selection, the command should return everything from the given starting point up to the end of the selection. Tk takes care of returning the information to the application that requested it. In most cases the entire selection is retrieved in one invocation of the command; for very large selections, however, Tk makes several separate invocations so that it can transmit the selection back to the requester in manageable pieces.

The preceding example simply added a new target to a widget that already provided some built-in selection support. If selection support is being added to a widget that has no built-in support at all, additional Tcl code is needed to claim ownership of the selection and to respond to deselections. For example, suppose that there is a group of three radiobuttons named .a, .b, and .c and that the buttons have already been configured with their −variable and −value options to store information about the selected button in a global variable named state. Now suppose that you want to tie the radiobuttons to the selection, so that (a) whenever a button becomes selected it claims the X selection, (b) selection retrievals return the contents of state, and (c) when some other widget claims the selection away from the buttons, state is cleared and all the buttons become deselected. The following code implements these features:

```
selection handle .a getValue STRING
proc getValue {offset maxBytes} {
    global state
    set last [expr $offset+$maxBytes-1]
    string range $state $offset $last
}
foreach w {.a .b .c} {
    $w config -command {selection own .a selGone}
}
proc selGone {} {
    global state
    set state {}
}
```

The selection handle command and the getValue procedure are similar to the previous example: they respond to STRING selection requests for .a by returning the contents of the state variable. The foreach loop specifies a -command option for each of the widgets. This causes the selection own command to be invoked whenever the user clicks on any of the radiobuttons, and the selection own command claims ownership of the selection for widget .a (.a will officially own the selection regardless of which radiobutton gets selected and it returns state in response to selection requests). The selection own command also specifies that procedure selGone should be invoked whenever the selection is claimed away by some other widget. selGone sets state to an empty string. All of the radiobuttons monitor state for changes, so when it gets cleared the radiobuttons deselect themselves.

Chapter 21
The Input Focus

At any given time one window of an application is designated as the *input focus window*, or *focus window* for short. All keystrokes received by the application are directed to the focus window and processed according to its event bindings; if the focus window has no bindings for the keystroke, the keystroke is ignored. This chapter describes Tk's focus command, which is used to control the input focus. Table 21.1 summarizes the syntax of the focus command.

Note: *The focus window is only used for key press and key release events. Mouse-related events, such as enter, leave, button press, and button release, are always delivered to the window under the mouse, regardless of the focus window. Furthermore, the focus window determines only what happens once a keystroke event arrives at a particular application; it does not determine which of the applications on the display receives keystrokes. The choice of a focus application is made by the window manager, not Tk.*

21.1 Focus model: explicit vs. implicit

There are two possible ways of handling the input focus, known as the *implicit* and *explicit* focus models. In the implicit model the focus follows the mouse: keystrokes are directed to the window under the mouse pointer and the focus window changes implicitly when the mouse moves from one window to another. In the explicit model the focus window is set explicitly and doesn't change until it is explicitly reset; mouse motions do not automatically change the focus.

Tk implements the explicit focus model, for several reasons. First, the explicit model allows you to move the mouse cursor out of the way when you're typing in a window;

focus	
	Returns the path name of the application's focus window, or an empty string if there is no focus window.
focus *window*	
	Sets the application's focus window to *window*.
focus default ?*window*?	
	If *window* is specified, it becomes the default focus window, which will receive the input focus whenever the focus window is destroyed. In this case the command returns an empty string. If *window* is specified as none, there will be no default focus window. If *window* is omitted, the command returns the current default focus window, or none if there is no default.
focus none	
	Clears the focus window; keystrokes will be ignored until the focus is reset.

Table 21.1. A summary of the focus command.

with the implicit model you'd have to keep the mouse in the window while you type. Second, and more important, the explicit model allows an application to change the focus window without the user moving the mouse. For example, when an application pops up a dialog box that requires type-in, such as one that prompts for a file name, it can set the input focus to the appropriate window in the dialog without you having to move the mouse, and it can move the focus back to its original window when you're finished with the dialog box. This allows you to keep your hands on the keyboard. Similarly, when you're typing in a form the application can move the input focus to the next entry in the form each time you type a tab, so that you can keep your hands on the keyboard and work more efficiently. Last, if you want an implicit focus model, it can always be achieved with event bindings that change the focus each time the mouse cursor enters a new window.

Tk applications don't need to worry about the input focus very often because the default bindings for text-oriented widgets already take care of the most common situations. For example, when you click button 1 over an entry or text widget the widget automatically makes itself the focus window. As an application designer you need to set the focus only in cases like those in the previous paragraph where you want to move the focus among the windows of your application to reflect the flow of work.

21.2 Setting the input focus

To set the input focus, invoke the focus command with a widget name as argument:

```
focus .dialog.entry
```

From this point on, all keystrokes received by the application will be directed to
`.dialog.entry` and the previous focus window will no longer receive keystrokes. The
new focus window will display some sort of highlight, such as a blinking insertion cursor,
to indicate that it has the focus and the previous focus window will stop displaying its
highlight.

Here is a script that implements tabbing among four entries in a form:

```
set tabList {.form.e1 .form.e2 .form.e3 .form.e4}
foreach w $tabList {
    bind $w <Tab> {tab $tabList}
}
proc tab list {
    set i [lsearch -exact $list [focus]]
    incr i
    if {$i >= [llength $list]} {
        set i 0
    }
    focus [lindex $list $i]
}
```

This script assumes that the four entry windows have already been created. It uses the
variable `tabList` to describe the order of traversal among the entries and arranges for
the procedure `tab` to be invoked whenever a tab is typed in any of the entries. The `tab`
procedure invokes `focus` with no arguments to determine which window has the focus,
finds where this window is in the list that gives the order of tabbing, and sets the input
focus to the next window in the list. The procedure `tab` could be used for many different
forms just by passing it a different `list` argument for each form. The order of focusing
can also be changed at any time by changing the value of the `tabList` variable.

21.3 Clearing the focus

The command `focus none` clears the input focus for the application. Once this command has been executed, keystrokes for the application will be discarded.

21.4 The default focus

When the focus window is destroyed, Tk automatically sets the input focus for the application to a window called the *default focus window*. The default focus window is initially
none, which means that there will be no focus window after the focus window is deleted
and keystrokes will be discarded until the focus window is set again.

The `focus default` command can be used to specify a default focus window and
to query the current default:

```
      focus default
⇒   none
      focus default .entry
      focus default
⇒   .entry
```

Once this script has been completed, `.entry` will receive the input focus whenever the input focus window is destroyed.

21.5   Shortcuts

If an application provides keyboard shortcuts (for example, you can type Control-s to save the file or Control-q to quit the application), it will need special attention to bindings and the input focus. First, the shortcut bindings must be present in every window where you want them to apply. For example, suppose that an editor has a main text window plus several entry windows for searching and replacement. You will create bindings for shortcuts like Control-q in the main text window, but you will probably want most or all of the bindings to apply in the auxiliary windows also, so you'll have to define the shortcut bindings in each of these windows too.

In addition, an application with shortcuts should never let the focus become `none`, since that prevents any of the shortcuts from being processed. If no other focus window is available, I suggest setting the focus to the main window of the application; of course, you'll have to define shortcut bindings for `.` so that they are available in this mode. In addition, I recommend setting the default focus window to `.` or some other suitable window so that the focus isn't lost when dialog boxes and other windows are deleted.

Chapter 22
Window Managers

For each display running the X Window System there is a special process called the *window manager*. The main function of the window manager is to control the arrangement of all the top-level windows on each screen. In this respect it is similar to a geometry manager except that instead of managing internal windows within an application it manages the top-level windows of all applications. The window manager allows each application to request particular locations and sizes for its top-level windows, which can be overridden interactively by users. Window managers also serve several purposes besides geometry management: they add decorative frames around top-level windows; they allow windows to be iconified and deiconified; and they notify applications of certain events, such as user requests to destroy the window.

X allows for the existence of many different window managers that implement different styles of layout, provide different kinds of decoration and icon management, and so on. Some common examples of window managers are mwm (which is used for the examples in this book), twm, and tvtwm. Only a single window manager runs on a display at any given time, and the user gets to choose which one. To allow any application to work smoothly with any window manager, X defines a protocol for the interactions between applications and window managers. The protocol is defined by the Inter-Client Communication Conventions Manual (ICCCM), which is included as part of the Scheifler and Gettys book. With Tk you use the wm command to communicate with the window manager; Tk implements the wm command using the ICCCM protocols so that any Tk-based application should work with any window manager. Table 22.1 summarizes the wm command.

```
wm aspect window ?xThin yThin xFat yFat?
                Set or query window's aspect ratio. If an aspect ratio is specified, it
                constrains interactive resizes so that window's width/height will be at least
                as great as xThin/yThin and no greater than xFat/yFat.
wm client window ?name?
                Set or query the WM_CLIENT_MACHINE property for window, which gives
                the name of the machine on which window's application is running.
wm command window ?value?
                Set or query the WM_COMMAND property for window, which contains the
                command line used to initiate window's application.
wm deiconify window
                Arrange for window to be displayed in normal fashion.
wm focusmodel window ?model?
                Set or query the focus model for window. model must be active or
                passive.
wm frame window
                If window has been reparented by the window manager, returns the X
                identifier of the top-level window in the frame. If window hasn't been
                reparented, returns the X identifier for window.
wm geometry window ?value?
                Set or query the requested geometry for window. value must have the
                form =widthxheight±x±y (any of =, widthxheight, or ±x±y can be
                omitted).
wm group window ?leader?
                Set or query the window group to which window belongs. leader must be
                the name of a top-level window, or an empty string to remove window
                from its current group.
wm iconbitmap window ?bitmap?
                Set or query the bitmap for window's icon.
wm iconify window
                Arrange for window to be displayed in iconic form.
wm iconmask window ?bitmap?
                Set or query the mask bitmap for window's icon.
wm iconname window ?string?
                Set or query the string to be displayed in window's icon.
wm iconposition window ?x y?
                Set or query the hints about where on the screen to display window's icon.
wm iconwindow window ?icon?
                Set or query the window to use as icon for window. icon must be the path
                name of a top-level window.
wm maxsize window ?width height?
                Set or query the maximum permissible dimensions for window during
                interactive resize operations.
```

Table 22.1. A summary of the wm command. In all of these commands window must be the name of a top-level window. Many of the commands, such as wm aspect or wm group, are used to set and query various parameters related to window management. For these commands, if the parameters are specified as null strings, the parameters are removed completely; if the parameters are omitted, the command returns the current settings for the parameters.

```
wm minsize window ?width height?
               Set or query the minimum permissible dimensions for window during
               interactive resize operations.
wm overrideredirect window ?boolean?
               Set or query the override-redirect flag for window.
wm positionfrom window ?whom?
               Set or query the source of the position specification for window. whom must
               be program or user.
wm protocol window ?protocol? ?script?
               Arrange for script to be executed whenever the window manager sends a
               message to window with the given protocol. protocol must be the
               name of an atom for a window manager protocol, such as
               WM_DELETE_WINDOW, WM_SAVE_YOURSELF, or WM_TAKE_FOCUS. If
               script is an empty string, the current handler for protocol is deleted. If
               script is omitted, the current script for protocol is returned (or an
               empty string if there is no handler for protocol). If both protocol and
               script are omitted, the command returns a list of all protocols with
               handlers defined for window.
wm sizefrom window ?whom?
               Set or query the source of the size specification for window. whom must be
               program or user.
wm state window
               Returns the current state of window: normal, iconic, or withdrawn.
wm title window ?string?
               Set or query the title string to display in the decorative border for window.
wm transient window ?master?
               Set or query the transient status of window. master must be the name of a
               top-level window on whose behalf window is working as a transient.
wm withdraw window
               Arrange for window not to appear on the screen at all, either in normal or
               iconic form.
```

Table 22.1, continued.

22.1 Window sizes

Even if a Tk application never invokes the wm command, Tk will still communicate with the window manager on the application's behalf so that its top-level windows appear on the screen. By default each top-level window appears in its *natural size*, which is the size it requested using the normal Tk mechanisms for geometry management. Tk forwards the natural size to the window manager and most window managers will honor the request. If the natural size of a top-level window should change, Tk forwards the new size to the window manager and the window manager will resize the window to correspond to the latest request. By default the user cannot resize windows interactively: window sizes will be determined solely by their natural sizes.

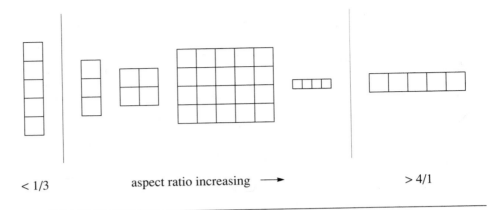

< 1/3   aspect ratio increasing $\longrightarrow$ > 4/1

Figure 22.1. The aspect ratio of a window is its width divided by its height. After the command "wm aspect .w 1 3 4 1" the window manager will allow the user to resize .w to any of the shapes between the two dotted lines but not to those outside the dotted lines.

If you want to allow interactive resizing, you must invoke wm minsize and/or wm maxsize to specify a range of acceptable sizes. For example the script

```
wm minsize .w 100 50
wm maxsize .w 400 150
```

allows .w to be resized but constrains it to be 100 to 400 pixels wide and 50 to 150 pixels high. If the command

```
wm minsize .w 1 1
```

is invoked, there will effectively be no lower limit on the size of .w. If you set a minimum size without a maximum size, the maximum size will be the size of the display; if you set a maximum size without a minimum size, the minimum size will be unconstrained. You can disable interactive resizing again by clearing all of the size bounds:

```
wm minsize .w {} {}
wm maxsize .w {} {}
```

In addition to constraining the dimensions of a window you can also constrain its aspect ratio (width divided by height) using the wm aspect command. For example,

```
wm aspect .w 1 3 4 1
```

tells the window manager not to let the user resize the window to an aspect ratio less than 1/3 or greater than 4. See Figure 22.1 for examples of various aspect ratios.

If the user interactively resizes a top-level window, the window's natural size will be ignored from that point on. Regardless of how the internal needs of the window change, its size will remain as set by the user. A similar effect occurs if you invoke the wm geometry command, as in the following example:

```
wm geometry .w 300x200
```

This command forces .w to be 300 pixels wide and 200 pixels high just as if the user had resized the window interactively. The natural size for .w will be ignored and the size specified in the wm geometry command overrides any size that the user might have specified interactively (but the user can resize the window again to override the size in the wm geometry command).

Note: *The only difference between the wm geometry command and an interactive resize is that wm geometry is not subject to the constraints specified by wm minsize, wm maxsize, and wm aspect.*

If you would like to restore a window to its natural size you can invoke wm geometry with an empty geometry string:

```
wm geometry .w {}
```

This causes Tk to forget any size specified by the user or by wm geometry, so the window returns to its natural size.

22.2   Gridded windows

In some cases it doesn't make sense to resize a window to arbitrary pixel sizes. For example, consider the application in Figure 22.2. When the user resizes the top-level window the text widget changes size in response. Ideally the text widget should always contain an integral number of characters in each dimension, and sizes that result in partial characters should be rounded off.

Gridded geometry management accomplishes this effect. When gridding is enabled for a top-level window its dimensions will be constrained to lie on an imaginary grid. The geometry of the grid is determined by one of the widgets contained in the top-level window (e.g., the text widget in Figure 22.2) so that the widget always holds an integral number of its internal objects. Usually the widget that controls the gridding is a text-oriented widget such as an entry or listbox or text.

To enable gridding, set the -setgrid option to 1 in the controlling widget. The following code was used in the example in Figure 22.2, where the text widget is .t:

```
.t configure -setgrid 1
```

This command has several effects. First, it automatically makes the main window resizable, even if no wm minsize or wm maxsize command has been invoked. Second, it constrains the size of the main window so that .t will always hold an integral number of characters in its font. Third, it changes the meaning of dimensions used in Tk. These dimensions now represent grid units rather than pixels. For example, the command

```
wm geometry . 50x30
```

sets the size of the main window so that .t is 50 characters wide and 30 lines high, and dimensions in the wm minsize and wm maxsize commands will also be grid units.

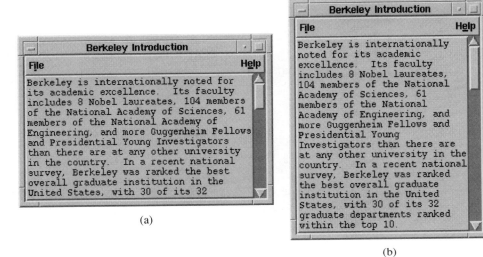

(a)

(b)

Figure 22.2. An example of gridded geometry management. If the user interactively resizes the window from the dimensions in (a) to those in (b), the window manager will round off the dimensions so that the text widget holds an integral number of characters in each dimension.

Many window managers display the dimensions of a window on the screen while it is being resized; these dimensions will be given in grid units too.

Note: *Gridding only works well for windows with fixed-size objects, such as a text window with a monospace font. If different characters have different sizes, the window's size won't necessarily be an integral number of characters.*

Furthermore, in order for gridding to work correctly you must have configured the internal geometry management of the application so that the controlling window stretches and shrinks in response to changes in the size of the top-level window, e.g., by packing it with options "-expand 1 -fill both".

22.3 Window positions

Controlling the position of a top-level window is simpler than controlling its size. Users can move windows interactively, and an application can also move its own windows using the wm geometry command. For example, the command

```
wm geometry .w +100+200
```

positions .w so that its upper-left corner is at pixel (100,200) on the display. If either of the + characters is replaced with a −, the coordinates are measured from the right and bottom sides of the display. For example,

```
wm geometry .w -0-0
```

positions .w at the lower-right corner of the display.

Note: *If you are using a virtual-root window manager such as* tvtwm, *the positions you specify in a* wm geometry *command may either be relative to the screen or to the virtual root window. Consult the documentation for your window manager to see which of these is the case. With some window managers, such as* tvtwm, *you can use options to the window manager along with the* wm positionfrom *command to control which interpretation is used.*

22.4 Window states

At any given time each top-level window is in one of three states. In the *normal* or *deiconified* state the window appears on the screen. In the *iconified* state the window does not appear on the screen, but a small icon is displayed instead. In the *withdrawn* state neither the window nor its icon appears on the screen and the window is ignored completely by the window manager.

New top-level windows start off in the normal state. You can use the facilities of your window manager to iconify a window interactively, or you can invoke the wm iconify command within the window's application, for example

```
wm iconify .w
```

If you invoke wm iconify immediately, before the window first appears on the screen, it starts off in the iconic state. The command wm deiconify causes a window to revert to normal state again.

The command wm withdraw places a window in the withdrawn state. If invoked immediately, before a window has appeared on the screen, the window will start off withdrawn. The most common use for this command is to prevent the main window of an application from ever appearing on the screen (in some applications the main window serves no purpose and the user interface is presented with a collection of top-level windows). Once a window has been withdrawn, it can be returned to the screen with either wm deiconify or wm iconify.

The wm state command returns the current state for a window:

```
wm iconify .w
wm state .w
```
⇒ *iconic*

22.5 Decorations

When a window appears on the screen in the normal state, the window manager usually adds a decorative frame around the window. The frame typically displays a title for the window and contains interactive controls for resizing the window, moving it, and so on. For example, the window in Figure 22.2 was decorated by the mwm window manager.

The wm title command allows you to set the title that is displayed in a window's decorative frame. For example, the command

```
wm title . "Berkeley Introduction"
```

was used to set the title for the window in Figure 22.2.

The wm command provides several options for controlling what is displayed when a window is iconified. First, you can use wm iconname to specify a title to display in the icon. Second, some window managers allow you to specify a bitmap to be displayed in the icon. The wm iconbitmap command allows you to set this bitmap, and wm iconmask allows you to create nonrectangular icons by specifying that certain bits of the icon are transparent. Third, some window managers allow you to use one window as the icon for another; wm iconwindow sets up such an arrangement if your window manager supports it. Finally, you can specify a position on the screen for the icon with the wm iconposition command.

Note: *Almost all window managers support* wm iconname *and* wm iconposition *but fewer support* wm iconbitmap *and almost no window managers support* wm iconwindow *very well. Don't assume that these features work until you've tried them with your own window manager.*

22.6 Window manager protocols

There are times when the window manager needs to inform an application that an important event has occurred or is about to occur so that the application can do something to deal with the event. In X terminology these events are called *window manager protocols*. The window manager passes an identifier for the event to the application and the application can do what it likes in response (including nothing). The two most useful protocols are WM_DELETE_WINDOW and WM_SAVE_YOURSELF. The window manager invokes the WM_DELETE_WINDOW protocol when it wants the application to destroy the window; usually this means that the user asked the window manager to kill the window. The WM_SAVE_YOURSELF protocol is invoked when the X server is about to be shut down or the window is about to be lost for some other reason. It gives the application a chance to save its state on disk before its X connection disappears. For information about other protocols, refer to ICCCM documentation.

The wm protocol command arranges for a script to be invoked whenever a particular protocol is triggered. For example, the command

```
wm protocol . WM_DELETE_WINDOW {
    puts stdout "I don't wish to die"
}
```

arranges for a message to be printed on standard output whenever the window manager asks the application to kill its main window. In this case, the window will not actually be destroyed. If you don't specify a handler for WM_DELETE_WINDOW, Tk will destroy the window automatically. WM_DELETE_WINDOW is the only protocol where Tk takes default action on your behalf; for other protocols, like WM_SAVE_YOURSELF, nothing will happen unless you specify an explicit handler.

22.7 Special handling: transients, groups, and override-redirect

You can ask the window manager to provide three kinds of special treatment for windows. First, you can mark a top-level window as *transient* with a command like the following:

```
wm transient .w .
```

This indicates to the window manager that .w is a short-lived window such as a dialog box, working on behalf of the application's main window. The last argument to wm transient (which is . in the example) is referred to as the *master* for the transient window. The window manager may treat transient windows differently than other windows by providing less decoration or by iconifying and deiconifying them whenever their master is iconified or deiconified.

In situations where several long-lived windows work together you can use the wm group command to tell the window manager about the group. The following script tells the window manager that the windows .top1, .top2, .top3, and .top4 are working together as a group, and .top1 is the group *leader*:

```
foreach i {.top2 .top3 .top4} {
    wm group $i .top1
}
```

The window manager can then treat the group as a unit, and it may give special treatment to the leader. For example, when the group leader is iconified all the other windows in the group might be removed from the display without displaying icons for them: the leader's icon represents the whole group in this case. When the leader's icon is deiconified again, all the windows in the group might return to the display. The exact treatment of groups is up to the window manager, and different window managers may handle them differently. The leader for a group need not actually appear on the screen (e.g., it could be withdrawn).

In some extreme cases it is important for a top-level window to be completely ignored by the window manager: no decorations, no interactive manipulation of the window via the window manager, no iconifying, and so on. The best example of such a window is a pop-up menu. In these cases, the windows should be marked as *override-redirect* using a command similar to the following:

```
wm overrideredirect .popup true
```

This command must be invoked before the window has actually appeared on the screen.

Note: *Menus automatically mark themselves as override-redirect so you don't need to do this for them. The* wm overrideredirect *command is hardly ever used.*

22.8   Session management

The wm command provides two options for communicating with session managers: wm client and wm command. These commands pass information to the session manager about the application running in the window; they are typically used by the session manager to display information to the user and to save the state of the session so that it can be recreated in the future. wm client identifies the machine on which the application is running, and wm command identifies the shell command used to invoke the application. For example,

```
wm client . sprite.berkeley.edu
wm command . {browse /usr/local/bin}
```

indicates that the application is running on the machine sprite.berkeley.edu and was invoked with the shell command browse /usr/local/bin.

22.9   A warning about window managers

Although the desired behavior of window managers is supposedly described in the X ICCCM document, the ICCCM is not always clear and no window manager that I know of implements everything exactly as described in the ICCCM. For example, the mwm window manager doesn't always deal properly with changes in the minimum and maximum sizes for windows after they've appeared on the screen, and the twm window manager treats the aspect ratio backwards; neither window manager positions windows on the screen exactly where they requested.

One of the main sources of trouble is Tk's dynamic nature, which allows you to change anything anytime. Almost all applications except those based on Tk set all the information about a window before it appears on the screen and they never change it after that. Because of this, window manager code to handle dynamic changes hasn't been debugged very well. You can avoid problems by setting as much of the information as possible before the window first appears on the screen and avoiding changes.

Chapter 23
The Send Command

The selection mechanism described in Chapter 20 provides a simple way for one application to retrieve data from another application. This chapter describes the send command, which provides a more powerful form of communication between applications. With send, any Tk application can invoke arbitrary Tcl scripts in any other Tk application on the display; these commands can both retrieve information and also take actions that modify the state of the target application. Table 23.1 summarizes send and three other related commands.

23.1 Basics

To use send, all you have to do is give the name of an application and a Tcl script to execute in the application. For example, consider the following command:

```
send tgdb {break tkButton.c 200}
```

The first argument to send is the name of the target application and the second argument is a Tcl script to execute in that application. Tk locates the named application (an imaginary Tcl-based version of the gdb debugger in this case), forwards the script to that application, and arranges for the script to be executed in the application's interpreter. In this example the script sets a breakpoint at a particular line in a particular file. The result or error generated by the script is passed back to the originating application and returned by the send command.

send is synchronous: it doesn't complete until the script has been executed in the remote application and the result has been returned. send defers the processing of X

243

```
selection get APPLICATION
             Returns the name of the Tk application that currently has the selection, or
             generates an error if the selection is not in a Tk application.

send appName arg ?arg ...?
             Concatenates all the arg's with spaces as separators, then executes the
             resulting script in the interpreter of the application given by appName. The
             result of that execution is returned as the result of the send command.

winfo interps
             Returns a list whose elements are the names of all the Tk applications on
             the display containing the application's main window.
winfo name .
             Returns the name of the current application, suitable for use in send
             commands issued by other applications.
```

Table 23.1. A summary of send and related commands.

---

events while it waits for the remote application to respond, so the application will not respond to its user interface during this time. After the send command completes and the application returns to normal event processing, any waiting events will be processed. A sending application *will* respond to send requests from other applications while waiting for its own send to complete. This means, for example, that the target of the send can send a command back to the initiator while processing the script, without danger of deadlock.

One of the most common uses of send is to try simple experiments in Tk applications that are already running, such as changing a color or modifying the command associated with a button. Most Tk applications don't present an interface for typing Tcl commands directly to the application. However, you can always issue commands to such applications by starting an interactive wish application and then invoking send. For example, the following command changes the background color of a particular window in an application named scan:

```
send scan {.menubar.file configure -bg blue}
```

Chapter 27 contains an example script that uses send to build a more powerful and convenient remote controller.

23.2 Hypertools

send is intended to encourage the development of small reusable applications called *hypertools*. Many of today's windowing applications are monoliths that bundle several different packages into a single program. For example, debuggers often contain editors to display the source files being debugged, and spreadsheets often contain charting packages or communication packages or even databases. Unfortunately, each of these packages can only be used from within the monolithic program that contains it.

With send each of these packages can be built as a separate stand-alone program. Related programs can communicate by sending commands to each other. For example, a debugger can send a command to an editor to highlight the current line of execution, or a spreadsheet can send a script to a charting package to chart a dataset derived from the spreadsheet, or a mail reader can send a command to a multimedia application to play a video clip associated with the mail. With send it should be possible to reuse existing programs in unforeseen ways. For example, once a Tk-based audio-video application becomes available, any existing Tk application can be made into a multimedia application just by adding a few scripts that send commands to the audio-video application. The term "hypertools" reflects this ability to connect applications in interesting ways and to reuse them in ways not foreseen by their original designers.

When designing Tk applications, I encourage you to focus on doing one or a few things well; don't try to bundle everything in one program. Instead, provide different functions in different hypertools that can be controlled via send and reused independently.

23.3 Application names

To send to an application, you have to know its name. Each application on the display has a unique name, which it can choose in any way it pleases as long as it is unique. In many cases the application name is just the name of the program that created the application. For example, wish uses the application name wish by default; or, if it is running under the control of a script file, it uses the name of the script file as its application name. In programs like editors that are associated with a file or object, the application name typically has two parts: the name of the application and the name of the file or object on which it is operating. For example, if an editor named mx is displaying a file named tk.h, the application's name is likely to be "mx tk.h".

If an application requests a name that is already in use, Tk adds an extra number to the end of the new name to keep it from conflicting with the existing name. For example, if you start up wish twice on the same display, the first instance will have the name wish and the second instance will have the name "wish #2". Similarly, if you open a second editor window on the same file it will end up with a name like "mx tk.h #2".

Tk provides three commands that return information about the names of applications. First, the command

```
    winfo name .
⇒ wish #2
```

returns the name of the invoking application. Second, the command

```
        winfo interps
    ⇒   wish {wish #2} {mx tk.h}
```

returns a list whose elements are the names of all the applications defined on the display.
Third, the command

```
        selection get APPLICATION
```

returns the name of the Tk application that currently owns the selection; if no Tk application currently owns the selection, then the command generates an error.

Note: *At present the application name is set by the application's C code when it initializes the Tk*
            toolkit; it cannot be changed.

23.4   Security issues

The send command is potentially a major security loophole. Any application that uses
your display can send scripts to any Tk application on that display, and the scripts can
use the full power of Tcl to read and write your files or invoke subprocesses with the
authority of your account. Ultimately this security problem must be solved in the X display server, since even applications that don't use Tk can be tricked into abusing your
account by sufficiently sophisticated applications on the same display. However, without
Tk it is relatively difficult to create invasive applications; with Tk and send it is trivial.

You can protect yourself fairly well if you employ a key-based protection scheme for
your display like xauth instead of a host-based scheme like xhost. xauth generates an
obscure authorization string and tells the server not to allow an application to use the display unless it can produce the string. Typically the string is stored in a file that can only be
read by a particular user, so this restricts use of the display to the one user. If you want to
allow other users to access your display, you can give them a copy of your authorization
file, or you can change the protection on your authorization file so that it is group-read-
able.

Unfortunately, many people use the xhost program for protection: it specifies a set
of machine names to the server and any process running on any of those machines can
establish connections with the server. Anyone with an account on any of the listed
machines can connect to your server. To prevent these people from sending to your applications and abusing your account, Tk checks to see if xhost-style protection is being
used on the display; if so, Tk refuses to accept incoming send commands. If you currently use xhost for protection, you should learn about xauth and switch to it as soon
as possible. If for some reason you need to use the send command even though you're
using xhost for protection, you can do this by compiling Tk with a special flag; see the
Tk Makefile for details.

Chapter 24
Modal Interactions

Usually the user of a Tk application has complete control over what operations to perform and in what order. The application offers a variety of panels and controls and the user selects among them. However, there are times when it's useful to restrict the user's range of choices or force the user to do things in a certain order; these are called *modal interactions*. The best example of a modal interaction is a dialog box: the application is carrying out some function requested by the user such as writing information to a file when it discovers that it needs additional input from the user, such as the name of the file to write. It displays a dialog box and forces the user to respond to the dialog box, for example, by selecting a file name, before proceeding. After the user responds, the application completes the operation and returns to its normal mode of operation where the user can do anything he or she pleases.

Tk provides two mechanisms for use in modal interactions. First, the grab command allows you to restrict the user temporarily so that he or she can interact with only a few of the application's windows (for example, only the dialog box). Second, the tkwait command allows you to suspend the evaluation of a script until a particular event has occurred, such as the user responding to a dialog box, and then continue the script after this has happened. These commands are summarized in Table 24.1.

A word of caution is in order here. Although modal interactions are sometimes useful, most experts agree that they should be kept to a minimum. Users can become frustrated if their range of choices is constantly being limited by modes, and mode switches can be confusing.

```
grab ?-global? window
              Same as grab set command.
grab current ?window?
              Returns the name of the current grab window for window's display or an
              empty string if there is no grab for that display. If window is omitted,
              returns a list of all windows grabbed by this application for all displays.
grab release window
              Releases the grab on window, if there is one.
grab set ?-global? window
              Sets a grab on window, releasing any previous grab on window's display.
              If -global is specified, the grab is global; otherwise it is local.
grab status window
              Returns none if no grab is currently set on window, local if a local grab
              is set, and global if a global grab is set.

tkwait variable varName
              Waits until variable varName changes value, then returns.
tkwait visibility window
              Waits until the visibility state of window changes, then returns.
tkwait window window
              Waits until window is destroyed, then returns.
```

Table 24.1. A summary of the grab and tkwait commands.

24.1 Grabs

Mouse events such as button presses and mouse motion are normally delivered to the window under the pointer. However, it is possible for a window to claim ownership of the mouse so that mouse events are delivered only to that window and its descendants in the Tk window hierarchy. This is called a *grab*. When the mouse is over one of the windows in the grab subtree, mouse events are delivered and processed just as if no grab were in effect. When the mouse is outside the grab subtree, button presses and releases and mouse motion events are delivered to the grab window instead of the window under the mouse, and window entry and exit events are discarded. Thus a grab prevents the user from interacting with windows outside the grab subtree.

The grab command sets and releases grabs. For example, if you've created a dialog box named .dlg and you want to prevent the user from interacting with any window except .dlg and its subwindows, you can invoke the command

```
grab set .dlg
```

After the user has responded to the dialog box, you can release the grab with the command

```
grab release .dlg
```

If the dialog box is destroyed after the user has responded to it, there's no need to invoke grab release: Tk releases the grab automatically when the grab window is destroyed.

Tk provides two forms of grab, local and global. A *local grab* affects only the grabbing application: if the user moves the pointer into some other application on the display, he or she can interact with the other application as usual. You should always try to use local grabs, and they are the default in the grab set command. A *global grab* takes over the entire display so that you cannot interact with any application except the one that set the grab. To request a global grab, specify the -global switch to grab set as in the following command:

```
grab set -global .dlg
```

Global grabs are rarely needed and they are tricky to use (if you forget to release the grab your display will lock up so that it is unusable). One place where global grabs are used is for pull-down menus.

Note: *X will not let you set a global grab on a window unless it is visible. Section 24.3 describes how to use the* tkwait visibility *command to wait for a window to become visible. Local grabs are not subject to the visibility restriction.*

The most common way to use grabs is to set a grab on a top-level window so that only a single panel or dialog box is active during the grab. However, it is possible for the grab subtree to contain additional top-level windows; when this happens all of the panels or dialogs corresponding to those top-level windows will be active during the grab.

24.2   Keyboard handling during grabs

Local grabs have no effect on the way the keyboard is handled: keystrokes received anywhere in the application are forwarded to the focus window as usual. Most likely you will set the focus to a window in the grab subtree when you set the grab. Windows outside the grab subtree can't receive any mouse events so they are unlikely to claim the focus away from the grab subtree. Thus the grab is likely to have the effect of restricting the keyboard focus to the grab subtree; however, you are free to move the focus anywhere you wish. If you move the pointer into another application, the focus will move to that other application just as if there had been no grab.

During global grabs Tk also sets a grab on the keyboard so that keyboard events go to the grabbing application even if the pointer is over some other application. This means that you cannot use the keyboard to interact with any other application. Once keyboard events arrive at the grabbing application they are forwarded to the focus window in the usual fashion.

24.3   Waiting: the tkwait command

The second aspect of a modal interaction is waiting. Typically you will want to suspend a script during a modal interaction and resume it when the interaction is complete. For example, if you display a file selection dialog during a file write operation, you will probably want to wait for the user to respond to the dialog, then complete the file write using the name supplied in the dialog interaction. Or, when you start up an application you might wish to display an introductory panel that describes the application and keep this panel visible while the application initializes itself; before going off to do the main initialization you'll want to be sure that the panel is visible on the screen. The tkwait command can be used to wait in situations like these.

tkwait has three forms, each of which waits for a different event to occur. The first form waits for a window to be destroyed, as in the following command:

```
tkwait window .dlg
```

This command will not return until .dlg has been destroyed. You might invoke this command after creating a dialog box and setting a grab on it; the command won't return until after the user has interacted with the dialog in a way that causes it to be destroyed. While tkwait is waiting, the application responds to events so the user can interact with the application's windows. In the dialog box example bindings must exist to destroy the dialog once the user's response is complete (e.g., the user clicks on the OK button). The bindings for the dialog box might also save additional information in variables (such as the name of a file or an identifier for the button that was pressed). This information can be used once tkwait returns.

The following script creates a panel with two buttons labeled OK and Cancel, waits for the user to click on one of the buttons, and then deletes the panel:

```
toplevel .panel
button .panel.ok -text OK -command {
    set label OK
    destroy .panel
}
button .panel.cancel -text Cancel -command {
    set label Cancel
    destroy .panel
}
pack .panel.ok -side left
pack .panel.cancel -side right
grab set .panel
tkwait window .panel
```

When the tkwait command returns, the variable label will contain the label of the button on which you clicked.

The second form for tkwait waits for the visibility state of a window to change. For example, the command

```
tkwait visibility .intro
```

will not return until the visibility state of .intro has changed. Typically this command is invoked just after a new window has been created, in which case it won't return until the window has become visible on the screen. tkwait visibility can be used to wait for a window to become visible before setting a global grab on it, or to make sure that an introductory panel is on the screen before invoking a lengthy initialization script. Like all forms of `tkwait`, `tkwait visibility` will respond to events while waiting.

The third form of `tkwait` provides a general mechanism for implementing other forms of waiting. In this form, the command doesn't return until a given variable has been modified. For example, the command

```
tkwait variable x
```

will not return until variable x has been modified. This form of `tkwait` is typically used in conjunction with event bindings that modify the variable. For example, the following procedure uses `tkwait variable` to implement something analogous to `tkwait window` except that you can specify more than one window and the procedure will return as soon as any of the named windows has been deleted (it returns the name of the window that was deleted):

```
proc waitWindows args {
    global dead
    foreach w $args {
        bind $w <Destroy> "set dead $w"
    }
    tkwait variable dead
    return $dead
}
```

Chapter 25
More on Configuration Options

Configuration options for widgets were introduced in previous chapters. You can specify configuration options when creating new widgets and modify them with the `configure` action for widget commands. This chapter describes two additional facilities related to options. The first part of this chapter describes the option database, which can be used to specify default values for options. The second part of the chapter describes the full syntax of the `configure` widget command: it can be used to retrieve information about options as well as to modify options. Table 25.1 summarizes the commands for manipulating configuration options. For a complete list of the options available for a particular widget class, see the reference documentation for the corresponding class command, such as `button`.

25.1 The option database

The option database supplies values for configuration options that aren't specified explicitly by the application designer. The option database is consulted when widgets are created: for each option not specified on the command line, the widget queries the option database and uses the value from the database, if there is one. If there is no value in the option database, the widget class supplies a default value. Values in the option database are usually provided by the user to personalize applications, for example, to specify consistently larger fonts. Tk supports the RESOURCE_MANAGER property and `.Xdefaults` file in the same way as other X toolkits like Xt.

The option database shouldn't be needed very often in Tk applications because widgets have reasonable default values for their options. If options do need to be changed, it will often be easier to make the changes by invoking `configure` widget commands

```
class window ?optionName value optionName value ...?
                Creates a new widget with class class and path name window, and sets
                options for the new widget as given by optionName-value pairs.
                Unspecified options are filled in using the option database or widget
                defaults. Returns window as result.
```

```
window configure
                Returns a list whose elements are sublists describing all of the options for
                window. Each sublist describes one option in the form described next.
window configure optionName
                Returns a list describing option optionName for window. The list will
                normally contain five values: optionName, the option's name in the option
                database, its class, its default value, and its current value. If the option is a
                synonym for another option, the list contains two values: the option name
                and the database name for the synonym.
window configure optionName value ?optionName value ...?
                Sets the value for each optionName of window to the corresponding
                value.
```

```
option add pattern value ?priority?
                Adds a new option to the option database as specified by pattern and
                value. priority must be either a number between 0 and 100 or a
                symbolic name (see the reference documentation for details on symbolic
                names).
option clear
                Removes all entries from the option database.
option get window dbName dbClass
                If the option database contains a pattern that matches window, dbName,
                and dbClass, returns the value for the highest priority matching pattern.
                Otherwise returns an empty string.
option readfile fileName ?priority?
                Reads fileName, which must have the standard format for a .Xdefaults
                file, and adds all the options specified in that file to the option database at
                priority level priority.
```

Table 25.1. The commands for manipulating widget configuration options.

from a Tcl script, rather than creating entries in your .Xdefaults file. The option database exists primarily to provide cultural compatibility with other X toolkits; I suggest that you use it as little as possible.

25.2 Option database entries

The option database contains any number of entries, where each entry consists of two strings: a *pattern* and a *value*. The pattern specifies one or more widgets and options, and the value is a string to use for options that match the pattern.

In its simplest form a pattern consists of an application name, an optional widget name, and an option name, all separated by dots. For example, here are two patterns in this form:

```
wish.a.b.foreground
wish.background
```

The first pattern applies to the `foreground` option in the widget `.a.b` in the application `wish`. In the second pattern the widget name is omitted, so the pattern applies to the main widget for `wish`. Each of these patterns applies to only a single option for a single widget.

Patterns may also contain classes or wildcards, which allow them to match many different options or widgets. Any component of the widget name may be replaced by a class, in which case the pattern matches any widget that is an instance of that class. For example, the pattern below applies to all children of `.a` that are checkbuttons:

```
wish.a.Checkbutton.foreground
```

Application and option names may also be replaced with classes. The class for an application is the class of its main window, which is currently `Tk` for all Tk applications; names and classes for applications are discussed in more detail in Chapter 22. Individual options also have classes. For example, the class for the `foreground` option is `Foreground`. Several other options such as `selector` (the color used for displaying selectors in radiobuttons and checkbuttons) also have the class `Foreground`, so the following pattern applies to any of these options for any checkbutton widget that is a child of `.a` in `wish`:

```
wish.a.Checkbutton.Foreground
```

Last, patterns may contain * wildcard characters. A * matches any number of window names or classes, as in the following examples:

```
*Foreground
wish*Button.foreground
```

The first pattern applies to any option in any widget of any application as long as the option's class is `Foreground`. The second pattern applies to the `foreground` option of any button widget in the `wish` application. The * wildcard may only be used for window or application names; it cannot be used for the option name (it wouldn't make much sense to specify the same value for all options of a widget).

Note: *This syntax for patterns is the same as that supported by the standard X resource database mechanisms in the X11R3 and X11R4 releases. The `?` wildcard, which was added in the X11R5 release, is not yet supported by Tk's option database.*

The database name for an option is usually the same as the name you would use in a widget creation command or a configure widget command, except that there is no leading – and capital letters are used to mark internal word boundaries. For example, the database name for the `-borderwidth` option is `borderWidth`. The class for an option is usually the same as its database name except that the first letter is capitalized. For example, the class for the `-borderwidth` option is `BorderWidth`. It's important to remember that in Tk classes *always* start with an initial capital letter; any name starting with an initial capital letter is assumed to be a class.

25.3   The RESOURCE_MANAGER property and .Xdefaults file

When a Tk application starts up, Tk automatically initializes the option database. If there is a RESOURCE_MANAGER property on the root window for the display, the database is initialized from it. Otherwise Tk checks the user's home directory for an .Xdefaults file and uses it if it exists. The initialization information has the same form whether it comes from the RESOURCE_MANAGER property or the .Xdefaults file. The syntax described here is the same as that supported by other toolkits such as Xt.

Each line of initialization data specifies one entry in the resource database in a form such as the following:

```
*Foreground: blue
```

The line consists of a pattern (*Foreground in the example) followed by a colon, white space, and a value to associate with the pattern (blue in the example). If the value is too long to fit on one line, it can be placed on multiple lines with each line but the last ending in a backslash-newline sequence:

```
*Gizmo.text: This is a very long initial \
value to use for the text option in all \
"Gizmo" widgets.
```

The backslashes and newlines will not be part of the value.

Blank lines are ignored, as are lines whose first nonblank character is # or !.

25.4   Priorities in the option database

It is possible for several patterns in the option database to match a particular option. When this happens Tk uses a two-part priority scheme to determine which pattern applies. Tk's mechanism for resolving conflicts is different from the standard mechanism supported by the Xt toolkit, but I think it is simpler and easier to work with.

For the most part the priority of an option in the database is determined by the order in which it was entered into the database: newer options take priority over older ones. When specifying options (for example, by typing them into your .Xdefaults file) you should specify the more general options first, with more specific overrides following later. For example, if you want button widgets to have a background color of Bisque1 and all other widgets to have white backgrounds, put the following lines in your .Xdefaults file:

```
*background: white
*Button.background: Bisque1
```

The `*background` pattern matches any option that the `*Button.background` pattern matches, but the `*Button.background` pattern has higher priority since it was specified last. If the order of the patterns had been reversed, all widgets (including buttons) would have white backgrounds and the `*Button.background` pattern would have no effect.

In some cases it may not be possible to specify general patterns before specific ones (for example, you might add a more general pattern to the option database after it has already been initialized with a number of specific patterns from the RESOURCE_MANAGER property). To accommodate these situations, each entry also has an integer priority level between 0 and 100, inclusive. An entry with a higher priority level takes precedence over entries with lower priority levels, regardless of the order in which they were inserted into the option database. Priority levels are not used very often in Tk; refer to the reference documentation for complete details on how they work.

Tk's priority scheme is different from the scheme used by other X toolkits such as Xt. Xt gives higher priority to the most specific pattern, e.g., `.a.b.foreground` is more specific than `*foreground` so it receives higher priority regardless of the order in which the patterns appear. In most cases this won't be a problem: you can specify options for Xt applications using the Xt rules and options for Tk applications using the Tk rules. In cases where you want to specify options that apply both to Tk applications and Xt applications, use the Xt rules but make sure that the patterns considered higher priority by Xt also appear later in your `.Xdefaults` file. In general, you shouldn't need to specify very many options to Tk applications (the defaults should always be reasonable), so the issue of pattern priority shouldn't come up often.

Note: *The option database is queried only for options not specified explicitly in the widget creation command. This means that the user cannot override any option that is specified in a widget creation command. If you want to specify a value for an option but allow the user to override that value through the RESOURCE_MANAGER property, you should specify the value for the option using the* `option` *command described in the next section.*

25.5 The option command

The `option` command allows you to manipulate the option database while an application is running. The command `option add` will create a new entry in the database. It takes two or three arguments. The first two arguments are the pattern and value for the new entry and the third argument, if specified, is a priority level for the new entry. For example,

```
option add *Button.background Bisque1
```

adds an entry that sets the background color for all button widgets to `Bisque1`. Changes to the option database affect only the application in which `option add` was invoked, and they apply only to new widgets created in the future; the database changes will not affect widgets that already exist.

The `option clear` command will remove all entries from the option database. On the next access to the database, it will be reinitialized from the RESOURCE_MANAGER property or the .Xdefaults file.

The command `option readfile` will read a file in the format described earlier for the RESOURCE_MANAGER property and make entries in the option database for each line. For example, the following command augments the option database with the information in file newOptions:

```
option readfile newOptions
```

The `option readfile` command can also be given a priority level as an extra argument after the file name.

To query whether there is an entry in the option database that applies to a particular option, use the `option get` command:

```
option get .a.b background Background
```

This command takes three arguments: the path name of a widget (`.a.b`), the database name for an option (`background`), and the class for that option (`Background`). The command searches the option database to see if any entries match the given window, option, and class. If so, the value of the highest priority matching option is returned. If no entry matches, then an empty string is returned.

25.6 The configure widget command

Every widget class supports a `configure` widget command. This command comes in three forms, which can be used both to change the values of options and also to retrieve information about the widget's options.

If a `configure` widget command is given two additional arguments, it changes the value of an option as in the following example:

```
.button configure -text Quit
```

If the `configure` widget command is given just one extra argument, it returns information about the named option:

```
.button configure -text
```
⇒ *-text text Text { } Quit*

The return value is normally a list with five elements. The first element of the list is the name of the option as you'd specify it on a Tcl command line when creating or configuring a widget. The second and third elements are a name and class to use for looking up the option in the option database. The fourth element is the default value provided by the widget class (a single space character in the preceding example), and the fifth element is the current value of the option. If you wish to retrieve just the current value of an option, you can use `lindex` to extract it from the list:

```
lindex [.button configure -text] 4
```
⇒ *Quit*

Some widget options are just synonyms for other options (e.g., the `-bg` option for buttons is the same as the `-background` option). Configuration information for a synonym is returned as a list with two elements consisting of the option's command-line name and the option database name of its synonym:

```
.button configure -bg
```
⇒ *-bg background*

If the `configure` widget command is invoked with no additional arguments, it returns information about all of the widget's options as a list of lists with one sublist for each option:

```
.button configure
```
⇒ *{-activebackground activeBackground Foreground Black Black}*
{-activeforeground activeForeground Background White White}
{-anchor anchor Anchor center center} {-background background
Background White White} {-bd borderWidth} {-bg background}
{-bitmap bitmap Bitmap {} {}} {-borderwidth borderWidth
BorderWidth 2 2} {-command command Command {} {}} {-cursor cursor
Cursor {} {}} {-disabledforeground disabledForeground
DisabledForeground {} {}} {-fg foreground} {-font font Font
-Adobe-Helvetica-Bold-R-Normal-*-120-*
-Adobe-Helvetica-Bold-R-Normal-*-120-*} {-foreground foreground
Foreground Black Black} {-height height Height 0 0} {-padx padX
Pad 1 1} {-pady padY Pad 1 1} {-relief relief Relief raised
raised} {-state state State normal normal} {-text text Text { }
Quit} {-textvariable textVariable Variable {} {}} {-width width
Width 0 0}

Chapter 26
Odds and Ends

This chapter describes seven additional Tk commands: `destroy`, which deletes widgets; `after`, which delays execution or schedules a script for execution later; `update`, which forces operations that are normally delayed, such as screen updates, to be done immediately; `winfo`, which provides a variety of information about windows, such as their dimensions and children; `raise` and `lower`, which change the stacking order of windows, and `tk`, which provides access to various internals of the Tk toolkit. Table 26.1 summarizes these commands. This chapter also describes several global variables that are read or written by Tk and may be useful to Tk applications.

26.1 Destroying widgets

The `destroy` command deletes one or more widgets. It takes any number of widget names as arguments, for example:

```
destroy .dlg1 .dlg2
```

This command destroys `.dlg1` and `.dlg2`, including their widget state and the widget commands named after the windows. It also recursively destroys their children. The command "`destroy .`" destroys all of the widgets in the application; when this happens most Tk applications will exit.

`after` *ms*
Delays for *ms* milliseconds before returning.
`after` *ms arg* ?*arg arg* ...?
Concatenates all the *arg* values (with spaces as separators) and arranges for the resulting script to be executed after *ms* milliseconds have elapsed. Returns without waiting for the script to be executed.
`destroy` *window* ?*window window* ...?
Deletes each of the *windows* plus all of the windows descended from them. The corresponding widget commands (and all widget states) are also deleted.
`lower` *window* ?*belowThis*?
Changes *window*'s position in the stacking order so that it is just below the window given by *belowThis*. If *belowThis* is omitted, move *window* to the bottom of the stacking order.
`raise` *window* ?*aboveThis*?
Changes *window*'s position in the stacking order so that it is just above the window given by *aboveThis*. If *aboveThis* is omitted, move *window* to the top of the stacking order.
`tk colormodel` *window* ?*value*?
Sets the color model for *window*'s screen to value, which must be either `color` or `monochrome`. If *value* isn't specified, returns the current color model for *window*'s screen.
`update` ?*idletasks*?
Brings the display up to date and processes all pending events. If `idletasks` is specified, no events are processed except those in the idle task queue (delayed updates).
`winfo` *option* ?*arg arg* ...?
Returns various pieces of information about windows, depending on the *option* argument. See reference documentation for details.

Table 26.1. A summary of the commands discussed in this chapter.

26.2 Time delays

The `after` command allows you to incorporate timing into your Tk applications. It has two forms. If you invoke `after` with a single argument, the argument specifies a delay in milliseconds, and the command delays for that number of milliseconds before returning. For example,

```
after 500
```

delays for 500 milliseconds before returning. If you specify additional arguments, as in the command

```
after 5000 {puts "Time's up!"}
```

then the `after` command returns immediately without any delay. However, it concatenates all of the additional arguments (with spaces between them) and arranges for the resulting script to be evaluated after the specified delay. The script will be evaluated at global level as an event handler, just like the scripts for bindings. In the previous example, a message will be printed on standard output after 5 seconds. There may be any number of `after` scripts pending at once.

This script uses `after` to build a general-purpose blinking utility:

```
proc blink {w option value1 value2 interval} {
    $w config $option $value1
    after $interval [list blink $w $option \
            $value2 $value1 $interval]
}
blink .b -bg red black 500
```

The `blink` procedure takes five arguments, which are the name of a widget, the name of an option for that widget, two values for that option, and a blink interval in milliseconds. The procedure arranges for the option to switch back and forth between the two values at the given blink interval. It does this by immediately setting the option to the first value and arranging for itself to be invoked again at the end of the next interval with the two option values reversed, so that option is set to the other value. The procedure reschedules itself each time it is called, so it executes periodically forever. `blink` runs "in background": it always returns immediately, then gets reinvoked by Tk's timer code after the next interval expires. This allows the application to do other things while the blinking is occurring.

26.3 The update command

Tk normally delays operations such as screen updates until the application is idle. For example, if you invoke a widget command to change the text in a button, the button will not redisplay itself immediately. Instead it schedules the redisplay to be done later and returns immediately. At some point the application becomes *idle,* which means that all existing events have been processed and the application is in the event loop and about to wait for another event to occur. At this point all of the delayed operations are carried out. Tk delays redisplays because it saves work when the same window is modified repeatedly: with delayed redisplay the window only gets redrawn once at the end. Tk also delays many other operations, such as geometry recalculations and window creation.

For the most part the delays are invisible. Interactive applications rarely do very much work at a time, so Tk becomes idle again very quickly and updates the screen before the user can perceive any delay. However, there are times when the delays are inconvenient. For example, if a script is going to execute for a long time, you may wish to bring the screen up to date at certain times during the execution of the script. The update command allows you to do this. If you invoke the command

```
update idletasks
```

then all of the delayed operations such as redisplays are carried out immediately; the command will not return until they have finished.

The following procedure uses update to flash a widget synchronously:

```
proc flash {w option value1 value2 interval count} {
    for {set i 0} {$i < $count} {incr i} {
        $w config $option $value1
        update idletasks
        after $interval
        $w config $option $value2
        update idletasks
        after $interval
    }
}
```

This procedure is similar to blink except that it runs in the foreground instead of the background: it flashes the option a given number of times and doesn't return until the flashing is complete. Tk never becomes idle during the execution of this procedure (the after command doesn't return to the event loop while it waits for the time to elapse) so the update commands are needed to force the widget to be redisplayed. Without the update commands no changes would appear on the screen until the script completed, at which point the widget's option would change to value2.

If you invoke update without the idletasks argument, all pending events are processed too. You might do this in the middle of a long calculation to allow the application to respond to user interactions (for example, the user might invoke a Cancel button to abort the calculation).

26.4 Information about widgets

The winfo command provides information about widgets. It has more than 40 different forms for retrieving different kinds of information. For example,

```
winfo exists .w
```

returns a 0 or 1 value to indicate whether widget .w exists;

```
winfo children .menu
```

returns a list whose elements are the children of .menu;

```
winfo screenmmheight .dialog
```

returns the height of .dialog's screen in millimeters; and

```
winfo class .w
```

returns the class of widget `.w` , such as `Button` or `Text`. Refer to the Tk reference documentation for details on all of the options provided by `winfo`.

26.5 Raise and lower

As mentioned in Section 15.1, a stacking order determines the layering of widgets on the screen. If two sibling widgets overlap, the stacking order determines which one appears on top of the other. Widgets are normally stacked in order of their creation: each new widget goes at the top of the stacking order, obscuring any of its siblings that were created before it. The `raise` and `lower` commands allow you to change the stacking order of widgets:

```
raise .w
raise .w .x
lower .w
lower .w .x
```

The first command raises `.w` so that it is at the top of the stacking order (it obscures all of its siblings). The second places `.w` just above `.x` in the stacking order. The third command lowers `.w` to the bottom of the stacking order (it is obscured by all of its siblings) and the last command places `.w` just below `.x` in the stacking order.

Note: *You can use `raise` and `lower` for top-level widgets as well as internal widgets, but this does not work for all window managers. Some window managers (in particular, some versions of `olwm` and `olvwm`) prevent applications from raising and lowering their top-level windows; with these window managers you must raise or lower top-level widgets manually using window manager functions.*

26.6 The tk command: color models

The `tk` command provides access to various aspects of Tk's internal state. At present only one aspect is accessible: the *color model*. At any given time Tk treats each screen as being either a color or monochrome screen; this is the screen's color model. When creating widgets, Tk uses different defaults for configuration options depending on the color model of the screen. If you specify a color other than black or white for a screen whose color model is monochrome, Tk rounds the color to either black or white.

Tk normally picks a color model for a screen based on the number of bits per pixel for that screen: if the screen has only a few bits per pixel (currently four or fewer) Tk uses a monochrome color model; if the screen has many bits per pixel, Tk treats the screen as color. You can invoke the `tk` command to change Tk's color model from the default. For example, the following command sets the color model for the main window's screen to monochrome:

```
tk colormodel . monochrome
```

If the color model for a screen is color and Tk finds itself unable to allocate a color for a window on that screen (e.g., because the colormap is full), Tk generates an error that is processed using the standard `tkerror` mechanism described in Section 18.8. Tk then changes the color model to monochrome and retries the allocation so the application can continue in monochrome mode. If the application finds a way to free up more colors, it can reset the color model back to color again.

26.7 Variables managed by Tk

Several global variables are significant to Tk, either because it sets them or because it reads them and adjusts its behavior accordingly. You may find the following variables useful:

`tk_version`	Set by Tk to its current version number. Has a form like 3.2, where 3 is the major version number and 2 is a minor version number. Changes in the major version number imply incompatible changes in Tk.
`tk_library`	Set by Tk to hold the path name of the directory containing a library of standard Tk scripts and demonstrations. This variable is set from the TK_LIBRARY environment variable, if it exists, or from a compiled-in default otherwise.
`tk_strictMotif`	If set to 1 by the application, Tk goes out of its way to observe strict Motif compliance. Otherwise Tk deviates slightly from Motif (e.g., by highlighting active elements when the mouse cursor passes over them).

In addition to these variables, which may be useful to the application, Tk also uses the associative array `tk_priv` to store information for its private use. Applications should not normally use or modify any of the values in `tk_priv`.

Chapter 27
Examples

This chapter presents two relatively complete examples that illustrate many of the features of Tk. The first example is a procedure that generates a dialog box, waits for the user to respond, and returns the user's response. The second example is an application that allows you to control other Tk applications remotely: it connects itself to an application so that you can type commands to the other application and see the results.

27.1 A procedure that generates dialog boxes

The first example is a Tcl procedure named `dialog` that creates dialog boxes like those shown in Figure 27.1. Each dialog contains a text message at the top plus an optional bitmap to the left of the text. At the bottom of the dialog box is a row containing any number of buttons. One of the buttons may be specified as the default button, in which case it is displayed in a sunken frame. `dialog` creates a dialog box of this form, then waits for the user to respond by clicking on a button. Once the user has responded, `dialog` destroys the dialog box and returns the index of the button that was invoked. If the user types a return and a default button was specified, the index of the default button is returned. `dialog` sets a grab so that the user must respond to the dialog box before interacting with the application in any other way.

Figures 27.2 and 27.3 show the Tcl code for `dialog`; the code is also available on-line in the file `dialog.tcl` in the Tk library area. `dialog` takes six or more arguments. The first argument, w, gives the name to use for the dialog's top-level window. The second argument, `title`, gives a title for the window manager to display in the dialog's decorative frame. The third argument, `text`, gives a message to display on the right side of the

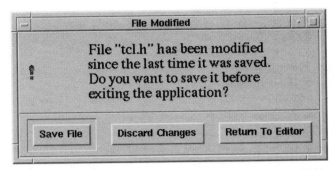

```
dialog .d {File Modified} {File "tcl.h" has been modified since\
    the last time it was saved. Do you want to save it before\
    exiting the application?} warning 0 {Save File} \
    {Discard Changes} {Return To Editor}
```

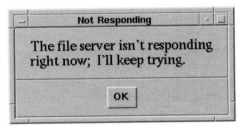

```
dialog .d {Not Responding} {The file server isn't responding\
    right now; I'll keep trying.} {} -1 OK
```

Figure 27.1. Two examples of dialog boxes created by the `dialog` procedure. Underneath each dialog box is the command that created it.

dialog. The fourth argument, `bitmap`, gives the name of a bitmap to display on the left side of the dialog; if it is specified as an empty string, then no bitmap is displayed. The fifth argument, `default`, gives the index of a default button, or −1 if there is to be no default button. The sixth and additional arguments contain the strings to display in the buttons.

The code for `dialog` divides into five major parts, each headed by a comment in the figures. The first part of the procedure creates the dialog's top-level window. It sets up information for the window manager, such as the title for the window's frame and the text to display in the dialog's icon. Then it creates two frames, one for the bitmap and message at the top of the dialog, and the other for the row of buttons at the bottom.

```
proc dialog {w title text bitmap default args} {
    global button

    # 1. Create the top-level window and divide it into top
    # and bottom parts.

    toplevel $w -class Dialog
    wm title $w $title
    wm iconname $w Dialog
    frame $w.top -relief raised -bd 1
    pack $w.top -side top -fill both
    frame $w.bot -relief raised -bd 1
    pack $w.bot -side bottom -fill both

    # 2. Fill the top part with the bitmap and message.

    message $w.top.msg -width 3i -text $text\
            -font -Adobe-Times-Medium-R-Normal-*-180-*
    pack $w.top.msg -side right -expand 1 -fill both\
            -padx 3m -pady 3m
    if {$bitmap != ""} {
        label $w.top.bitmap -bitmap $bitmap
        pack $w.top.bitmap -side left -padx 3m -pady 3m
    }

    # 3. Create a row of buttons at the bottom of the dialog.

    set i 0
    foreach but $args {
        button $w.bot.button$i -text $but -command\
                "set button $i"
        if {$i == $default} {
            frame $w.bot.default -relief sunken -bd 1
            raise $w.bot.button$i
            pack $w.bot.default -side left -expand 1\
                    -padx 3m -pady 2m
            pack $w.bot.button$i -in $w.bot.default\
                    -side left -padx 2m -pady 2m\
                    -ipadx 2m -ipady 1m
        } else {
            pack $w.bot.button$i -side left -expand 1\
                    -padx 3m -pady 3m -ipadx 2m -ipady 1m
        }
        incr i
    }
```

Figure 27.2. A Tcl procedure that generates dialog boxes with a text message, optional bitmap, and any number of buttons. Continued in Figure 27.3.

```
# 4. Set up a binding for <Return>, if there's a default,
# set a grab, and claim the focus too.

if {$default >= 0} {
    bind $w <Return> "$w.bot.button$default flash; \
        set button $default"
}
set oldFocus [focus]
grab set $w
focus $w

# 5. Wait for the user to respond, then restore the focus
# and return the index of the selected button.

tkwait variable button
destroy $w
focus $oldFocus
return $button
}
```

Figure 27.3. Procedure to generate dialog boxes, cont'd.

The second part of `dialog` creates a message widget to hold the dialog's text string and a label widget to hold its bitmap, if any. The widgets are packed on the right and left sides of the top frame, respectively.

The third part of the procedure creates the row of buttons. Since `args` was used as the name of the last argument to `dialog`, the procedure can take any number of arguments greater than or equal to five; `args` will be a list whose elements are all the additional arguments after `default`. For each of these arguments, `dialog` creates a button that displays the argument value as its text. The default button, if any, is packed in a special sunken ring (`$w.bot.default`). If a default ring is created, the `raise` command must be used to ensure that the button is displayed above the frame (without the `raise` command the frame will be on top of the button, since it is created later). The buttons are packed with the `-expand` option so that they spread themselves evenly across the width of the dialog box; if there is only a single button, then it is centered. Each button is configured so that when the user clicks on it the global variable `button` is set to the index of that button.

Note: *It is important that the value of the* `-command` *option be specified in quotes, not curly braces, so that* `$i` *(the button's index) is substituted into the command immediately. If the value were surrounded by braces, the value of* `$i` *wouldn't be substituted until the command is actually executed; this would use the value of global variable* i *(which might not even exist), not the variable* i *from the* `dialog` *procedure.*

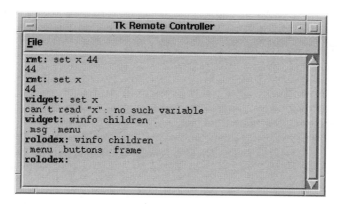

Figure 27.4. The rmt application allows a user to type interactively to any Tk application on the display. It contains a menu for selecting an application plus a text widget for typing commands and displaying results. In this example the user has issued commands to three different applications: first the rmt application itself, then an application named widget, and finally one named rolodex (the prompt on each command line indicates the name of the application that executed the command).

The fourth part of dialog (Figure 27.3) sets up a binding so that typing a return to the dialog box flashes the default button and sets the button variable just as if the button had been invoked. It also sets the input focus to the dialog box and sets a local grab on the dialog box to give it control over both the keyboard and the mouse.

The last part of the procedure waits for the user to interact with the dialog. It does this by waiting for the button variable to change value, which will happen when the user clicks on a button in the dialog box or types a return. When the tkwait command returns, the button variable contains the index of the selected button. dialog then destroys the dialog box (which also releases its grab), restores the input focus to its old window, and returns.

27.2 A remote-control application

The second example is an application called rmt, which allows you to type Tcl commands interactively to any Tk application on the display. Figure 27.4 shows what rmt looks like on the screen. It contains a menu that can be used to select an application plus a text widget and a scrollbar. At any given time rmt is "connected" to one application; lines that you type in the text widget are forwarded to the current application using send and the results are displayed in the text widget. rmt displays the name of the current application in the prompt at the beginning of each command line. You can change the current application by selecting an entry in the menu, in which case the prompt changes to display the new application's name. You can also type commands to the `rmt` application itself by selecting `rmt` as the current application. When `rmt` starts up it connects to itself.

The `wish` script that creates `rmt` is shown in Figures 27.5 through 27.8; it is also available on-line in the file `demos/rmt` in the Tk library area. The script is designed to be placed into a file and executed directly. It contains about 100 lines of Tcl code in all, which divide into seven major parts. It makes extensive use of the facilities of text widgets, including marks and tags.

The first part of the `rmt` script sets up the overall window structure, consisting of a menu bar, a text widget, and a scrollbar. It also passes information to the window manager, such as titles to appear in the window's decorative frame and icon. The command

```
wm minsize . 1 1
```

enables interactive resizing by the user as described in Section 22.1. Since the text widget has been packed with `-expand` set to 1 and `-fill` to `both`, any extra space created by the user goes to the text widget; since it is last in the packing order, it also shrinks if the user resizes the application to a smaller size. The `-setgrid` option for the text widget enables gridding as described in Section 22.2: interactive resizing always leaves the text widget with dimensions that are an integral number of characters.

The command

```
.t tag configure bold -font \
    -Adobe*-Courier-Bold-R-Normal-*-120-*
```

creates a tag named `bold` for the text widget and associates a bold font with that tag. The script applies this tag to the characters in the prompts so that they appear in boldface, whereas the commands and results appear in a normal font.

The second part of the script fills in the menu with two entries. The top entry displays a cascaded submenu with the names of all applications, and the bottom entry is a command entry that causes `rmt` to exit. The cascaded submenu is named `.mBar.file.m.apps`; its `-postcommand` option causes the script `fillApps-Menu` to be executed each time the submenu is posted on the screen. `fillAppsMenu` is a Tcl procedure defined near the bottom of Figure 27.5; it deletes any existing entries in the submenu, extracts the names of all applications on the display with `winfo interps`, and then creates one entry in the menu for each application name. When one of these entries is invoked by the user, the procedure `newApp` is invoked with the application's name as argument..

Note: *The command "`list newApp $i`" creates a Tcl list with two elements. As described in Section 6.7, when a list is executed as a command each element of the list becomes one word for the command. Thus this form guarantees that newApp is invoked with a single argument consisting of the value of $i at the time the menu entry is created, even if $i contains spaces or other special characters.*

The third part of the `rmt` script, shown in Figure 27.6, creates event bindings for the text widget. Tk defines several default bindings for texts, which handle mouse clicks, character

```
#!/usr/local/bin/wish -f

# 1. Create basic application structure:  menu bar on top of
# text widget, scrollbar on right.

frame .mBar -relief raised -bd 2
pack .mBar -side top -fill x
scrollbar .s -relief flat -command ".t yview"
pack .s -side right -fill y
text .t -relief raised -bd 2 -yscrollcommand ".s set" \
    -setgrid true
.t tag configure bold -font \
    Adobe-Courier-Bold-R-Normal-*-120-*
pack .t -side left -fill both -expand 1
wm title . "Tk Remote Controller"
wm iconname . "Tk Remote"
wm minsize . 1 1


# 2. Create menu button and menus.

menubutton .mBar.file -text File -underline 0\
        -menu .mBar.file.m
menu .mBar.file.m
.mBar.file.m add cascade -label "Select Application" \
    -underline 0 -accelerator => -menu .mBar.file.m.apps
.mBar.file.m add command -label "Quit" -underline 0 \
    -command exit
menu .mBar.file.m.apps -postcommand fillAppsMenu
pack .mBar.file -side left
tk_menuBar .mBar .mBar.file

proc fillAppsMenu {} {
    catch {.mBar.file.m.apps delete 0 last}
    foreach i [lsort [winfo interps]] {
        .mBar.file.m.apps add command -label $i \
            -command [list newApp $i]
    }
}
```

Figure 27.5. A script that generates `rmt`, an application for remotely controlling other Tk applications. This figure contains basic window setup code. The script continues in Figures 27.6, Figure 27.7, and 27.8.

insertion, and common editing keystrokes such as backspace. However, `rmt`'s text widget has different behavior than that provided by the default bindings, so the code in Figure 27.6 overrides many of the defaults. You don't need to understand the details of the bindings; they have been copied from the defaults in Tk's startup script (file `tk.tcl` in the Tk

```
# 3. Create bindings for text widget to allow commands to
# be entered and information to be selected.  New characters
# can only be added at the end of the text (can't ever move
# insertion point).

bind .t <1> {
    set tk_priv(selectMode) char
    .t mark set anchor @%x,%y
    if {[lindex [%W config -state] 4] == "normal"} {focus %W}
}
bind .t <Double-1> {
    set tk_priv(selectMode) word
    tk_textSelectTo .t @%x,%y
}
bind .t <Triple-1> {
    set tk_priv(selectMode) line
    tk_textSelectTo .t @%x,%y
}
bind .t <Return> {.t insert insert \n; invoke}
bind .t <BackSpace> backspace
bind .t <Control-h> backspace
bind .t <Delete> backspace
bind .t <Control-v> {
    .t insert insert [selection get]
    .t yview -pickplace insert
    if [string match *.0 [.t index insert]] {
        invoke
    }
}
```

Figure 27.6. Bindings for the rmt application. These are modified versions of the default Tk bindings, so they use existing Tk facilities such as the variable tk_priv and the procedure tk_textSelectTo.

library area) and modified so that (a) the user can't move the insertion cursor (it always has to be at the end of the text), (b) the procedure backspace is invoked instead of Tk's normal text backspace procedure, and (c) the procedure invoke is called whenever the user types a return or copies in text that ends with a newline.

The fourth part of the rmt script is a procedure called backspace. It implements backspacing in a way that disallows backspacing over the prompt (see Figure 27.7). backspace checks to see if the character just before the insertion cursor is the last character of the most recent prompt. If not, it deletes the character; if so, it does nothing, so that the prompt never gets erased. To keep track of the most recent prompt, rmt sets a mark named promptEnd at the position of the last character in the most recent prompt (see the prompt procedure given later for the code that sets promptEnd).

```
# 4. Procedure to backspace over one character, as long as
# the character isn't part of the prompt.

proc backspace {} {
    if {[.t index promptEnd]
            != [.t index {insert - 1 char}]} {
        .t delete {insert - 1 char} insert
        .t yview -pickplace insert
    }
}

# 5. Procedure that's invoked when return is typed:  if
# there's not yet a complete command (e.g. braces are open)
# then do nothing.  Otherwise, execute command (locally or
# remotely), output the result or error message, and issue
# a new prompt.

proc invoke {} {
    global app
    set cmd [.t get {promptEnd + 1 char} insert]
    if [info complete $cmd] {
        if {$app == [winfo name .]} {
            catch [list uplevel #0 $cmd] msg
        } else {
            catch [list send $app $cmd] msg
        }
        if {$msg != ""} {
            .t insert insert $msg\n
        }
        prompt
    }
    .t yview -pickplace insert
}

proc prompt {} {
    global app
    .t insert insert "$app: "
    .t mark set promptEnd {insert - 1 char}
    .t tag add bold {insert linestart} promptEnd
}
```

Figure 27.7. Procedures for backspacing, executing commands, and outputting prompts for rmt.

The fifth part of the rmt script handles command invocation; it consists of two procedures, invoke and prompt (Figure 27.7). The invoke procedure is called whenever a newline character is added to the text widget, either because the user typed a return or because the selection was copied into the widget and it ended with a newline. invoke

```
# 6. Procedure to select a new application.  Also changes
# the prompt on the current command line to reflect the new
# name.

proc newApp appName {
    global app
    set app $appName
    .t delete {promptEnd linestart} promptEnd
    .t insert promptEnd "$appName:"
    .t tag add bold {promptEnd linestart} promptEnd
}

# 7. Miscellaneous initialization.

set app [winfo name .]
prompt
focus .t
```

Figure 27.8. Code to select a new application for rmt, plus miscellaneous initialization code.

extracts the command from the text widget (everything from the end of the prompt to the current insertion point) and then invokes info complete to make sure that the command is complete. If the command contains unmatched braces or unmatched quotes, invoke returns without executing the command so the user can enter the rest of the command; after each return is typed invoke checks again, and after the command is complete it is invoked. The command is invoked by executing it locally or sending it to the appropriate application. If the command returns a non-empty string (either as a normal result or as an error message), the string is added to the end of the text widget. Finally, invoke outputs a new prompt and scrolls the view in the text to keep the insertion cursor visible.

The prompt procedure is responsible for outputting prompts. It just adds characters to the text widget, sets the promptEnd mark to the last character in the prompt, and then applies the bold tag to all the characters in the prompt so that they'll appear in a bold font.

The sixth part of the rmt script consists of the newApp procedure in Figure 27.8. newApp is invoked to change the current application. It sets the global variable app, which identifies the current application, then overwrites the most recent prompt to display the new application's name.

The last part of rmt consists of miscellaneous initialization (see Figure 27.8). It connects the application to itself initially, outputs the initial prompt, and sets the input focus to the text window.

Part III:

Writing Tcl Applications in C

Chapter 28
Philosophy

Given a choice between implementing a particular piece of functionality as a Tcl script or as C code, it is generally better to implement it as a script, using `wish` or `tclsh`, for example. Scripts are usually easier to write, they can be modified dynamically, and you can debug them more quickly because you don't have to recompile after each bug fix. However, there are three reasons why it is sometimes better to implement a new function in C. First, you may need to access low-level facilities that aren't accessible in Tcl scripts. For example, the Tcl built-in commands do not provide access to network sockets, so if you want to talk to a network at this level you will have to write C code to do it. Second, you may be concerned about efficiency. For example, if you need to peform intensive numerical calculations or operate on large arrays of data, you will be able to do it more efficiently in C than in Tcl. The third reason for implementing in C is complexity. If you are manipulating complex data structures or writing a large amount of code, the task will probably be more manageable in C than in Tcl. Tcl provides very little structure; this makes it easy to connect different things together but hard to manage large complex scripts. C provides more structure, which is cumbersome when you're implementing small things but indispensable when you're implementing big complicated things.

This part of the book describes how to write C code that extends an existing application or creates a whole new application. A Tcl application consists of the Tcl library plus some application-specific code, as shown in Figure 28.1. The Tcl library includes a parser for Tcl scripts, procedures to execute all of the core commands such as `set` and `if`, and a set of utility procedures for use in accessing Tcl variables, parsing arguments, manipulating Tcl lists, evaluating Tcl expressions, and so on.

The application-specific code consists of three parts. Most of the code will consist of procedures to implement new Tcl commands. The second piece of application code per-

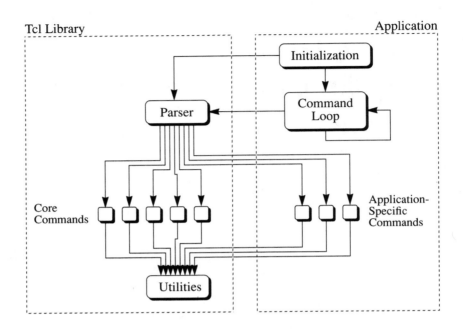

Figure 28.1. The Tcl library provides a parser for the Tcl language, a set of core commands, and several utility procedures. The application provides additional commands plus procedures to collect scripts for evaluation. The scripts are evaluated by Tcl and then passed to command procedures (either in Tcl or the application) for execution.

forms initializations such as registering the application's new commands with the Tcl parser. The third part of the application is a command loop that collects Tcl scripts and passes them to the Tcl parser for evaluation. For example, tclsh reads commands from standard input or from a file; wish also allows scripts to be associated with X events and evaluates the scripts when the corresponding events occur. When the Tcl parser receives a script, it parses it, performs substitutions, and then invokes a procedure (either in Tcl or in the application) to execute each command.

This chapter discusses several high-level issues to consider when designing a Tcl application, such as what new Tcl commands to implement, how to name objects, and what form to use for command results. The following chapters present the specific C interfaces provided by the Tcl library. The information in this part of the book applies to both Tcl and Tk applications. For example, to create a new Tk widget, you will need to create new Tcl commands with the facilities described here.

28.1   C vs. Tcl: primitives

To make a Tcl application as flexible and powerful as possible, you should organize its C code as a set of new Tcl commands that provide a clean set of *primitive operations*. You need not implement every imaginable feature in C, since new features can always be implemented later as Tcl scripts. The purpose of the C code is to provide basic operations that make it easy to implement a wide variety of useful scripts. If your C code lumps several functions together into a single command, it will not be possible to write scripts that use the functions separately and your application will not be very flexible or extensible. Instead, each command should provide a single function and you should combine them with Tcl scripts. You will probably find that many of your application's essential features are implemented as scripts.

As an example of the trade-offs between C and Tcl, consider a program to manipulate weather reports. Suppose that information about current weather is available for a large number of measurement stations from one or more network sites using a well-defined network protocol, and you want to write a Tcl application to manipulate this information. Users of your application might wish to answer questions such as:

- What is the complete weather report for station X?

- What is the current temperature at station X?

- Which station in the country has the highest current temperature?

- At which stations is it currently raining?

You'll need to write some C code for this application in order to retrieve weather reports over the network. What form should these new commands take?

One approach is to implement each of the functions in C as a separate Tcl command. For example, you might provide a command that retrieves the weather report from a station, formats it into prose, and prints it on standard output. Unfortunately this command can be used for only one purpose; you would have to provide a second command for situations where you want to retrieve a report without printing it out (for example, to find all the stations where it is raining).

Instead, I would implement just one new command in C, called `weather`. The first argument to `weather` is either `stations` or `report`: `weather stations` returns a list of all the stations for which weather reports are available, and `weather report` returns a complete weather report for a particular station given by an additional argument. The `weather` command doesn't directly answer any of the preceding questions, but it makes it easy to answer them all. For example, Tcl already has a `puts` command that can be used to print information on standard output, so the first feature (printing a weather report for a station) can be implemented with a script that calls `weather report`, formats the report, and prints it with `puts`. The second feature (printing just the temperature) can be implemented by extracting the temperature from the result of `weather report` and then printing it alone. The third and fourth features (finding the hottest station and

finding all stations where it is raining) can be implemented with scripts that invoke
`weather report` for each station and extract and print relevant information. Many
other features could also be implemented as Tcl scripts, such as printing a sorted list of the
10 stations with the highest temperatures.

The preceding paragraph suggests that lower level commands are better than higher
level ones. However, if the commands are at too low a level, Tcl scripts will become
unnecessarily complicated and you may lose opportunities for efficient implementation.
For example, instead of providing a single command that retrieves a weather report, you
might provide separate Tcl commands for each step of the protocol that retrieves a report:
one command to connect to a server, one command to select a particular station, one command to request a report for the selected station, and so on. Although this results in more
primitive commands, it is probably a mistake. The extra commands don't provide any
additional functionality and they make it more tedious to write Tcl scripts. Furthermore,
suppose that network communication delays are high, so that it takes a long time to get a
response from a weather server, but the server allows you to request reports for several
stations at once and get them all back in about the same time as a single report. In this situation you might want an even higher level interface, perhaps a Tcl command that takes
any number of stations as arguments and retrieves reports for all of them at once. This
would allow the C code to amortize the communication delays across several report
retrievals and it might permit a much more efficient implementation of operations such as
finding the station with the highest temperature.

To summarize, you should pick commands that are primitive enough so that all of the
application's key functions are available individually through Tcl commands. On the other
hand, you should pick commands that are at a high enough level to hide unimportant
details and capitalize on opportunities for efficient implementation.

28.2 Object names

The easiest way to think about your C code is in terms of *objects*. The C code in a Tcl
application typically implements a few new kinds of objects, which are manipulated by
the application's new Tcl commands. In the C code of your application you will probably
refer to the objects using pointers to the C structures that represent the objects, but you
can't use pointers in Tcl scripts. String names will have to be used in the Tcl scripts and the
C code that implements your commands will have to translate from those strings to internal pointers. For example, the objects in the weather application are weather stations; the
`weather stations` command returns a list of station names, and the
`weather report` command takes a station name as an argument.

I recommend using names that convey meaningful information to humans. For example, Tk uses hierarchical path names like `.menu.help` for widgets; the name of the widget indicates its position in the widget hierarchy. Tcl uses names like `file3` or `file4`
for open files; these names don't convey a lot of information, but they at least include the

letters `file` to suggest that they're used for file access, and the number is the POSIX file descriptor number for the open file. For the weather application I'd recommend using the official U.S. Weather Service station names, such as `SFO` or `LAX`. Or, if those turn out to be too cryptic, I recommend using something more readable like city names.

The easiest way to manage object names is with hash tables. With this approach you create one hash table for each kind of object, and the hash table maps from object names to C structure pointers. When you create a new object you enter its name into the hash table along with the address of its C structure. When the name is used later to manipulate the object, you look the name up in the hash table to find the corresponding C structure. This approach allows you to format names in any way you wish, and it detects any attempt to use a nonexistent name. The Tcl library implements flexible hash tables that make it easy for you to use this approach (see Chapter 35).

28.3 Commands: action-oriented vs. object-oriented

There are two approaches you can use when defining commands in your application, which I call *action-oriented* and *object-oriented*. In the action-oriented approach there is one command for each action that can be taken on an object, and the command takes an object name as an argument. The weather application is action-oriented: the `weather report` command corresponds to an action (retrieve weather report) and it takes a weather station name as an argument. Tcl's file commands are also action-oriented: there are separate commands for opening files, reading, writing, closing, etc.

In the object-oriented approach there is one command for each object, and the name of the command is the name of the object. When the command is invoked its first argument specifies the operation to perform on the object. Tk's widgets work this way: if there is a button widget `.b`, there is also a command named `.b`; you can invoke `.b flash` to flash the widget or `.b invoke` to evaluate its Tcl script.

The action-oriented approach is best when there are a great many objects or the objects are unpredictable or short-lived. For example, it wouldn't make sense to implement string operations using an object-oriented approach because there would have to be one command for each string, and in practice Tcl applications have large numbers of strings that are created and deleted continuously. The weather application uses the action-oriented approach because there are only a few actions and potentially a large number of stations. In addition, the application probably doesn't need to maintain information for each station all the time; it uses the station name to look up weather information when requested.

The object-oriented approach works well when the number of objects isn't too great (e.g., a few tens or hundreds) and the objects are well defined and exist for at least moderate amounts of time. Tk's widgets fit this description. The object-oriented approach has the advantage that it doesn't pollute the command name space with lots of commands for individual actions. For example, in the action-oriented approach the command `delete` might be defined for one kind of object, thereby preventing its use for any other kind of object. In the object-oriented approach you need only ensure that your object names don't conflict with existing commands or other object names. For example, Tk claims all command names starting with . for its widget commands. The object-oriented approach also makes it possible for different objects to implement the same action in different ways. For example, if .t is a text widget and .l is a listbox widget in Tk, the commands ".t yview 0" and ".l yview 0" are implemented in very different ways even though they produce the same logical effect (adjust the view to make the topmost line visible at the top of the window).

Note: *Although Tcl's file commands are implemented using the action-oriented approach, in retrospect I wish that I had used the object-oriented model, since open files fit that model nicely.*

28.4 Representing information

The information passed into and out of your Tcl commands should be formatted for easy processing by Tcl scripts, not necessarily for maximum human readability. For example, the command that retrieves a weather report shouldn't return English prose describing the weather. Instead, it should return the information in a structured form that makes it easy to extract the different components under the control of a Tcl script. You might return the report as a list consisting of pairs of elements, where the first element of each pair is a keyword and the second element is a value associated with that keyword, such as:

```
temp 53 hi 68 lo 37 precip 0.02 sky part
```

This indicates that the current temperature at the station is 53 degrees, the high and low for the last 24 hours were 68 and 37 degrees, 0.02 inches of rain has fallen in the last 24 hours, and the sky is partly cloudy. Or, the command might store the report in an associative array where each keyword is used as the name of an array element and the corresponding value is stored in that element. Either of these approaches would make it easy to extract components of the report. You can always reformat the information to make it more readable before displaying it to the user.

On the other hand, you should not gratuitously sacrifice readability. For example, the above list could have been encoded as

```
53 68 37 0.02 4
```

where the first element is always the current temperature, the second and third elements are the 24-hour high and low, and so on. In this case the last element represents the sky conditions numerically, where 4 means partly cloudy. This approach is unnecessarily confusing and will not make your scripts any more efficient, since Tcl stores numbers as strings anyway.

In some cases, the easiest way to represent information is with Tcl scripts that can be evaluated. For example, if an application needs to save its state in a disk file, I suggest formatting the file as a Tcl script. This allows you to reload the state simply by `sourceing` the file.

Chapter 29
Interpreters and Script Evaluation

This chapter describes how to create and delete interpreters and how to use them to evaluate Tcl scripts. Table 29.1 summarizes the library procedures discussed in this chapter.

29.1 Interpreters

The central data structure manipulated by the Tcl library is a C structure of type `Tcl_Interp`. I'll refer to these structures (or pointers to them) as *interpreters*. Almost all of the Tcl library procedures take a pointer to a `Tcl_Interp` structure as an argument. An interpreter embodies the execution state of a Tcl script, including commands implemented in C, Tcl procedures, variables, and an execution stack that reflects partially evaluated commands and Tcl procedures. Most Tcl applications use only a single interpreter but it is possible for a single process to manage several independent interpreters; for example, if an editor application is displaying several different files, it might make sense to use a separate interpreter for each file.

29.2 A simple Tcl application

The following program illustrates how to create and use an interpreter. It is a simple but complete Tcl application that evaluates a Tcl script stored in a file and prints the result or error message, if any.

```
Tcl_Interp *Tcl_CreateInterp(void)
            Creates a new interpreter and returns a token for it.
void Tcl_DeleteInterp(Tcl_Interp *interp)
            Deletes an interpreter.
```
```
int Tcl_Eval(Tcl_Interp *interp, char *script)
            Evaluates script in interp and returns its completion code. A result or
            error string will be in interp->result.
int Tcl_EvalFile(Tcl_Interp *interp, char *fileName)
            Evaluates the contents of file fileName in interp and returns its
            completion code. A result or error string will be in interp->result.
int Tcl_GlobalEval(Tcl_Interp *interp, char *script)
            Evaluates script in interp at the global level and returns its completion
            code. A result or error string will be in interp->result.
int Tcl_VarEval(Tcl_Interp *interp, char *string,
    char *string, ... (char *) NULL)
            Concatenates all of the string arguments into a single string, evaluates
            the resulting script in interp, and returns its completion code. A result or
            error string will be in interp->result.
int Tcl_RecordAndEval(Tcl_Interp *interp, char *script,
    int flags)
            Records script as an event in interp's history list and evaluates it if
            flags is zero (TCL_NO_EVAL means don't evaluate the script). Returns a
            completion code such as TCL_OK and leaves a result or error message in
            interp->result.
```

Table 29.1. Tcl library procedures for creating and deleting interpreters and for evaluating Tcl scripts.

```
/* simple.c -- Tcl application to evaluate script file. */
#include <stdio.h>
#include <stdlib.h>
#include <tcl.h>

main(int argc, char *argv[]) {
    Tcl_Interp *interp;
    int code;

    if (argc != 2) {
        fprintf(stderr, "Wrong # arguments: ");
        fprintf(stderr, "should be \"%s fileName\"\n",
                argv[0]);
        exit(1);
    }

    interp = Tcl_CreateInterp();
    code = Tcl_EvalFile(interp, argv[1]);
    if (*interp->result != 0) {
```

```
            printf("%s\n", interp->result);
        }
    if (code != TCL_OK) {
        exit(1);
    }
    exit(0);
}
```

If Tcl has been installed properly at your site, you can copy this C code into a file named `simple.c` and compile it with the following shell command:

```
cc simple.c -ltcl -lm
```

After you've compiled the program you can evaluate a script file `test.tcl` by typing the following command to your shell:

```
a.out test.tcl
```

The code for `simple.c` starts out with `#include` statements for `stdio.h` and `tcl.h`. You'll need to include `tcl.h` in every file that uses Tcl structures or procedures, because it defines structures such as `Tcl_Interp` and declares the Tcl library procedures. After checking to be sure that a file name was specified on the command line, the program invokes `Tcl_CreateInterp` to create a new interpreter. The new interpreter will contain all of the built-in commands described in Part I but no Tcl procedures or variables. It will have an empty execution stack. `Tcl_CreateInterp` returns a pointer to the `Tcl_Interp` structure for the interpreter, which is used as a token for the interpreter when calling other Tcl procedures. Most of the fields of the `Tcl_Interp` structure are hidden so that they cannot be accessed outside the Tcl library. The only accessible fields are those that describe the result of the last script evaluation; they'll be discussed shortly.

Next `simple.c` calls `Tcl_EvalFile` with the interpreter and the name of the script file as arguments. `Tcl_EvalFile` reads the file and evaluates its contents as a Tcl script, just as if you had invoked the Tcl `source` command with the file name as an argument. When `Tcl_EvalFile` returns, the execution stack for the interpreter will once again be empty.

`Tcl_EvalFile` returns two pieces of information: an integer *completion code* and a string. The completion code is returned as the result of the procedure. It will be either `TCL_OK`, which means that the script completed normally, or `TCL_ERROR`, which means that an error of some sort occurred (for example, the script file couldn't be read or the script aborted with an error). The second piece of information returned by `Tcl_Eval-File` is a string, a pointer to which is returned in `interp->result`. If the completion code is `TCL_OK`, `interp->result` points to the script's result; if the completion code is `TCL_ERROR`, `interp->result` points to a message describing the error.

Note: *The result string belongs to Tcl. It may or may not be dynamically allocated. You can read it and copy it, but you should not modify it and you should not save pointers to it. There is always a valid string pointed to by* `interp->result`, *but Tcl may overwrite the string or reallocate its memory during the next call to* `Tcl_EvalFile` *or any of the other procedures that evaluate scripts. Chapter 30 discusses the result string in more detail.*

If the result string is nonempty, `simple.c` prints it, regardless of whether it is an error message or a normal result. Then the program exits. It follows the UNIX style of exiting with a status of 1 if an error occurred and 0 if it completed successfully.

When the script file is evaluated only the built-in Tcl commands are available: no Tk commands will be available in this application and no application-specific commands have been defined.

29.3   Other evaluation procedures

Tcl provides three other procedures besides `Tcl_EvalFile` for evaluating scripts. Each of these procedures takes an interpreter as its first argument and each returns a completion code and string just like `Tcl_EvalFile`. `Tcl_Eval` is similar to `Tcl_EvalFile` except that its second argument is a Tcl script rather than a file name:

```
char cmd[] = "set a 44";
...
code = Tcl_Eval(interp, cmd);
```

For various arcane reasons, the script passed to `Tcl_Eval` must be writable (`Tcl_Eval` may make temporary modifications to it, which it undoes before returning). This is the reason for creating the script as an initialized character array in this example; if the second argument to `Tcl_Eval` is `"set a 44"` instead of `cmd` and your compiler places constant strings in read-only memory, then a core dump will occur.

`Tcl_VarEval` takes a variable number of string arguments terminated with a NULL argument. It concatenates the strings and evaluates the result as a Tcl script. For example, the following statement has the same effect as the previous one:

```
code = Tcl_VarEval(interp, "set a ", "44",
        (char *) NULL);
```

`Tcl_GlobalEval` is similar to `Tcl_Eval` except that it evaluates the script at global variable context (as if the execution stack were empty) even when procedures are active. It is used in special cases such as the `uplevel` command and Tk's event bindings.

If you want a script to be recorded on the Tcl history list, call `Tcl_RecordAnd-Eval` instead of `Tcl_Eval`:

```
char *script;
int code;
...
code = Tcl_RecordAndEval(interp, script, 0);
```

`Tcl_RecordAndEval` is identical to `Tcl_Eval` except that it records the script as a new entry on the history list before invoking it. Tcl records only the scripts passed to `Tcl_RecordAndEval`, so you can select which ones to record. Typically you'll record only commands that were typed interactively. The last argument to `Tcl_RecordAndEval` is normally 0; if you specify `TCL_NO_EVAL` instead, Tcl will record the script without actually evaluating it.

Each call to a procedure such as `Tcl_Eval` or `Tcl_VarEval` must be for a complete script. For example, the following code fragment will not work:

```
char part1[] = "set ";
char part2[] = "a ";
char part3[] = "44";
Tcl_Eval(interp, part1);
Tcl_Eval(interp, part2);
Tcl_Eval(interp, part3);
```

This code attempts to execute a single Tcl command by passing it in pieces to `Tcl_Eval`. However, `Tcl_Eval` will attempt to process each piece as a self-contained script. This will result in an error in the first piece because no arguments are given to `set`, and errors in the second and third pieces because there are no commands named a or 44. In this particular case `Tcl_VarEval` should be used instead:

```
code = Tcl_VarEval(interp, part1, part2, part3,
    (char *) NULL);
```

Of course, there is still a single call to evaluate the entire command, but `Tcl_VarEval` allows you to specify the command in multiple pieces.

29.4   Deleting interpreters

The procedure `Tcl_DeleteInterp` may be called to destroy an interpreter and all its associated state. It is invoked with an interpreter as argument:

```
Tcl_DeleteInterp(interp);
```

Once `Tcl_DeleteInterp` returns you should never use the interpreter again. In applications like `simple.c`, which use a single interpreter throughout their lifetime, there is no need to delete the interpreter, because the `exit` call at the end of the main program implicitly destroys all of the program's structures under POSIX.

Chapter 30
Creating New Tcl Commands

Each Tcl command is implemented by a *command procedure* written in C. When a Tcl command is invoked during script evaluation, Tcl calls its command procedure to carry out the command. This chapter provides basic information on how to write command procedures, how to register command procedures in an interpreter, and how to manage the interpreter's result string. Table 30.1 summarizes the Tcl library procedures discussed in this chapter.

30.1 Command procedures

The interface to a command procedure is defined by the `Tcl_CmdProc` procedure prototype:

```
typedef int Tcl_CmdProc(ClientData clientData,
        Tcl_Interp *interp, int argc, char *argv[]);
```

A command procedure is invoked when its corresponding Tcl command is executed, and it is passed four arguments. The first, `clientData`, is discussed in Section 30.5. The second, `interp`, is the interpreter in which the command was executed. The third and fourth arguments have the same meaning as the `argc` and `argv` arguments to a C main program: `argc` specifies the total number of words in the Tcl command and `argv` is an array of pointers to the values of the words. Tcl processes all the special characters such as $ and [] before invoking command procedures so the values in `argc` reflect any substitutions that were specified for the command. The command name is included in `argc` and `argv`, and `argv[argc]` is NULL. A command procedure returns two values, just like

```
void Tcl_CreateCommand(Tcl_Interp *interp, char *cmdName,
     Tcl_CmdProc *cmdProc, ClientData clientData,
     Tcl_CmdDeleteProc *deleteProc)
```
> Defines a new command in interp with name cmdName. When the command is invoked cmdProc will be called with clientData as argument; if the command is ever deleted, deleteProc will be called.

```
int Tcl_DeleteCommand(Tcl_Interp *interp, char *cmdName)
```
> If cmdName is a command or procedure in interp, then deletes it and returns 0. Otherwise returns -1.

```
void Tcl_SetResult(Tcl_Interp *interp, char *string,
     Tcl_FreeProc *freeProc)
```
> Arranges for string (or a copy of it) to become the result for interp. freeProc identifies a procedure to call to eventually free the result, or it may be TCL_STATIC, TCL_DYNAMIC, or TCL_VOLATILE.

```
void Tcl_AppendResult(Tcl_Interp *interp, char *string,
     char *string, ... (char *) NULL)
```
> Appends each of the string arguments to the current result string in interp.

```
void Tcl_AppendElement(Tcl_Interp *interp, char *string)
```
> Formats string as a Tcl list element and appends it to the result string in interp, with a preceding separator space if needed.

```
void Tcl_ResetResult(Tcl_Interp *interp)
```
> Resets interp's result to the default empty state, freeing up any dynamically allocated memory associated with it.

Table 30.1. Tcl library procedures for creating and deleting commands and for manipulating the result string.

Tcl_Eval and Tcl_EvalFile. It returns an integer completion code such as TCL_OK or TCL_ERROR as its result and leaves a result string or error message in interp->result.

Here is the command procedure for a new command called eq that compares its two arguments for equality:

```
int EqCmd(ClientData clientData, Tcl_Interp *interp,
        int argc, char *argv[]) {
    if (argc != 3) {
        interp->result = "wrong # args";
        return TCL_ERROR;
    }
    if (strcmp(argv[1], argv[2]) == 0) {
        interp->result = "1";
    } else {
        interp->result = "0";
    }
    return TCL_OK;
}
```

EqCmd checks to see that it was called with exactly two arguments (three words, including the command name), and if not it stores an error message in interp->result and returns TCL_ERROR. Otherwise it compares its two argument strings and stores a string in interp->result to indicate whether or not they were equal; then it returns TCL_OK to indicate that the command completed normally. EqCmd does not use its clientData argument, but this argument plays an important role in many other Tcl commands, as you will see shortly.

Note: *A command procedure should treat the contents of the argv array as read-only. In general it is not safe for a command procedure to modify these strings.*

30.2 Registering commands

In order for a command procedure to be invoked by Tcl, you must register it by calling Tcl_CreateCommand. Here is the simple program from Section 29.2, augmented with a call to Tcl_CreateCommand:

```
/* simple2.c -- define new command, then evaluate script. */
#include <stdio.h>
#include <tcl.h>

main(int argc, char *argv[]) {
    Tcl_Interp *interp;
    int code;

    if (argc != 2) {
        fprintf(stderr, "Wrong # arguments: ");
        fprintf(stderr, "should be \"%s fileName\"\n",
                argv[0]);
        exit(1);
    }

    interp = Tcl_CreateInterp();
    Tcl_CreateCommand(interp, "eq", EqCmd,
            (ClientData) NULL, (Tcl_CmdDeleteProc *) NULL);
    code = Tcl_EvalFile(interp, argv[1]);
    if (*interp->result != 0) {
        printf("%s\n", interp->result);
    }
    if (code != TCL_OK) {
        exit(1);
    }
    exit(0);
}
```

The first argument to Tcl_CreateCommand identifies the interpreter in which the command will be used. The second argument specifies the name for the command and the third argument specifies its command procedure. The fourth and fifth arguments are discussed in Section 30.5; they can be specified as NULL for simple commands like this one. Tcl_CreateCommand creates a new command for interp named eq; if a command by that name already exists, it is silently deleted. Whenever eq is invoked in interp, Tcl will call EqCmd to carry out its function.

If the code for EqCmd is included in the same file with the main procedure, it can be compiled and invoked just like the simple program in Section 29.2. However, scripts for this application can use the new eq command:

```
    eq abc def
⇒   0
    eq 1 1
⇒   1
    set w .dlg
    set w2 .dlg.ok
    eq $w.ok $w2
⇒   1
```

When processing scripts, Tcl carries out all of the command-line substitutions before calling the command procedure, so when EqCmd is called for the last eq command above both argv[1] and argv[2] are .dlg.ok.

Tcl_CreateCommand is usually called by applications during initialization to register application-specific commands. In addition, new commands can be created at any time while an application is running. For example, the proc command creates a new command for each Tcl procedure that is defined, and Tk creates a widget command for each new widget. In Sections 30.5 and 30.7 you will see examples where the command procedure for one command creates a new command.

Commands created by Tcl_CreateCommand are indistinguishable from Tcl's built-in commands. Each built-in command has a command procedure with the same form as EqCmd, and you can redefine a built-in command by calling Tcl_CreateCommand with the name of the command and a new command procedure.

30.3 The result protocol

The EqCmd procedure returns a result by setting interp->result to point to a static string. However, the result string can also be managed in several other ways. Tcl defines a protocol for setting and using the result, which allows for dynamically allocated results and provides a small static area to avoid memory-allocation overheads in simple cases.

The full definition of the Tcl_Interp structure, as visible outside the Tcl library, is

```
typedef struct Tcl_Interp {
    char *result;
    Tcl_FreeProc *freeProc;
    int errorLine;
} Tcl_Interp;
```

The first field, `result`, points to the interpreter's current result. The second field, `freeProc`, is used when freeing dynamically allocated results; it will be discussed later. The third field, `errorLine`, is related to error handling and is described in Section 33.2.

When Tcl invokes a command procedure the `result` and `freeProc` fields always have well-defined values. `interp->result` points to a small character array that is part of the interpreter structure and the array has been initialized to hold an empty string (one whose first character is zero, i.e., `""`). `interp->freeProc` is zero. This state is referred to as the *initialized state* for the result. Not only is this the state of the result when command procedures are invoked, but many Tcl library procedures also expect the interpreter's result to be in the initialized state when they are invoked. If a command procedure wishes to return an empty string as its result, it simply returns without modifying `interp->result` or `interp->freeProc`.

A command procedure can specify a nonempty result in three ways. First, it can modify `interp->result` to point to any string whose value will not change before the next Tcl command procedure is invoked. This might be a static string as in EqCmd or a dynamically allocated string. For example, Tk stores the name of each widget in a dynamically allocated record associated with the widget, and it returns widget names by setting `interp->result` to the name string in the widget record. This string is dynamically allocated, but widgets are deleted only by Tcl commands so the string is guaranteed not to be recycled before the next Tcl command executes. If a string is stored in automatic storage associated with the command procedure, you should not return its address in `interp->result`, since the value of the string will change as soon as some other procedure reuses the stack space.

The second way to set a result is to use the preallocated space in the `Tcl_Interp` structure. In its initialized state `interp->result` points to this space. If a command procedure wishes to return a small result it can copy it to the location pointed to by `interp->result`. For example, the following procedure implements a command `numwords` that returns a decimal string giving a count of its arguments:

```
int NumwordsCmd(ClientData clientData,
        Tcl_Interp *interp, int argc, char *argv[]) {
    sprintf(interp->result, "%d", argc);
    return TCL_OK;
}
```

The size of the preallocated space is guaranteed to be at least 200 bytes; you can retrieve the exact size with the symbol `TCL_RESULT_SIZE` defined by `tcl.h`. It is generally safe to use this area for printing a few numbers and/or short strings, but it is *not* safe to copy long strings to the preallocated space.

The third way to set a result is to allocate memory with a storage allocator such as `malloc`, store the result string there, and set `interp->result` to the address of the memory. To ensure that the memory is eventually freed, you must also set `interp->freeProc` to the address of a procedure that Tcl can call to free the memory, such as `free`. In this case the dynamically allocated memory becomes the property of Tcl. After Tcl has finished using the result, it will free it by invoking the procedure specified by `interp->freeProc`. This procedure must match the following procedure prototype:

```
typedef void Tcl_FreeProc(char *blockPtr);
```

The procedure will be invoked with a single argument containing the address that you stored in `interp->result`. In most cases you will use `malloc` for dynamic allocation and thus set `interp->freeProc` to `free`, but the mechanism is general enough to support other storage allocators too.

30.4 Procedures for managing the result

Tcl provides several library procedures for manipulating the result. These procedures all obey the protocol described in the previous section, and you may find them more convenient than setting `interp->result` and `interp->freeProc` directly. The first procedure is `Tcl_SetResult`, which simply implements the protocol just described. For example, EqCmd could have replaced the statement

```
interp->result = "wrong # args";
```

with a call to `Tcl_SetResult` as follows:

```
Tcl_SetResult(interp, "wrong # args", TCL_STATIC);
```

The first argument to `Tcl_SetResult` is an interpreter. The second argument is a string to use as result, and the third argument gives additional information about the string. `TCL_STATIC` means that the string is static, so `Tcl_SetResult` just stores its address into `interp->result`. A value of `TCL_VOLATILE` for the third argument means that the string is about to change (for example, it is stored in the procedure's stack frame) so a copy must be made for the result. `Tcl_SetResult` will copy the string into the preallocated space if it fits, otherwise it will allocate new memory to use for the result and copy the string there (setting `interp->freeProc` appropriately). If the third argument is `TCL_DYNAMIC` it means that the string was allocated with `malloc` and should become the property of Tcl: `Tcl_SetResult` will set `interp->freeProc` to `free` as described earlier. Finally, the third argument may be the address of a procedure suitable for use in `interp->freeProc`; in this case the string is dynamically allocated and Tcl will eventually call the specified procedure to free it.

The second procedure for managing the result is `Tcl_AppendResult`, which makes it easy to build up results in pieces. It takes any number of strings as arguments and appends them to the interpreter's result in order. As the result grows in length `Tcl_Ap-`

pendResult allocates new memory for it. `Tcl_AppendResult` may be called repeatedly to build up long results incrementally, and it does this efficiently even if the result becomes very large (for example, it allocates extra memory so that it doesn't have to copy the existing result into a larger area on each call). Here is an implementation of the `concat` command that uses `Tcl_AppendResult`:

```
int ConcatCmd(ClientData clientData,
        Tcl_Interp *interp, int argc, char *argv[]) {
    int i;
    if (argc == 1) {
        return TCL_OK;
    }
    Tcl_AppendResult(interp, argv[1], (char *) NULL);
    for (i = 2; i < argc; i++) {
        Tcl_AppendResult(interp, " ", argv[i],
                (char *) NULL);
    }
    return TCL_OK;
}
```

The `NULL` argument in each call to `Tcl_AppendResult` marks the end of the strings to append. Since the result is initially empty, the first call to `Tcl_AppendResult` just sets the result to `argv[1]`; each additional call appends one more argument preceded by a separator space.

`Tcl_AppendElement` is similar to `Tcl_AppendResult` except that it adds only one string to the result at a time and it appends it as a list element instead of a raw string. It's useful for creating lists. For example, here is a simple implementation of the `list` command:

```
int ListCmd(ClientData clientData, Tcl_Interp *interp,
        int argc, char *argv[]) {
    int i;
    for (i = 1; i < argc; i++) {
        Tcl_AppendElement(interp, argv[i]);
    }
    return TCL_OK;
}
```

Each call to `Tcl_AppendElement` adds one argument to the result. The argument is converted to a proper list element before appending it to the result (for example, it is enclosed in braces if it contains space characters). `Tcl_AppendElement` also adds a separator space if it is needed before the new element (no space is added if the result is currently empty or if its characters are " {", which means that the new element will be the first element of a sublist). For example, if `ListCmd` is invoked with four arguments, `list`, `abc`, `x y`, and `}`, it produces the following result:

```
abc {x y} \}
```

Like `Tcl_AppendResult`, `Tcl_AppendElement` enlarges the result space if needed and does it in a way that is efficient even for large results and repeated calls.

If you set the result for an interpreter and then decide that you want to discard it (for example, an error has occurred and you want to replace the current result with an error message), you should call the procedure `Tcl_ResetResult`. It will invoke `interp->freeProc` if needed and restore the interpreter's result to its initialized state. You can then store a new value in the result in any of the usual ways. You need not call `Tcl_ResetResult` if you're going to use `Tcl_SetResult` to store the new result, because `Tcl_SetResult` takes care of freeing any existing result.

30.5 ClientData and deletion callbacks

The fourth and fifth arguments to `Tcl_CreateCommand`, `clientData` and `deleteProc`, were not discussed in Section 30.2 but they are useful when commands are associated with objects. The `clientData` argument is used to pass a one-word value to a command procedure (typically the address of the C data structure for an object). Tcl saves the `clientData` value and uses it as the first argument to the command procedure. The type `ClientData` is large enough to hold either an integer or a pointer value.

`clientData` values are used in conjunction with *callback procedures*. A callback is a procedure whose address is passed to a Tcl library procedure and saved in a Tcl data structure. Later, at some significant time, the address is used to invoke the procedure ("call it back"). A command procedure is an example of a callback: Tcl associates the procedure address with a Tcl command name and calls the procedure whenever the command is invoked. When a callback is specified in Tcl or Tk a `clientData` argument is provided along with the procedure address and the `clientData` value is passed to the callback as its first argument.

The `deleteProc` argument to `Tcl_CreateCommand` specifies a deletion callback. If its value isn't NULL, it is the address of a procedure for Tcl to invoke when the command is deleted. The procedure must match the following prototype:

```
typedef void Tcl_CmdDeleteProc(ClientData clientData);
```

The deletion callback takes a single argument, which is the `clientData` value specified when the command was created. Deletion callbacks are used for purposes such as freeing the object associated with a command.

Figure 30.1 shows how `clientData` and `deleteProc` can be used to implement counter objects. The application containing this code must register `CounterCmd` as a Tcl command using the following call:

```
Tcl_CreateCommand(interp, "counter", CounterCmd,
        (ClientData) NULL, (Tcl_CmdDeleteProc *) NULL);
```

New counters can then be created by invoking the `counter` Tcl command; each invocation creates a new object and returns a name for that object:

```
counter
```
⇒ *ctr0*

```
typedef struct {
    int value;
} Counter;

int CounterCmd(ClientData clientData, Tcl_Interp *interp,
        int argc, char *argv[]) {
    Counter *counterPtr;
    static int id = 0;
    if (argc != 1) {
        interp->result = "wrong # args";
        return TCL_ERROR;
    }
    counterPtr = (Counter *) malloc(sizeof(Counter));
    counterPtr->value = 0;
    sprintf(interp->result, "ctr%d", id);
    id++;
    Tcl_CreateCommand(interp, interp->result, ObjectCmd,
            (ClientData) counterPtr, DeleteCounter);
    return TCL_OK;
}

int ObjectCmd(ClientData clientData, Tcl_Interp *interp,
        int argc, char *argv[]) {
    Counter *counterPtr = (Counter *) clientData;
    if (argc != 2) {
        interp->result = "wrong # args";
        return TCL_ERROR;
    }
    if (strcmp(argv[1], "get") == 0) {
        sprintf(interp->result, "%d", counterPtr->value);
    } else if (strcmp(argv[1], "next") == 0) {
        counterPtr->value++;
    } else {
        Tcl_AppendResult(interp, "bad counter command \"",
                argv[1], "\": should be get or next",
                (char *) NULL);
        return TCL_ERROR;
    }
    return TCL_OK;
}

void DeleteCounter(ClientData clientData) {
    free((char *) clientData);
}
```

Figure 30.1. An implementation of counter objects.

```
     counter
⇒  ctr1
```

`CounterCmd` is the command procedure for `counter`. It allocates a structure for the new counter and initializes its value to zero. Then it creates a name for the counter using the static variable `id`, arranges for that name to be returned as the command's result, and increments `id` so that the next new counter will get a different name.

This example uses the object-oriented style described in Section 28.3, where there is one command for each counter object. As part of creating a new counter, `CounterCmd` creates a new Tcl command named after the counter. It uses the address of the `Counter` structure as the `clientData` for the command and specifies `DeleteCounter` as the deletion callback for the new command.

Counters can be manipulated by invoking the commands named after them. Each counter supports two options to its command: `get`, which returns the current value of the counter, and `next`, which increments the counter's value. Once `ctr0` and `ctr1` are created as shown earlier, the following Tcl commands can be invoked:

```
     ctr0 next; ctr0 next; ctr0 get
⇒  2
     ctr1 get
⇒  0
     ctr0 clear
⇒  bad counter command "clear": should be get or next
```

The procedure `ObjectCmd` implements the Tcl commands for all existing counters. It is passed a different `clientData` argument for each counter, which it casts back to a value of type `Counter *`. `ObjectCmd` checks `argv[1]` to see which command option was invoked. If it was `get`, it returns the counter's value as a decimal string; if it was `next`, it increments the counter's value and leaves `interp->result` untouched so that the result is an empty string. If an unknown command was invoked, `ObjectCmd` calls `Tcl_AppendResult` to create an error message.

Note: *It is not safe to create the error message with a statement like*

```
     sprintf(interp->result, "bad counter command \"%s\": "
            "should be get or next", argv[1]);
```

This is unsafe because `argv[1]` has unknown length. It could be so long that `sprintf` overflows the space allocated in the interpreter and corrupts memory . `Tcl_AppendResult` is safe because it checks the lengths of its arguments and allocates as much space as needed for the result.

To destroy a counter from Tcl you can delete its Tcl command, for example:

```
     rename ctr0 {}
```

As part of deleting the command Tcl will invoke `DeleteProc`, which frees up the memory associated with the counter.

This object-oriented implementation of counter objects is similar to Tk's implementation of widgets: there is one Tcl command to create a new instance of a counter or widget, and one Tcl command for each existing counter or widget. A single command procedure implements all of the counter or widget commands for a particular type of object, receiving a `clientData` argument that identifies a specific counter or widget. A different mechanism is used to delete Tk widgets than for counters above, but in both cases the command corresponding to the object is deleted at the same time as the object.

30.6 Deleting commands

Tcl commands can be removed from an interpreter by calling `Tcl_DeleteCommand`. For example, the statement below will delete the `ctr0` command in the same way as the `rename` command used earlier:

```
Tcl_DeleteCommand(interp, "ctr0");
```

If the command has a deletion callback, it will be invoked before the command is removed. Any command may be deleted, including built-in commands, application-specific commands, and Tcl procedures.

30.7 How Tcl procedures work

All Tcl commands, including those in the Tcl core such as `set`, `if`, and `proc`, use the mechanism described in this chapter. For example, consider the creation and execution of a Tcl procedure:

```
proc inc x {expr $x+1}
inc 23
```
⇒ *24*

Figure 30.2 shows the flow of control in these two commands. When the `proc` command is evaluated, Tcl invokes its command procedure. The `proc` command procedure is part of the Tcl library but it has the same arguments and results described in Section 30.1. The `proc` command procedure allocates a new data structure to describe `inc`, including information about `inc`'s arguments and body. Then the `proc` command procedure invokes `Tcl_CreateCommand` to create the Tcl command for `inc`. It specifies a special procedure called `InterpProc` (which is part of the Tcl library) as the command procedure for `inc`, and it uses the address of the new data structure as the `clientData` for the command. Then the `proc` command procedure returns.

When the `inc` command is evaluated Tcl invokes `InterpProc` as the command procedure for the command. `InterpProc` uses its `clientData` argument to gain access to the data structure for `inc`, then invokes `Tcl_Eval` to evaluate `inc`'s body. Before calling `Tcl_Eval`, `InterpProc` creates a new variable scope for the procedure,

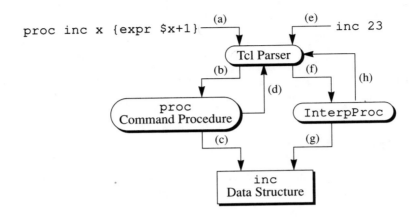

Figure 30.2. The creation and invocation of a Tcl procedure: (a) the `proc` command is invoked; (b) the Tcl parser invokes the command procedure associated with `proc`; (c) the `proc` command procedure creates a data structure to hold the Tcl script that is `inc`'s body; (d) `inc` is registered as a new Tcl command; (e) `inc` is invoked; (f) the Tcl parser invokes `InterpProc` as the command procedure for `inc`; (g) `InterpProc` retrieves the body of `inc` from the data structure; and (h) the body of `inc` is passed to `Tcl_Eval` for evaluation.

uses its `argv` argument to retrieve the first argument to the `inc` command, and assigns this value to the `x` variable in the new scope. When the `Tcl_Eval` call completes, `InterpProc` destroys the procedure's variable scope and returns the completion code from `Tcl_Eval`.

All Tcl procedures have `InterpProc` as their command procedure. However, each Tcl procedure has a different `clientData`, which refers to the structure for that procedure.

Chapter 31
Tcl_AppInit and Packages

Section 29.2 explained how you can create a new Tcl application by writing a `main` procedure that calls `Tcl_CreateInterp` and invokes Tcl scripts in that interpreter. If you want to include additional Tcl commands in such an application, you can do so by calling `Tcl_CreateCommand` to register the commands, as described in Section 30.2.

However, in most cases you'll probably want to include your new commands in an existing Tcl application such as `tclsh` or `wish`. These applications have fancier main procedures that provide many useful features. For example, the `main` procedure for `tclsh` copies its command-line arguments into Tcl variables and reads commands interactively from standard input if desired. The `main` procedure for `wish` also provides these functions, and in addition it creates a Tk application including a main widget.

This chapter discusses the procedure `Tcl_AppInit`, which makes it easy to reuse the existing main program for `tclsh` or `wish` while adding a few new Tcl commands of your own. The chapter also describes how to organize a related set of commands as a *package* that you can distribute to other people for incorporation into their applications.

31.1 Tcl_AppInit

`Tcl_AppInit` is a procedure that performs application-specific initialization, such as creating new commands. The `main` procedures for `tclsh` and `wish` invoke `Tcl_App-Init` after they have peformed all of their own initializations but before they start evaluating Tcl scripts (Figure 31.1). The overall idea is for the procedure `main` to carry out functions that are the same in all `tclsh`-like (or `wish`-like) applications, while `Tcl_AppInit` carries out the functions that may differ from application to application.

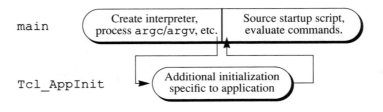

Figure 31.1. Tcl_AppInit is invoked by main just before it starts evaluating Tcl commands; the same main procedure is used by many different applications, with different versions of Tcl_AppInit for each application.

The version of Tcl_AppInit used by tclsh looks like this:

```
int Tcl_AppInit(Tcl_Interp *interp) {
    if (Tcl_Init(interp) == TCL_ERROR) {
        return TCL_ERROR;
    }
    tcl_RcFileName = "~/.tclshrc";
    return TCL_OK;
}
```

Tcl_AppInit is invoked with a single argument consisting of the Tcl interpreter for the application. If Tcl_AppInit completes normally it returns TCL_OK, and if it encounters an error it returns TCL_ERROR and leaves an error message in interp->result (in this case the application will print the error message and exit). This particular version of Tcl_AppInit does two things. First it calls the procedure Tcl_Init, which performs additional Tcl initialization (it sources a script from the Tcl library to define the unknown procedure and set up the autoloading mechanism). The argument and result for Tcl_Init are the same as those for Tcl_AppInit. The second thing done by Tcl_AppInit is to set the global variable tcl_RcFileName, which gives the name of a user-specific startup script. This variable is initially set to NULL by main; if Tcl_AppInit modifies tcl_RcFileName, and if the application is running interactively (rather than from a script file), then main will source the file named by tcl_RcFileName.

To create a new Tcl application, all you have to do is write your Tcl_AppInit procedure and compile it with the Tcl library. For example, you can regenerate the tclsh application by making yourself a copy of the file tclAppInit.c from the Tcl source directory, which contains the preceding code for Tcl_AppInit. Then compile this file and link it with the Tcl library:

```
cc tclAppInit.c -ltcl -lm -o mytclsh
```

The resulting application will be identical to the system version of tclsh: it will support interactive input, script files, and all of the other features of tclsh.

Note: This example assumes that Tcl has been installed in the standard way on your system.

Note: If you type the code for Tcl_AppInit into a file instead of copying tclAppInit.c from the Tcl source directory, you'll need to add the following lines before the procedure declaration:

```
#include "tcl.h"
extern int main();
int *tclDummyMainPtr = (int *) main;
```

The last two lines are needed on many systems to force the linker to include the main procedure from the Tcl library.

Now suppose that you wish to define two additional Tcl commands, cmd1 and cmd2, in your application, and that the resulting application is to be called myapp. You can do this by copying tclAppInit.c to myAppInit.c and replacing the Tcl_AppInit code with the following code:

```
int Cmd1Proc(ClientData clientData, Tcl_Interp *interp,
        int argc, char *argv[]) {
... implementation of cmd1 ...
}

int Cmd2Proc(ClientData clientData, Tcl_Interp *interp,
        int argc, char *argv[]) {
... implementation of cmd2 ...
}

int Tcl_AppInit(Tcl_Interp *interp) {
    if (Tcl_Init(interp) == TCL_ERROR) {
        return TCL_ERROR;
    }
    Tcl_CreateCommand(interp, "cmd1", Cmd1Proc,
            (ClientData) NULL, (Tcl_CmdDeleteProc *) NULL);
    Tcl_CreateCommand(interp, "cmd2", Cmd2Proc,
            (ClientData) NULL, (Tcl_CmdDeleteProc *) NULL);
    tcl_RcFileName = "~/.myapprc";
    return TCL_OK;
}
```

This code differs from the Tcl_AppInit code given previously in three ways. First, there are two extra procedures, Cmd1Proc and Cmd2Proc. These are the command procedures for the new commands. Second, there are two calls to Tcl_CreateCommand in Tcl_AppInit, which register the new commands in interp. Finally, this version of Tcl_AppInit sets tcl_RcFileName to ~/.myapprc so that the new application has a different user startup file from tclsh.

The following command will compile this new application:

```
cc myAppInit.c -ltcl -lm -o myapp
```

This will produce an executable named myapp that is just like tclsh except that it has the new commands cmd1 and cmd2 and it reads a different user startup file.

You can do several other things in `Tcl_AppInit` besides register new commands. First, you can evaluate an application-specific Tcl script by calling `Tcl_Eval` or `Tcl_EvalFile`. Second, you can process command-line arguments, which are available through the following Tcl variables:

argv0
: If the application was invoked to run interactively, this holds the name of the application, such as `tclsh` or `wish` or `myapp`; if a script file was specified when the application was invoked, this holds the name of the script file.

argv
: A Tcl list containing all of the command-line arguments except the command name (element 0 is the argument immediately after the command name).

argc
: The number of elements in `argv`.

You can access these variables either by evaluating a Tcl script or directly from C by invoking the library procedures `Tcl_GetVar` and `Tcl_SplitList`, which are described in Sections 34.3 and 32.3, respectively. Third, you can omit the call to `Tcl_Init` if you want a bare-bones application that doesn't have things like autoloading. The last thing you might wish to do in `Tcl_AppInit` is initialize additional packages. This is described in Section 31.2.

If you want to add your new commands to `wish` instead of `tclsh`, you should use the same approach except start from the file `tkAppInit.c` in the Tk source directory instead of `tclAppInit.c`. The version of `Tcl_AppInit` in `tkAppInit.c` contains a call to `Tk_Init` for Tk-specific initialization (this procedure just sources Tk's startup script, which creates the default class bindings). You'll also have to link with the Tk and X libraries:

```
cc myAppInit.c -ltk -ltcl -lX11 -lm -o myapp
```

This will produce an application just like `wish` except for the presence of your new commands.

31.2 Defining packages

The previous section described how to use `Tcl_AppInit` if your new commands are intended for use only in a single application. However, it is much better if you can implement new commands in a general-purpose way so they can be used in many different Tcl applications. Ideally you will even distribute your new commands freely, like Tcl and Tk, so that they can be used by other people in the Tcl community. To do this, you should structure the new commands as a *package*.

A package consists of the command procedures that implement a set of related Tcl commands, plus any supporting code needed by them. To make it easy for other people to use your package and to allow many different packages to be used together in a single Tcl application, you should take three extra steps when writing your package: use name prefixes, write an initialization procedure, and support multiple interpreters. These issues are discussed separately in the rest of this section.

31.2.1 Package prefixes

Package prefixes make it possible for a single application to incorporate many different packages without experiencing naming conflicts. For example, suppose that you are writing a package to provide access to a relational database, and that it must include a procedure that opens a connection to a database server. It would be a bad idea to name the procedure Open; this name is so generic that it is likely to be used in some other package too, in which case it wouldn't be possible to use both packages in the same application. Instead, use a name like Rdb_Open where Rdb_ is the package prefix; use the same prefix for every other global name in the package too. Package prefixes help to avoid name conflicts between packages: as long as two packages have different prefixes, they can be used together in a single application without conflicts between their names.

Here are some conventions that I recommend you follow when choosing and using prefixes. These conventions are used internally by Tcl and Tk and many packages.

- Choose prefixes that are moderately short (3 to 6 characters) and end in an underscore, like Rdb_. Try to avoid totally generic prefixes like File_, since these may be used by someone else too.

- For global procedures and types, capitalize only the first letter of the prefix, as in Rdb_Open or Nfs_FileHandle. Capitalize the letter after the prefix and the first letter of each additional word of the name, such as the H in Nfs_FileHandle.

- If you must use global variables, don't capitalize any of the letters in the prefix, as in nfs_NumOpenFiles.

- If a variable or procedure is only used internally in your package, declare it static; in this case you can use whatever name you wish, since it won't conflict with global names.

- If your package is split among several files and there are internal variables or procedures that need to be used in all of the files, these variables and procedures can't be declared static (if they are, they'll be usable only in a single file). For these names, use a prefix but omit the underscore, such as RdbCheckAccess. Alternatively, you can move the underscore to the beginning of the name, as in _RdbCheckAccess. This convention makes it easy to tell which features of your applications are exported and which ones are for internal use only.

- Use the same prefix for the Tcl commands provided by your package, except all lowercase, as in rdb_query. If a package provides only a single Tcl command, you can just use the prefix as the name of the command, as in rdb.

- For Tcl command procedures, name the procedure after the command, except with capitalization as described earlier in this list and a Cmd suffix. For example, the command procedure for the rdb_query command should have the name Rdb_QueryCmd.

31.2.2 Package initialization procedures

For each package there should be one C procedure that is invoked to initialize the package in an existing Tcl interpreter. This procedure is called the *package initialization procedure*. Its name should consist of the package prefix followed by Init, as in Rdb_Init. Package initialization procedures should take a single argument consisting of a Tcl interpreter and they should return a Tcl completion code, just like Tcl_AppInit. For example, here is a hypothetical initialization procedure for the Rdb package:

```
int Rdb_Init(Tcl_Interp *interp) {
    Tcl_CreateCommand(interp, "rdb_connect",
            Rdb_ConnectCmd, (ClientData) NULL,
            (Tcl_CmdDeleteProc *) NULL);
    Tcl_CreateCommand(interp, "rdb_query",
            Rdb_QueryCmd, (ClientData) NULL,
            (Tcl_CmdDeleteProc *) NULL);
    ...
    return Tcl_EvalFile(interp,
            "/usr/local/lib/rdb/init.tcl");
}
```

This procedure does two things. First, it registers all of the commands provided by the package. Second, it sources a startup script associated with the package. Many packages will not need to have startup scripts, in which case the call to Tcl_EvalFile can be omitted from the initialization procedure. However, if a package defines Tcl procedures in addition to commands, you'll need to source a startup script to create the procedures (or modify auto_path so that they can be autoloaded). Alternatively, you can include a Tcl script as a string in the code of your package and evaluate it with Tcl_Eval.

If you have defined an initialization procedure for your package, all that needs to be done to use your package in a Tcl application is to call its initialization procedure in Tcl_AppInit and include the package's object file(s) when linking. For example, here is the Tcl_AppInit for a Tcl application that uses the Rdb package:

```
int Tcl_AppInit(Tcl_Interp *interp) {
    if (Tcl_Init(interp) == TCL_ERROR) {
        return TCL_ERROR;
    }
    if (Rdb_Init(interp) == TCL_ERROR) {
        return TCL_ERROR;
    }
    tcl_RcFileName = "~/.myapprc";
    return TCL_OK;
}
```

The complete application can then be compiled with a command such as

```
cc myAppInit.c rdb.o -ltcl -lm -o myapp
```

(this assumes that the Rdb package has already been compiled into the object file
`rdb.o`). If an application uses several packages, its `Tcl_AppInit` invokes each of their
initialization procedures and all of their object files are included when the application is
compiled.

31.2.3   Multiple interpreters

Although most Tcl applications have only a single interpreter, some applications will use
more than one. Because of this, you should design your packages to work in an environment containing several intepreters. If a package is used in multiple interpreters, its initialization procedure will be called once for each interpreter. If there are certain initializations
that you don't wish to redo for each interpreter (such as initializating data structures that
will be shared among interpreters), you must keep track of the fact that these structures
have already been initialized.

    If you wish to keep separate state information for each interpreter, you should not use
global variables for this, since they will be shared among all the interpreters. Instead, use
the `clientData` for the Tcl commands to hold a pointer to the state information for the
particular interpreter. For example, suppose the Rdb package is to keep separate information about open connections for each interpreter in which it is used. The package might
then include code like the following:

```
typedef struct RdbInfo {
    int numOpenConnections;
    ... other state information for interpreter ...
} RdbInfo;

int Rdb_Init(Tcl_Interp *interp) {
    RdbInfo *rdbPtr;
    rdbPtr = (RdbInfo *) malloc(sizeof(RdbInfo));
    rdbPtr->numOpenConnections = 0;
    ... initialize other fields of structure ...
    Tcl_CreateCommand(interp, "rdb_connect",
            Rdb_ConnectCmd, (ClientData) rdbPtr,
            (Tcl_CmdDeleteProc *) NULL);
    Tcl_CreateCommand(interp, "rdb_query",
            Rdb_QueryCmd, (ClientData) rdbPtr,
            (Tcl_CmdDeleteProc *) NULL);
    ... register other commands ...
    return Tcl_EvalFile(interp,
            "/usr/local/lib/rdb/init.tcl");
}
```

```
int Rdb_ConnectCmd(ClientData clientData, Tcl_Interp *interp,
        int argc, char *argv[]) {
    RdbInfo *rdbPtr;
    rdbPtr = (RdbInfo *) clientData;
    ...
}
...
```

The RdbInfo structure is private to the Rdb package. It holds all of the state information for a single interpreter, such as the number of connections open in that interpreter. When the package is initialized for an interpreter, a new RdbInfo structure is allocated and initialized. The address of this structure is used as the clientData for all of the Rdb commands in the interpreter. When a particular command is invoked, such as rdb_connect, the command procedure casts its clientData argument back into a pointer to an RdbInfo structure, then uses the information in the structure to carry out the command. There is a different RdbInfo structure for each interpreter.

Chapter 32
Parsing

This chapter describes Tcl library procedures for parsing and evaluating strings in various forms such as integers, expressions and lists. These procedures are typically used by command procedures to process the words of Tcl commands. See Table 32.1 for a summary.

32.1 Numbers and Booleans

Tcl provides three procedures for parsing numbers and Boolean values: `Tcl_GetInt`, `Tcl_GetDouble`, and `Tcl_GetBoolean`. Each of these procedures takes three arguments: an interpreter, a string, and a pointer to a place to store the value of the string. Each of the procedures returns `TCL_OK` or `TCL_ERROR` to indicate whether the string was parsed successfully. For example, this command procedure uses `Tcl_GetInt` to implement a `sum` command:

```
int SumCmd(ClientData clientData, Tcl_Interp *interp,
        int argc, char *argv[]) {
    int num1, num2;
    if (argc != 3) {
        interp->result = "wrong # args";
        return TCL_ERROR;
    }
    if (Tcl_GetInt(interp, argv[1], &num1) != TCL_OK) {
        return TCL_ERROR;
    }
    if (Tcl_GetInt(interp, argv[2], &num2) != TCL_OK) {
```

```
int Tcl_GetInt(Tcl_Interp *interp, char *string, int *intPtr)
          Parses string as an integer, stores value at *intPtr, and returns
          TCL_OK. If an error occurs while parsing, returns TCL_ERROR and stores an
          error message in interp->result.
int Tcl_GetDouble(Tcl_Interp *interp, char *string,
    double *doublePtr)
          Same as Tcl_GetInt except parses string as a floating-point value and
          stores value at *doublePtr.
int Tcl_GetBoolean(Tcl_Interp *interp, char *string, int *intPtr)
          Same as Tcl_GetInt except parses string as a Boolean and stores 0/1
          value at *intPtr. See Table 32.2 for legal values for string.
```

```
int Tcl_ExprString(Tcl_Interp *interp, char *string)
          Evaluates string as an expression, stores value as string in
          interp->result, and returns TCL_OK. If an error occurs during
          evaluation, returns TCL_ERROR and stores an error message in
          interp->result.
int Tcl_ExprLong(Tcl_Interp *interp, char *string,
    long *longPtr)
          Same as Tcl_ExprString except stores value as a long integer at
          *longPtr. An error occurs if the value can't be converted to an integer.
int Tcl_ExprDouble(Tcl_Interp *interp, char *string,
    double *doublePtr)
          Same as Tcl_ExprString except stores value as double-precision
          floating-point value at *doublePtr. An error occurs if the value can't be
          converted to a floating-point number.
int Tcl_ExprBoolean(Tcl_Interp *interp, char *string,
    int *intPtr)
          Same as Tcl_ExprString except stores value as 0/1 integer at *intPtr.
          An error occurs if the value can't be converted to a Boolean value.
```

```
int Tcl_SplitList(Tcl_Interp *interp, char *list, int *argcPtr,
    char ***argvPtr)
          Parses list as a Tcl list and creates an array of strings whose values are
          the elements of list. Stores count of number of list elements at *argcPtr
          and pointer to array at *argvPtr. Returns TCL_OK. If an error occurs
          while parsing list, returns TCL_ERROR and stores an error message in
          interp->result. Space for string array is dynamically allocated; caller
          must eventually pass *argvPtr to free.
char *Tcl_Merge(int argc, char **argv)
          Inverse of Tcl_SplitList. Returns pointer to Tcl list whose elements are
          the members of argv. Result is dynamically allocated; caller must
          eventually pass it to free.
```

Table 32.1. A summary of Tcl library procedures for parsing and expression evaluation.

```
        return TCL_ERROR;
    }
    sprintf(interp->result, "%d", num1+num2);
    return TCL_OK;
}
```

SumCmd expects each of the command's two arguments to be an integer. It calls
`Tcl_GetInt` to convert them from strings to integers, sums the values, and converts the
result back to a decimal string in `interp->result`. `Tcl_GetInt` accepts strings in
decimal (e.g., `492`), hexadecimal (e.g., `0x1ae`), or octal (e.g., `017`) formats, and allows
them to be signed and preceded by white space. If the string is in one of these formats,
`Tcl_GetInt` returns TCL_OK and stores the value of the string in the location pointed
to by its last argument. If the string can't be parsed correctly, `Tcl_GetInt` stores an
error message in `interp->result` and returns TCL_ERROR; in this case SumCmd
returns TCL_ERROR to its caller with `interp->result` still pointing to the error message from `Tcl_GetInt`.

Here are some examples of invoking the `sum` command in Tcl scripts:

```
    sum 2 3
```
⇒ *5*
```
    sum 011 0x14
```
⇒ *29*
```
    sum 3 6z
```
⇒ *expected integer but got "6z"*

`Tcl_GetDouble` is similar to `Tcl_GetInt` except that it expects the string to
consist of a floating-point number such as `-2.2` or `3.0e-6` or `7`. It stores the double-precision value of the number at the location given by its last argument or returns an error in
the same way as `Tcl_GetInt`. `Tcl_GetBoolean` is similar except that it converts
the string to a 0 or 1 integer value, which it stores at the location given by its last argument. Any of the true values listed in Table 32.2 converts to 1 and any of the false values
converts to 0.

True Values	False Values
1	0
true	false
on	off
yes	no

Table 32.2. Legal values for Boolean strings parsed by `Tcl_GetBoolean`. Any of the values may
be abbreviated or capitalized.

Many other Tcl and Tk library procedures are similar to `Tcl_GetInt` in the way they use an `interp` argument for error reporting. These procedures all expect the interpreter's result to be in its initialized state when they are called. If they complete successfully, they leave the result in its initialized state (or, in a few cases, they return an answer in `interp->result`); if an error occurs, they put an error message in `interp->result`. The procedures' return values indicate whether they succeeded, usually as a `TCL_OK` or `TCL_ERROR` completion code but sometimes in other forms such as a `NULL` string pointer. When an error occurs, all the caller needs to do is return a failure itself, leaving the error message in the interpreter's result.

32.2 Expression evaluation

Tcl provides four library procedures that evaluate expressions of the form described in Chapter 5: `Tcl_ExprString`, `Tcl_ExprLong`, `Tcl_ExprDouble`, and `Tcl_ExprBoolean`. These procedures are similar except that they return the result of the expression in different forms as indicated by their names. Here is a command procedure that uses `Tcl_ExprString` to implement a simplified version of the `expr` command that allows only a single argument:

```
int ExprCmd(ClientData clientData, Tcl_Interp *interp,
        int argc, char *argv[]) {
    if (argc != 2) {
        interp->result = "wrong # args";
        return TCL_ERROR;
    }
    return Tcl_ExprString(interp, argv[1]);
}
```

`ExprCmd` merely checks its argument count and then calls `Tcl_ExprString`. `Tcl_ExprString` evaluates its second argument as a Tcl expression and returns the value as a string in `interp->result`. Like `Tcl_GetInt`, it returns `TCL_OK` if it evaluated the expression successfully; if an error occurs, it leaves an error message in `interp->result` and returns `TCL_ERROR`.

`Tcl_ExprLong`, `Tcl_ExprDouble`, and `Tcl_ExprBoolean` are similar to `Tcl_ExprString` except that they return the expression's result as a long integer, double-precision floating-point number, or 0/1 integer, respectively. Each of the procedures takes an additional argument that points to a place to store the result. For these procedures the result must be convertible to the requested type. For example, if abc is passed to `Tcl_ExprLong`, `Tcl_ExprLong` will return an error because abc has no integer value. If the string 40 is passed to `Tcl_ExprBoolean` it will succeed and store 1 in the value word (any nonzero integer is considered to be true).

32.3 **Manipulating lists**

Tcl provides several procedures for manipulating lists, of which the most useful are
Tcl_SplitList and Tcl_Merge. Given a string in the form of a Tcl list,
Tcl_SplitList extracts the elements and returns them as an array of string pointers.
For example, here is an implementation of Tcl's lindex command that uses
Tcl_SplitList:

```
int LindexCmd(ClientData clientData,
        Tcl_Interp *interp, int argc, char *argv[]) {
    int index, listArgc;
    char **listArgv;
    if (argc != 3) {
        interp->result = "wrong # args";
        return TCL_ERROR;
    }
    if (Tcl_GetInt(interp, argv[2], &index) != TCL_OK) {
        return TCL_ERROR;
    }
    if (Tcl_SplitList(interp, argv[1], &listArgc,
            &listArgv) != TCL_OK) {
        return TCL_ERROR;
    }
    if ((index >= 0) && (index < listArgc)) {
        Tcl_SetResult(interp, listArgv[index],
                TCL_VOLATILE);
    }
    free((char *) listArgv);
    return TCL_OK;
}
```

LindexCmd checks its argument count, calls Tcl_GetInt to convert argv[2] (the
index) into an integer, then calls Tcl_SplitList to parse the list. Tcl_SplitList
returns a count of the number of elements in the list to listArgc. It also creates an array
of pointers to the values of the elements and stores a pointer to that array in listArgv. If
Tcl_SplitList encounters an error in parsing the list (for example, unmatched
braces), it returns TCL_ERROR and leaves an error message in interp->result; otherwise it returns TCL_OK.

Tcl_SplitList calls malloc to allocate space for the array of pointers and for
the string values of the elements; the caller must free up this space by passing listArgv
to free. The space for both pointers and strings is allocated in a single block of memory
so only a single call to free is needed. LindexCmd calls Tcl_SetResult to copy the
desired element into the interpreter's result. It specifies TCL_VOLATILE to indicate that
the string value is about to be destroyed (its memory will be freed); Tcl_SetResult
will make a copy of the listArgv[index] for interp's result. If the specified index
is outside the range of elements in the list, LindexCmd leaves interp->result in its
initialized state, which returns an empty string.

Tcl_Merge is the inverse of Tcl_SplitList. Given argc and argv information describing the elements of a list, it returns a malloc'ed string containing the list. Tcl_Merge always succeeds so it doesn't need an interp argument for error reporting. Here is an implementation of the list command that uses Tcl_Merge:

```
int ListCmd2(ClientData clientData, Tcl_Interp *interp,
        int argc, char *argv[]) {
    interp->result = Tcl_Merge(argc-1, argv+1);
    interp->freeProc = (Tcl_FreeProc *) free;
    return TCL_OK;
}
```

ListCmd2 takes the result from Tcl_Merge and stores it in the interpreter's result. Since the list string is dynamically allocated ListCmd2 sets interp->freeProc to free so that Tcl will call free to release the storage for the list when it is no longer needed.

Chapter 33
Exceptions

Many Tcl commands, such as `if` and `while`, have arguments that are Tcl scripts. The command procedures for these commands invoke `Tcl_Eval` recursively to evaluate the scripts. If `Tcl_Eval` returns a completion code other than `TCL_OK`, an *exception* is said to have occurred. Exceptions include `TCL_ERROR`, which was described in Chapter 29, plus several others that have not been mentioned yet. This chapter introduces the full set of exceptions and describes how to unwind nested evaluations and leave useful information in the `errorInfo` and `errorCode` variables. See Table 33.1 for a summary of procedures related to exception handling.

33.1 Completion codes

Table 33.2 lists the full set of Tcl completion codes defined by Tcl. If a command procedure returns anything other than `TCL_OK`, Tcl aborts the evaluation of the script containing the command and returns the code as the result of `Tcl_Eval` (or `Tcl_EvalFile`, etc.). `TCL_OK` and `TCL_ERROR` have already been discussed; they are used for normal returns and errors, respectively. The completion codes `TCL_BREAK` or `TCL_CONTINUE` occur if `break` or `continue` commands are invoked by a script; in both of these cases the interpreter's result is an empty string. The `TCL_RETURN` completion code occurs if `return` is invoked; in this case the interpreter's result is the intended result of the enclosing procedure. Additional completion codes may be defined by application-specific commands.

As an example of how to generate a `TCL_BREAK` completion code, here is the command procedure for the `break` command:

```
void Tcl_AddErrorInfo(Tcl_Interp *interp, char *message)
            Adds message to stack trace being formed in the errorInfo variable.
void Tcl_SetErrorCode(Tcl_Interp *interp, char *field1,
    char *field2, ... (char *) NULL)
            Creates a list whose elements are the field arguments, and sets the
            errorCode variable to the contents of the list.
```

Table 33.1. A summary of Tcl library procedures for setting errorInfo and errorCode.

Completion Code	Meaning
TCL_OK	Command completed normally.
TCL_ERROR	Unrecoverable error occurred.
TCL_BREAK	break command was invoked.
TCL_CONTINUE	continue command was invoked.
TCL_RETURN	return command was invoked.
anything else	Defined by application.

Table 33.2. Completion codes that may be returned by command procedures and procedures that evaluate scripts, such as Tcl_Eval.

```
int BreakCmd(ClientData clientData, Tcl_Interp *interp,
        int argc, char *argv[]) {
    if (argc != 1) {
        interp->result = "wrong # args";
        return TCL_ERROR;
    }
    return TCL_BREAK;
}
```

TCL_BREAK, TCL_CONTINUE, and TCL_RETURN are used to unwind nested script evaluations back to an enclosing looping command or procedure invocation. Under most circumstances a procedure that receives any completion code other than TCL_OK from Tcl_Eval should immediately return that same completion code to its caller without modifying the interpreter's result. However, a few commands process some of the special completion codes without returning them upward. For example, here is an implementation of the while command:

```
int WhileCmd(ClientData clientData, Tcl_Interp *interp,
        int argc, char *argv[]) {
    int bool;
    int code;
    if (argc != 3) {
        interp->result = "wrong # args";
        return TCL_ERROR;
    }
    while (1) {
        Tcl_ResetResult(interp);
        if (Tcl_ExprBoolean(interp, argv[1], &bool)
                != TCL_OK) {
            return TCL_ERROR;
        }
        if (bool == 0) {
            return TCL_OK;
        }
        code = Tcl_Eval(interp, argv[2]);
        if (code == TCL_CONTINUE) {
            continue;
        } else if (code == TCL_BREAK) {
            return TCL_OK;
        } else if (code != TCL_OK) {
            return code;
        }
    }
}
```

After checking its argument count, WhileCmd enters a loop where each iteration evaluates the command's first argument as an expression and its second argument as a script. If
an error occurs while evaluating the expression, WhileCmd returns the error. If the
expression evaluates successfully but its value is 0, the command terminates with a normal
return. Otherwise it evaluates the script argument. If the completion code is TCL_CON-
TINUE, WhileCmd goes on to the next loop iteration. If the code is TCL_BREAK, WhileCmd ends the execution of the command and returns TCL_OK to its caller. If
Tcl_Eval returns any other completion code besides TCL_OK, WhileCmd simply
reflects that code upward. This causes the proper unwinding to occur on TCL_ERROR or
TCL_RETURN codes, and it will also unwind if any new completion codes are added in
the future.

　　If an exceptional return unwinds all the way through the topmost script being evaluated, Tcl checks the completion code to be sure it is either TCL_OK or TCL_ERROR. If
not, Tcl turns the return into an error with an appropriate error message. Furthermore, if a
TCL_BREAK or TCL_CONTINUE exception unwinds all the way out of a procedure, Tcl
also turns it into an error. For example:

```
break
⇒ invoked "break" outside of a loop
```

```
proc badbreak {} {break}
badbreak
```
⟹ *invoked "break" outside of a loop*

Thus applications need not worry about completion codes other than TCL_OK and TCL_ERROR when evaluating scripts from the topmost level.

33.2 Augmenting the stack trace in errorInfo

When an error occurs Tcl modifies the errorInfo global variable to hold a stack trace of the commands that were being evaluated at the time of the error. It does this by calling the procedure Tcl_AddErrorInfo, which has the following prototype:

```
void Tcl_AddErrorInfo(Tcl_Interp *interp, char *message);
```

The first call to Tcl_AddErrorInfo after an error sets errorInfo to the error message stored in interp->result and then appends message. Each subsequent call for the same error appends message to errorInfo's current value. Whenever a command procedure returns TCL_ERROR, Tcl_Eval calls Tcl_AddErrorInfo to log information about the command that was being executed. If there are nested calls to Tcl_Eval, each one adds information about its command as it unwinds, so that a stack trace forms in errorInfo.

Command procedures can call Tcl_AddErrorInfo themselves to provide additional information about the context of the error. This is particularly useful for command procedures that invoke Tcl_Eval recursively. For example, consider the following Tcl procedure, which is a buggy attempt to find the length of the longest element in a list:

```
proc longest list {
    set i [llength $list]
    while {$i >= 0} {
        set length [string length [lindex $list $i]]
        if {$length > $max} {
            set max $length
        }
        incr i -1
    }
    return $max
}
```

This procedure is buggy because it never initializes the variable max, so an error will occur when the if command attempts to read it. If the procedure is invoked with the command "longest {a 12345 xyz}", the following stack trace will be stored in errorInfo after the error:

```
can't read "max": no such variable
    while executing
"if {$length > $max} {
        set max $length
    }"
    ("while" body line 3)
    invoked from within
"while {$i >= 0} {
        set length [string length [lindex $list $i]]
        if {$length > $max} {
            set max $length
        }
        incr i
    }"
    (procedure "longest" line 3)
    invoked from within
"longest {a 12345 xyz}"
```

All of the information is provided by `Tcl_Eval` except for the two lines with comments in parentheses. The first parenthesized message was generated by the command procedure for `while`, and the second was generated by the Tcl code that evaluates procedure bodies. If you used the implementation of `while` on page 321 instead of the built-in Tcl implementation, then the first parenthesized message would be missing. The C code below is a replacement for the last `else` clause in `WhileCmd`; it uses `Tcl_AppendResult` to add the parenthetical remark.

```
    ...
    } else if (code != TCL_OK) {
        if (code == TCL_ERROR) {
            char msg[50];
            sprintf(msg, "\n    (\"while\" body line %d)",
                    interp->errorLine);
            Tcl_AddErrorInfo(interp, msg);
        }
        return code;
    }
    ...
```

The `errorLine` field of `interp` is set by `Tcl_Eval` whenever a command procedure returns `TCL_ERROR`; it gives the line number of the command that produced the error. A line number of 1 corresponds to the first line of the script being evaluated, which is the line containing the open brace in this example; the `if` command that generated the error is on line 3.

For simple Tcl commands you shouldn't need to invoke `Tcl_AddErrorInfo`: the information provided by `Tcl_Eval` will be sufficient. However, if you write code that calls `Tcl_Eval`, I recommend calling `Tcl_AddErrorInfo` whenever `Tcl_Eval` returns an error, to provide information about why `Tcl_Eval` was invoked and also to include the line number of the error.

Note: *You must call* `Tcl_AddErrorInfo` *rather than trying to set the* `errorInfo` *variable directly, because* `Tcl_AddErrorInfo` *contains special code to detect the first call after an error and clear out the old contents of* `errorInfo`.

33.3   Setting errorCode

The last piece of information set after an error is the `errorCode` variable, which provides information about the error in a form that's easy to process with Tcl scripts. It is intended for use in situations where a script is likely to catch the error, determine what went wrong, and attempt to recover from it if possible. If a command procedure returns an error to Tcl without setting `errorCode`, Tcl sets it to NONE. If a command procedure wishes to provide information in `errorCode`, it should invoke `Tcl_SetErrorCode` before returning TCL_ERROR.

`Tcl_SetErrorCode` takes as arguments an interpreter and any number of string arguments ending with a null pointer. It forms the strings into a list and stores the list as the value of `errorCode`. For example, suppose that you have written several commands to implement gizmo objects, and that there are several errors that could occur in commands that manipulate the objects, such as an attempt to use a nonexistent object. If one of your command procedures detects a nonexistent object error, it might set `errorCode` as follows:

```
Tcl_SetErrorCode(interp, "GIZMO", "EXIST",
            "no object by that name", (char *) NULL);
```

This will leave the value "GIZMO EXIST {no object by that name}" in `errorCode`. GIZMO identifies a general class of errors (those associated with gizmo objects), EXIST is the symbolic name for the particular error that occurred, and the last element of the list is a human-readable error message. You can store whatever you want in `errorCode` as long as the first list element doesn't conflict with other values already in use, but the overall idea is to provide symbolic information that can easily be processed by a Tcl script. For example, a script that accesses gizmos might catch errors and if the error is a nonexistent gizmo it might automatically create a new gizmo.

Note: *It is important to call* `Tcl_SetErrorCode` *rather than setting* `errorCode` *directly with* `Tcl_SetVar`. *This is because* `Tcl_SetErrorCode` *also sets other information in the interpreter so that* `errorCode` *isn't later set to its default value; if you set* `errorCode` *directly, Tcl will override your value with the default value NONE.*

Chapter 34
Accessing Tcl Variables

This chapter describes how you can access Tcl variables from C code. Tcl provides library procedures to set variables, read their values, and unset them. It also allows you to "link" a Tcl variable to a C variable so that changes in one are visible in the other. Tcl also provides a tracing mechanism that you can use to monitor and restrict variable accesses. Table 34.1 summarizes the library procedures that are discussed in the chapter.

34.1 Naming variables

Most of the procedures related to variables come in pairs such as `Tcl_SetVar` and `Tcl_SetVar2`. The two procedures in each pair differ only in the way in which they name a Tcl variable. In the first procedure of each pair, such as `Tcl_SetVar`, the variable is named with a single string argument, `varName`. This form is typically used when a variable name has been specified as an argument to a Tcl command. The string can name a scalar variable such as `x` or `fieldName`, or it can name an element of an array, such as `a(42)` or `area(South America)`. No substitutions or modifications are performed on the name. For example, if `varName` is `a($i)` Tcl will not use the value of variable `i` as the element name within array `a`; it will use the string `$i` literally as the element name (of course, in most cases variable names come from the arguments to Tcl commands, so substitutions will already have been performed by the Tcl parser).

The second procedure of each pair has a name ending in 2, such as `Tcl_SetVar2`. In these procedures the variable name is separated into two arguments: `name1` and `name2`. If the variable is a scalar, `name1` is the name of the variable and `name2` is NULL. If the variable is an array element, `name1` is the name of the array and `name2` is the name

```
char *Tcl_SetVar(Tcl_Interp *interp, char *varName,
    char *newValue, int flags)
char *Tcl_SetVar2(Tcl_Interp *interp, char *name1, char *name2,
    char *newValue, int flags)
```
Sets the value of the variable to newValue, creating the variable if it didn't already exist. Returns the new value of the variable or NULL in case of error.

```
char *Tcl_GetVar(Tcl_Interp *interp, char *varName,
    int flags)
char *Tcl_GetVar2(Tcl_Interp *interp, char *name1, char *name2,
    int flags)
```
Returns the current value of the variable, or NULL in case of error.

```
int Tcl_UnsetVar(Tcl_Interp *interp, char *varName,
    int flags)
int Tcl_UnsetVar2(Tcl_Interp *interp, char *name1, char *name2,
    int flags)
```
Removes the variable from interp and returns TCL_OK. If the variable doesn't exist, TCL_ERROR is returned.

```
int Tcl_LinkVar(Tcl_Interp *interp, char *varName, char *addr,
    int type)
```
Associates Tcl variable varName with the C variable at *addr and maintains consistency between their values. type specifies how to interpret the C variable; it must be TCL_LINK_INT, TCL_LINK_DOUBLE, TCL_LINK_BOOLEAN, or TCL_LINK_STRING, optionally OR'ed with TCL_LINK_READ_ONLY.

```
void Tcl_UnlinkVar(Tcl_Interp *interp, char *varName)
```
Removes the association created by Tcl_LinkVar for Tcl variable varName, if there was one.

Table 34.1. Tcl library procedures for manipulating variables. Most of the procedures come in pairs; in one procedure the variable is named with a single string (which may specify either a scalar or an array element) and in the other procedure the variable is named with separate array and element names (name1 and name2, respectively). If name2 is NULL, the variable must be a scalar.

of the element within the array. This form of procedure is less commonly used but it is slightly faster than the first form (procedures like Tcl_SetVar are implemented by calling procedures like Tcl_SetVar2).

34.2 Setting variable values

Tcl_SetVar and Tcl_SetVar2 are used to set the value of a variable. For example,

```
    Tcl_SetVar(interp, "a", "44", 0);
```
will set the value of variable a in interp to the string 44. If there does not yet exist a variable named a, a new one is created. The variable is set in the current execution context: if a Tcl procedure is currently being executed, the variable will be a local one for that

```
int Tcl_TraceVar(Tcl_Interp *interp, char *varName,
    int flags, Tcl_VarTraceProc *proc, ClientData clientData)
int Tcl_TraceVar2(Tcl_Interp *interp, char *name1, char *name2,
    int flags, Tcl_VarTraceProc *proc, ClientData clientData)
            Arrange for proc to be invoked whenever one of the operations specified
            by flags is performed on the variable. Returns TCL_OK or TCL_ERROR.
void Tcl_UntraceVar(Tcl_Interp *interp, char *varName,
    int flags, Tcl_VarTraceProc *proc, ClientData clientData)
void Tcl_UntraceVar2(Tcl_Interp *interp, char *name1,
    char *name2, int flags, Tcl_VarTraceProc *proc,
    ClientData clientData)
            Removes the trace on the variable that matches proc, clientData, and
            flags, if there is one.
ClientData Tcl_VarTraceInfo(Tcl_Interp *interp, char *varName,
    int flags, Tcl_VarTraceProc *proc,
    ClientData prevClientData)
ClientData Tcl_VarTraceInfo2(Tcl_Interp *interp, char *name1,
    char *name2, int flags, Tcl_VarTraceProc *proc,
    ClientData prevClientData)
            If prevClientData is NULL, returns the ClientData associated with
            the first trace on the variable that matches flags and proc (only the
            TCL_GLOBAL_ONLY bit of flags is used); otherwise returns the
            ClientData for the next trace matching flags and proc after the one
            whose ClientData is prevClientData. Returns NULL if there are no
            (more) matching traces.
```

Table 34.1, continued.

procedure; if no procedure is currently being executed, the variable will be a global variable. If the operation completed successfully, the return value from Tcl_SetVar is a pointer to the variable's new value as stored in the variable table. (This value is static enough to be used as an interpreter's result.) If an error occurred, such as specifying the name of an array without also specifying an element name, NULL is returned.

The last argument to Tcl_SetVar or Tcl_SetVar2 consists of an OR'ed combination of flag bits. Table 34.2 lists the symbolic values for the flags. If the TCL_GLOBAL_ONLY flag is specified, the operation always applies to a global variable, even if a Tcl procedure is currently being executed. TCL_LEAVE_ERR_MSG controls how errors are reported. Normally, Tcl_SetVar and Tcl_SetVar2 just return NULL if an error occurs. However, if TCL_LEAVE_ERR_MSG has been specified, the procedures will also store an error message in the interpreter's result. This last form is useful when the procedure is invoked from a command procedure that plans to abort if the variable access fails.

The flag TCL_APPEND_VALUE means that the new value should be appended to the variable's current value instead of replacing it. Tcl implements the append operation in a way that is relatively efficient, even in the face of repeated appends to the same variable. If

Flag Name	Meaning
TCL_GLOBAL_ONLY	Reference global variable, regardless of current execution context.
TCL_LEAVE_ERR_MSG	If operation fails, leave error message in interp->result.
TCL_APPEND_VALUE	Append new value to existing value instead of overwriting.
TCL_LIST_ELEMENT	Convert new value to a list element before setting or appending.

Table 34.2. Values that may be OR'ed together in the flags arguments to Tcl_SetVar and Tcl_SetVar2. Other procedures permit subsets of these flags.

the variable doesn't yet exist, TCL_APPEND_VALUE has no effect and the variable is set as usual.

The last flag, TCL_LIST_ELEMENT, means that the new value should be converted to a proper list element (for example, by enclosing in braces if necessary) before setting or appending. If both TCL_LIST_ELEMENT and TCL_APPEND_VALUE are specified, a separator space is also added before the new element if needed.

Here is an implementation of the lappend command that uses Tcl_SetVar:

```
int LappendCmd(ClientData clientData, Tcl_Interp *interp,
        int argc, char *argv[]) {
    int i;
    char *varValue;
    if (argc < 3) {
        interp->result = "wrong # args";
        return TCL_ERROR;
    }
    for (i = 2; i < argc; i++) {
        varValue = Tcl_SetVar(interp, argv[1], argv[i],
                TCL_LIST_ELEMENT|TCL_APPEND_VALUE
                |TCL_LEAVE_ERR_MSG);
        if (varValue == NULL) {
            return TCL_ERROR;
        }
    }
    interp->result = varValue;
    return TCL_OK;
}
```

It simply calls Tcl_SetVar once for each argument and lets Tcl_SetVar do all the work of converting the argument to a list value and appending it to the variable. If an error occurs, Tcl_SetVar leaves an error message in interp->result and Lappend-

Cmd returns the message to Tcl. If the command completes successfully, it returns the variable's final value as its result (the value of the variable returned by `Tcl_SetVar` is static enough to make `interp->result` point directly to it). For example, suppose the following Tcl command is invoked:

```
set a 44
lappend a x {b c}
⇒  44 x {b c}
```

When LappendCmd is invoked `argc` will be 4, `Argv[2]` will be x, and `argv[3]` will be "b c" (the braces are removed by the Tcl parser). LappendCmd makes two calls to `Tcl_SetVar`; during the first call no conversion is necessary to produce a proper list element, but during the second call `Tcl_SetVar` adds braces back around "b c" before appending it to the variable.

34.3 Reading variables

The procedures `Tcl_GetVar` and `Tcl_GetVar2` may be used to retrieve variable values. For example,

```
char *value;
...
value = Tcl_GetVar(interp, "a", 0);
```

will store in `value` a pointer to the current value of variable a. The string pointed to by `value` belongs to Tcl and should not be modified; furthermore, the string is only valid up until the next call to `Tcl_SetVar` or `Tcl_SetVar2` for the variable. If the variable doesn't exist or some other error occurs, NULL is returned. `Tcl_GetVar` and `Tcl_GetVar2` support the TCL_GLOBAL_ONLY and TCL_LEAVE_ERR_MSG flags in the same way as `Tcl_SetVar`.

The following command procedure uses `Tcl_GetVar` and `Tcl_SetVar` to implement the `incr` command:

```
int IncrCmd(ClientData clientData, Tcl_Interp *interp,
        int argc, char *argv[]) {
    int value, inc;
    char *string, *varValue, newValue[20];
    if ((argc != 2) && (argc != 3)) {
        interp->result = "wrong # args";
        return TCL_ERROR;
    }
    if (argc == 2) {
        inc = 1;
    } else if (Tcl_GetInt(interp, argv[2], &inc)
            != TCL_OK) {
        return TCL_ERROR;
    }
    string = Tcl_GetVar(interp, argv[1],
```

```
                        TCL_LEAVE_ERR_MSG);
            if (string == NULL) {
                return TCL_ERROR;
            }
            if (Tcl_GetInt(interp, string, &value) != TCL_OK) {
                return TCL_ERROR;
            }
            sprintf(newValue, "%d", value + inc);
            varValue = Tcl_SetVar(interp, argv[1], newValue,
                    TCL_LEAVE_ERR_MSG);
            if (varValue == NULL) {
                return TCL_ERROR;
            }
            interp->result = varValue;
            return TCL_OK;
        }
```

IncrCmd does very little work itself. It just calls library procedures and aborts if errors occur. The first call to Tcl_GetInt converts the increment from text to binary. Tcl_GetVar retrieves the original value of the variable, and another call to Tcl_Get-Int converts that value to binary. IncrCmd adds the increment to the variable's value and calls sprintf to convert the result back to text. Tcl_SetVar stores this value in the variable, and IncrCmd returns the new value as its result.

34.4 Unsetting variables

To remove a variable, call Tcl_UnsetVar or Tcl_UnsetVar2. For example, either of the calls

```
        Tcl_UnsetVar(interp, "population(Michigan)", 0);
```

or

```
        Tcl_UnsetVar2(interp, "population", "Michigan", 0);
```

will remove the element Michigan from the array population. These calls have the same effect as the Tcl command

```
        unset population(Michigan)
```

Tcl_UnsetVar and Tcl_UnsetVar2 return TCL_OK if the variable was successfully removed and TCL_ERROR if the variable didn't exist or couldn't be removed for some other reason. TCL_GLOBAL_ONLY and TCL_LEAVE_ERR_MSG may be specified as flags to these procedures. If an array name is given without an element name, the entire array is removed.

34.5   Linking Tcl and C variables

Tcl provides a mechanism called *variable linking* that allows you to associate a Tcl variable with a C variable. Whenever the Tcl variable is read the value will be supplied from the C variable, and whenever the Tcl variable is written the new value will be stored in the C variable as well. The procedure `Tcl_LinkVar` creates a link. For example, consider the following C code:

```
int value = 32;
...
Tcl_LinkVar(interp, "x", (char *) &value, TCL_LINK_INT);
```

This links Tcl variable x to the C variable `value`. Whenever the Tcl variable x is read, Tcl will convert `value` to a decimal string and return the string as the value of x (32 in the preceding example). If `value` is modified, the new value will be returned the next time that Tcl variable x is read. Whenever Tcl variable x is written x's new value will be converted from a decimal string to an integer and stored in `value`. If a Tcl script attempts to write a value into x that isn't a proper integer, the write will be rejected with an error:

```
set x red
```
⇒ *can't set "x": variable must have integer value*

The last argument to `Tcl_LinkVar` indicates the type of the C variable. In the previous example the type is `TCL_LINK_INT`, which indicates that the C variable is an integer and only proper integer values may be stored in the Tcl variable. The type may also be one of the following:

`TCL_LINK_DOUBLE`	The C variable is of type `double`, and the Tcl variable may have only proper real values.
`TCL_LINK_BOOLEAN`	The C variable is treated as an integer Boolean value (it will read as 0 or 1 from Tcl) and the Tcl variable may have only proper Boolean values (see Table 32.2).
`TCL_LINK_STRING`	The C variable has type `char *` (the argument to `Tcl_LinkVar` is a pointer to a pointer). If the C variable's value is not null, it must point to a string allocated with `malloc`. When the Tcl variable is modified, the old string will be freed and a new one will be allocated to hold the variable's new value. The Tcl variable may be assigned any string value.

The flag `TCL_LINK_READ_ONLY` may also be OR'ed with the type, as in the following example:

```
Tcl_LinkVar(interp, "x", (char *) &value,
        TCL_LINK_INT|TCL_LINK_READ_ONLY);
```

This makes the Tcl variable read-only: any attempt to modify the variable from Tcl will be rejected with an error.

The procedure `Tcl_UnlinkVar` removes a variable link previously established by `Tcl_LinkVar`. For example, the following statement removes the link created above:

```
Tcl_UnlinkVar(interp, "x");
```
If the Tcl variable is unset, Tcl automatically recreates the variable again; it cannot be permanently unset until the link is removed.

34.6 Setting and unsetting variable traces

Variable traces allow you to specify a C procedure to be invoked whenever a variable is read, written, or unset. Traces can be used for many purposes. For example, in Tk you can configure a button widget so that it displays the value of a variable and updates itself automatically when the variable is modified. This feature is implemented with variable traces. You can also use traces for debugging, to create read-only variables, and for many other purposes.

The procedures Tcl_TraceVar and Tcl_TraceVar2 create variable traces, as in the following example:

```
Tcl_TraceVar(interp, "x", TCL_TRACE_WRITES, WriteProc,
        (ClientData) NULL);
```
This creates a write trace on variable x in interp, which means that WriteProc will be invoked whenever x is modified. The third argument to Tcl_TraceVar is an OR'ed combination of flag bits that select the operations to trace: TCL_TRACE_READS for reads, TCL_TRACE_WRITES for writes, and TCL_TRACE_UNSETS for unsets. In addition, the flag TCL_GLOBAL_ONLY may be specified to force the variable name to be interpreted as global. Tcl_TraceVar and Tcl_TraceVar2 normally return TCL_OK; if an error occurs, they leave an error message in interp->result and return TCL_ERROR.

The library procedures Tcl_UntraceVar and Tcl_UntraceVar2 remove variable traces. For example, the following call will remove the trace set above:

```
Tcl_UntraceVar(interp, "x", TCL_TRACE_WRITES,
        WriteProc, (ClientData) NULL);
```
Tcl_UntraceVar finds the specified variable, looks for a trace that matches the flags, trace procedure, and clientData specified by its arguments, and removes the trace if it exists. If no matching trace exists, Tcl_UntraceVar does nothing. Tcl_Untrace-Var and Tcl_UntraceVar2 accept the same flag bits as Tcl_TraceVar.

34.7 Trace callbacks

Trace callback procedures such as WriteProc in the previous section must match the following prototype:

```
typedef char *Tcl_VarTraceProc(ClientData clientData,
        Tcl_Interp *interp, char *name1, char *name2,
        int flags);
```

The `clientData` and `interp` arguments will be the same as the corresponding arguments passed to `Tcl_TraceVar` or `Tcl_TraceVar2`. `clientData` typically points to a structure containing information needed by the trace callback. `name1` and `name2` give the name of the variable in the same form as the arguments to `Tcl_SetVar2`. `flags` consists of an OR'ed combination of bits. Either `TCL_TRACE_READS`, `TCL_TRACE_WRITES`, or `TCL_TRACE_UNSETS` is set to indicate which operation triggered the trace, and `TCL_GLOBAL_ONLY` is set if the variable is a global variable that isn't accessible from the current execution context; the trace callback must pass this flag back into procedures like `Tcl_GetVar2` if it wishes to access the variable. The bits `TCL_TRACE_DESTROYED` and `TCL_INTERP_DESTROYED` are set in special circumstances as described in Section 34.10.

For read traces, the callback is invoked just before `Tcl_GetVar` or `Tcl_GetVar2` returns the variable's value; if the callback modifies the value of the variable, the modified value will be returned. For write traces the callback is invoked after the variable's value has been changed. The callback can modify the variable to override the change, and this modified value will be returned as the result of `Tcl_SetVar` or `Tcl_SetVar2`. For unset traces the callback is invoked after the variable has been unset, so the callback cannot access the variable. Unset callbacks can occur when a variable is explicitly unset, when a procedure returns (thereby deleting all of its local variables) or when an interpreter is destroyed (thereby deleting all of the variables in the interpreter).

A trace callback procedure can invoke `Tcl_GetVar2` and `Tcl_SetVar2` to read and write the value of the traced variable. All traces on the variable are temporarily disabled while the callback executes so calls to `Tcl_GetVar2` and `Tcl_SetVar2` will not trigger additional trace callbacks. As mentioned earlier, unset traces aren't invoked until after the variable has been deleted, so attempts to read the variable during unset callbacks will fail. However, it is possible for an unset callback procedure to write the variable, in which case a new variable will be created.

This code sets a write trace that prints out the new value of variable x each time it is modified:

```
Tcl_TraceVar(interp, "x", TCL_TRACE_WRITES, Print,
        (ClientData) NULL);
...
char *Print(ClientData clientData, Tcl_Interp *interp,
        char *name1, char *name2, int flags) {
    char *value;
    value = Tcl_GetVar2(interp, name1, name2,
            flags & TCL_GLOBAL_ONLY);
    if (value != NULL) {
        if (name2 == NULL) {
            printf("new value of %s is %s\n", name1,
                    value);
        } else {
            printf("new value of %s(%s) is %s\n", name1,
                    name2, value);
        }
    }
    return NULL;
}
```

Print must pass the TCL_GLOBAL_ONLY bit of its flags argument to Tcl_Get-
Var2 in order to make sure that the variable can be accessed properly. Tcl_GetVar2
should never return an error, but Print checks for one anyway and doesn't try to print
the variable's value if an error occurs.

Trace callbacks normally return NULL values; a non-NULL value signals an error. In
this case the return value must be a pointer to a static string containing an error message.
The traced access will abort and the error message will be returned to whomever initiated
that access. For example, if the access was invoked by a set command or $-substitution,
a Tcl error will result; if the access was invoked via Tcl_GetVar, Tcl_GetVar will
return NULL and also leave the error message in interp->result if the
TCL_LEAVE_ERR_MSG flag was specified.

The code below uses a trace to make variable x read-only with value 192:

```
Tcl_TraceVar(interp, "x", TCL_TRACE_WRITES, Reject,
        (ClientData) "192");
...
char *Reject(ClientData clientData, Tcl_Interp *interp,
        char *name1, char *name2, int flags) {
    char *correct = (char *) clientData;
    Tcl_SetVar2(interp, name1, name2, correct,
                flags & TCL_GLOBAL_ONLY);
    return "variable is read-only";
};
```

Reject is a trace callback that is invoked whenever x is written. It returns an error message to abort the write access. Since x has already been modified before Reject is
invoked, Reject must undo the write by restoring the variable's correct value. The correct value is passed to the trace callback using its clientData argument. This imple-

mentation allows the same procedure to be used as the write callback for many different read-only variables; a different correct value can be passed to Reject for each variable.

34.8   Whole-array traces

You can create a trace on an entire array by specifying an array name to Tcl_TraceVar or Tcl_TraceVar2 without an element name. This creates a whole-array trace: the callback procedure will be invoked whenever any of the specified operations is invoked on any element of the array. If the entire array is unset, the callback will be invoked just once, with name1 containing the array name and name2 NULL.

34.9   Multiple traces

Multiple traces can exist for the same variable. When this happens, each of the relevant callbacks is invoked on each variable access. The callbacks are invoked in order from the one most recently created to the oldest. If there are both whole-array traces and individual element traces, the whole-array callbacks are invoked before element callbacks. If an error is returned by one of the callbacks, no subsequent callbacks are invoked.

34.10   Unset callbacks

Unset callbacks are different from read and write callbacks in several ways. First of all, unset callbacks cannot return an error condition; they must always succeed. Second, two extra flags are defined for unset callbacks: TCL_TRACE_DESTROYED and TCL_INTERP_DESTROYED. When a variable is unset all of its traces are deleted; unset traces on the variable will still be invoked, but they will be passed the TCL_TRACE_DE-STROYED flag to indicate that the trace has now been deleted and won't be invoked anymore. If an array element is unset and there is a whole-array unset trace for the element's array, the unset trace is not deleted and the callback will be invoked without the TCL_TRACE_DESTROYED flag set.

 If the TCL_INTERP_DESTROYED flag is set during an unset callback it means that the interpreter containing the variable has been destroyed. In this case the callback must be careful not to use the interpreter at all, since the interpreter's state is in the process of being deleted. The callback should merely clean up its own internal data structures.

34.11   Nonexistent variables

It is legal to set a trace on a variable that does not yet exist. The variable will continue to appear not to exist (attempts to read it will fail), but the trace's callback will be invoked during operations on the variable. For example, you can set a read trace on an undefined variable and then, on the first access to the variable, assign it a default value.

34.12   Querying trace information

The procedures `Tcl_VarTraceInfo` and `Tcl_VarTraceInfo2` can be used to determine whether a particular kind of trace has been set on a variable and, if so, to retrieve its `ClientData` value. For example, consider the following code:

```
ClientData clientData;
...
clientData = Tcl_VarTraceInfo(interp, "x", 0, Reject,
        (ClientData) NULL);
```

`Tcl_VarTraceInfo` will see if there is a trace on variable x that has `Reject` as its trace callback. If so, it will return the `ClientData` value associated with the first (most recently created) such trace; if not it will return NULL. Given the code in Section 34.7, this call will tell whether x is read-only; if so, it will return the variable's read-only value. If there are multiple traces on a variable with the same callback, you can step through them all in order by making multiple calls to `Tcl_VarTraceInfo`, as in the following code:

```
ClientData clientData;
...
clientData = NULL;
while (1) {
    clientData = Tcl_VarTraceInfo(interp, "x", 0,
            Reject, clientData);
    if (clientData == NULL) {
        break;
    }
    ... process trace ...
}
```

In each call to `Tcl_VarTraceInfo` after the first, the previous `ClientData` value is passed in as the last argument. `Tcl_VarTraceInfo` finds the trace with this value, then returns the `ClientData` for the next trace. When it reaches the last trace it returns NULL.

Chapter 35
Hash Tables

A *hash table* is a collection of *entries*, where each entry consists of a *key* and a *value*. No two entries may have the same key. Given a key, a hash table can very quickly locate its entry and hence the associated value. Tcl contains a general-purpose hash table package that it uses in several places internally. For example, all of the commands in an interpreter are stored in a hash table where the key for each entry is a command name and the value is a pointer to information about the command. All of the global variables are stored in another hash table where the key for each entry is the name of a variable and the value is a pointer to information about the variable.

Tcl exports its hash table facilities through a set of library procedures so that applications can use them too (see Table 35.1 for a summary). The most common use for hash tables is to associate names with objects. In order for an application to implement a new kind of object, it must give the objects textual names for use in Tcl commands. When a command procedure receives an object name as an argument it must locate the C data structure for the object. Typically there will be one hash table for each type of object, where the key for an entry is an object name and the value is a pointer to the C data structure that represents the object. When a command procedure needs to find an object it looks up its name in the hash table. If there is no entry for the name, the command procedure returns an error.

For the examples in this chapter I will use a hypothetical application that implements objects called "gizmos." Each gizmo is represented internally with a structure declared like this:

```
typedef struct Gizmo {
    ... fields of gizmo object ...
} Gizmo;
```

```
void Tcl_InitHashTable(Tcl_HashTable *tablePtr, int keyType)
          Creates a new hash table and stores information about the table at
          *tablePtr. keyType is either TCL_STRING_KEYS,
          TCL_ONE_WORD_KEYS, or an integer greater than 1.
void Tcl_DeleteHashTable(Tcl_HashTable *tablePtr)
          Deletes all the entries in the hash table and frees up related storage.
```

```
Tcl_HashEntry *Tcl_CreateHashEntry(Tcl_HashTable *tablePtr,
     char *key, int *newPtr)
          Returns a pointer to the entry in tablePtr whose key is key, creating a
          new entry if needed. *newPtr is set to 1 if a new entry was created or 0 if
          the entry already existed.
Tcl_HashEntry *Tcl_FindHashEntry(Tcl_HashTable *tablePtr,
     char *key)
          Returns a pointer to the entry in tablePtr whose key is key, or NULL if
          no such entry exists.
void Tcl_DeleteHashEntry(Tcl_HashEntry *entryPtr)
          Deletes an entry from its hash table.
```

```
ClientData Tcl_GetHashValue(Tcl_HashEntry *entryPtr)
          Returns the value associated with a hash table entry.
void Tcl_SetHashValue(Tcl_HashEntry *entryPtr,
     ClientData value)
          Sets the value associated with a hash table entry.
char *Tcl_GetHashKey(Tcl_HashTable *tablePtr,
     Tcl_HashEntry *entryPtr)
          Returns the key associated with a hash table entry.
```

```
Tcl_HashEntry *Tcl_FirstHashEntry(Tcl_HashTable *tablePtr,
     Tcl_HashSearch *searchPtr)
          Starts a search through all the elements of a hash table. Stores information
          about the search at *searchPtr and returns the hash table's first entry or
          NULL if it has no entries.
Tcl_HashEntry *Tcl_NextHashEntry(Tcl_HashSearch *searchPtr)
          Returns the next entry in the search identified by searchPtr or NULL if all
          entries in the table have been returned.
```

```
char *Tcl_HashStats(Tcl_HashTable *tablePtr)
          Returns a string giving usage statistics for tablePtr. The string is
          dynamically allocated and must be freed by the caller.
```

Table 35.1. A summary of Tcl library procedures for managing hash tables.

The application uses names like gizmo42 to refer to gizmos in Tcl commands, where
each gizmo has a different number at the end of its name. The application follows the
action-oriented approach described in Section 28.3 by providing a collection of Tcl commands to manipulate the objects, such as gcreate to create a new gizmo, gdelete to
delete an existing gizmo, gsearch to find gizmos with certain characteristics, and so on.

35.1   Keys and values

Tcl hash tables support three different kinds of keys. All of the entries in a single hash table must use the same kind of key, but different tables may use different kinds. The most common form of key is a string. In this case each key is a null-terminated string of arbitrary length, such as `gizmo18` or `Waste not want not`. Different entries in a table may have keys of different length. The gizmo implementation uses strings as keys.

The second form of key is a one-word value. In this case each key may be any value that fits in a single word, such as an integer. One-word keys are passed into Tcl using values of type `char *` so the keys are limited to the size of a character pointer.

The last form of key is an array. In this case each key is an array of integers (C `int` type). All keys in the table must be the same size.

The values for hash table entries are items of type `ClientData`, which are large enough to hold either an integer or a pointer. In most applications, such as the gizmo example, hash table values are pointers to records for objects. These pointers are cast into `ClientData` items when storing them in hash table entries, and they are cast back from `ClientData` to object pointers when retrieved from the hash table.

35.2   Creating and deleting hash tables

Each hash table is represented by a C structure of type `Tcl_HashTable`. Space for this structure is allocated by the client, not by Tcl; these structures are usually global variables or elements of other structures. When calling hash table procedures you provide a pointer to a `Tcl_HashTable` structure as a token for the hash table. You should never use or modify any of the fields of a `Tcl_HashTable` directly. Use the Tcl library procedures and macros for this.

Here is how a hash table might be created for the gizmo application:

```
Tcl_HashTable gizmoTable;
...
Tcl_InitHashTable(&gizmoTable, TCL_STRING_KEYS);
```

The first argument to `Tcl_InitHashTable` is a `Tcl_HashTable` pointer and the second argument is an integer that specifies the sort of keys that will be used for the table. `TCL_STRING_KEYS` means that strings will be used as the keys for the table. If `TCL_ONE_WORD_KEYS` is specified, it means that single-word values such as integers or pointers will be used as keys. If the second argument is neither `TCL_STRING_KEYS` or `TCL_ONE_WORD_KEYS`, then it must be an integer value greater than one; this means that keys are arrays with the given number of `int`'s in each array. `Tcl_InitHash-Table` initializes the structure to refer to an empty hash table with keys as specified.

`Tcl_DeleteHashTable` removes all the entries from a hash table and frees the memory that was allocated for the table (except space for the `Tcl_HashTable` structure itself, which is the property of the client). For example, the following statement could be used to delete the hash table we just initialized:

```
Tcl_DeleteHashTable(&gizmoTable);
```

35.3 Creating entries

The procedure `Tcl_CreateHashEntry` creates an entry with a given key and `Tcl_SetHashValue` sets the value associated with the entry. For example, the following code might be used to implement the `gcreate` command, which makes a new gizmo object:

```
int GcreateCmd(ClientData clientData,
        Tcl_Interp *interp, int argc, char *argv[]) {
    static unsigned int id = 1;
    int new;
    Tcl_HashEntry *entryPtr;
    Gizmo *gizmoPtr;
    ... check argc, etc ...
    do {
        sprintf(interp->result, "gizmo%u", id);
        id++;
        entryPtr = Tcl_CreateHashEntry(&gizmoTable,
                interp->result, &new);
    } while (!new);
    gizmoPtr = (Gizmo *) malloc(sizeof(Gizmo));
    Tcl_SetHashValue(entryPtr, gizmoPtr);
    ... initialize *gizmoPtr, etc ...
    return TCL_OK;
}
```

This code creates a name for the object by concatenating `gizmo` with the value of the static variable `id`. It returns the name of the new object as the result of the Tcl command (the result string is small, so `GcreateCmd` just writes it into the static area pointed to by `interp->result`, as described on page 297). `GcreateCmd` then increments `id` so that each new object will have a unique name. `Tcl_CreateHashEntry` is called to create a new entry with a key equal to the object's name; it returns a token for the entry. Under normal conditions there will not already exist an entry with the given key, in which case `Tcl_CreateHashEntry` sets new to 1 to indicate that it created a new entry. However, it is possible for `Tcl_CreateHashEntry` to be called with a key that already exists in the table. In `GcreateCmd` this can only happen if a very large number of objects are created, so that `id` wraps around to zero again. If this happens, `Tcl_CreateHashEntry` sets new to 0; `GcreateCmd` will try again with the next larger `id` until it eventually finds a name that isn't already in use.

After creating the hash table entry `GcreateCmd` allocates memory for the object's record and invokes `Tcl_SetHashValue` to store the record address as the value of the hash table entry. `Tcl_SetHashValue` is actually a macro, not a procedure; its first argument is a token for a hash table entry and its second argument, the new value for the entry, can be anything that fits in the space of a `ClientData` value. After setting the value of the hash table entry `GcreateCmd` initializes the new object's record.

Note: *Tcl's hash tables restructure themselves as you add entries. A table won't use much memory for the hash buckets when it has only a small number of entries, but it will increase the size of the bucket array as the number of entries increases. Tcl's hash tables should operate efficiently even when they have a very large number of entries.*

35.4 Finding existing entries

The procedure `Tcl_FindHashEntry` locates an existing entry in a hash table. It is similar to `Tcl_CreateHashEntry` except that it won't create a new entry if the key doesn't exist in the hash table. `Tcl_FindHashEntry` is typically used to find an object given its name. For example, the gizmo implementation might contain a utility procedure called `GetGizmo`, which is something like `Tcl_GetInt` except that it translates its string argument to a `Gizmo` pointer instead of an integer:

```
Gizmo *GetGizmo(Tcl_Interp *interp, char *string) {
    Tcl_HashEntry *entryPtr;
    entryPtr = Tcl_FindHashEntry(&gizmoTable, string);
    if (entryPtr == NULL) {
        Tcl_AppendResult(interp, "no gizmo named \"",
                string, "\"", (char *) NULL);
        return NULL;
    }
    return (Gizmo *) Tcl_GetHashValue(entryPtr);
}
```

`GetGizmo` looks up a gizmo name in the gizmo hash table. If the name exists, `GetGizmo` extracts the value from the entry using the macro `Tcl_GetHashValue`, converts it to a `Gizmo` pointer, and returns it. If the name doesn't exist, `GetGizmo` stores an error message in `interp->result` and returns NULL.

`GetGizmo` can be invoked from any command procedure that needs to look up a gizmo object. For example, suppose there is a command `gtwist` that performs a "twist" operation on gizmos, and that it takes a gizmo name as its first argument. The command might be implemented like this:

```
int GtwistCmd(ClientData clientData,
        Tcl_Interp *interp, int argc, char *argv[]) {
    Gizmo *gizmoPtr;
    ... check argc, etc ...
    gizmoPtr = GetGizmo(interp, argv[1]);
    if (gizmoPtr == NULL) {
        return TCL_ERROR;
    }
    ... perform twist operation ...
    return TCL_OK;
}
```

35.5 Searching

Tcl provides two procedures that you can use to search through all of the entries in a hash table. `Tcl_FirstHashEntry` starts a search and returns the first entry, and `Tcl_NextHashEntry` returns successive entries until the search is complete. For example, suppose you wish to provide a `gsearch` command that searches through all existing gizmos and returns a list of the names of the gizmos that meet a certain set of criteria. This command might be implemented as follows:

```
int GsearchCmd(ClientData clientData,
        Tcl_Interp *interp, int argc, char *argv[]) {
    Tcl_HashEntry *entryPtr;
    Tcl_HashSearch search;
    Gizmo *gizmoPtr;
    ... process arguments to choose search criteria ...
    for (entryPtr = Tcl_FirstHashEntry(&gizmoTable,
            &search); entryPtr != NULL;
            entryPtr = Tcl_NextHashEntry(&search)) {
        gizmoPtr = (Gizmo *) Tcl_GetHashValue(entryPtr);
        if (...object satisfies search criteria...) {
            Tcl_AppendElement(interp,
                    Tcl_GetHashKey(&gizmoTable, entryPtr));
        }
    }
    return TCL_OK;
}
```

A structure of type `Tcl_HashSearch` is used to keep track of the search; it is possible to carry out multiple searches simultaneously, using a different `Tcl_HashSearch` structure for each. `Tcl_FirstHashEntry` initializes this structure and returns a token for the first entry in the table (or NULL if the table is empty). `Tcl_NextHashEntry` uses the information in the structure to step through successive entries in the table; each call to `Tcl_NextHashEntry` returns a pointer to the next entry (in no particular order), and NULL is returned when the end of the table is reached. For each entry GsearchCmd extracts the value from the entry, converts it to a `Gizmo` pointer, and sees if that object meets the criteria specified in the command's arguments. If so, GsearchCmd uses the Tcl_GetHashKey macro to get the name of the object (i.e., the entry's key) and invokes Tcl_AppendElement to append the name to the interpreter's result as a list element.

Note: *It is not safe to modify the structure of a hash table during a search. If you create or delete entries, you should terminate any searches in progress.*

35.6 Deleting entries

The procedure Tcl_DeleteHashEntry will delete an entry from a hash table. For example, the following procedure uses Tcl_DeleteHashEntry to implement a gdelete command, which takes any number of arguments and deletes the gizmo objects they name:

```
int GdeleteCmd(ClientData clientData,
        Tcl_Interp *interp, int argc, char *argv[]) {
    Tcl_HashEntry *entryPtr;
    Gizmo *gizmoPtr;
    int i;
    for (i = 1; i < argc; i++) {
        entryPtr = Tcl_FindHashEntry(&gizmoTable,
                argv[i]);
        if (entryPtr == NULL) {
            continue;
        }
        gizmoPtr = (Gizmo *) Tcl_GetHashValue(entryPtr);
        Tcl_DeleteHashEntry(entryPtr);
        ... clean up *gizmoPtr ...
        free((char *) gizmoPtr);
    }
    return TCL_OK;
}
```

GdeleteCmd checks each of its arguments to see if it is the name of a gizmo object. If not, the argument is ignored. Otherwise GdeleteCmd extracts a gizmo pointer from the hash table entry and calls Tcl_DeleteHashEntry to remove the entry from the hash table. Then it performs internal cleanup on the gizmo object if needed and frees the object's record.

35.7 Statistics

The procedure Tcl_HashStats returns a string containing various statistics about the structure of a hash table. For example, it might be used to implement a gstat command for gizmos:

```
int GstatCmd(ClientData clientData, Tcl_Interp *interp,
        int argc, char *argv[]) {
    if (argc != 1) {
        interp->result = "wrong # args";
        return TCL_ERROR;
    }
    interp->result = Tcl_HashStats(&gizmoTable);
    interp->freeProc = (Tcl_FreeProc *) free;
    return TCL_OK;
}
```

The string returned by `Tcl_HashStats` is dynamically allocated and must be passed to `free`; GstatCmd uses this string as the command's result and sets `interp->freeProc` so that Tcl will free the string.

The string returned by `Tcl_HashStats` contains information such as the following:

```
1416 entries in table, 1024 buckets
number of buckets with 0 entries: 60
number of buckets with 1 entries: 591
number of buckets with 2 entries: 302
number of buckets with 3 entries: 67
number of buckets with 4 entries: 5
number of buckets with 5 entries: 0
number of buckets with 6 entries: 0
number of buckets with 7 entries: 0
number of buckets with 8 entries: 0
number of buckets with 9 entries: 0
number of buckets with more than 10 entries: 0
average search distance for entry: 1.4
```

You can use this information to see how efficiently the entries are stored in the hash table. For example, the last line indicates the average number of entries that Tcl will have to check during hash table lookups, assuming that all entries are accessed with equal probability.

Chapter 36
String Utilities

This chapter describes Tcl's library procedures for manipulating strings, including a dynamic string mechanism that allows you to build up arbitrarily long strings, a procedure for testing whether a command is complete, and a procedure for doing simple string matching. Table 36.1 summarizes these procedures.

36.1 Dynamic strings

A *dynamic string* is a string that can be appended to without bound. As you append information to a dynamic string, Tcl automatically enlarges the memory area allocated for it. If the string is short, Tcl avoids dynamic memory allocation altogether by using a small static buffer to hold the string. Tcl provides 10 procedures and macros for manipulating dynamic strings:

Tcl_DStringInit initializes a dynamic string to an empty string.

Tcl_DStringAppend adds characters to a dynamic string.

Tcl_DStringAppendElement adds a new list element to a dynamic string.

Tcl_DStringStartSublist and Tcl_DStringEndSublist can be used to create sublists within a dynamic string.

Tcl_DStringValue returns the current value of a dynamic string.

Tcl_DStringLength returns the current length of a dynamic string.

Tcl_DStringTrunc truncates a dynamic string.

```
void Tcl_DStringInit(Tcl_DString *dsPtr)
            Initializes dsPtr's value to an empty string (previous contents of dsPtr
            are discarded without cleanup).
char *Tcl_DStringAppend(Tcl_DString *dsPtr, char *string,
    int length)
            Appends length bytes from string to dsPtr's value and returns new
            value of dsPtr. If length is less than zero, appends all of string.
char *Tcl_DStringAppendElement(Tcl_DString *dsPtr, char *string)
            Converts string to proper list element and appends to dsPtr's value
            (with separator space if needed). Returns new value of dsPtr.
Tcl_DStringStartSublist(Tcl_DString *dsPtr)
            Adds characters to dsPtr ("  {", for example) to initiate a sublist.
Tcl_DStringEndSublist(Tcl_DString *dsPtr)
            Adds characters to dsPtr ("}", for example) to terminate a sublist.
char *Tcl_DStringValue(Tcl_DString *dsPtr)
            Returns a pointer to the current value of dsPtr.
int Tcl_DStringLength(Tcl_DString *dsPtr)
            Returns the number of characters in dsPtr, not including the terminating
            null character.
void Tcl_DStringTrunc(Tcl_DString *dsPtr, int newLength)
            If dsPtr has more than newLength characters, shortens it to include only
            the first newLength characters.
void Tcl_DStringFree(Tcl_DString *dsPtr)
            Frees up any memory allocated for dsPtr and reinitializes dsPtr's value
            to an empty string.
void Tcl_DStringResult(Tcl_Interp *interp, Tcl_DString *dsPtr)
            Moves the value of dsPtr to interp->result and reinitializes dsPtr's
            value to an empty string.
```

```
int Tcl_CommandComplete(char *cmd)
            Returns 1 if cmd holds one or more complete commands, 0 if the last
            command in cmd is incomplete due to open braces etc.
```

```
int Tcl_StringMatch(char *string, char *pattern)
            Returns 1 if string matches pattern using glob-style rules for pattern
            matching, 0 otherwise.
```

Table 36.1. Tcl library procedures for manipulating strings.

Tcl_DStringFree releases any storage allocated for a dynamic string and reinitializes the string.

Tcl_DStringResult moves the value of a dynamic string to the result string for an interpreter and reinitializes the dynamic string.

The code below uses several of these procedures to implement a map command, which takes a list and generates a new list by applying some operation to each element of the original list. map takes two arguments: a list and a Tcl command. For each element in the list, it executes the given command with the list element appended as an additional argument. It takes the results of all the commands and generates a new list from them, and then returns this list as its result. Here are some examples of how you might use the map command:

```
proc inc x {expr $x+1}
map {4 18 16 19 -7} inc
```
⇒ *5 19 17 20 -6*
```
proc addz x {return "$x z"}
map {a b {a b c}} addz
```
⇒ *{a z} {b z} {a b c z}*

Here is the command procedure that implements map:

```
int MapCmd(ClientData clientData, Tcl_Interp *interp,
        int argc, char *argv[]) {
    Tcl_DString command, newList;
    int listArgc, i, result;
    char **listArgv;
    if (argc != 3) {
        interp->result = "wrong # args";
        return TCL_ERROR;
    }
    if (Tcl_SplitList(interp, argv[1], &listArgc,
            &listArgv) != TCL_OK) {
        return TCL_ERROR;
    }
    Tcl_DStringInit(&newList);
    Tcl_DStringInit(&command);
    for (i = 0; i < listArgc; i++) {
        Tcl_DStringAppend(&command, argv[2], -1);
        Tcl_DStringAppendElement(&command, listArgv[i]);
        result = Tcl_Eval(interp,
                Tcl_DStringValue(&command));
        Tcl_DStringFree(&command);
        if (result != TCL_OK) {
            Tcl_DStringFree(&newList);
            free((char *) listArgv);
            return result;
        }
        Tcl_DStringAppendElement(&newList, interp->result);
    }
    Tcl_DStringResult(interp, &newList);
    free((char *) listArgv);
    return TCL_OK;
}
```

MapCmd uses two dynamic strings. One holds the result list and the other holds the command to execute in each step. The first dynamic string is needed because the length of the command is unpredictable, and the second one is needed to store the result list as it builds up (this information can't be placed immediately in interp->result because the interpreter's result will be overwritten by the command that is evaluated to process the next list element). Each dynamic string is represented by a structure of type `Tcl_DString`. The structure holds information about the string such as a pointer to its current value, a small array to use for small strings, and a length. Tcl doesn't allocate `Tcl_DString` structures; it is up to you to allocate the structure (as a local variable, for example) and pass its address to the dynamic string library procedures. You should never access the fields of a `Tcl_DString` structure directly; use the macros and procedures provided by Tcl.

After checking its argument count, extracting all of the elements from the initial list, and initializing its dynamic strings, MapCmd enters a loop to process the elements of the list. For each element it first creates the command to execute for that element. It does this by calling `Tcl_DStringAppend` to append the part of the command provided in `argv[2]`, then it calls `Tcl_DStringAppendElement` to append the list element as an additional argument. These procedures are similar in that both add new information to the dynamic string. However, `Tcl_DStringAppend` adds the information as raw text whereas `Tcl_DStringAppendElement` converts its string argument to a proper list element and adds that list element to the dynamic string (with a separator space, if needed). It's important to use `Tcl_DStringAppendElement` for the list element so that it becomes a single word of the Tcl command being formed. If `Tcl_DString-Append` were used instead and the element were "a b c" as in the example on page 347, then the command passed to `Tcl_Eval` would be "addz a b c", which would result in an error (too many arguments to the addz procedure). When `Tcl_DString-AppendElement` is used the command is "addz {a b c}", which parses correctly.

Once MapCmd has created the command to execute for an element, it invokes `Tcl_Eval` to evaluate the command. The `Tcl_DStringFree` call frees any memory that was allocated for the command string and resets the dynamic string to an empty value for use in the next command. If the command returned an error, MapCmd returns that same error; otherwise it uses `Tcl_DStringAppendElement` to add the result of the command to the result list as a new list element.

MapCmd calls `Tcl_DStringResult` after all of the list elements have been processed. This transfers the value of the string to the interpreter's result in an efficient way (for example, if the dynamic string uses dynamically allocated memory, `Tcl_DStringResult` just copies a pointer to the result to `interp->result` rather than allocating new memory and copying the string).

Before returning, MapCmd must be sure to free any memory allocated for the dynamic strings. It turns out that this has already been done by `Tcl_DStringFree` for command and by `Tcl_DStringResult` for newList.

36.2 **Command completeness**

When an application reads commands typed interactively, it must wait until a complete command has been entered before evaluating it. For example, suppose an application is reading commands from standard input and the user types the following three lines:

```
foreach i {1 2 3 4 5} {
    puts "$i*$i is [expr $i*$i]"
}
```

If the application reads each line separately and passes it to Tcl_Eval, a "missing close-brace" error will be generated by the first line. Instead, the application should collect input until all the commands read are complete (for example, there are no unmatched braces or quotes) then execute all of the input as a single script. The procedure Tcl_CommandComplete makes this possible. It takes a string as argument and returns 1 if the string contains syntactically complete commands or 0 if the last command isn't yet complete.

The C procedure that follows uses dynamic strings and Tcl_CommandComplete to read and evaluate a command typed on standard input. It collects input until all the commands read are complete, then it evaluates the command(s) and returns the completion code from the evaluation. It uses Tcl_RecordAndEval to evaluate the command so that the command is recorded on the history list.

```
int DoOneCmd(Tcl_Interp *interp) {
    char line[200];
    Tcl_DString cmd;
    int code;
    Tcl_DStringInit(&cmd);
    while (1) {
        if (fgets(line, sizeof(line), stdin) == NULL) {
            break;
        }
        Tcl_DStringAppend(&cmd, line, -1);
        if (Tcl_CommandComplete(Tcl_DStringValue(&cmd))) {
            break;
        }
    }
    code = Tcl_RecordAndEval(interp,
            Tcl_DStringValue(&cmd), 0);
    Tcl_DStringFree(&cmd);
    return code;
}
```

In the foreach example, DoOneCmd will collect all three lines before evaluating them. If an end-of-file occurs fgets will return NULL and DoOneCmd will evaluate the command even if it isn't complete yet.

Note: *Tcl_CommandComplete checks only for completeness in the sense of parsing correctly. It doesn't guarantee that the script will behave correctly. For example, if a user accidentally splits a command like "set x y" over two lines by typing a newline after the x, each line will be considered to be complete. The first line will simply query the variable instead of modifying it, and the second line will invoke a command y, which will probably generate an error.*

36.3 String matching

The procedure Tcl_StringMatch provides the same functionality as the string match Tcl command. Given a string and a pattern, it returns 1 if the string matches the pattern using glob-style matching and 0 otherwise. For example, here is a command procedure that uses Tcl_StringMatch to implement a simplified version of lsearch that provides only glob-style matching. It returns the index of the first element in a list that matches a pattern, or −1 if no element matches:

```
int LsearchCmd(ClientData clientData,
        Tcl_Interp *interp, int argc, char *argv[]) {
    int listArgc, i, result;
    char **listArgv;
    if (argc != 3) {
        interp->result = "wrong # args";
        return TCL_ERROR;
    }
    if (Tcl_SplitList(interp, argv[1], &listArgc,
            &listArgv) != TCL_OK) {
        return TCL_ERROR;
    }
    result = -1;
    for (i = 0; i < listArgc; i++) {
        if (Tcl_StringMatch(listArgv[i], argv[2])) {
            result = i;
            break;
        }
    }
    sprintf(interp->result, "%d", result);
    free((char *) listArgv);
    return TCL_OK;
}
```

Chapter 37
POSIX Utilities

This chapter describes several utilities that you may find useful if you use POSIX system calls in your C code. The procedures can be used to expand tilde (~) notation in file names, to generate messages for POSIX errors and signals, and to manage subprocesses. See Table 37.1 for a summary of the procedures.

37.1 Tilde expansion

Tcl and Tk allow you to use ~ notation when specifying file names, and if you write new commands that manipulate files then you should support tildes also. For example, the command

```
open ~ouster/.login
```

opens the file named `.login` in the home directory of user `ouster`, and

```
open ~/.login
```

opens a file named `.login` in the home directory of the current user (as given by the HOME environment variable). Unfortunately, tildes are not supported by the POSIX system calls that open files. For example, in the first `open` command the name presented to the `open` system call must be something like

```
/users/ouster/.login
```

where `~ouster` has been replaced by the home directory for `ouster`. The procedure that carries out this substitution is `Tcl_TildeSubst`. It is used internally by Tcl and Tk to process file names before using them in system calls, and you may find it useful if you write C code that deals with POSIX files.

```
char *Tcl_TildeSubst(Tcl_Interp *interp, char *name,
    Tcl_DString *resultPtr)
```
> If name starts with ~, returns a new name with the ~ and following characters replaced with the corresponding home directory name. If name doesn't start with ~, returns name. Uses *resultPtr if needed to hold new name (caller need not initialize *resultPtr, but must free it by calling Tcl_DStringFree). If an error occurs, returns NULL and leaves an error message in interp->result.

```
char *Tcl_PosixError(Tcl_Interp *interp)
```
> Sets the errorCode variable in interp based on the current value of errno, and returns a string identifying the error.

```
char *Tcl_ErrnoId(void)
```
> Returns a symbolic name corresponding to the current value of errno, such as ENOENT.

```
char *Tcl_SignalId(int sig)
```
> Returns the symbolic name for sig, such as SIGINT.

```
char *Tcl_SignalMsg(int sig)
```
> Returns a human-readable message describing signal sig.

```
int Tcl_CreatePipeline(Tcl_Interp *interp, int argc,
    char *argv[], int **pidPtr, int *inPipePtr,
    int *outPipePtr, int *errFilePtr)
```
> Creates a process pipeline, returns a count of the number of processes created, and stores at *pidPtr the address of a malloc-ed array of process identifiers. If an error occurs, returns −1 and leaves an error message in interp->result. inPipePtr, outPipePtr, and errFilePtr are used to control default I/O redirection.

```
void Tcl_DetachPids(int numPids, int *pidPtr)
```
> Passes responsibility for numPids at *pidPtr to Tcl: Tcl will allow them to run in backround and reap them in some future call to Tcl_ReapDetachedProcs.

```
void Tcl_ReapDetachedProcs(void)
```
> Checks to see if any detached processes have exited; if so, cleans up their state.

Table 37.1. Tcl library procedures for dealing with POSIX system calls.

For example, the implementation of the open command contains code something like the following:

```
int fd;
Tcl_DString buffer;
char *fullName;
...
fullName = Tcl_TildeSubst(interp, argv[1], &buffer);
if (fullName == NULL) {
    return TCL_ERROR;
}
fd = open(fullName, ...);
Tcl_DStringFree(&buffer);
...
```

Tcl_TildeSubst takes as arguments an interpreter, a file name that may start with a tilde, and a dynamic string. It returns a new file name, which is either the original name (if it didn't start with ~), a new tilde-expanded name, or NULL if an error occurred; in the last case an error message is left in the interpreter's result.

If Tcl_TildeSubst has to generate a new name, it uses the dynamic string given by its final argument to store the name. When Tcl_TildeSubst is called, the dynamic string should either be uninitialized or empty. Tcl_TildeSubst initializes it and then uses it for the new name if needed. After the caller has finished using the new file name, it must invoke Tcl_DStringFree to release any memory that was allocated for the dynamic string.

37.2 Generating messages

When an error or signal occurs in the C code of a Tcl application, the application should report the error or signal back to the Tcl script that triggered it, usually as a Tcl error. To do this, information about the error or signal must be converted from the binary form used in C to a string form for use in Tcl scripts. Tcl provides four procedures to do this: Tcl_PosixError, Tcl_ErrnoId, Tcl_SignalId, and Tcl_SignalMsg.

Tcl_PosixError provides a simple "all in one" mechanism for reporting errors in system calls. Tcl_PosixError examines the C variable errno to determine what kind of error occurred, calls Tcl_SetErrorCode to set the errorCode variable appropriately, and returns a human-readable string suitable for use in an error message. For example, consider the following fragment of code, which might be part of a command procedure:

```
FILE *f;
...
f = fopen("prolog.ps", "r");
if (f == NULL) {
    Tcl_AppendResult(interp, "couldn't open prolog.ps: ",
            Tcl_PosixError(interp), (char *) NULL);
    return TCL_ERROR;
}
```

If the file doesn't exist or isn't readable, an error will occur when `fopen` invokes a system call to open the file. An integer code will be stored in the `errno` variable to identify the error, and `fopen` will return a null pointer. The preceding code detects such errors and invokes `Tcl_PosixError`. For example, if the file didn't exist, `Tcl_PosixError` will set `errorCode` to

```
POSIX ENOENT {no such file or directory}
```

and return the string "`no such file or directory`". This code incorporates `Tcl_PosixError`'s return value into its own error message, which it stores in `interp->result`. In the case of a nonexistent file, the code will return "`couldn't open prolog.ps: no such file or directory`" as its error message.

`Tcl_ErrnoId` returns the official POSIX name for the error indicated by `errno`. The names are the symbolic ones defined in the header file `errno.h`. For example, if `errno`'s value is ENOENT, `Tcl_ErrnoId` will return the string ENOENT. The return value from `Tcl_ErrnoId` is the same as the value that `Tcl_PosixError` stores in the second element of `errorCode`.

`Tcl_SignalId` and `Tcl_SignalMsg` each take a POSIX signal number as argument, and each returns a string describing the signal. `Tcl_SignalId` returns the official POSIX name for the signal as defined in `signal.h`, and `Tcl_SignalMsg` returns a human-readable message describing the signal. For example,

```
Tcl_SignalId(SIGILL)
```

returns the string `SIGILL`, and

```
Tcl_SignalMsg(SIGILL)
```

returns "`illegal instruction`".

37.3 Creating subprocesses

`Tcl_CreatePipeline` is the procedure that does most of the work of creating subprocesses for `exec` and `open`. It creates one or more subprocesses in a pipeline configuration. It has the following arguments and result:

```
int Tcl_CreatePipeline(Tcl_Interp *interp, int argc,
        char *argv[], int **pidPtr, int *inPipePtr,
        int *outPipePtr, int *errFilePtr)
```

The `argc` and `argv` arguments describe the commands for the subprocesses in the same form they would be specified to `exec`. Each string in `argv` becomes one word of one command, except for special strings like > and | that are used for I/O redirection and separators between commands. `Tcl_CreatePipeline` normally returns a count of the number of subprocesses created, and it stores at `*pidPtr` a pointer to an array containing the process identifiers for the new processes. The array is dynamically allocated and must be freed by the caller by passing it to `free`. If an error occurred while spawning the subprocesses (for example, `argc` and `argv` specified that output should be redirected to a file but the file couldn't be opened), `Tcl_CreatePipeline` returns −1 and leaves an error message in `interp->result`.

The last three arguments to `Tcl_CreatePipeline` are used to control I/O to and from the pipeline if `argv` and `argc` don't specify I/O redirection. If these arguments are NULL, the first process in the pipeline will take its standard input from the standard input of the parent, the last process will write its standard output to the standard output of the parent, and all of the processes will use the parent's standard error channel for their error messages. If `inPipePtr` is not NULL, it points to an integer; `Tcl_CreatePipeline` will create a pipe, connect its output to the standard input of the first subprocess, and store a writable file descriptor for its input at `*inPipePtr`. If `outPipePtr` is not NULL, standard output goes to a pipe and a readable descriptor for the pipe is stored at `*out-PipePtr`. If `errFilePtr` is not NULL, `Tcl_CreatePipeline` creates a temporary file and connects the standard error files for all of the subprocesses to that file; a readable descriptor for the file will be stored at `*errFilePtr`. `Tcl_CreatePipe-line` removes the file before it returns, so the file will only exist as long as it is open.

If `argv` specifies input or output redirection, this overrides the requests made in the arguments to `Tcl_CreatePipeline`. For example, if `argv` redirects standard input, no pipe is created for standard input; if `inPipePtr` is not NULL, −1 is stored at `*inPipePtr` to indicate that standard input was redirected. If `argv` redirects standard output, no pipe is created for it; if `outPipePtr` is not NULL, −1 is stored at `*out-PipePtr`. If `argv` redirects some or all of the standard error output and `errFilePtr` is not NULL, the file will still be created and a descriptor will be returned, even though it's possible that no messages will actually appear in the file.

37.4 Background processes

`Tcl_DetachPids` and `Tcl_ReapDetachedProcs` are used to keep track of processes executing in the background. If an application creates a subprocess and abandons it (i.e., the parent never invokes a system call to wait for the child to exit), the child executes in background and when it exits it becomes a *zombie*. It remains a zombie until its parent officially waits for it or until the parent exits. Zombie processes occupy space in the system's process table, so if you create enough of them you will overflow the process table and make it impossible for anyone to create more processes. To keep this from happening, you must invoke a system call such as `waitpid`, which will return the exit status of the zombie process. Once the status has been returned the zombie relinquishes its slot in the process table.

To prevent zombies from overflowing the process table you should pass the process identifiers for background processes to `Tcl_DetachPids`:

```
Tcl_DetachPids(int numPids, int *pidPtr);
```

The `pidPtr` argument points to an array of process identifiers and `numPids` gives the size of the array. Each of these processes now becomes the property of Tcl and the caller should not refer to them again. Tcl will assume responsibility for waiting for the processes after they exit.

In order for Tcl to clean up background processes you may need to call `Tcl_Reap-DetachedProcs` from time to time. `Tcl_ReapDetachedProcs` invokes the `waitpid` kernel call on each detached process so that its state can be cleaned up if it has exited. If some of the detached processes are still executing, `Tcl_ReapDetached-Procs` doesn't actually wait for them to exit; it only cleans up the processes that have already exited. Tcl automatically invokes `Tcl_ReapDetachedProcs` each time `Tcl_CreatePipeline` is invoked, so under normal circumstances you won't ever need to invoke it. However, if you create processes without calling `Tcl_CreatePipe-line` (e.g., by invoking the `fork` system call) and subsequently pass the processes to `Tcl_DetachPids`, then you should also invoke `Tcl_ReapDetachedProcs` from time to time. For example, a good place to call `Tcl_ReapDetachedProcs` is in the code that creates new subprocesses.

Part IV:

Tk's C Interfaces

Chapter 38
Introduction

Like Tcl, Tk is a C library package, and it provides a collection of procedures that you can invoke from an enclosing application. Although you can do many interesting things with Tk without writing any C code, just by writing `wish` scripts, you will probably find that most large graphical user interface applications require some C code too. The most common reason for using Tk's C interfaces is to build new kinds of widgets. For example, if you write a Tk-based spreadsheet you will probably need a new widget to display the contents of the spreadsheet; if you write a charting package you'll probably build one or two new widgets to display charts and graphs in various forms; and so on. Some of these widgets could probably be implemented with existing Tk widgets such as canvases or texts, but for big jobs a new widget tailored to the needs of your application can probably do the job more simply and efficiently than any of Tk's general-purpose widgets. Typically you will build one or two new widget classes to display your application's new objects, then combine your custom widgets with Tk's built-in widgets to create the full user interface of the application.

The chapters in this part of the book will show how to use Tk's library procedures to write new widgets in C. In addition, Chapter 45 provides a brief introduction to writing new geometry managers. You can also use the Tk library procedures to access window system features that aren't supported by the existing Tcl commands, such as setting the border width of a top-level window. In any event, the new features you implement should appear as Tcl commands so that you can use them in scripts. Both the philosophical issues and the library procedures discussed in Part III apply to this part of the book as well.

This chapter provides an overview of the internal structure of a widget and introduces a simple "square" widget. The remaining chapters in Part IV go over each of the main procedures of a widget in detail, introducing the related Tk library procedures and showing the code for the square widget. By the end of this part of the book you will have seen the complete source code for the square widget.

38.1   What's in a widget?

All widget classes have the same basic structure, consisting of a widget record and six C procedures that implement the widget's look and feel. More complex widgets may have additional data structures and procedures, but all widgets have at least these basic components.

A *widget record* is the C data structure that represents the state of a widget. It includes all of the widget's configuration options plus anything else the widget needs for its own internal use. For example, the widget record for a label widget contains the label's text or bitmap, its background and foreground colors, its relief, and so on. Each instance of a widget has its own widget record, but all widgets of the same class have widget records with the same structure. One of the first things to do when designing a new widget class is to design the widget record for that class.

Of the six core procedures that make up a widget, two are Tcl command procedures. The first of these is called the *class command procedure*; it implements the Tcl command that creates new widgets of this class. The command's name is the same as the class name, and the command should have the standard syntax described in Section 15.5 for class commands. The class command procedure initializes a new widget record, creates the window for the new widget, and creates the widget command for the new widget. It is described in more detail in Chapters 39 and 40.

The second command procedure is the *widget command procedure*. It implements the widget commands for all widgets of this class. Chapter 40 discusses how to write widget command procedures and shows the widget command procedure for square widgets.

The third core procedure for a widget class is its *configure procedure*. Given one or more options in string form, such as −background red, the configure procedure parses the options and fills in the widget record with corresponding internal representations such as an XColor structure. The configure procedure is invoked by the create procedure and the widget command procedure to handle configuration options specified on their command lines. Chapter 40 describes the facilities provided by Tk for writing configure procedures.

The fourth core procedure is the *event procedure*. It is invoked by Tk's event dispatcher and typically handles exposures (events indicating that part of the window needs to be redrawn), window size changes, focus changes, and the destruction of the window. Chapter 41 describes the Tk event dispatcher, including its facilities for managing X events plus additional features for timers, event-driven file I/O, and idle callbacks.

The fifth core procedure is the *display procedure*. It is invoked to redraw part or all of the widget on the screen after window exposures, changes in configuration options, and changes in the input focus. Chapter 42 discusses several issues related to redisplay, such as deferred redisplay, double-buffering with pixmaps, and Tk's support for 3-D effects.

The last of a widget's core procedures is its *destroy procedure*. This procedure is called when the widget is destroyed and is responsible for freeing all of the resources allocated for the widget, including the memory for its widget record and X resources such as colors and pixmaps. Widget destruction is tricky because the widget could be in use at the time it is destroyed; Chapter 43 describes how deferred destruction is used to avoid potential problems.

The C code that implements widgets is event-driven, in that it consists of short responses to user interactions and other events. Each of the core procedures responds to events of some sort. The create, widget command, and configure procedures all respond to Tcl commands. The event procedure responds to X events, and the display and destroy procedures are invoked by the command and event procedures.

38.2 The relationship between Tk and Xlib

Xlib is the C library package that provides the lowest level of access to the X Window System. Tk is implemented using Xlib but it hides most of the Xlib procedures from the C code in widgets, as shown in Figure 38.1. For example, Xlib provides a procedure `XCreateWindow` to create new windows, but you should not use it; instead, call `Tk_CreateWindowFromPath`. `Tk_CreateWindowFromPath` calls `XCreateWindow` but also does additional things such as associating a textual name with the window. Similarly, you shouldn't normally call Xlib procedures such as `XAllocColor` to allocate colors and other resources; call the corresponding Tk procedures such as `Tk_GetColor` instead. In the case of colors, Tk calls Xlib to allocate the color, but it also remembers the colors that are allocated; if you use the same color in many different places, Tk will communicate with the X server only once.

However, Tk does not totally hide Xlib from you. When widgets redisplay themselves they make direct calls to Xlib procedures such as `XDrawLine` and `XDrawString`. Fur-

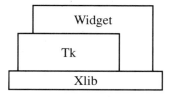

Figure 38.1. Tk hides many of the Xlib interfaces from widgets, but widgets still invoke Xlib directly for a few purposes such as drawing on the screen.

thermore, many of the structures manipulated by Tk are the same as the structures provided by Xlib, such as graphics contexts and window attributes. Thus you'll need to know quite a bit about Xlib in order to write new widgets with Tk. This book assumes that you are familiar with the following concepts from Xlib:

- Window attributes such as `background_pixel`, which are stored in `XSetWindowAttributes` structures.
- Resources related to graphics, such as pixmaps, colors, graphics contexts, and fonts.
- Procedures for displaying, such as `XDrawLine` and `XDrawString`.
- Event types and the `XEvent` structure.

Refer to Xlib documentation such as the Scheifler and Gettys book for specifics about the Xlib structures and procedures. If you haven't used Xlib before I'd suggest waiting to read about Xlib until you need the information. That way you can focus on just the information you need and avoid learning about the parts of Xlib that are hidden by Tk.

Besides Xlib, you shouldn't need to know anything about any other X toolkit or library. For example, Tk is completely independent from the Xt toolkit so you don't need to know anything about Xt.

38.3 Square: an example widget

I will use a simple widget called "square" for examples throughout Part IV. The square widget displays a colored square on a background as shown in Figure 38.2. The widget supports several configuration options, such as colors for the background and for the square, a relief for the widget, and a border width used for both the widget and the square. It also provides three widget commands: `configure`, which is used in the standard way to query and change options; `position`, which fetches and sets the position of the square's upper-left corner relative to the upper-left corner of the window; and `size`, which fetches and sets the square's size. Figure 38.2 illustrates the `position` and `size` commands.

Given these simple commands many other features can be written as Tcl scripts. For example, the following script arranges for the square to center itself over the mouse cursor when Button 1 is pressed and to track the mouse as long as Button 1 is held down. It assumes that the square widget is named `.s`.

```
proc center {x y} {
    set a [.s size]
    .s position [expr $x-($a/2)] [expr $y-($a/2)]
}
bind .s <ButtonPress-1> {center %x %y}
bind .s <B1-Motion> {center %x %y}
```

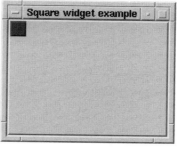

```
square .s
pack .s
wm title .s "Square widget example"
```

(a)

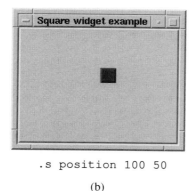

`.s position 100 50`

(b)

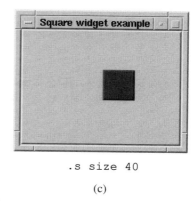

`.s size 40`

(c)

Figure 38.2. A sequence of scripts and the displays that they produce. Figure (a) creates a square widget, Figure (b) invokes the `position` widget command to move the square within its widget, and Figure (c) changes the size of the square from the default size of 20.

Note: *For this particular widget it would probably make more sense to use configuration options such as* `-position` *and* `-size` *instead of the* `position` *and* `size` *commands; I used widget commands in order to illustrate how to write widget commands.*

You will see all of the C code for the square widget in the remaining chapters of Part IV; there are about 320 lines in all. The square widget doesn't use all of the features of Tk but it illustrates the basic things you must do to create a new widget. For examples of more complex widgets you can look at the source code for some of Tk's widgets; they have the same basic structure as the square widget and they use the same library procedures that you will read about in the chapters that follow.

38.4 tk.h

Each C source file that uses any of Tk's facilities should include the following statement near the beginning of the file:

```
#include <tk.h>
```

The include file tk.h declares all of the structures, procedures, and symbolic values supported by Tk.

38.5 Design for reusability

When building a new widget, try to make it as flexible and general purpose as possible, so that other people will be able to use your widget in ways that you didn't foresee when you created it. Here are a few specific things to think about:

1. Store all the information about the widget in its widget record. Try not to use static or global variables to hold widget state, since they may make it impossible to have more than one instance of the widget in any given application. Even if you don't envision using more than one instance per application, don't do anything to rule this out.

2. Make sure that all of the primitive operations on your widget are available through its widget command. Don't hard-wire the widget's behavior in C. Instead, define the behavior as a set of class bindings using the bind command. This will make it easy to change and extend the widget's behavior.

3. Provide escapes to Tcl. Look for interesting ways to embed Tcl commands in your widget and invoke them in response to various events. For example, the actions for button widgets and menu items are stored as Tcl commands that are evaluated when the widgets are invoked, and canvases and texts allow you to associate Tcl commands with their internal objects in order to give them behaviors.

4. Organize the code for your widget in one or a few files that can easily be linked into other applications besides the one you're writing, and follow the conventions described in Section 31.2 for creating packages. For example, all of the variables and procedures for the square widget are defined as static, so that their names are not visible outside the file containing the square code. The only externally visible procedure is the initialization procedure Square_Init, which registers the class command for square widgets (see Section 39.7).

5. Document your widget code carefully, so that other people can use your code as the starting point for building other widgets.

Chapter 39
Creating Windows

This chapter presents Tk's basic library procedures for creating windows. It describes the Tk_Window type, which is used as a token for windows, then introduces the Tk procedures for creating and deleting windows. Tk provides several macros for retrieving information about windows, which are introduced next. Then the chapter discusses what should be in the create procedure for a widget, using the square widget as an example. The chapter closes with a discussion of delayed window creation. See Table 39.1 for a summary of the procedures discussed in this chapter.

39.1 Windows and Tk_Windows

Xlib uses a token of type Window to refer to each window. These tokens are returned by procedures in Xlib that create windows, and they must be used when communicating with Xlib (for example, to draw graphics in a window).

Tk uses a token of type Tk_Window to represent each window. When you create a new window Tk returns a Tk_Window token, and you must pass this token back to Tk when invoking Tk procedures to manipulate the window. Tk keeps several pieces of information for each window, such as its name and current size, and you can access this information using the Tk_Window token. There is one Window for each Tk_Window, and Tk allocates the Window automatically on your behalf; you should not normally invoke Xlib procedures to create windows. You can retrieve the Window for a Tk_Window using the Tk_WindowId macro described in Section 39.5.

```
Tk_Window Tk_CreateMainWindow(Tcl_Interp *interp,
    char *screenName, char *appName, char *className)
```
Creates a new application and returns a token for the application's main window. screenName gives the screen on which to create the main window (if NULL, Tk picks default), appName gives a base name for the application, and className gives the class of the application (and also the main widget). If an error occurs, returns NULL and stores an error message in interp->result.

```
Tk_Window Tk_CreateWindowFromPath(Tcl_Interp *interp,
    Tk_Window tkwin, char *pathName, char *screenName)
```
Creates a new window in tkwin's application whose path name is pathName. If screenName is NULL the new window will be an internal window; otherwise it will be a top-level window on screenName. Returns a token for the new window. If an error occurs, returns NULL and stores an error message in interp->result.

```
Tk_Window Tk_CreateWindow(Tcl_Interp *interp,
    Tk_Window parent, char *name, char *screenName)
```
Same as Tk_CreateWindowFromPath, except that the new window is specified with a parent and a name within that parent, rather than a complete path name.

```
void Tk_SetClass(Tk_Window tkwin, char *class)
```
Sets tkwin's class to class.

```
void Tk_DestroyWindow(TkWindow tkwin)
```
Destroys tkwin and all of its descendants in the window hierarchy.

```
Tk_Window Tk_NameToWindow(Tcl_Interp *interp, char *pathName,
    Tk_Window tkwin)
```
Returns the token for the window whose path name is pathName in the same application as tkwin. If no such name exists, returns NULL and stores an error message in interp->result.

```
void Tk_MakeWindowExist(TkWindow tkwin)
```
Forces the creation of the X window for tkwin, if it doesn't already exist.

Table 39.1. A summary of basic procedures for window creation and deletion.

39.2 Creating Tk_Windows

Tk applications typically use two procedures for creating windows: Tk_CreateMain-Window and Tk_CreateWindowFromPath. Tk_CreateMainWindow creates a new application; it is usually invoked in the main program of an application. Before invoking Tk_CreateMainWindow you should create a Tcl interpreter to use for the application. Tk_CreateMainWindow takes four arguments, consisting of the interpreter plus three strings:

```
Tk_Window Tk_CreateMainWindow(Tcl_Interp *interp,
            char *screenName, char *appName, char *className);
```

The `screenName` argument gives the name of the screen on which to create the main window. It can have any form acceptable to your X server. For example, on most UNIX-like systems `unix:0` selects the default screen of display 0 on the local machine, or `ginger.cs.berkeley.edu:0.0` selects screen 0 of display 0 on the machine whose network address is `ginger.cs.berkeley.edu`. `screenName` may be specified as NULL, in which case Tk picks a default server. On UNIX-like systems the default server is normally determined by the `DISPLAY` environment variable.

The third argument to `Tk_CreateMainWindow` is a name to use for the application, such as `clock` for a clock program or "`mx foo.c`" for an editor named `mx` editing a file `foo.c`. This is the name that other applications will use to send commands to the new application. Each application must have a unique name; if `appName` is already in use by some other application, Tk adds a suffix like #2 to make the name unique. Thus the actual name of the application may be something like "`clock #3`" or "`mx foo.c #4`". You can determine the actual name for the application by calling the `Tk_Name` macro or by invoking the Tcl command "`winfo name .`".

The last argument to `Tk_CreateMainWindow` is a class name, which is typically the name of the application except with an initial capital letter (for example, `Mx` might be the class name for an application named `mx`). This is used both as the class for the application and as the class for the main widget. Among other things, the class name is used when matching patterns in the option database.

`Tk_CreateMainWindow` creates a toplevel widget to use as the application's main widget, registers the application's name so that other applications can send commands to it, and adds all of Tk's commands to the interpreter. It returns the `Tk_Window` token for the main window. If an error occurs (for example, `screenName` doesn't exist or the X server refused to accept a connection), `Tk_CreateMainWindow` returns NULL and leaves an error message in `interp->result`.

`Tk_CreateWindowFromPath` adds a new window to an existing application. It is the procedure that is usually called when creating new widgets and it has the following prototype:

```
Tk_Window Tk_CreateWindowFromPath(Tcl_Interp *interp,
            Tk_Window tkwin, char *pathName, char *screenName);
```

The `tkwin` argument is a token for an existing window; its only purpose is to identify the application in which to create the new window. `pathName` gives the full path name for the new window, such as `.a.b.c`. A window by this name must not already exist, but its parent (for example, `.a.b`) must exist. If `screenName` is NULL, the new window is an internal window; otherwise the new window will be a top-level window on the indicated screen. `Tk_CreateWindowFromPath` returns a token for the new window unless an error occurs, in which case it returns NULL and leaves an error message in `interp->result`.

39.3   Setting a window's class

The procedure `Tk_SetClass` assigns a particular class name to a window. For example,

```
Tk_SetClass(tkwin, "Foo");
```

sets the class of window `tkwin` to `Foo`. Class names are used by Tk for several purposes such as finding options in the option database and matching events to bindings. The class name for a widget should normally be the same as the name of the Tcl command that creates widgets of that class except with an initial capital letter, such as `Checkbutton` for checkbutton widgets or `Canvas` for canvases. Typically, `Tk_SetClass` is called just after calling `Tk_CreateWindowFromPath`.

39.4   Deleting windows

The procedure `Tk_DestroyWindow` takes a `Tk_Window` as argument and deletes the window. It also deletes all of the window's children recursively. Deleting the main window of an application will delete all of the windows in the application, and most applications will exit when they notice that all of their windows have been deleted.

39.5   Basic operations on Tk_Windows

Given a textual path name for a window, `Tk_NameToWindow` may be used to find the `Tk_Window` token for the window:

```
Tk_Window Tk_NameToWindow(Tcl_Interp *interp, char *pathName,
        Tk_Window tkwin);
```

`pathName` is the name of the desired window, such as `.a.b.c`, and `tkwin` is a token for any window in the application of interest (it isn't used except to select a specific application). Normally `Tk_NameToWindow` returns a token for the given window, but if no such window exists it returns `NULL` and leaves an error message in `interp->result`.

Tk maintains several pieces of information about each `Tk_Window` and provides a set of C macros that you can use to access the information. See Table 39.2 for a summary of all the macros. Each macro takes a `Tk_Window` as an argument and returns the corresponding piece of information for the window. For example, if `tkwin` is a `Tk_Window`, then

```
int width;
...
width = Tk_Width(tkwin);
```

returns an integer value giving the current width of `tkwin` in pixels. Here are a few of the more commonly used macros:

Macro Name	Result Type	Meaning
Tk_Attributes	XSetWindowAttributes *	Window attributes such as border pixel and cursor.
Tk_Changes	XWindowChanges *	Window position, size, stacking order.
Tk_Class	Tk_Uid	Name of window's class.
Tk_Colormap	Colormap	Colormap for window.
Tk_Depth	int	Bits per pixel.
Tk_Display	Display	X display for window.
Tk_Height	int	Current height of window in pixels.
Tk_InternalBorderWidth	int	Width of internal border in pixels.
Tk_IsMapped	int	1 if window mapped, 0 otherwise.
Tk_IsTopLevel	int	1 if top-level, 0 if internal.
Tk_Name	Tk_Uid	Name within parent. For main window, returns application name.
Tk_Parent	Tk_Window	Parent, or NULL for main window.
Tk_PathName	char *	Full path name of window.
Tk_ReqWidth	int	Requested width in pixels.
Tk_ReqHeight	int	Requested height in pixels.
Tk_Screen	Screen *	X screen for window.
Tk_ScreenNumber	int	Index of window's screen.
Tk_Visual	Visual *	Information about window's visual characteristics.
Tk_Width	int	Current width of window in pixels.
Tk_WindowId	Window	X identifier for window.
Tk_X	int	X-coordinate of window within parent.
Tk_Y	int	Y-coordinate of window within parent.

Table 39.2. Macros defined by Tk for retrieving window state. Each macro takes a Tk_Window as argument and returns a result whose type is given in the second column. All of these macros are fast (they simply return fields from Tk's internal structures and don't require any interactions with the X server).

- `Tk_Width` and `Tk_Height` return the window's dimensions; this information is used during redisplay for purposes such as centering text.
- `Tk_WindowId` returns the X identifier for the window, which is needed when invoking Xlib procedures during redisplay.
- `Tk_Display` returns a pointer to Xlib's `Display` structure corresponding to the window; it is also needed when invoking Xlib procedures.

Some of the macros, like `Tk_InternalBorderWidth` and `Tk_ReqWidth`, are only used by geometry managers (see Chapter 45) and others such as `Tk_Visual` are rarely used by anyone.

39.6   Class command procedures

The class command procedure for a widget must do five things:

- Create a new `Tk_Window`.
- Create and initialize a widget record.
- Set up event handlers.
- Create a widget command for the widget.
- Process configuration options for the widget.

The class command procedure implements a Tcl command named after the widget's class, and its `clientData` argument should be the `Tk_Window` token for the main window of the application (this is needed in order to identify the application to `Tk_CreateWindowFromPath`).

Figure 39.1 shows the code for `SquareCmd`, which is the class command procedure for square widgets. After checking its argument count, `SquareCmd` creates a new window for the widget and invokes `Tk_SetClass` to assign it a class of `Square`. The middle part of `SquareCmd` allocates a widget record for the new widget and initializes it. Tk does not impose any constraints on the structure of a widget record, but in practice many of the fields are the same from widget class to widget class. The widget record for squares has the following definition:

```
typedef struct {
    Tk_Window tkwin;
    Display *display;
    Tcl_Interp *interp;
    int x, y;
    int size;
    int borderWidth;
    Tk_3DBorder bgBorder;
    Tk_3DBorder fgBorder;
    int relief;
    GC gc;
    int updatePending;
} Square;
```

The first field of the record is the Tk_Window for the widget. The next field, display, identifies the X display for the widget (it is needed during cleanup after the widget is deleted). interp holds a pointer to the interpreter for the application. The x and y fields give the position of the upper-left corner of the square in pixels relative to the upper-left corner of the window, and the size field specifies the square's size in pixels. The last six fields are used for displaying the widget; they will be discussed in Chapters 40 and 42.

After initializing the new widget record SquareCmd calls Tk_CreateEvent-Handler; this arranges for SquareEventProc to be called whenever the widget needs to be redrawn or when various other events occur, such as deleting its window or changing its size; events will be discussed in more detail in Chapter 41. Next Square-Cmd calls Tcl_CreateCommand to create the widget command for the widget. The widget's name is the name of the command, SquareWidgetCmd is the command procedure, and a pointer to the widget record is the clientData for the command. Then SquareCmd calls SquareConfigure to process the configuration options specified as arguments to the command; Chapter 40 describes how the configuration options are handled. If an error occurs in processing the configuration options, SquareCmd destroys the window and returns an error. Otherwise it returns success with the widget's path name in interp->result.

Note: *Strictly speaking, not all of the fields of a widget record need to be initialized explicitly in the create procedure, since they will be overwritten by the configure procedure. However, the rules for exactly which fields need to be initialized are complicated; I strongly recommend that you initialize all of the fields to be safe. Pointers or tokens for Tk structures should be initialized to NULL, and X resources such as graphics contexts should be initialized to None.*

39.7   Package initialization

In order for SquareCmd to be invoked in a Tk application, a new Tcl command must be created with SquareCmd as its command procedure. The best way to do this is to

```
static int SquareCmd(ClientData clientData,
        Tcl_Interp *interp, int argc, char *argv[]) {
    Tk_Window main = (Tk_Window) clientData;
    Square *squarePtr;
    Tk_Window tkwin;

    if (argc < 2) {
        Tcl_AppendResult(interp, "wrong # args: should be \"",
                argv[0], " pathName ?options?\"", (char *) NULL);
        return TCL_ERROR;
    }

    tkwin = Tk_CreateWindowFromPath(interp, main, argv[1],
            (char *) NULL);
    if (tkwin == NULL) {
        return TCL_ERROR;
    }
    Tk_SetClass(tkwin, "Square");

    squarePtr = (Square *) malloc(sizeof(Square));
    squarePtr->tkwin = tkwin;
    squarePtr->display = Tk_Display(tkwin);
    squarePtr->interp = interp;
    squarePtr->x = squarePtr->y = 0;
    squarePtr->size = 20;
    squarePtr->borderWidth = 0;
    squarePtr->bgBorder = squarePtr->fgBorder = NULL;
    squarePtr->relief = TK_RELIEF_FLAT;
    squarePtr->gc = None;
    squarePtr->updatePending = 0;

    Tk_CreateEventHandler(tkwin,
            ExposureMask|StructureNotifyMask, SquareEventProc,
            (ClientData) squarePtr);
    Tcl_CreateCommand(interp, Tk_PathName(tkwin),
        SquareWidgetCmd, (ClientData) squarePtr,
        (Tcl_CmdDeleteProc *) NULL);
    if (SquareConfigure(interp, squarePtr, argc-2, argv+2, 0)
            != TCL_OK) {
        Tk_DestroyWindow(squarePtr->tkwin);
        return TCL_ERROR;
    }
    interp->result = Tk_PathName(tkwin);
    return TCL_OK;
```

. The class command procedure for square widgets. This procedure implements the
  mand.

ment the square widget as a package according to the rules described in Section 31.2, with a package initialization procedure that creates the new Tcl command:

```
int Square_Init(Tcl_Interp *interp) {
    Tcl_CreateCommand(interp, "square", SquareCmd,
            (ClientData) Tk_MainWindow(interp),
            (Tcl_CmdDeleteProc *) NULL);
    return TCL_OK;
}
```

This procedure can then be invoked from an application's `Tcl_AppInit` procedure in the standard fashion described in Chapter 31. `Square_Init` uses a module prefix in its name, and it is the only procedure in the square widget implementation that must be visible outside the square widget. All of the other procedures, such as `SquareCmd`, are declared `static` so that they aren't visible outside the square widget; because of this, their names need not follow any particular convention.

39.8 Delayed window creation

`Tk_CreateMainWindow` and `Tk_CreateWindowFromPath` create the Tk data structures for a window, but they do not communicate with the X server to create an actual X window. If you create a `Tk_Window` and immediately fetch its X window identifier using `Tk_WindowId`, the result will be `None`. Tk doesn't normally create the X window for a `Tk_Window` until the window is mapped by a geometry manager (see Chapter 45). The reason for delaying window creation is performance. When a `Tk_Window` is initially created, all of its attributes are set to default values. However, many of these attributes will be modified almost immediately when the widget configures itself. It's more efficient to delay the window's creation until all of its attributes have been set, rather than first creating the window and then asking the X server to modify the attributes later.

Delayed window creation is normally invisible to widgets, since the only time a widget needs to know the X identifier for a window is when it invokes Xlib procedures to display it. This doesn't happen until after the window has been mapped, so the X window will have been created by then. If for some reason you should need the X window identifier before a `Tk_Window` has been mapped, you can invoke `Tk_MakeWindowExist`:

```
void Tk_MakeWindowExist(tkwin);
```

This forces the X window for `tkwin` to be created immediately if it hasn't been created yet. Once `Tk_MakeWindowExist` returns, `Tk_WindowId` can be used to retrieve the `Window` token for it.

Chapter 40
Configuring Widgets

The phrase "configuring a widget" refers to all of the setup that must be done prior to actually drawing the widget's contents on the screen. A widget is configured initially when it is created and it may be reconfigured by invoking its widget command. One of the largest components of configuring a widget is processing configuration options such as −borderwidth 1m. For each option the textual value must be translated to an internal form suitable for use in the widget. For example, distances specified in floating-point millimeters must be translated to integer pixel values and font names must be mapped to corresponding XFontStruct structures. Configuring a widget also includes other tasks such as preparing X graphics contexts to use when drawing the widget and setting attributes of the widget's window, such as its background color.

This chapter describes the Tk library procedures for configuring widgets, and it presents the square widget's configure procedure and widget command procedure. Chapter 42 will show how to draw a widget once configuration is complete.

40.1 Tk_ConfigureWidget

Tk provides three library procedures, Tk_ConfigureWidget, Tk_Configure-Info, and Tk_FreeOptions, that do most of the work of processing configuration options (see Table 40.1). To use these procedures you first create a *configuration table* that describes all of the configuration options supported by your widget class. For each option there is one entry in the configuration table and a corresponding field in the widget record. When creating a new widget, you pass this table to Tk_ConfigureWidget along with argc/argv information describing the configuration options (i.e., all the arguments in

```
int Tk_ConfigureWidget(Tcl_Interp *interp, Tk_Window tkwin,
    Tk_ConfigSpec *specs, int argc, char *argv[], char *widgRec,
    int flags)
```
Processes a set of arguments from a Tcl command (`argc` and `argv`) using a table of allowable configuration options (`specs`) and sets the appropriate fields of a widget record (`widgRec`). `tkwin` is the widget's window. Normally returns TCL_OK; if an error occurs, returns TCL_ERROR and leaves an error message in `interp->result`. `flags` is normally 0 or TK_CONFIG_ARGV_ONLY (see reference documentation for other possibilities).

```
int Tk_ConfigureInfo(Tcl_Interp *interp, Tk_Window tkwin,
    Tk_ConfigSpec *specs, char *widgRec, char *argvName,
    int flags)
```
Finds the configuration option in `specs` whose command-line name is `argvName`, locates the value of that option in `widgRec`, and generates in `interp->result` a list describing that configuration option. If `argvName` is NULL, generates a list of lists describing all of the options in `specs`. Normally returns TCL_OK; if an error occurs, returns TCL_ERROR and leaves an error message in `interp->result`. `flags` is normally 0 (see the reference documentation for other possibilities).

```
void Tk_FreeOptions(Tk_ConfigSpec *specs, char *widgRec,
    Display *display, int flags)
```
Frees any resources in `widgRec` that are referenced by `specs`. `display` must be the widget's display. `flags` is normally 0 but can be used to select particular entries in `specs` (see reference documentation for details).

```
int Tk_Offset(type, field)
```
This is a macro that returns the offset of a field named `field` within a structure whose type is `type`. Used when creating configuration tables.

Table 40.1. A summary of Tk_ConfigureWidget and related procedures and macros.

the creation command after the widget name). You also provide a pointer to the widget record for the widget. `Tk_ConfigureWidget` processes each option in `argv` according to the information in the configuration table: it converts string values to appropriate internal forms, allocates resources such as fonts and colors if necessary, and stores the results into the widget record. For options that aren't explicitly specified in `argv`, `Tk_ConfigureWidget` checks the option database and uses the value specified there, if there is one. For options that still haven't been set, `Tk_ConfigureWidget` uses default values specified in the configuration table.

When the `configure` widget command is invoked to change options, you call `Tk_ConfigureWidget` again with the `argc`/`argv` information describing the new option values. `Tk_ConfigureWidget` will process the arguments according to the table and modify the information in the widget record accordingly. When the `config-`

ure widget command is invoked to read out the current settings of options, you call Tk_ConfigureInfo. It generates a Tcl result describing one or all of the widget's options in exactly the right form, so all you have to do is return this result from the widget command procedure.

Finally, when a widget is deleted you invoke Tk_FreeOptions. Tk_FreeOptions scans through the table to find options for which resources have been allocated, such as fonts and colors. For each such option it uses the information in the widget record to free up the resource.

40.1.1   Tk_ConfigSpec tables

Most of the work in processing options is in creating the configuration table. The table is an array of records, each with the following structure:

```
typedef struct {
    int type;
    char *argvName;
    char *dbName;
    char *dbClass;
    char *defValue;
    int offset;
    int specFlags;
    Tk_CustomOption *customPtr;
} Tk_ConfigSpec;
```

The type field specifies the internal form into which the option's string value should be converted. For example, TK_CONFIG_INT means the option's value should be converted to an integer and TK_CONFIG_COLOR means that the option's value should be converted to a pointer to an XColor structure. For TK_CONFIG_INT the option's value must have the syntax of a decimal, hexadecimal, or octal integer and for TK_CONFIG_COLOR the option's value must have one of the forms for colors described in Section 16.1.3. For TK_CONFIG_COLOR Tk will allocate an XColor structure, which must later be freed (e.g., by calling Tk_FreeOptions). More than 20 different option types are defined by Tk; see the reference documentation for details on each of the supported types.

argvName is the option's name as specified on command lines, such as -background or -font. The dbName and dbClass fields give the option's name and class in the option database. The defValue field gives a default value to use for the option if it isn't specified on the command line and there isn't a value for it in the option database. The default is specified as a string in the same way it might be typed in a Tcl command; NULL means there is no default for the option.

The offset field tells where in the widget record to store the converted value of the option. It is specified as a byte displacement from the beginning of the record. You should use the Tk_Offset macro to generate values for this field. For example,

```
Tk_Offset(Square, relief)
```

produces an appropriate offset for the relief field of a record whose type is Square.

The `specFlags` field contains an OR-ed combination of flag bits that provide additional control over the handling of the option. A few of the flags are discussed later; see the reference documentation for a complete listing. Finally, the `customPtr` field provides additional information for application-defined options. It is used only when the type is `TK_CONFIG_CUSTOM` and should be `NULL` in other cases. See the reference documentation for details on defining custom option types.

Here is the configuration table for square widgets:

```
static Tk_ConfigSpec configSpecs[] = {
    {TK_CONFIG_BORDER, "-background", "background",
        "Background", "#cdb79e",
        Tk_Offset(Square, bgBorder), TK_CONFIG_COLOR_ONLY,
        (Tk_CustomOption *) NULL},
    {TK_CONFIG_BORDER, "-background", "background",
        "Background", "white", Tk_Offset(Square, bgBorder),
        TK_CONFIG_MONO_ONLY, (Tk_CustomOption *) NULL},
    {TK_CONFIG_SYNONYM, "-bd", "borderWidth", (char *) NULL,
        (char *) NULL, 0, 0, (Tk_CustomOption *) NULL},
    {TK_CONFIG_SYNONYM, "-bg", "background", (char *) NULL,
        (char *) NULL, 0, 0, (Tk_CustomOption *) NULL},
    {TK_CONFIG_PIXELS, "-borderwidth", "borderWidth",
        "BorderWidth", "1m", Tk_Offset(Square, borderWidth),
        0, (Tk_CustomOption *) NULL},
    {TK_CONFIG_SYNONYM, "-fg", "foreground", (char *) NULL,
        (char *) NULL, 0, 0, (Tk_CustomOption *) NULL},
    {TK_CONFIG_BORDER, "-foreground", "foreground",
        "Foreground", "#b03060",
        Tk_Offset(Square, fgBorder), TK_CONFIG_COLOR_ONLY,
        (Tk_CustomOption *) NULL},
    {TK_CONFIG_BORDER, "-foreground", "foreground",
        "Foreground", "black",
        Tk_Offset(Square, fgBorder), TK_CONFIG_MONO_ONLY,
        (Tk_CustomOption *) NULL},
    {TK_CONFIG_RELIEF, "-relief", "relief", "Relief",
        "raised", Tk_Offset(Square, relief), 0,
        (Tk_CustomOption *) NULL},
    {TK_CONFIG_END, (char *) NULL, (char *) NULL,
        (char *) NULL, (char *) NULL, 0, 0,
        (Tk_CustomOption *) NULL}
};
```

This table illustrates three additional features of `Tk_ConfigSpecs` structures. First, there are two entries each for the `-background` and `-foreground` options. The first entry for each option has the `TK_CONFIG_COLOR_ONLY` flag set, which causes Tk to use that option if the display is a color display and to ignore it if the display is monochrome. The second entry specifies the `TK_CONFIG_MONO_ONLY` flag so it is only used for monochrome displays. This feature allows different default values to be specified for color and mono displays (the current color model for the window determines whether it should be treated as color or monochrome; see Section 26.6). Second, the options `-bd`,

-bg, and -fg have type TK_CONFIG_SYNONYM. This means that each of these options is a synonym for some other option; the dbName field identifies the other option and the other fields are ignored. For example, if the -bd option is specified, Tk will actually use the table entry for the -borderwidth option. Third, the last entry in the table must have type TK_CONFIG_END; Tk depends on this to locate the end of the table.

40.1.2 Invoking Tk_ConfigureWidget

Suppose that Tk_ConfigureWidget is invoked as follows:

```
Tcl_Interp *interp;
Tk_Window tkwin;
char *argv[] = {"-relief", "sunken", "-bg", "blue"};
Square *squarePtr;
int code;
...
code = Tk_ConfigureWidget(interp, tkwin, configSpecs,
          4, argv, (char *) squarePtr, 0);
```

A call much like this will occur if a square widget is created with the Tcl command

```
square .s -relief sunken -bg blue
```

The -relief option will be processed according to type TK_CONFIG_RELIEF, which dictates that the option's value must be a valid relief such as raised or sunken. In this case the value specified is sunken; Tk_ConfigureWidget converts this string value to the integer value TK_RELIEF_SUNKEN and stores that value in squarePtr->relief. The -bg option will be processed according to the config-Specs entry for -background, which has type TK_CONFIG_BORDER. This type requires that the option's value be a valid color name; Tk creates a data structure suitable for drawing graphics in that color in tkwin, and it computes additional colors for drawing light and dark shadows to produce three-dimensional effects. All of this information is stored in the new structure and a token for that structure is stored in the bgBorder field of squarePtr. In Chapter 42 you'll see how this token is used to draw the widget.

Since the -borderwidth and -foreground options weren't specified in argv, Tk_ConfigureWidget looks them up in the option database using the information for those options in configSpecs. If it finds values in the option database, it will use them in the same way as if they had been supplied in argv.

If an option isn't specified in the option database, Tk_ConfigureWidget uses the default value specified in its table entry. For example, for -borderwidth it will use the default value 1m. Since the option has type TK_CONFIG_PIXELS, this string must specify a screen distance in one of the forms described in Section 16.1.2. 1m specifies a distance of one millimeter; Tk converts this to the corresponding number of pixels and stores the result as an integer in squarePtr->borderWidth. If the default value for an option is NULL, Tk_ConfigureWidget does nothing at all if there is no value in either argv or the option database; the value in the widget record will be unchanged.

40.1.3   Errors

Tk_ConfigureWidget normally returns TCL_OK. If an error occurs, it returns
TCL_ERROR and leaves an error message in interp->result. The most common
form of error is a value that doesn't make sense for the option type, such as abc for the
-bd option. Tk_ConfigureWidget returns as soon as it encounters an error, which
means that some of the fields of the widget record may not have been set yet.

40.1.4   Reconfiguring

Tk_ConfigureWidget gets invoked not only when a widget is created but also during
the configure widget command. When reconfiguring you will not want to consider the
option database or default values. You will want to process only the options that are specified explicitly in argv, leaving all the unspecified options with their previous values. To
accomplish this, specify TK_CONFIG_ARGV_ONLY as the last argument to Tk_Con-
figureWidget:

```
code = Tk_ConfigureWidget(interp, tkwin, configSpecs,
        argc, argv, (char *) squarePtr,
        TK_CONFIG_ARGV_ONLY);
```

40.1.5   Tk_ConfigureInfo

If a configure widget command is invoked with a single argument, or with no arguments, then it must return configuration information. For example, if .s is a square widget, then

```
.s configure -background
```
should return a list of information about the -background option and
```
.s configure
```
should return a list of lists describing all the options, as described in Section 25.6.
Tk_ConfigureInfo does all the work of generating this information in the proper format. For the square widget it might be invoked as follows:

```
code = Tk_ConfigureInfo(interp, squarePtr->tkwin,
        configSpecs, (char *) squarePtr, argv[2], 0);
```
argv[2] specifies the name of a particular option (e.g., -background in the first
configure widget command). If information is to be returned about all options, as in
the second configure widget command, then NULL should be specified as the option
name. Tk_ConfigureInfo sets interp->result to hold the proper value and
returns TCL_OK. If an error occurs (because a bad option name was specified, for example), Tk_ConfigureInfo stores an error message in interp->result and returns
TCL_ERROR. In either case, the widget command procedure can leave
interp->result as it is and return code as its completion code.

40.1.6 Tk_FreeOptions

Tk_FreeOptions will free all of the information in a widget record that is related to configuration options. It is invoked when a widget is deleted. For some option types, such as TK_CONFIG_BORDER, Tk_ConfigureWidget allocates resources that must eventually be freed. Tk_FreeOptions takes care of this:

```
void Tk_FreeOptions(Tk_ConfigSpec *specs, char *widgRec,
        Display *display, int flags);
```

specs and widgRec should be the same as in calls to Tk_ConfigureWidget. display identifies the X display containing the widget (it is needed for freeing certain options) and flags should normally be 0. Tk_FreeOptions will scan specs looking for entries such as TK_CONFIG_BORDER whose resources must be freed. For each such entry it checks the widget record to be sure a resource is actually allocated (for example, if the value of a string resource is NULL, it means that no memory is allocated). If there is a resource allocated, Tk_FreeOptions passes the value from the widget record to an appropriate procedure to free up the resource and resets the value in the widget record to a state such as NULL to indicate that it has been freed.

40.1.7 Other uses for configuration tables

Configuration tables can also be used for things other than widgets. They are suitable for any situation where textual information must be converted to an internal form and stored in fields of a structure, particularly if the information is specified in the same form as for widget options, e.g.,

```
-background blue -width 1m
```

Tk uses configuration tables internally for menu entries, canvas items, and display attributes of tags in text widgets.

40.2 Resource caches

The X Window System provides a number of different resources for applications to use. Windows are one example; others include graphics contexts, fonts, pixmaps, colors, and cursors. An application must allocate resources before using them and free resources when they're no longer needed. X was designed to make resource allocation and deallocation as cheap as possible, but it is still expensive in many situations because it requires communication with the X server (for example, font allocation requires communication with the server to make sure the font exists). If an application uses the same resource in several different places, such as the same font in many different windows, it is wasteful to allocate separate resources for each use; this wastes time communicating with the server and it wastes space in the X server, which must keep track of the copies of the resource.

Tk provides a collection of *resource caches* in order to reduce the costs of resource management. When your application needs a particular resource you shouldn't call Xlib to allocate it; call the corresponding Tk procedure instead. Tk keeps track of all the resources used by the application and allows them to be shared. If you use the same font in many different widgets, Tk will call Xlib to allocate a font for the first widget, but it will reuse this font for all the other widgets. When the resource is no longer needed anywhere in the application (for example, all the widgets using the font have been destroyed) then Tk will invoke the Xlib procedure to free the resource. This approach saves time as well as memory in the X server.

If you allocate a resource through Tk you must treat it as read-only since it may be shared. For example, if you allocate a graphics context with `Tk_GetGC` you must not change the background color of the graphics context, since this would affect the other uses of the graphics context. If a widget finds that it needs different resouces (for example, because it has been reconfigured), it should free the old resource and allocate a new one. In the rare cases where you really need to modify a resource after creating it, you should not use Tk's resource caches; call Xlib directly to allocate the resource so that you can have a private copy.

Most of the resources for a widget are allocated automatically by `Tk_ConfigureWidget`, and `Tk_ConfigureWidget` uses the Tk resource caches. The following subsections describe how to use the Tk resource caches directly, without going through `Tk_ConfigureWidget`.

40.2.1 Graphics contexts

Graphics contexts are the resource that you are most likely to allocate directly. They are needed whenever you draw information on the screen and `Tk_ConfigureWidget` does not provide facilities for allocating them. The procedure `Tk_GetGC` allocates a graphics context and is similar to the Xlib procedure `XCreateGC`:

```
GC Tk_GetGC(Tk_Window tkwin, unsigned long valueMask,
        XGCValues *valuePtr);
```

The `tkwin` argument specifies the window in which the graphics context will be used. `valueMask` and `valuePtr` specify the fields of the graphics context. `valueMask` is an OR-ed combination of bits such as `GCForeground` or `GCFont` that indicate which fields of `valuePtr` are significant. `valuePtr` specifies values of the selected fields. Refer to Scheifler and Gettys for details on the possible values for `valueMask` and `valuePtr`. `Tk_GetGC` returns the X resource identifier for a graphics context that matches `valueMask` and `valuePtr`. The graphics context will have default values for all of the unspecified fields.

When you're finished with a graphics context you must free it by calling `Tk_FreeGC`:

```
void Tk_FreeGC(Display *display, GC gc);
```

The `display` argument indicates the display for which the graphics context was allocated and the `gc` argument identifies the graphics context (`gc` must have been the return value from some previous call to `Tk_GetGC`). There must be exactly one call to `Tk_FreeGC` for each call to `Tk_GetGC`.

In most cases the configure procedure of a widget will allocate all of the graphics contexts needed by the widget, so that they are readily available when the widget redraws itself. If the widget's `configure` widget command is invoked to change its configuration options, the configure procedure is called to carry out the command; it allocates new graphics contexts and frees the old ones. When the widget is destroyed its destroy procedure calls `Tk_FreeGC` to release all of the graphics contexts.

40.2.2 Other resources

Although resources other than graphics contexts are normally allocated and deallocated automatically by `Tk_ConfigureWidget` and `Tk_FreeOptions`, you can also allocate them explicitly using Tk library procedures. For each resource there are three procedures. The first procedure (such `Tk_GetColor`) takes a textual description of the resource in the same way it might be specified as a configuration option and returns a suitable resource or an error. The second procedure (such as `Tk_FreeColor`) takes a resource allocated by the first procedure and frees it. The third procedure (such as `Tk_NameOfColor`) takes a resource and returns the textual description that was used to allocate it. The following resources are supported in this way:

Bitmaps: the procedures `Tk_GetBitmap`, `Tk_FreeBitmap`, and `Tk_NameOf-Bitmap` manage `Pixmap` resources with depth one. You can also invoke `Tk_DefineBitmap` to create new internally defined bitmaps, and `Tk_SizeOf-Bitmap` returns the dimensions of a bitmap.

Colors: the procedures `Tk_GetColor`, `Tk_FreeColor`, and `Tk_NameOfColor` manage `XColor` structures. You can also invoke `Tk_GetColorByValue` to specify a color with integer intensities rather than a string.

Cursors: the procedures `Tk_GetCursor`, `Tk_FreeCursor`, and `Tk_Name-OfCursor` manage `Cursor` resources. You can also invoke `Tk_GetCursorFrom-Data` to define a cursor based on binary data in the application.

Fonts: the procedures `Tk_GetFontStruct`, `Tk_FreeFontStruct`, and `Tk_NameOfFontStruct` manage `XFontStruct` structures.

3D borders: the procedures `Tk_Get3DBorder`, `Tk_Free3DBorder`, and `Tk_NameOf3DBorder` manage `Tk_3DBorder` resources, which are used to draw objects with beveled edges that produce 3D effects. Associated with these procedures are other procedures such as `Tk_Draw3DRectangle` that draw objects on the screen (see Section 42.3). In addition you can invoke `Tk_3DBorderColor` to retrieve the `XColor` structure for the border's base color.

40.3 Tk_Uids

When invoking procedures like `Tk_GetColor` you provide a textual description of the resource to allocate, such as `red` for a color. However, this textual description is not a normal C string but rather a *unique identifier*, which is represented with the type `Tk_Uid`:

```
typedef char *Tk_Uid;
```

A `Tk_Uid` is actually a pointer to a character array, just like a normal C string, and a `Tk_Uid` can be used anywhere that a string can be used. However, `Tk_Uid`'s have the property that any two `Tk_Uid`'s with the same string value also have the same pointer value: if a and b are `Tk_Uid`'s and

```
(strcmp(a,b) == 0)
```

then

```
(a == b)
```

and vice versa. Tk uses `Tk_Uid`'s to specify resources because they permit fast comparisons for equality.

If you use `Tk_ConfigureWidget` to allocate resources, you won't have to worry about `Tk_Uid`'s (Tk automatically translates strings from the configuration table into `Tk_Uid`'s). But if you call procedures like `Tk_GetColor` directly, you'll need to use `Tk_GetUid` to turn strings into unique identifiers:

```
Tk_Uid Tk_GetUid(char *string);
```

Given a string argument, `Tk_GetUid` returns the corresponding `Tk_Uid`. `Tk_GetUid` maintains a hash table for all the unique identifiers that have been used so far and returns a pointer to the key stored in the hash table; it makes a new entry in the table if there isn't already one for `string`.

Note: *If you pass strings directly to procedures like `Tk_GetColor` without converting them to unique identifiers, you will get unpredictable results. One common symptom is that the application uses the same resource over and over even though you think you've specified different values for each use. Typically what happens is that the same string buffer was used to store all of the different values. Tk just compares the string address rather than its contents, so the values appear to Tk to be the same.*

40.4 Other translators

Tk provides several other library procedures that translate from strings in various forms to internal representations. These procedures are similar to the resource managers in Section 40.2 except that the internal forms are not resources that require freeing, so typically there is just a "get" procedure and a "name of" procedure with no "free" procedure. Tk provides the following translators (see the reference documentation for details):

Anchors: Tk_GetAnchor and Tk_NameOfAnchor translate between strings containing anchor positions such as center or ne and integers with values defined by symbols such as TK_ANCHOR_CENTER or TK_ANCHOR_NE.

Cap styles: Tk_GetCapStyle and Tk_NameOfCapStyle translate between strings containing X cap styles (butt, projecting, or round) and integers with values defined by the X symbols CapButt, CapProjecting, and CapRound.

Join styles: Tk_JoinStyle and Tk_NameOfJoinStyle translate between strings containing X join styles (bevel, miter, or round) and integers with values defined by the X symbols JoinBevel, JoinMiter, and JoinRound.

Justification styles: Tk_GetJustify and Tk_NameOfJustify translate between strings containing styles of justification (left, right, center, or fill) and integers with values defined by the symbols TK_JUSTIFY_LEFT, TK_JUSTIFY_RIGHT, TK_JUSTIFY_CENTER, and TK_JUSTIFY_FILL.

Reliefs: Tk_GetRelief and Tk_NameOfRelief translate between strings containing relief names (raised, sunken, flat, groove, or ridge) and integers with values defined by the symbols TK_RELIEF_RAISED, TK_RELIEF_SUNKEN, etc.

Screen distances: Tk_GetPixels and Tk_GetScreenMM process strings that contain screen distances in any of the forms described in Section 16.1.2, such as 1.5m or 2. Tk_GetPixels returns an integer result in pixel units, and Tk_GetScreenMM returns a real result whose units are millimeters.

Window names: Tk_NameToWindow translates from a string containing a window path name such as .dlg.quit to the Tk_Window token for the corresponding window.

X atoms: Tk_InternAtom and Tk_GetAtomName translate between strings containing the names of X atoms (e.g., RESOURCE_MANAGER) and X Atom tokens. Tk keeps a cache of atom names to avoid communication with the X server.

40.5   Changing window attributes

Tk provides a collection of procedures for modifying a window's attributes (for example, background color or cursor) and configuration (for example, position or size). These procedures are summarized in Table 40.2. The procedures have the same arguments as the Xlib procedures with corresponding names. They perform the same functions as the Xlib procedures except that they also retain a local copy of the new information so that it can be returned by the macros described in Section 39.5. For example, Tk_ResizeWindow is similar to the Xlib procedure XResizeWindow in that it modifies the dimensions of a window. However, it also remembers the new dimensions so they can be accessed with the Tk_Width and Tk_Height macros.

```
Tk_ChangeWindowAttributes(Tk_Window tkwin,
    unsigned int valueMask, XSetWindowAttributes *attsPtr)
```

```
Tk_ConfigureWindow(Tk_Window tkwin, unsigned int valueMask,
    XWindowChanges *valuePtr)
```

```
Tk_DefineCursor(Tk_Window tkwin, Cursor cursor)
```

```
Tk_MoveWindow(Tk_Window tkwin, int x, int y)
```

```
Tk_MoveResizeWindow(Tk_Window tkwin, int x, int y,
    unsigned int width, unsigned int height)
```

```
Tk_ResizeWindow(Tk_Window tkwin, unsigned int width,
    unsigned int height)
```

```
Tk_SetWindowBackground(Tk_Window tkwin, unsigned long pixel)
```

```
Tk_SetWindowBackgroundPixmap(Tk_Window tkwin, Pixmap pixmap)
```

```
Tk_SetWindowBorder(Tk_Window tkwin, unsigned long pixel)
```

```
Tk_SetWindowBorderPixmap(Tk_Window tkwin, Pixmap pixmap)
```

```
Tk_SetWindowBorderWidth(Tk_Window tkwin, int width)
```

```
Tk_SetWindowColormap(Tk_Window tkwin, Colormap colormap)
```

```
Tk_UndefineCursor(Tk_Window tkwin)
```

Table 40.2. Tk procedures for modifying attributes and window configuration information.
Tk_ChangeWindowAttributes and Tk_ConfigureWindow allow any or all of the attributes or
configuration to be set at once (valueMask selects which values should be set); the other
procedures set selected fields individually.

Of the procedures in Table 40.2, only Tk_SetWindowBackground is commonly
invoked by widgets. A widget will typically provide a -background option with a type
of TK_CONFIG_BORDER, which causes a field in the widget record to be set. However,
this doesn't automatically set the window's background color; it just fills in a field in the
widget record. As you will see in Section 40.6, the configure procedure must then extract
the color from the widget record and invoke Tk_SetWindowBackground to install
that color as the background for the widget.

The other procedures in Table 40.2 are rarely invoked directly by widgets. For exam-
ple, the cursor for a widget can be handled with a configuration option of
TK_CONFIG_ACTIVE_CURSOR, in which case Tk_ConfigureWidget calls
Tk_DefineCursor automatically to install the cursor. Widgets should definitely *not*

```
static int SquareConfigure(Tcl_Interp *interp,
        Square *squarePtr, int argc, char *argv[], int flags) {
    if (Tk_ConfigureWidget(interp, squarePtr->tkwin, configSpecs,
            argc, argv, (char *) squarePtr, flags) != TCL_OK) {
        return TCL_ERROR;
    }
    Tk_SetWindowBackground(squarePtr->tkwin,
            Tk_3DBorderColor(squarePtr->bgBorder)->pixel);
    if (squarePtr->gc == None) {
        XGCValues gcValues;
        gcValues.function = GXcopy;
        gcValues.graphics_exposures = False;
        squarePtr->gc = Tk_GetGC(squarePtr->tkwin,
                GCFunction|GCGraphicsExposures, &gcValues);
    }
    Tk_GeometryRequest(squarePtr->tkwin, 200, 150);
    Tk_SetInternalBorder(squarePtr->tkwin,
            squarePtr->borderWidth);
    if (!squarePtr->updatePending) {
        Tk_DoWhenIdle(SquareDisplay, (ClientData) squarePtr);
        squarePtr->updatePending = 1;
    }
    return TCL_OK;
}
```

Figure 40.1. The configure procedure for square widgets. It is invoked by the creation procedure and by the widget command procedure to set and modify configuration options.

invoke Tk_MoveWindow, Tk_ResizeWindow, or Tk_MoveResizeWindow: only geometry managers should change the size or location of a window.

40.6 The square configure procedure

Figure 40.1 contains the code for the square widget's configure procedure. Its argv argument contains pairs of strings that specify configuration options. Most of the work is done by Tk_ConfigureWidget. Once Tk_ConfigureWidget returns, SquareConfigure extracts the color associated with the -background option and calls Tk_SetWindowBackground to install it as the background color for the widget's window. Then it allocates a graphics context to use during redisplay for copying bits from an off-screen pixmap into the window (the usage of the off-screen pixmap is explained in Chapter 42). Next SquareConfigure calls Tk_GeometryRequest and Tk_SetInternalBorderWidth to provide information to its geometry manager (as discussed in Chapter 45). Finally, it arranges for the widget to be redisplayed, as discussed in Chapter 42.

40.7 The square widget command procedure

Figure 40.2 contains the C code for SquareWidgetCmd, which implements widget
commands for square widgets. The clientData argument to the procedure is a pointer
to the widget record for a particular square widget; if there are multiple square widgets in
an application, they all use SquareWidgetCmd as their widget command procedure,
but there is a different clientData value for each widget command.

The main portion of the procedure consists of a series of if statements that compare
argv[1] successively to configure, position, and size, which are the three
actions defined for squares. If argv[1] matches one of these strings, the corresponding
code is executed; otherwise an error is generated.

The configure action is handled in one of three ways, depending on how many
additional arguments it receives. If no additional arguments are present, SquareWidgetCmd calls Tk_ConfigureInfo to return descriptive information for all of the widget's configuration options. If a single additional argument is provided,
SquareWidgetCmd calls Tk_ConfigureInfo to return information about that particular option. If two or more additional arguments are provided, SquareWidgetCmd
passes the additional arguments to SquareConfigure for processing; SquareWidgetCmd specifies the TK_CONFIG_ARGV_ONLY flag, which SquareConfigure
passes on to Tk_ConfigureWidget so that options not specified explicitly by argv
are left as is.

The position and size widget commands change the geometry of the square displayed in the widget, and they have similar implementations. If new values for the geometry are specified, each command calls Tk_GetPixels to convert the argument(s) to
pixel distances. The size widget command also checks to make sure that the new size is
within a particular range of values. Then both commands invoke KeepInWindow, which
adjusts the position of the square if necessary to ensure that it is fully visible in the widget's window (see Figure 40.3). Finally, the commands print the current values into
interp->result to return them.

SquareWidgetCmd invokes the procedures Tk_Preserve and Tk_Release as
a way of preventing the widget record from being destroyed while the widget command is
executing. Chapter 43 discusses these procedures in more detail. The square widget is so
simple that the calls aren't actually needed, but virtually all real widgets do need them so I
put them in SquareWidgetCmd too.

```
static int SquareWidgetCmd(ClientData clientData,
        Tcl_Interp *interp, int argc, char *argv[]) {
    Square *squarePtr = (Square *) clientData;
    int result = TCL_OK;

    if (argc < 2) {
        Tcl_AppendResult(interp, "wrong # args: should be \"",
                argv[0], " option ?arg arg ...?\"",
                (char *) NULL);
        return TCL_ERROR;
    }

    Tk_Preserve((ClientData) squarePtr);
    if (strcmp(argv[1], "configure") == 0) {
        if (argc == 2) {
            result = Tk_ConfigureInfo(interp, squarePtr->tkwin,
                    configSpecs, (char *) squarePtr,
                    (char *) NULL, 0);
        } else if (argc == 3) {
            result = Tk_ConfigureInfo(interp, squarePtr->tkwin,
                    configSpecs, (char *) squarePtr, argv[2], 0);
        } else {
            result = SquareConfigure(interp, squarePtr, argc-2,
                    argv+2, TK_CONFIG_ARGV_ONLY);
        }
    } else if (strcmp(argv[1], "position") == 0) {
        if ((argc != 2) && (argc != 4)) {
            Tcl_AppendResult(interp, "wrong # args: should be \"",
                    argv[0], " position ?x y?\"", (char *) NULL);
            goto error;
        }
        if (argc == 4) {
            if ((Tk_GetPixels(interp, squarePtr->tkwin, argv[2],
                    &squarePtr->x) != TCL_OK) ||
                    (Tk_GetPixels(interp, squarePtr->tkwin,
                    argv[3], &squarePtr->y) != TCL_OK)) {
                goto error;
            }
            KeepInWindow(squarePtr);
        }
        sprintf(interp->result, "%d %d", squarePtr->x,
                squarePtr->y);
    } else if (strcmp(argv[1], "size") == 0) {
```

Figure 40.2. The widget command procedure for square widgets (continued).

```
    if ((argc != 2) && (argc != 3)) {
        Tcl_AppendResult(interp, "wrong # args: should be \"",
                argv[0], " size ?amount?\"", (char *) NULL);
        goto error;
    }
    if (argc == 3) {
        int i;
        if (Tk_GetPixels(interp, squarePtr->tkwin, argv[2],
                &i) != TCL_OK) {
            goto error;
        }
        if ((i <= 0) || (i > 100)) {
            Tcl_AppendResult(interp, "bad size \"", argv[2],
                    "\"", (char *) NULL);
            goto error;
        }
        squarePtr->size = i;
        KeepInWindow(squarePtr);
    }
    sprintf(interp->result, "%d", squarePtr->size);
} else {
    Tcl_AppendResult(interp, "bad option \"", argv[1],
            "\": must be configure, position, or size",
            (char *) NULL);
    goto error;
}
if (!squarePtr->updatePending) {
    Tk_DoWhenIdle(SquareDisplay, (ClientData) squarePtr);
    squarePtr->updatePending = 1;
}
Tk_Release((ClientData) squarePtr);
return result;

error:
    Tk_Release((ClientData) squarePtr);
    return TCL_ERROR;
}
```

Figure 40.2, continued.

```
static void KeepInWindow(Square *squarePtr) {
    int gap, bd;
    bd = 0;
    if (squarePtr->relief != TK_RELIEF_FLAT) {
        bd = squarePtr->borderWidth;
    }
    gap = (Tk_Width(squarePtr->tkwin) - bd)
            - (squarePtr->x + squarePtr->size);
    if (gap < 0) {
        squarePtr->x += gap;
    }
    gap = (Tk_Height(squarePtr->tkwin) - bd)
            - (squarePtr->y + squarePtr->size);
    if (gap < 0) {
        squarePtr->y += gap;
    }
    if (squarePtr->x < bd) {
        squarePtr->x = bd;
    }
    if (squarePtr->y < bd) {
        squarePtr->y = bd;
    }
}
```

Figure 40.3. The KeepInWindow procedure adjusts the location of the square to make sure that it is visible in the widget's window.

Chapter 41
Events

This chapter describes Tk's library procedures for event handling. The code you will write for event handling divides into three parts. The first part consists of code that creates event handlers: it informs Tk that certain callback procedures should be invoked when particular events occur. The second part consists of the callbacks themselves. The third part consists of top-level code that invokes the Tk event dispatcher to process events.

Tk supports three kinds of events: X events, file events, and timer events. Tk also allows you to create *idle callbacks*, which cause procedures to be invoked when Tk runs out of other things to do; idle callbacks are used to defer redisplays and other computations until all pending events have been processed. Tk's procedures for event handling are summarized in Table 41.1.

If you are not already familiar with X events, you may need to read about them in the Scheifler and Gettys book before reading this chapter.

41.1 X events

The X window server generates a number of different events to report interesting things that occur in the window system, such as mouse presses or changes in a window's size. Chapter 18 showed how you can use Tk's `bind` command to write event handlers as Tcl scripts. This section describes how to write event handlers in C. Typically you will use C handlers for only five kinds of X events:

```
void Tk_CreateEventHandler(Tk_Window tkwin, unsigned long mask,
    Tk_EventProc *proc, ClientData clientData)
```
> Arranges for proc to be invoked whenever any of the events selected by mask occurs for tkwin.
```
void Tk_DeleteEventHandler(Tk_Window tkwin, unsigned long mask,
    Tk_EventProc *proc, ClientData clientData)
```
> Deletes the event handler that matches mask, proc, and clientData, if such a handler exists.

```
void Tk_CreateFileHandler(int fd, int mask, Tk_FileProc *proc,
    ClientData clientData)
```
> Arranges for proc to be invoked whenever one of the conditions indicated by mask occurs for the file whose descriptor number is fd.
```
void Tk_DeleteFileHandler(int fd)
```
> Deletes the file handler for fd, if one exists.

```
Tk_TimerToken Tk_CreateTimerHandler(int milliseconds,
    Tk_TimerProc *proc, ClientData clientData)
```
> Arranges for proc to be invoked after milliseconds have elapsed. Returns a token that can be used to cancel the callback.
```
void Tk_DeleteTimerHandler(Tk_TimerToken token)
```
> Cancels the timer callback indicated by token, if it hasn't yet triggered.

```
void Tk_DoWhenIdle(Tk_IdleProc *proc, ClientData clientData)
```
> Arranges for proc to be invoked when Tk has nothing else to do.
```
void Tk_CancelIdleCall(Tk_IdleProc *proc, ClientData clientData)
```
> Deletes any existing idle callbacks for proc and clientData.

```
void Tk_CreateGenericHandler(Tk_GenericProc *proc,
    ClientData clientData)
```
> Arranges for proc to be invoked whenever any X event is received by this process.
```
void Tk_DeleteGenericHandler(Tk_GenericProc *proc,
    ClientData clientData)
```
> Deletes the generic handler given by proc and clientData, if such a handler exists.

```
void Tk_MainLoop(void)
```
> Processes events until all the windows created by this process have been destroyed.
```
int Tk_DoOneEvent(int flags)
```
> Processes a single event of any sort and then returns. flags is normally 0 but may be used to restrict the events that will be processed or to return immediately if there are no pending events.

Table 41.1. A summary of the Tk library procedures for event handling.

Expose: these events notify the widget that part or all of its window needs to be redisplayed.

ConfigureNotify: these events occur when the window's size or position changes so that it can adjust its layout accordingly (for example, centered text may have to be repositioned).

FocusIn and FocusOut: these events notify the widget that it has gained or lost the input focus, so it can turn on or off its insertion cursor.

DestroyNotify: these events notify the widget that its window has been destroyed, so it should free up the widget record and any associated resources.

The responses to these events are fairly standard and it is unlikely that users or application developers will want to change the responses so it makes sense to hard-code them in C. For most other events, such as key presses and mouse actions, it is better to define the handlers in Tcl with the bind command. As a widget writer you can create class bindings to give the widget its default behavior, then users can modify the class bindings or augment them with additional widget-specific bindings. By using Tcl as much as possible you'll make your widgets more flexible.

The procedure Tk_CreateEventHandler is used by widgets to register interest in X events:

```
void Tk_CreateEventHandler(Tk_Window tkwin,
        unsigned long mask, Tk_EventProc *proc,
        ClientData clientData);
```

The tkwin argument identifies a particular window and mask is an OR'ed combination of bits like KeyPressMask and StructureNotifyMask that select the events of interest (refer to the Scheifler and Gettys book for details on the mask values that are available). When one of the requested events occurs for tkwin, Tk will invoke proc to handle the event. proc must match the following prototype:

```
typedef void Tk_EventProc(ClientData clientData,
    XEvent *eventPtr);
```

Its first argument will be the same as the clientData value that was passed to Tk_CreateEventHandler and the second argument will be a pointer to a structure containing information about the event (see Scheifler and Gettys for details on the contents of an XEvent structure). Any number of event handlers can exist for a given window and mask but there can be only one event handler with a particular tkwin, mask, proc, and clientData. If a particular event matches the tkwin and mask for more than one handler, all of the matching handlers are invoked, in the order in which they were created.

For example, the C code for the square widget deals with Expose, ConfigureNotify, and DestroyNotify events. To process these events, the following code is present in the create procedure for squares (see Figure 39.1 on page 372):

```
Tk_CreateEventHandler(squarePtr->tkwin,
        ExposureMask|StructureNotifyMask, SquareEventProc,
        (ClientData) squarePtr);
```

The ExposureMask bit selects Expose events and StructureNotifyMask selects both ConfigureNotify and DestroyNotify events, plus several other types of events. The address of the widget's record is used as the clientData for the callback, so it will be passed to SquareEventProc as its first argument.

Figure 41.1 contains the code for SquareEventProc, the event procedure for square widgets. Whenever an event occurs that matches ExposureMask or StructureNotifyMask, Tk will invoke SquareEventProc. SquareEventProc casts its clientData argument back into a Square * pointer, then checks to see what kind of event occurred. For Expose events SquareEventProc arranges for the widget to be redisplayed. For ConfigureNotify events, SquareEventProc calls KeepIn-Window to make sure that the square is still visible in the window (see Figure 40.3 on page 391), then SquareEventProc arranges for the widget to be redrawn. For

```
static void SquareEventProc(ClientData clientData,
        XEvent *eventPtr) {
    Square *squarePtr = (Square *) clientData;
    if (eventPtr->type == Expose) {
        if (!squarePtr->updatePending) {
            Tk_DoWhenIdle(SquareDisplay, (ClientData) squarePtr);
            squarePtr->updatePending = 1;
        }
    } else if (eventPtr->type == ConfigureNotify) {
        KeepInWindow(squarePtr);
        if (!squarePtr->updatePending) {
            Tk_DoWhenIdle(SquareDisplay, (ClientData) squarePtr);
            squarePtr->updatePending = 1;
        }
    } else if (eventPtr->type == DestroyNotify) {
        Tcl_DeleteCommand(squarePtr->interp,
                Tk_PathName(squarePtr->tkwin));
        squarePtr->tkwin = NULL;
        if (squarePtr->updatePending) {
            Tk_CancelIdleCall(SquareDisplay,
                    (ClientData) squarePtr);
        }
        Tk_EventuallyFree((ClientData) squarePtr, SquareDestroy);
    }
}
```

Figure 41.1. The event procedure for square widgets.

`DestroyNotify` events `SquareEventProc` starts the process of destroying the widget and freeing its widget record; this process is discussed in more detail in Chapter 43.

If you need to cancel an existing X event handler, invoke `Tk_DeleteEvent-Handler` with the same arguments that you passed to `Tk_CreateEventHandler` when you created the handler:

```
void Tk_DeleteEventHandler(Tk_Window tkwin,
        unsigned long mask, Tk_EventProc *proc,
        ClientData clientData);
```

This deletes the handler corresponding to `tkwin`, `mask`, `proc`, and `clientData` so that its callback will not be invoked anymore. If no such handler exists, the procedure does nothing. Tk automatically deletes all of the event handlers for a window when the window is destroyed, so most widgets never need to call `Tk_DeleteEventHandler`.

41.2   File events

Event-driven programs like Tk applications should not block for long periods of time while executing any one operation, because this prevents other events from being serviced. For example, if a Tk application attempts to read from its standard input at a time when no input is available, the application will block until input appears. During this time the process will be suspended by the operating system so it cannot service X events. This means, for example, that the application will not be able to respond to mouse actions nor will it be able to redraw itself. Such behavior is likely to be annoying to the user, since he or she expects to be able to interact with the application at any time.

File handlers provide an event-driven mechanism for reading and writing files that may have long I/O delays. The procedure `Tk_CreateFileHandler` creates a new file handler:

```
void Tk_CreateFileHandler(int fd, int mask,
        Tk_FileProc *proc, ClientData clientData);
```

The `fd` argument gives the number of a POSIX file descriptor (0 for standard input, 1 for standard output, and so on). `mask` indicates when `proc` should be invoked. It is an OR'ed combination of the following bits:

TK_READABLE means that Tk should invoke `proc` whenever data are waiting to be read on `fd`.

TK_WRITABLE means that Tk should invoke `proc` whenever `fd` is capable of accepting more output data.

TK_EXCEPTION means that Tk should invoke `proc` whenever an exceptional condition is present for `fd`.

`proc` must match the following prototype:

```
typedef void Tk_FileProc(ClientData clientData, int mask);
```

The `clientData` argument will be the same as the `clientData` argument to `Tk_CreateFileHandler` and `mask` will contain a combination of the bits `TK_READABLE`, `TK_WRITABLE`, and `TK_EXCEPTION` to indicate the state of the file at the time of the callback. Only one file handler can exist for a given file at a time; if you call `Tk_CreateFileHandler` at a time when a handler for `fd` exists, the new handler replaces the old one.

To delete a file handler, call `Tk_DeleteFileHandler` with the same `fd` argument that was used to create the handler:

```
void Tk_DeleteFileHandler(int fd);
```

This removes the handler for `fd` so that its callback will not be invoked again.

Note: *You can temporarily disable a file handler by calling* `Tk_CreateFileHandler` *with a mask of 0. You can call* `Tk_CreateFileHandler` *again to reset the mask when you want to re-enable the handler. This approach is more efficient than calling* `Tk_DeleteFileHandler` *to delete the handler.*

With file handlers you can do event-driven file I/O. Rather than opening a file, reading it from start to finish, and then closing the file, you open the file, create a file handler for it, and then return. When the file is readable the callback will be invoked. It issues exactly one read request for the file, processes the data returned by the read, and then returns. When the file becomes readable again (perhaps immediately), the callback will be invoked again. Eventually, when the entire file has been read, the file will become readable and the read call will return an end-of-file condition. At this point the file can be closed and the file handler deleted. With this approach, your application will still be able to respond to X events even if there are long delays in reading the file.

For example, `wish` uses a file handler to read commands from its standard input. The main program for `wish` creates a file handler for standard input (file descriptor 0) with the following statement:

```
...
Tcl_DStringInit(&command);
Tk_CreateFileHandler(0, TK_READABLE, StdinProc,
        (ClientData) NULL);
...
```

In addition to registering `StdinProc` as the callback for standard input, this code initializes a dynamic string that will be used to buffer lines of input until a complete Tcl command is ready for evaluation. Then the main program enters the event loop as described in Section 41.6. When data become available on standard input, `StdinProc` will be invoked. Its code is as follows:

```
void StdinProc(ClientData clientData, int mask) {
    int count, code;
    char input[1000];
    count = read(0, input, 1000);
    if (count <= 0) {
        ... handle errors and end of file ...
    }
    Tcl_DStringAppend(&command, input, count);
    if (Tcl_CmdComplete(Tcl_DStringValue(&command)) {
        code = Tcl_Eval(interp,
                Tcl_DStringValue(&command));
        Tcl_DStringFree(&command);
        ...
    }
    ...
}
```

After reading from standard input and checking for errors and end-of-file, StdinProc adds the new data to the dynamic string's current contents. Then it checks to see if the dynamic string contains a complete Tcl command (it won't, for example, if a line such as "foreach i $x {" has been entered but the body of the foreach loop hasn't yet been typed). If the command is complete, StdinProc evaluates the command and clears the dynamic string for the next command.

Note: *It is usually best to use nonblocking I/O with file handlers, just to be absolutely sure that I/O operations don't block. To request nonblocking I/O, specify the flag O_NONBLOCK to the* fcntl *POSIX system call. If you use file handlers for writing to files with long output delays, such as pipes and network sockets, it is essential that you use nonblocking I/O; otherwise if you supply too much data in a* write *system call, the output buffers will fill and the process will be put to sleep.*

Note: *For ordinary disk files it isn't necessary to use the event-driven approach described in this section, because reading and writing these files rarely incurs noticeable delays. File handlers are useful primarily for files such as terminals, pipes, and network connections, which can block for indefinite periods of time.*

41.3 Timer events

Timer events trigger callbacks after particular time intervals. For example, entry widgets use timer events to display blinking insertion cursors. When the entry gains the input focus, it displays the insertion cursor and creates a timer callback that will trigger in a few tenths of a second. The timer callback erases the insertion cursor and reschedules itself for a few tenths of a second later. The next time the callback is invoked it turns the insertion cursor on again. This process repeats indefinitely so that the cursor blinks on and off. When the widget loses the input focus it cancels the timer callback and erases the insertion cursor.

The procedure `Tk_CreateTimerHandler` creates a timer callback:

```
Tk_TimerToken Tk_CreateTimerHandler(int milliseconds,
          Tk_TimerProc *proc, ClientData clientData);
```

The `milliseconds` argument specifies how many milliseconds should elapse before the callback is invoked. `Tk_CreateTimerHandler` returns immediately, and its return value is a token that can be used to cancel the callback. After the given interval has elapsed Tk will invoke `proc`, which must match the following prototype:

```
void Tk_TimerProc(ClientData clientData);
```

Its argument will be the `clientData` passed to `Tk_CreateTimerHandler`. `Proc` is only called once, after which Tk deletes the callback automatically. If you want `proc` to be called over and over at regular intervals, `proc` should reschedule itself by calling `Tk_CreateTimerHandler` each time it is invoked.

Note: *There is no guarantee that* `proc` *will be invoked at exactly the specified time. If the application is busy processing other events when the specified time occurs,* `proc` *won't be invoked until the next time the application invokes the event dispatcher, as described in Section 41.6.*

`Tk_DeleteTimerHandler` cancels a timer callback:

```
void Tk_DeleteTimerHandler(Tk_TimerToken token);
```

It takes a single argument, which is a token returned by a previous call to `Tk_CreateTimerHandler`, and deletes the callback so that it will never be invoked. It is safe to invoke `Tk_DeleteTimerHandler` even if the callback has already been invoked; in this case the procedure has no effect.

41.4 Idle callbacks

The procedure `Tk_DoWhenIdle` creates an *idle callback*:

```
void Tk_DoWhenIdle(Tk_IdleProc *proc, ClientData clientData);
```

This arranges for `proc` to be invoked the next time the application becomes idle. The application is idle when Tk's main event-processing procedure, `Tk_DoOneEvent`, is called and no X events, file events, or timer events are ready. Normally when this occurs `Tk_DoOneEvent` will suspend the process until an event occurs. However, if idle callbacks exist, all of them are invoked. Idle callbacks are also invoked when the `update` Tcl command is invoked. The `proc` for an idle callback must match the following prototype:

```
typedef void Tk_IdleProc(ClientData clientData);
```

It returns no result and takes a single argument, which will be the `clientData` argument passed to `Tk_DoWhenIdle`.

`Tk_CancelIdleCall` deletes an idle callback so that it won't be invoked after all:

```
void Tk_CancelIdleCall(Tk_IdleProc *proc,
          ClientData clientData);
```

Tk_CancelIdleCall deletes all of the idle callbacks that match proc and client-Data (there can be more than one). If there are no matching idle callbacks, the procedure has no effect.

Idle callbacks are used to implement the delayed operations described in Section 26.3. The most common use of idle callbacks in widgets is for redisplay. It is generally a bad idea to redisplay a widget immediately when its state is modified, since this can result in multiple redisplays. For example, suppose the following set of Tcl commands is invoked to change the color, size, and location of a square widget .s:

```
.s configure -foreground purple
.s size 2c
.s position 1.2c 3.1c
```

Each of these commands modifies the widget in a way that requires it to be redisplayed, but it would be a bad idea for each command to redraw the widget. This would result in three redisplays, which are unnecessary and can cause the widget to flash as it steps through a series of changes. It is much better to wait until all of the commands have been executed and then redisplay the widget once. Idle callbacks provide a way of knowing when all of the changes have been made: the callback will not be invoked until all available events have been fully processed.

For example, the square widget uses idle callbacks for redisplaying itself. Whenever it notices that it needs to be redrawn it invokes the following code:

```
if (!squarePtr->updatePending) {
    Tk_DoWhenIdle(SquareDisplay, (ClientData) squarePtr);
    squarePtr->updatePending = 1;
}
```

This arranges for SquareDisplay to be invoked as an idle handler to redraw the widget. The updatePending field of the widget record keeps track of whether Square-Display has already been scheduled, so that it will be scheduled only once. When SquareDisplay is finally invoked it resets updatePending to zero.

41.5 Generic event handlers

The X event handlers described in Section 41.1 trigger only when particular events occur for a particular window managed by Tk. A *generic event handler* is one that is invoked for every X event received by the application, regardless of which display or window the event refers to. Generic handlers are used to deal with events that aren't associated with a particular window, such as MappingNotify events, and events for windows not managed by Tk, such as those in other applications. Generic event handlers are rarely needed and should be used sparingly.

To create a generic event handler, call Tk_CreateGenericHandler:

```
void Tk_CreateGenericHandler(Tk_GenericProc *proc,
        ClientData clientData);
```

This will arrange for `proc` to be invoked whenever any X event is received by the application. `proc` must match the following prototype:

```
typedef int Tk_GenericProc(ClientData clientData,
        XEvent *eventPtr);
```

Its `clientData` argument will be the `clientData` passed to `Tk_Create-GenericHandler` and `eventPtr` will be a pointer to the X event. Generic handlers are invoked before normal event handlers, and if there are multiple generic handlers then they are called in the order in which they were created. Each generic handler returns an integer result. If the result is nonzero it indicates that the handler has completely processed the event and no further handlers, either generic or normal, should be invoked for the event.

The procedure `Tk_DeleteGenericHandler` deletes generic handlers:

```
Tk_DeleteGenericHandler(Tk_GenericProc *proc,
        ClientData clientData);
```

Any generic handlers that match `proc` and `clientData` are removed, so that `proc` will not be invoked anymore.

Note: *Tk_CreateGenericHandler does nothing to ensure that the desired events are actually sent to the application. For example, if an application wishes to respond to events for a window in some other application, it must invoke XSelectInput to notify the X server that it wants to receive the events. Once the events arrive, Tk will dispatch them to the generic handler. However, an application should never invoke XSelectInput for a window managed locally by Tk, since this will interfere with Tk's event management.*

41.6 Invoking the event dispatcher

The preceding sections described the first two parts of event management: creating event handlers and writing callback procedures. The final part of event management is to invoke the Tk event dispatcher, which waits for events to occur and invokes the appropriate callbacks. If you don't invoke the dispatcher, no events will be processed and no callbacks will be invoked.

Tk provides two procedures for event dispatching: `Tk_MainLoop` and `Tk_DoOneEvent`. Most applications use only `Tk_MainLoop`. It takes no arguments and returns no result and it is typically invoked once, in the main program after initialization. `Tk_MainLoop` calls the Tk event dispatcher repeatedly to process events. When all available events have been processed, it suspends the process until more events occur, and it repeats this over and over. It returns only when every `Tk_Window` created by the process has been deleted (for example, after the "`destroy .`" command has been executed). A typical main program for a Tk application will create a Tcl interpreter, call `Tk_CreateMainWindow` to create a Tk application plus its main window, perform other application-specific initialization (such as evaluating a Tcl script to create the application's interface), and then call `Tk_MainLoop`. When `Tk_MainLoop` returns, the main program exits. Thus Tk provides top-level control over the application's execution and all of the application's useful work is carried out by event handlers invoked via `Tk_MainLoop`.

The second procedure for event dispatching is `Tk_DoOneEvent`, which provides a lower level interface to the event dispatcher:

```
int Tk_DoOneEvent(int flags)
```

The `flags` argument is normally 0 (or, equivalently, `TK_ALL_EVENTS`). In this case `Tk_DoOneEvent` processes a single event and then returns 1. If no events are pending, `Tk_DoOneEvent` suspends the process until an event arrives, processes that event, and then returns 1.

For example, `Tk_MainLoop` is implemented using `Tk_DoOneEvent`:

```
void Tk_MainLoop(void) {
    while (tk_NumMainWindows > 0) {
        Tk_DoOneEvent(0);
    }
}
```

The variable `tk_NumMainWindows` is maintained by Tk to count the total number of main windows (i.e., applications) managed by this process. `Tk_MainLoop` just calls `Tk_DoOneEvent` over and over until all the main windows have been deleted.

`Tk_DoOneEvent` is also used by commands such as `tkwait` that want to process events while waiting for something to happen. For example, the `tkwait window` command processes events until a given window has been deleted, then it returns. Here is the C code that implements this command:

```
int done;
...
Tk_CreateEventHandler(tkwin, StructureNotifyMask,
        WaitWindowProc, (ClientData) &done);
done = 0;
while (!done) {
    Tk_DoOneEvent(0);
}
...
```

The variable `tkwin` identifies the window whose deletion is awaited. The code creates an event handler that will be invoked when the window is deleted, then invokes `Tk_DoOneEvent` over and over until the `done` flag is set to indicate that `tkwin` has been deleted. The callback for the event handler is as follows:

```
void WaitWindowProc(ClientData clientData, XEvent *eventPtr) {
    int *donePtr = (int *) clientData;
    if (eventPtr->type == DestroyNotify) {
        *donePtr = 1;
    }
}
```

The clientData argument is a pointer to the flag variable. WaitWindowProc checks to make sure the event is a DestroyNotify event (StructureNotifyMask also selects several other kinds of events, such as ConfigureNotify), and if so, it sets the flag to one.

The flags argument to Tk_DoOneEvent can be used to restrict the kinds of events it will consider. If it contains any of the bits TK_X_EVENTS, TK_FILE_EVENTS, TK_TIMER_EVENTS, or TK_IDLE_EVENTS, then only the events indicated by the specified bits will be considered. Furthermore, if flags includes the bit TK_DONT_WAIT, or if no X, file, or timer events are requested, then Tk_DoOneEvent won't suspend the process; if no event is ready to be processed, it will return immediately with a 0 result to indicate that it had nothing to do. For example, the update idletasks command is implemented with the following code:

```
while (Tk_DoOneEvent(TK_IDLE_EVENTS) != 0) {
    /* empty loop body */
}
```

Chapter 42
Displaying Widgets

Tk provides relatively little support for actually drawing things on the screen. For the most part you just use Xlib functions like `XDrawLine` and `XDrawString`. The only procedures provided by Tk are those summarized in Table 42.1, which create three-dimensional effects by drawing light and dark shadows around objects. This chapter mainly discusses techniques for delaying redisplays and for using pixmaps to double-buffer redisplays. These techniques reduce redisplay overheads and help produce smooth visual effects with minimum flashing.

42.1 Delayed redisplay

The idea of delayed redisplay was introduced in Section 41.4. Rather than redrawing the widget every time its state is modified, you should use `Tk_DoWhenIdle` to schedule the widget's display procedure for execution later, when the application has finished processing all available events. This allows any other pending changes to the widget to be completed before it is redrawn.

Delayed redisplay requires you to keep track of what to redraw. For simple widgets such as the square widget or buttons or labels or entries, I recommend redrawing the entire widget whenever you must redraw any part of it. This eliminates the need to remember which parts to redraw and it will have fine performance for widgets like the ones mentioned earlier.

For larger and more complex widgets such as texts or canvases it isn't practical to redraw the whole widget after each change. This can take a substantial amount of time and cause annoying delays, particularly for operations like dragging where redisplays happen

```
void Tk_Fill3DRectangle(Display *display, Drawable drawable,
    Tk_3DBorder border, int x, int y, int width, int height,
    int borderWidth, int relief)
              Fills the area of drawable given by x, y, width, and height with the
              background color from border, then draws a 3D border borderWidth
              pixels wide around (but just inside) the rectangle. relief specifies the 3D
              appearance of the border.
void Tk_Draw3DRectangle(Display *display, Drawable drawable,
    Tk_3DBorder border, int x, int y, int width, int height,
    int borderWidth, int relief)
              Same as Tk_Fill3DRectangle except draws only the border.

void Tk_Fill3DPolygon(Display *display, Drawable drawable,
    Tk_3DBorder border, XPoint *pointPtr, int numPoints,
    int borderWidth, int leftRelief)
              Fills the area of a polygon in drawable with the background color from
              border. The polygon is specified by pointPtr and numPoints and need
              not be closed. Also draws a 3D border around the polygon. borderWidth
              specifies the width of the border, measured in pixels to the left of the
              polygon's trajectory (if negative, the border is drawn on the right).
              leftRelief specifies the 3D appearance of the border (for example,
              TK_RELIEF_RAISED means the left side of the trajectory appears higher
              than the right).
void Tk_Draw3DPolygon(Display *display, Drawable drawable,
    Tk_3DBorder border, XPoint *pointPtr, int numPoints,
    int borderWidth, int leftRelief)
              Same as Tk_Fill3DPolygon, except draws only the border without
              filling the interior of the polygon.
```

Table 42.1. A summary of Tk's procedures for drawing 3D effects. The drawable argument may be either a Window or Pixmap.

many times per second. For these widgets you should record which parts of the widget need to be redrawn in the widget record. The display procedure can then use this information to redraw only the affected parts.

I recommend recording what to redraw in the simplest (coarsest) way that gives adequate performance. Keeping redisplay information on a very fine grain is likely to add complexity to your widgets and probably won't improve performance noticeably over a coarser mechanism. For example, the Tk text widget does not record what to redraw on a character-by-character basis; instead, it keeps track of which lines on the screen need to be redrawn. The minimum amount that is ever redrawn is one whole line. Most redisplays involve only one or two lines, and today's workstations are fast enough to redraw hundreds of lines per second, so the widget can keep up with the user even if redraws are occurring dozens of times a second (such as when the user is dragging one end of the selection). Tk's canvases optimize redisplay by keeping a rectangular bounding box that includes all of the modified objects. If two small objects at opposite corners of the window are modified simultaneously, the redisplay area will include the entire window, but this doesn't happen very often. In more common cases, such as dragging a single small object, the bounding box approach requires only a small fraction of the window's area to be redrawn.

42.2 Double-buffering with pixmaps

If you want to achieve smooth visual effects, you should not draw graphics directly onto the screen. This causes annoying flashes because widgets usually redisplay themselves by first clearing an area to the background color and then drawing the foreground objects. While the widget is being redrawn the monitor is continuously refreshing itself from display memory, and sometimes the widget will be refreshed on the screen after it has been cleared but before the objects have been redrawn. For this one screen refresh, the widget will appear to be empty; by the time of the next refresh all of the objects will have been redrawn so they will appear again. The result is that the objects in the widget will appear to flash off, then on. This flashing is particularly noticeable during dynamic actions such as dragging or animation where redisplays happen frequently.

To avoid flashing it is best to use a technique called *double-buffering*, where you redisplay in two phases using an off-screen pixmap. The display procedure for the square widget, shown in Figure 42.1, uses this approach. It calls XCreatePixmap to allocate a pixmap the size of the window, then it calls Tk_Fill3DRectangle to redraw the widget in the pixmap. Once the widget has been drawn in the pixmap, the contents are copied to the screen by calling XCopyArea and the pixmap is freed by calling XFreePixmap. With this approach the screen makes a smooth transition from the widget's previous state to its new state. It is still possible for the screen to refresh itself during the copy from pixmap to screen but each pixel will be drawn in either its correct old value or its correct new value.

Note: *If you compile the square widget into* wish *you can use the dragging script from Section 38.3 to compare double-buffering with drawing directly on the screen. To make a version of the square widget that draws directly on the screen, just delete the calls to XCreatePixmap, XCopyArea, and XFreePixmap in SquareDisplay and replace the* pm *arguments to* Tk_Fill3DRectangle *with* TkWindowId(tkwin). *Or, you can use the version of the square widget that comes with the Tk distribution; it has a* −dbl *option that you can use to turn double-buffering on and off dynamically.*

42.3 Drawing procedures

Tk provides only four procedures for actually drawing graphics on the screen, which are summarized in Table 42.1. These procedures make it easy to produce the three-dimen-

```
static void SquareDisplay(ClientData clientData) {
    Square *squarePtr = (Square *) clientData;
    Tk_Window tkwin = squarePtr->tkwin;
    Display *display = Tk_Display(tkwin);
    Pixmap pm;
    squarePtr->updatePending = 0;
    if (!Tk_IsMapped(tkwin)) {
        return;
    }
    pm = XCreatePixmap(display, Tk_WindowId(tkwin),
            Tk_Width(tkwin), Tk_Height(tkwin), Tk_Depth(tkwin));
    Tk_Fill3DRectangle(display, pm, squarePtr->bgBorder,
        0, 0, Tk_Width(tkwin), Tk_Height(tkwin),
        squarePtr->borderWidth, squarePtr->relief);
    Tk_Fill3DRectangle(display, pm, squarePtr->fgBorder,
        squarePtr->x, squarePtr->y, squarePtr->size,
        squarePtr->size, squarePtr->borderWidth,
        squarePtr->relief);
    XCopyArea(display, pm, Tk_WindowId(tkwin),
        squarePtr->gc, 0, 0, Tk_Width(tkwin), Tk_Height(tkwin),
        0, 0);
    XFreePixmap(Tk_Display(tkwin), pm);
}
```

Figure 42.1. The display procedure for square widgets. It first clears
`squarePtr->updatePending` to indicate that there is no longer an idle callback for
`SquareDisplay` scheduled, then it makes sure that the window is mapped (if not, there's no need
to redisplay). It then redraws the widget in an off-screen pixmap and copies the pixmap onto the
screen when done.

sional effects required for Motif widgets, where light and dark shadows are drawn around
objects to make them look raised or sunken.

Before using any of the procedures in Table 42.1 you must allocate a Tk_3DBorder
object. A Tk_3DBorder records three colors (a base color for "flat" background surfaces
and lighter and darker colors for beveled edges) plus X graphics contexts for displaying
objects using those colors. Chapter 40 described how to allocate Tk_3DBorders, for
example by using a configuration table entry of type TK_CONFIG_BORDER or by calling
Tk_Get3DBorder.

Once you've created a Tk_3DBorder you can call Tk_Fill3DRectangle to
draw rectangular shapes with any of the standard reliefs:

```
void Tk_Fill3DRectangle(Display *display, Drawable drawable,
        Tk_3DBorder border, int x, int y, int width,
        int height, int borderWidth, int relief);
```

The display and drawable arguments specify the pixmap or window where the rectangle will be drawn. Display is usually specified as Tk_Display(tkwin) where

tkwin is the window being redrawn. Drawable is usually the off-screen pixmap being used for display, but it can also be Tk_WindowId(tkwin). border specifies the colors to be used for drawing the rectangle. x, y, width, height, and borderWidth specify the geometry of the rectangle and its border, all in pixel units (see Figure 42.2). Last, relief specifies the desired 3D effect, such as TK_RELIEF_RAISED or TK_RELIEF_RIDGE. Tk_Fill3DRectangle first fills the entire area of the rectangle with the "flat" color from border then it draws light and dark shadows border-Width pixels wide around the edge of the rectangle to produce the effect specified by relief.

Tk_Fill3DPolygon is similar to Tk_Fill3DRectangle except that it draws a polygon instead of a rectangle:

```
void Tk_Fill3DPolygon(Display *display, Drawable drawable,
        Tk_3DBorder border, XPoint *pointPtr, int numPoints,
        int borderWidth, int leftRelief);
```

display, drawable, and border all have the same meaning as for Tk_Fill3-DRectangle. pointPtr and numPoints define the polygon's shape (see Scheifler and Gettys for information about XPoint structures) and borderWidth gives the width of the border, all in pixel units. leftRelief defines the relief of the left side of the polygon's trajectory relative to its right side. For example, if leftRelief is specified as TK_RELIEF_RAISED, the left side of the trajectory will appear higher than the right side. If leftRelief is TK_RELIEF_RIDGE or TK_RELIEF_GROOVE, the border will be centered on the polygon's trajectory; otherwise it will be drawn on the left side of the polygon's trajectory if borderWidth is positive and on the right side if border-Width is negative. See Figure 42.2 for an example.

The procedures Tk_Draw3DRectangle and Tk_Draw3DPolygon are similar to Tk_Fill3DRectangle and Tk_Fill3DPolygon except that they draw only the border without filling the interior of the rectangle or polygon.

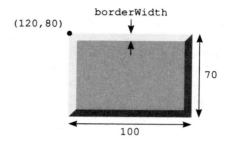

```
Tk_Fill3DRectangle(display, drawable, border, 120, 80, 100, 70,
    borderWidth, TK_RELIEF_RAISED);
```

(a)

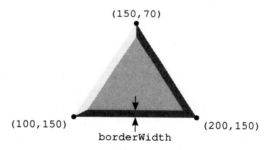

```
static XPoint points[] = {{200,150}, {150,70}, {100,150}};
Tk_Fill3DPolygon(display, drawable, border, points, 3,
    borderWidth, TK_RELIEF_RAISED);
```

(b)

Figure 42.2. Figure (a) shows a call to `Tk_Fill3DRectangle` and the graphic that is produced; the border is drawn entirely inside the rectangular area. Figure (b) shows a call to `Tk_Fill3DPolygon` and the resulting graphic. The relief `TK_RELIEF_RAISED` specifies that the left side of the path should appear higher than the right, and that the border should be drawn entirely on the left side of the path if `borderWidth` is positive.

Chapter 43
Destroying Widgets

This chapter describes how widgets should clean themselves up when they are destroyed. For the most part widget destruction is fairly straightforward: it is just a matter of freeing all of the resources associated with the widget. However, there is one complicating factor, which is that a widget might be in use at the time it is destroyed. This leads to a two-phase approach to destruction where some of the cleanup may have to be delayed until the widget is no longer in use. Tk's procedures for window destruction, most of which have to do with delayed cleanup, are summarized in Table 43.1.

43.1 Basics

Widgets can be destroyed in three different ways. First, the destroy Tcl command can be invoked; it destroys one or more widgets and all of their descendants in the window hierarchy. Second, C code in the application can invoke Tk_DestroyWindow, which has the same effect as the destroy command:

```
void Tk_DestroyWindow(Tk_Window tkwin);
```

Tk_DestroyWindow is not invoked very often but it is used, for example, to destroy a new widget immediately if an error is encountered while configuring it (see Figure 39.1 on page 372). The last way for a widget to be destroyed is for someone to delete its X window via the window manager.

A widget should handle all of these forms of window destruction in the same way, using a handler for DestroyNotify events. Tk makes sure that a DestroyNotify event is generated for each window that is destroyed and Tk does not free the Tk_Win-

```
void Tk_DestroyWindow(Tk_Window tkwin)
          Destroys tkwin and all of its descendants in the widget hierarchy.

void Tk_Preserve(ClientData clientData)
          Makes sure that clientData will not be freed until a matching call to
          Tk_Release has been made.
void Tk_Release(ClientData clientData)
          Cancels a previous Tk_Preserve call for clientData. May cause
          clientData to be freed.
void Tk_EventuallyFree(ClientData clientData,
     Tk_FreeProc *freeProc)
          Invokes freeProc to free clientData, unless Tk_Preserve has been
          called for it; in this case freeProc will not be invoked until each
          Tk_Preserve call has been cancelled with a call to Tk_Release.
```

Table 43.1. A summary of the Tk library procedures for destroying widgets and delaying object cleanup.

dow structure until after the handlers for the event have completed. When a widget receives a DestroyNotify event it typically does four things to clean itself up:

1. It deletes the widget command for the widget by calling Tcl_DeleteCommand.

2. It cancels any idle callbacks and timer handlers for the widget, such as the idle callback to redisplay the widget.

3. It frees any resources allocated for the widget. Most of this can be done by calling Tk_FreeOptions, but widgets usually have a few resources such as graphics contexts that are not directly associated with configuration options.

4. It frees the widget record.

For square widgets the first two of these actions are carried out in the event procedure, and the third and fourth actions are carried out in a separate procedure called SquareDestroy. SquareDestroy is the *destroy procedure* for square widgets; it is invoked indirectly from the event procedure using the mechanism discussed in Section 43.2. Its code is shown in Figure 43.1.

43.2 Delayed cleanup

The most delicate aspect of widget destruction is that the widget could be in use at the time it is destroyed; special precautions must be taken to delay most of the widget cleanup until the widget is no longer in use. For example, suppose that a dialog box .dlg contains a button that is created with the following command:

```
button .dlg.quit -text Quit -command "destroy .dlg"
```

```
static void SquareDestroy(ClientData clientData) {
    Square *squarePtr = (Square *) clientData;
    Tk_FreeOptions(configSpecs, (char *) squarePtr,
            squarePtr->display, 0);
    if (squarePtr->gc != None) {
        Tk_FreeGC(squarePtr->display, squarePtr->gc);
    }
    free((char *) squarePtr);
}
```

Figure 43.1. The destroy procedure for square widgets.

The purpose of this button is to destroy the dialog box. Now suppose that the user clicks on the button with the mouse. The binding for `<ButtonRelease-1>` invokes the button's `invoke` widget command:

    .dlg.quit invoke

The `invoke` widget command evaluates the button's `-command` option as a Tcl script, which destroys the dialog and all its descendants, including the button itself. When the button is destroyed a `DestroyNotify` event is generated, which causes the button's event procedure to be invoked to clean up the destroyed widget. Unfortunately it is not safe for the event procedure to free the button's widget record because the `invoke` widget command is still pending on the call stack and may need the widget record. If the event procedure frees the widget record, the widget command procedure will make wild references into memory. Thus in this situation it is important to wait until the widget command procedure completes before freeing the widget record.

However, a button widget might also be deleted at a time when there is no `invoke` widget command pending (e.g., the user might click on some other button, which destroys the entire application). In this case the cleanup must be done by the event procedure since there won't be any other opportunity for the widget to clean itself up. In other cases there could be several nested procedures each of which is using the widget record, so it won't be safe to clean up the widget record until the last of these procedures finishes.

To handle all of these cases cleanly, Tk provides a general-purpose mechanism for keeping track of whether an object is in use and delaying its cleanup until it is no longer being used. `Tk_Preserve` is invoked to indicate that an object is in use and should not be freed:

    void Tk_Preserve(ClientData clientData);

The `clientData` argument is a token for an object that might potentially be freed; typically it is the address of a widget record. For each call to `Tk_Preserve` there must eventually be a call to `Tk_Release`:

    void Tk_Release(ClientData clientData);

The `clientData` argument should be the same as the corresponding argument to `Tk_Preserve`. Each call to `Tk_Release` cancels a call to `Tk_Preserve` for the object; once all calls to `Tk_Preserve` have been cancelled it is safe to free the object.

When `Tk_Preserve` and `Tk_Release` are being used to manage an object you should call `Tk_EventuallyFree` to free the object:

```
void Tk_EventuallyFree(ClientData clientData,
        Tk_FreeProc *freeProc);
```

`clientData` must be the same as the `clientData` argument used in calls to `Tk_Preserve` and `Tk_Release`, and `freeProc` is a procedure that actually frees the object. `freeProc` must match the following prototype:

```
typedef void Tk_FreeProc(ClientData clientData);
```

Its `clientData` argument will be the `clientData` passed to `Tk_Eventually-Free`. If the object hasn't been protected with calls to `Tk_Preserve`, `Tk_Eventual-lyFree` will invoke `freeProc` immediately. If `Tk_Preserve` has been called for the object, `freeProc` won't be invoked immediately; instead it will be invoked later when `Tk_Release` is called. If `Tk_Preserve` has been called multiple times, then `freeProc` won't be invoked until each of the calls to `Tk_Preserve` has been cancelled by a separate call to `Tk_Release`.

I recommend that you use these procedures in the same way as in the square widget. Place a call to `Tk_Preserve` at the beginning of the widget command procedure and a call to `Tk_Release` at the end of the widget command procedure, as in Figure 40.2 (page 389). Be sure that you don't accidentally return from the widget command procedure without calling `Tk_Release`, since this would prevent the widget from ever being freed. Then divide the widget cleanup code into two parts. Put the code to delete the widget command, idle callbacks, and timer handlers directly into the event procedure as in Figure 41.1 on page 396; this code can be executed immediately without danger, and it prevents any new invocations of widget code. Put all the code to clean up the widget record into a separate delete procedure like `SquareDestroy`, and call `Tk_Eventu-allyFree` from the event procedure with the delete procedure as its `freeProc` argument.

This approach is a bit conservative but it's simple and safe. For example, most widgets have only one or two widget commands that could cause the widget to be destroyed, such as the `invoke` widget command for buttons. You could move the calls to `Tk_Pre-serve` and `Tk_Release` so that they occur only around code that might destroy the widget, such as a `Tcl_GlobalEval` call. This will save a bit of overhead by eliminating calls to `Tk_Preserve` and `Tk_Release` where they're not needed. However, `Tk_Preserve` and `Tk_Release` are fast enough that this optimization won't save much time and it means you'll constantly have to be on the lookout to add more calls to `Tk_Preserve` and `Tk_Release` if you modify the widget command procedure. If you place the calls at the beginning and end of the procedure you can modify the procedure later without having to worry about issues of widget cleanup. In fact, the square widget doesn't need calls to `Tk_Preserve` and `Tk_Release` at all, but I put them in anyway so that I won't have to remember to add them later if I modify the widget command procedure.

For most widgets the only place you'll need calls to `Tk_Preserve` and `Tk_Release` is in the widget command procedure. However, if you invoke procedures like `Tcl_Eval` or `Tk_DoOneEvent` anywhere else in the widget's code, you'll need additional `Tk_Preserve` and `Tk_Release` calls there too. For example, widgets like canvases and texts implement their own event binding mechanisms in C code; these widgets must invoke `Tk_Preserve` and `Tk_Release` around the calls to event handlers.

The problem of freeing objects while they're in use occurs in many contexts in Tk applications. For example, it's possible for the `-command` option for a button to change the button's `-command` option. This could cause the memory for the old value of the option to be freed while it's still being evaluated by the Tcl interpreter. To eliminate this problem, the button widget evaluates a copy of the script rather than the original. In general whenever you make a call whose behavior isn't completely predictable, such as a call to `Tcl_Eval` and its cousins, you should think about all the objects that are in use at the time of the call and take steps to protect them. In some cases making local copies may be the simplest solution, as with the `-command` option; in more complex cases I'd suggest using `Tk_Preserve` and `Tk_Release`; they can be used for objects of any sort, not just widget records.

Note: *`Tk_Preserve` and `Tk_Release` implement a form of short-term reference counts. They are implemented under the assumption that objects are in use for short periods of time such as the duration of a particular procedure call, so that there are only a few protected objects at any given time. You should not use them for long-term reference counts where there might be hundreds or thousands of objects that are protected at a given time, since they will be very slow in these cases.*

Chapter 44
Managing the Selection

This chapter describes how to manipulate the X selection from C code. The low-level protocols for claiming the selection and transmitting it between applications are defined by X's Inter-Client Communications Convention Manual (ICCCM) and are very complicated. Fortunately Tk takes care of all the low-level details for you and provides three simpler operations that you can perform on the selection:

- Create a *selection handler*, which is a callback procedure that can supply the selection when it is owned in a particular window and retrieved with a particular target.

- Claim ownership of the selection for a particular window.

- Retrieve the selection from its current owner in a particular target form.

Each of these three operations can be performed either with Tcl scripts or C code. Chapter 20 described how to manipulate the selection with Tcl scripts and much of that information applies here as well, such as the use of targets to specify different ways to retrieve the selection. Tcl scripts usually just retrieve the selection; claiming ownership and supplying the selection are rarely done from Tcl. In contrast, it's common to create selection handlers and claim ownership of the selection from C code but rare to retrieve the selection. See Table 44.1 for a summary of the Tk library procedures related to the selection.

44.1 Selection handlers

Each widget that supports the selection, such as an entry or text, must provide one or more *selection handlers* to supply the selection on demand. Each handler returns the selection in

```
void Tk_CreateSelHandler(Tk_Window tkwin, Atom target,
    Tk_SelectionProc *proc, ClientData clientData, Atom format)
```
    Arranges for `proc` to be invoked whenever the selection is owned by
    `tkwin` and is retrieved in the form given by `target`. `format` specifies the
    form in which Tk should transmit the selection to the requestor, and is
    usually `XA_STRING`.
```
void Tk_DeleteSelHandler(Tk_Window tkwin, Atom target)
```
    Removes the handler for `tkwin` and `target`, if one exists.

```
void Tk_OwnSelection(Tk_Window tkwin, Tk_LostSelProc *proc,
    ClientData clientData)
```
    Claims ownership of the selection for `tkwin` and notifies the previous
    owner, if any, that it has lost the selection. `proc` will be invoked later when
    `tkwin` loses the selection.
```
void Tk_ClearSelection(Tk_Window tkwin)
```
    Cancels any existing selection for the display containing `tkwin`.

```
int Tk_GetSelection(Tcl_Interp *interp, Tk_Window tkwin,
    Atom target, Tk_GetSelProc *proc, ClientData clientData)
```
    Retrieves the selection for `tkwin`'s display in the format specified by
    `target` and passes it to `proc` in one or more pieces. Returns `TCL_OK` or
    `TCL_ERROR` and leaves an error message in `interp->result` if an error
    occurs.

Table 44.1. A summary of Tk's procedures for managing the selection.

a particular target form. The procedure `Tk_CreateSelHandler` creates a new selection handler:

```
void Tk_CreateSelHandler(Tk_Window tkwin, Atom target,
        Tk_SelectionProc *proc, ClientData clientData,
        Atom format);
```

`tkwin` is the window from which the selection will be provided; the handler will be asked to supply the selection only when the selection is owned by `tkwin`. `target` specifies the target form in which the handler can supply the selection; the handler will be invoked only when the selection is retrieved with that target. `proc` is the address of the handler callback, and `clientData` is a value to pass to `proc`. `format` tells Tk how to transmit the selection to the requestor and is usually `XA_STRING` (see the reference documentation for other possibilities).

The callback procedure for a selection handler must match the following prototype:

```
typedef int Tk_SelectionProc(ClientData clientData,
        int offset, char *buffer, int maxBytes);
```

The `clientData` argument will be the `clientData` argument passed to `Tk_CreateSelHandler`; it is usually the address of a widget record. `proc` should place a null-terminated string at `buffer` containing up to `maxBytes` of the selection starting at byte offset within the selection. The procedure should return a count of the number of non-null bytes copied, which must be maxBytes unless there are fewer than maxBytes left in the selection. If the widget no longer has a selection (because, for example, the user deleted the selected range of characters), the selection handler should return –1.

Usually the entire selection will be retrieved in a single request: offset will be 0 and maxBytes will be large enough to accommodate the entire selection. However, very large selections will be retrieved in transfers of a few thousand bytes each. Tk will invoke the callback several times using successively higher values of offset to retrieve successive portions of the selection. If the callback returns a value less than maxBytes it means that the entire remainder of the selection has been returned. If its return value is maxBytes it means that there may be additional information in the selection so Tk will call it again to retrieve the next portion. You can assume that maxBytes will always be at least a few thousand.

For example, Tk's entry widgets have a widget record of type Entry with three fields that are used to manage the selection:

- string points to a null-terminated string containing the text in the entry.
- selectFirst is the index in string of the first selected byte (or –1 if nothing is selected).
- selectLast is the index of the last selected byte.

An entry will supply the selection in only one target form (STRING) so it only has a single selection handler. The create procedure for entries contains a statement like the following to create the selection handler, where entryPtr is a pointer to the widget record for the new widget:

```
Tk_CreateSelHandler(entryPtr->tkwin, XA_STRING,
        EntryFetchSelection, (ClientData) entryPtr,
        XA_STRING);
```

The callback for the selection handler is defined as follows:

```
int EntryFetchSelection(ClientData clientData, int offset,
        char *buffer, int maxBytes) {
    Entry *entryPtr = (Entry *) clientData;
    int count;
    if (entryPtr->selectFirst < 0) {
        return -1;
    }
    count = entryPtr->selectLast + 1 - entryPtr->selectFirst
        - offset;
    if (count > maxBytes) {
        count = maxBytes;
    }
    if (count <= 0) {
        count = 0;
    } else {
        strncpy(buffer, entryPtr->string +
```

```
                                    entryPtr->selectFirst + offset, count);
              }
              buffer[count] = 0;
              return count;
       }
```

If a widget wishes to supply the selection in several different target forms it should create a selection handler for each target. When the selection is retrieved, Tk will invoke the handler for the target specified by the retriever.

Tk automatically provides handlers for the following targets:

- APPLICATION: returns the name of the application, which can be used to send commands to the application containing the selection.
- MULTIPLE: used to retrieve the selection in multiple target forms simultaneously. Refer to ICCCM documentation for details.
- TARGETS: returns a list of all the targets supported by the current selection owner (including all the targets supported by Tk).
- TIMESTAMP: returns the time at which the selection was claimed by its current owner.
- WINDOW_NAME: returns the path name of the window that owns the selection.

A widget can override any of these default handlers by creating a handler of its own.

44.2 Claiming the selection

The previous section showed how a widget can supply the selection to a retriever. However, before a widget will be asked to supply the selection it must first claim ownership of the selection. This usually happens during widget commands that select something in the widget, such as the select widget command for entries and listboxes. To claim ownership of the selection, a widget should call Tk_OwnSelection:

```
       void Tk_OwnSelection(Tk_Window tkwin, Tk_LostSelProc *proc,
              (ClientData) clientData);
```

Tk_OwnSelection will communicate with the X server to claim the selection for tkwin; as part of this process the previous owner of the selection will be notified that it has lost the selection. tkwin will remain the selection owner until either some other window claims ownership, tkwin is destroyed, or Tk_ClearSelection is called. When tkwin loses the selection Tk will invoke proc so that the widget can deselect itself and display itself accordingly. proc must match the following prototype:

```
       typedef void Tk_LostSelProc(ClientData clientData);
```

The clientData argument will be the same as the clientData argument to Tk_OwnSelection; it is usually a pointer to the widget's record.

If a widget claims the selection and then eliminates its selection (for example, the selected text is deleted) the widget has three options. First, it can continue to service the selection and return 0 from its selection handlers; anyone who retrieves the selection will receive an empty string. Second, the widget can continue to service the selection and return –1 from its selection handlers; this will return an error ("no selection") to anyone who attempts to retrieve it. Third, the widget can call Tk_ClearSelection:

```
void Tk_ClearSelection(Tk_Window tkwin);
```

The tkwin argument identifies a display. Tk will claim the selection away from whatever window owned it (either in this application or any other application on tkwin's display) and leave the selection unclaimed, so that all attempts to retrieve it will result in errors. This approach will have the same effect as returning –1 from the selection handlers except that the selection handlers will never be invoked.

44.3 Retrieving the selection

If an application wishes to retrieve the selection, for example to insert the selected text into an entry, it usually does so with the selection get Tcl command. This section describes how to retrieve the selection at C level, but this facility is rarely needed. The only situation where I recommend writing C code to retrieve the selection is in cases where the selection may be very large and a Tcl script may be noticeably slow. This might occur in a text widget, for example, where a user might select a whole file in one window and then copy it into another window. If the selection has hundreds of thousands of bytes, a C implementation of the retrieval will be noticeably faster than a Tcl implementation.

To retrieve the selection from C code, invoke the procedure Tk_GetSelection:

```
typedef int Tk_GetSelection(Tcl_Interp *interp,
        Tk_Window tkwin, Atom target, Tk_GetSelProc *proc,
        ClientData clientData);
```

The interp argument is used for error reporting. tkwin specifies the window on whose behalf the selection is being retrieved (it selects a display to use for retrieval), and target specifies the target form for the retrieval. Tk_GetSelection doesn't return the selection directly to its caller. Instead, it invokes proc and passes it the selection. This makes retrieval a bit more complicated but it allows Tk to buffer data more efficiently. Large selections will be retrieved in several pieces, with one call to proc for each piece. Tk_GetSelection normally returns TCL_OK to indicate that the selection was successfully retrieved. If an error occurs, it returns TCL_ERROR and leaves an error message in interp->result.

proc must match the following prototype:

```
typedef int Tk_GetSelProc(ClientData clientData,
        Tcl_Interp *interp, char *portion);
```

The clientData and interp arguments will be the same as the corresponding arguments to Tk_GetSelection. portion points to a null-terminated ASCII string containing part or all of the selection. For small selections a single call will be made to proc with the entire contents of the selection. For large selections two or more calls will be made with successive portions of the selection. `proc` should return `TCL_OK` if it success-fully processes the current portion of the selection. If it encounters an error, it should return `TCL_ERROR` and leave an error message in `interp->result`; the selection retrieval will be aborted and this same error will be returned to `Tk_GetSelection`'s caller.

For example, here is code that retrieves the selection in target form `STRING` and prints it on standard output:

```
    ...
    if (Tk_GetSelection(interp, tkwin,
            Tk_InternAtom(tkwin, "STRING"), PrintSel,
            (ClientData) stdout) != TCL_OK) {
        ...
    }
    ...
int PrintSel(ClientData clientData, Tcl_Interp *interp,
        char *portion) {
    FILE *f = (FILE *) clientData;
    fputs(portion, f);
    return TCL_OK;
}
```

The call to `Tk_GetSelection` could be made, for example, in the widget command procedure for a widget, where `tkwin` is the `Tk_Window` for the widget and `interp` is the interpreter in which the widget command is being processed. The `clientData` argu-ment is used to pass a `FILE` pointer to `PrintSel`. The output could be written to a dif-ferent file by specifying a different `clientData` value.

Chapter 45
Geometry Management

Tk provides two groups of library procedures for geometry management. The first group of procedures implements a communication protocol between slave widgets and their geometry managers. Each widget calls Tk to provide geometry information such as the widget's preferred size and whether or not it has an internal grid. Tk then notifies the relevant geometry manager, so that the widget does not have to know which geometry manager is responsible for it. Each geometry manager calls Tk to identify the slave windows it will manage, so that Tk will know whom to notify when geometry information changes for the slaves. The second group of procedures is used by geometry managers to place slave windows. It includes facilities for mapping and unmapping windows and for setting their sizes and locations. All of these procedures are summarized in Table 45.1.

45.1 Requesting a size for a widget

Each widget is responsible for informing Tk of its geometry needs; Tk will make sure that this information is forwarded to any relevant geometry managers. A slave can provide three pieces of information: requested size, internal border, and grid. The first piece of information is provided by calling Tk_GeometryRequest:

```
void Tk_GeometryRequest(Tk_Window tkwin, int width,
        int height);
```

This indicates that the ideal dimensions for tkwin (in pixels) are width and height. Each widget should call Tk_GeometryRequest once when it is created and again whenever its preferred size changes (such as when its font changes); normally the calls to

```
void Tk_GeometryRequest(Tk_Window tkwin, int width, int height)
            Informs the geometry manager for tkwin that the preferred dimensions are
            width and height.
void Tk_SetInternalBorder(Tk_Window tkwin, int width)
            Informs any relevant geometry managers that tkwin has an internal border
            width pixels wide and that slave windows should not be placed in this
            border region.
void Tk_SetGrid(Tk_Window tkwin, int reqWidth, int reqHeight,
    int widthInc, int heightInc)
            Turns on gridded geometry management for tkwin's top-level window and
            specifies the grid geometry. The dimensions requested by
            Tk_GeometryRequest correspond to grid dimensions of reqWidth and
            reqHeight, and widthInc and heightInc specify the dimensions of a
            single grid cell.
```

```
void Tk_ManageGeometry(Tk_Window tkwin, Tk_GeometryProc *proc,
    ClientData clientData)
            Arranges for proc to be invoked whenever Tk_GeometryRequest is
            invoked for tkwin. Used by geometry managers to claim ownership of a
            slave window.
```

```
int Tk_ReqHeight(Tk_Window tkwin)
            Returns the height specified in the most recent call to
            Tk_GeometryRequest for tkwin (this is a macro, not a procedure).
int Tk_ReqWidth(Tk_Window tkwin)
            Returns the width specified in the most recent call to
            Tk_GeometryRequest for tkwin (this is a macro, not a procedure).
int Tk_InternalBorderWidth(Tk_Window tkwin)
            Returns the border width specified in the most recent call to
            Tk_SetInternalBorderWidth for tkwin (this is a macro, not a
            procedure).
```

```
void Tk_MapWindow(Tk_Window tkwin)
            Arranges for tkwin to be displayed on the screen whenever its ancestors
            are mapped.
void Tk_UnmapWindow(Tk_Window tkwin)
            Prevents tkwin and its descendants from appearing on the screen.
```

Table 45.1. A summary of Tk's procedures for geometry management. The top three procedures are invoked by widgets, while the others are used only by geometry managers. Continued on next page.

Tk_GeometryRequest are made by the widget's configure procedure. In addition, geometry managers will sometimes call Tk_GeometryRequest on a window's behalf. For example, the packer resets the requested size of a master window to match the needs of all of its slaves. This overrides the requested size set by the widget and results in the shrinkwrap effects shown in Chapter 17.

```
void Tk_MoveWindow(Tk_Window tkwin, int x, int y)
                Positions tkwin so that its upper-left pixel (including any borders) appears
                at coordinates x and y in its parent.
void Tk_MoveResizeWindow(Tk_Window tkwin, int x, int y,
        unsigned int width, unsigned int height)
                Changes tkwin's position within its parent and also its size.
void Tk_ResizeWindow(Tk_Window tkwin, unsigned int width,
        unsigned int height)
                Sets the inside dimensions of tkwin (not including its external border, if
                any) to width and height.
```

Table 45.1, continued.

45.2 Internal borders

The X window system allows each window to have a border that appears just outside the window. The official width and height of an X window are the inside dimensions, which describe the usable area of the window and don't include the border. Unfortunately, X requires the entire border of a window to be drawn with a single solid color or stipple. To achieve the Motif three-dimensional effects, the upper and left parts of the border have to be drawn differently than the lower and right parts. This means that X borders can't be used for Motif widgets. Instead, Motif widgets draw their own borders, typically using Tk procedures such as Tk_Draw3DRectangle. The border for a Motif widget is drawn around the perimeter of the widget but inside the official X area of the widget. This kind of border is called an *internal border*. Figure 45.1 shows the difference between external and internal borders.

If a widget has an internal border, its usable area (the part that's inside the internal border) is smaller than its official X area. This complicates geometry management in two ways. First, each widget has to include the border width (actually, twice the border width) in the width and height that it requests via Tk_GeometryRequest. Second, if a master window has an internal border, geometry managers should not place slave windows on top of the border; the usable area for arranging slaves should be the area inside the border. In order for this to happen, the geometry managers must know about the presence of the internal border. The procedure Tk_SetInternalBorder is provided for this purpose:

```
void Tk_SetInternalBorder(Tk_Window tkwin, int width);
```

This tells geometry managers that tkwin has an internal border that is width pixels wide and that slave widgets should not overlap the internal border. Widgets with internal borders normally call Tk_SetInternalBorder in their configure procedures at the same time that they call Tk_GeometryRequest. If a widget uses a normal X border, or

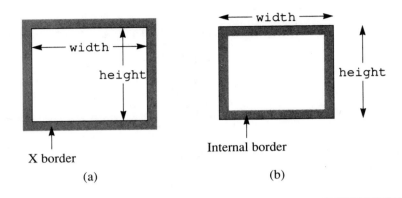

Figure 45.1. X borders and internal borders. Figure (a) shows an official X border, which is drawn by X outside the area of the window. Figure (b) shows an internal border drawn by a widget, where the area occupied by the border is part of the window's official area. In both figures `width` and `height` are the official X dimensions of the window.

if it has an internal border but doesn't mind slaves being placed on top of the border, then it need not call `Tk_SetInternalBorder`, or it can call it with a `width` of 0.

45.3 Grids

Gridded geometry management was introduced in Section 22.2. The goal is to allow the user to resize a top-level window interactively, but to constrain the resizing so that the window's dimensions always lie on a grid. Typically this means that a particular subwindow displaying fixed-width text always has a width and height that are an integral number of characters. The window manager implements constrained resizes, but the application must supply it with the geometry of the grid. In order for this to happen, the widget that determines the grid geometry must call `Tk_SetGrid`:

```
void Tk_SetGrid(Tk_Window tkwin, int gridWidth,
        int gridHeight, int widthInc, int heightInc);
```

The `gridWidth` and `gridHeight` arguments specify the number of grid units corresponding to the pixel dimensions requested in the most recent call to `Tk_GeometryRequest`. They allow the window manager to display the window's current size in grid units rather than pixels. The `widthInc` and `heightInc` arguments specify the number of pixels in a grid unit. Tk passes all of this information on to the window manager, and it will then constrain interactive resizes so that `tkwin`'s top-level window always has dimensions that lie on a grid defined by its requested geometry, `gridWidth`, and `gridHeight`.

Widgets that support gridding, such as texts, normally have a -setgrid option. If -setgrid is 0, the widget doesn't call Tk_SetGrid; this is done if gridded resizing isn't wanted (e.g., the widget uses a variable-width font) or if some other widget in the top-level window is to be the one that determines the grid. If -setgrid is 1, the widget calls Tk_SetGrid; typically this happens in the configure procedure at the same time that other geometry-related calls are made. If the widget's grid geometry changes (because its font has changed, for example), the widget calls Tk_SetGrid again.

45.4 Geometry managers

The remainder of this chapter describes the Tk library procedures that are used by geometry managers. It is intended to provide the basic information that you need to write a new geometry manager. This section provides an overview of the structure of a geometry manager and the following sections describe the Tk library procedures.

A typical geometry manager contains four main procedures. The first procedure is a *command procedure* that implements the geometry manager's Tcl command. Typically each geometry manager provides a single command that is used by the application designer to provide information to the geometry manager: pack for the packer, place for the placer, and so on. The command procedure collects information about slave and master windows managed by the geometry manager and allocates a C structure for each window to hold the information. For example, the packer uses a structure with two parts. The first part is used if the window is a master; it includes information such as a list of slaves for that master. The second part of the structure is used if the window is a slave; it includes information such as the side against which the slave is to be packed and padding and filling information. If a window is both a master and a slave, both parts are used. Each geometry manager maintains a hash table (using Tcl's hash table facilities) that maps from widget names to the C structure for geometry management.

The second procedure for a geometry manager is its *layout procedure*. This procedure performs all of the actual geometry calculations. It uses the information in the structures created by the command procedure, plus geometry information provided by all of the slaves, plus information about the current dimensions of the master. The layout procedure typically has two phases. In the first phase it scans all of the slaves of a given master, computes the ideal size for the master based on the needs of its slaves, and calls Tk_GeometryRequest to set the requested size of the master to the ideal size. This phase only exists for geometry managers like the packer that reflect geometry information upward through the widget hierarchy. For geometry managers like the placer, the first phase is skipped. In the second phase the layout procedure recomputes the geometries for all of the slaves of the master.

The third procedure is a *request callback* that Tk invokes whenever a slave managed by the geometry manager calls Tk_GeometryRequest. The callback arranges for the layout procedure to be executed, as will be described later.

The final procedure is an *event procedure* that is invoked when a master window is resized or when a master or slave window is destroyed. If a master window is resized, the event procedure arranges for the layout procedure to be executed to recompute the geometries of all of its slaves. If a master or slave window is destroyed, the event procedure deletes all of the information maintained by the geometry manager for that window. The command procedure creates event handlers that cause the event procedure to be invoked.

The layout procedure must be invoked after each call to the command procedure, the request callback, or the event procedure. This is usually accomplished with an idle callback, so that the layout procedure doesn't actually execute until all pending work is completed. The idle callback can save a lot of time in situations such as the initial creation of a complex panel. In this case the command procedure will be invoked once for each of many slave windows, but there won't be enough information to compute the final layout until all of the invocations have been made for all of the slaves. If the layout procedure were invoked immediately it would just waste time computing layouts that will be discarded almost immediately. With the idle callback, layout is deferred until complete information is available for all of the slaves.

45.5 Claiming ownership

A geometry manager uses the procedure `Tk_ManageGeometry` to indicate that it wishes to manage the geometry for a given slave window:

```
void Tk_ManageGeometry(Tk_Window tkwin,
        Tk_GeometryProc *proc, ClientData clientData);
```

From this point on, whenever `Tk_GeometryRequest` is invoked for `tkwin`, Tk will invoke `proc`. There can be only one geometry manager for a slave at a given time, so any previous geometry manager is cancelled. A geometry manager can also disown a slave by calling `Tk_ManageGeometry` with a null value for `proc`. `proc` must match the following prototype:

```
typedef void Tk_GeometryProc(ClientData clientData,
        Tk_Window tkwin);
```

The `clientData` and `tkwin` arguments will be the same as those passed to `Tk_ManageGeometry`. Usually `Tk_ManageGeometry` is invoked by the command procedure for a geometry manager, and usually `clientData` is a pointer to the structure holding the geometry manager's information about `tkwin`.

45.6 Retrieving geometry information

When a widget calls `Tk_GeometryRequest` or `Tk_SetInternalBorder`, Tk saves the geometry information in its data structure for the widget. The geometry manager's layout procedure can retrieve the requested dimensions of a slave with the macros `Tk_ReqWidth` and `Tk_ReqHeight`, and it can retrieve the width of a master's internal border with the macro `Tk_InternalBorderWidth`. It can also retrieve the master's actual dimensions with the `Tk_Width` and `Tk_Height` macros, which were originally described in Section 39.5.

Note: *Geometry managers need not worry about the gridding information provided with the* `Tk_SetGrid` *procedure. This information doesn't affect geometry managers at all. It is simply passed on to the window manager for use in controlling interactive resizes.*

45.7 Mapping and setting geometry

A geometry manager does two things to control the placement of a slave window. First, it determines whether the slave window is mapped or unmapped, and second, it sets the size and location of the window.

X allows a window to exist without appearing on the screen. Such a window is called *unmapped*: neither it nor any of its descendants will appear on the screen. In order for a window to appear, it and all of its ancestors (up through the nearest top-level window) must be *mapped*. All windows are initially unmapped. When a geometry manager takes responsibility for a window it must map it by calling `Tk_MapWindow`:

```
void Tk_MapWindow(Tk_Window tkwin);
```

Usually the geometry manager will call `Tk_MapWindow` in its layout procedure once it has decided where the window will appear. If a geometry manager decides not to manage a window anymore (e.g., in the `pack forget` command), it must unmap the window to remove it from the screen:

```
void Tk_UnmapWindow(Tk_Window tkwin);
```

Some geometry managers may temporarily unmap windows during normal operation. For example, the packer unmaps a slave if there isn't enough space in its master to display it; if the master is enlarged later, the slave will be mapped again.

Tk provides three procedures that a geometry manager's layout procedure can use to position slave windows:

```
void Tk_MoveWindow(Tk_Window tkwin, int x, int y);
void Tk_ResizeWindow(Tk_Window tkwin, unsigned int width,
        unsigned int height);
void Tk_MoveResizeWindow(Tk_Window tkwin, int x, int y,
        unsigned int width, unsigned int height);
```

`Tk_MoveWindow` moves a window so that its upper left corner appears at the given location in its parent; `Tk_ResizeWindow` sets the dimensions of a window without moving it; and `Tk_MoveResizeWindow` both moves a window and changes its dimensions.

The position specified to `Tk_MoveWindow` or `Tk_MoveResizeWindow` is a position in the slave's parent. However, most geometry managers allow the master for a slave to be not only its parent but any descendant of the parent. Typically the layout procedure will compute the slave's location relative to its master; before calling `Tk_Move-Window` or `Tk_MoveResizeWindow` it must translate these coordinates to the coordinate system of the slave's parent. The following code shows how to transform coordinates x and y from the master to the parent, assuming that `slave` is the slave window and `master` is its master:

```
int x, y;
Tk_Window slave, master, parent, ancestor;
...
for (ancestor = master; ancestor != Tk_Parent(slave);
        ancestor = Tk_Parent(ancestor)) {
    x += Tk_X(ancestor) + Tk_Changes(ancestor)->border_width;
    y += Tk_Y(ancestor) + Tk_Changes(ancestor)->border_width;
}
```

This code works up through the window hierarchy one level at a time, starting at the master window. At each level it translates the slave window's position from the coordinate system of a window to the coordinate system of its parent. When the parent of the slave is reached, the coordinates are in the correct coordinate system for configuring the slave. The macros `Tk_X`, `Tk_Y`, and `Tk_Changes` were defined in Table 39.2 on page 369; they are used to retrieve the coordinates of a particular window within its parent and the width of a window's X border.

45.8 Writing geometry managers

Writing a new geometry manager is not a very difficult task: most of the work is in the layout procedure, and overall it should be easier to write a new geometry manager than a new widget class. As with widget classes, though, I don't recommend that you start from scratch. I suggest that you first take a look at the code for one of Tk's geometry managers, then copy that code and modify it to create your own geometry manager.

Appendix
and
Index

Appendix A
Installing Tcl and Tk

The source code and reference documentation for Tcl and Tk are freely available. No license is required to use them and there are no restrictions on how you use them (for example, you can redistribute part or all of Tcl or Tk in products). This appendix describes how to retrieve the Tcl and Tk distributions and how to compile and install them on your local system.

A.1   Versions

Tcl and Tk are distributed separately, and each distribution has a version number. A version number consists of two integers separated by a period, such as 3.6 or 7.3. The first of the numbers is the *major version number* and the second is the *minor version number*. Each new release of Tcl or Tk gets a new version number. If the release is compatible with the previous release, it is called a *minor release*: the minor version number increments and the major version number stays the same. For example, Tk 3.2 was a minor release that followed Tk 3.1. Minor releases are compatible in the sense that C code and Tcl scripts written for the old release should also work under the new release without modifications. If a new release includes incompatible changes, it is called a *major release*: the major version number increments and the minor version number resets to zero. For example, Tcl 7.0 was a major release that followed Tcl 6.7. When you upgrade to a major release you will probably have to modify your scripts and C code to work with the new release.

Although Tcl can be used by itself, each release of Tk is designed to be used with a particular release of Tcl. When it starts up, Tk checks the Tcl release number to be sure

Geographic Location	Host Name	Directory
Western USA	`ftp.cs.berkeley.edu`	`/ucb/tcl`
Eastern USA	`ftp.x.org`	`/contrib`
Eastern USA	`ftp.uu.net`	`/languages/tcl`
Central USA	`harbor.ecn.purdue.edu`	`/pub/tcl`
Europe	`ftp.ibp.fr`	`/pub/tcl`
Australia	`syd.dit.csiro.au`	`/pub/tk`
Japan	`ftp2.fujixerox.co.jp`	`/pub/tcl`

Table A.1. FTP sites that are likely to contain the most recent releases of Tcl and Tk. This list was correct as of February 1994 but may change over time.

that it will work with Tk. The matching releases of Tcl and Tk don't necessarily have the same version numbers. For example, Tk 3.6 requires Tcl 7.3.

A.2   The master directory

Before retrieving Tcl and Tk you should pick a directory that will hold the distributions. If you are a system administrator and are planning to intall Tcl and Tk for public use, you might use a public directory such as `/usr/local/src/tcl`. If you are just retrieving Tcl and Tk for your own personal use, you might use a subdirectory of your home directory, such as `~/tcl`. I'll refer to this directory as the *master directory*.

Each distribution will occupy one subdirectory of the master directory, and the name of the subdirectory should be the name of the distribution, complete with version number. For example, if the master directory is `/usr/local/src/tcl`, Tcl 7.3 will be in the directory `/usr/local/src/tcl/tcl7.3` and Tk 3.6 will be in the directory `/usr/local/src/tcl/tk3.6`. If you also have version 2.1 of a contributed Tcl package named BLT, it will be in `/usr/local/src/tcl/blt2.1`, and so on. This structure allows several different versions of a given package to coexist, so users can upgrade to newer releases gradually.

A.3   Retrieving distributions with FTP

The Tcl and Tk distributions can be retrieved over the Internet from the University of California at Berkeley or from any of several other sites; see Table A.1 for a list of sites. You can use a mechanism called "anonymous FTP" (file transfer protocol) for retrievals; on most UNIX workstations you do this by running the `ftp` program from the master directory:

1. Pick a site from Table A.1 and invoke `ftp` with the host name as argument (for example, type `ftp ftp.cs.berkeley.edu` to your shell).

2. The `ftp` program will ask you for an account name. Type `anonymous`.

3. The `ftp` program will then ask you for a password. No password is required for anonymous FTP, but it is customary for you to type your e-mail address instead of a password in order to identify yourself to the remote host.

4. At this point you will be connected to the remote site. Type a `cd` command to change to the Tcl directory (for example, type `cd /ucb/tcl` if you are retrieving from `ftp.cs.berkeley.edu`).

5. Type the command `type image` to make sure that files are transferred in 8-bit binary mode.

6. Type one `get` command for each file you want to retrieve. Most files are stored as compressed `tar` files, so their names will end in `.tar.Z`. For example, to retrieve Tcl version 7.3, type `get tcl7.3.tar.Z`. If you're not sure which files to retrieve, you can type the command `ls` to see what files are available. Or you can retrieve the README file first; it contains a short description of each of the other files in the directory. It's probably best to use the latest versions of Tcl and Tk.

7. When you've retrieved all of the files you want, type `quit` to exit `ftp`.

At this point there will be one or more files with names like `tcl7.3.tar.Z` in the master directory. You can use the programs `zcat` and `tar` to unpack each distribution. For example, if you type

```
zcat tcl7.3.tar.Z | tar xf -
```

to your shell, the Tcl 7.3 distribution will get unpacked and a subdirectory `tcl7.3` will appear, which contains all of the Tcl source code and reference documentation. Once this is done you can delete the file `tcl7.3.tar.Z`.

A.4 Retrieving distributions with electronic mail

If you don't have direct access to the Internet, you will not be able to run the `ftp` program as described in the preceding section. However, if you can send and receive electronic mail, you can still retrieve distributions using a service called `ftpmail`. The `ftpmail` service runs at several sites in the Internet including `wrl.dec.com`. With `ftpmail` you can send an e-mail message indicating which files you would like from which hosts; the `ftpmail` server retrieves the files for you using FTP and mails their contents back to you. To find out more about how to use `ftpmail` just send a message to an `ftpmail` server (for example, mail to ftpmail@wrl.dec.com) whose body consists of the single line help. Directions will be sent back to you via e-mail.

A.5 Compiling and installing the distributions

The Tcl and Tk distributions include sources but no executable binaries. Thus you'll have to compile them before you can use them. There is a README file in the top-level directory for each distribution that contains complete information on how to configure, compile, and install that distribution. However, the distributions can be compiled on almost any UNIX-like workstation just by typing the following shell commands:

```
./configure
make
```

The first command runs a script that probes your system and sets configuration parameters; the second command compiles the distribution. I suggest trying these two commands before you read the README file, since they will almost always work. If these commands fail or you run into other troubles, you can go back and read through README in detail.

If you type the shell command

```
make install
```

from a Tcl or Tk distribution directory, then the binaries will be recompiled and all of the information needed to use the distribution will be installed in a standard place on your system. The default directory for installation is /usr/local, but you can change this by modifying the Makefile (there are instructions in the Makefile). Of course, to install you will need to have write permission on the install directory.

You can run Tcl or Tk without installing them, but in order to do this you will have to set the environment variables TCL_LIBRARY and TK_LIBRARY to tell Tcl and Tk where their library information is located. For example, if your master directory is ~/tcl and you are using Tcl 7.3 and Tk 3.6, you can set TCL_LIBRARY and TK_LIBRARY with the following commands to csh:

```
setenv TCL_LIBRARY ~/tcl/tcl7.3/library
setenv TK_LIBRARY ~/tcl/tk3.6/library
```

If you use sh as your shell, you can use the following commands instead:

```
TCL_LIBRARY=$HOME/tcl/tcl7.3/library
TK_LIBRARY=$HOME/tcl/tk3.6/library
export TCL_LIBRARY
export TK_LIBRARY
```

Once this has been done you can invoke programs like wish and tclsh directly from the directories where they were compiled. However, you will not be able to invoke a script directly unless you change its first line to refer to the directory containing the wish or tclsh executable (see Section 2.3).

A.6 Contributed extensions

Many people have written extensions for Tcl or Tk and made their work freely available to others in the Tcl/Tk community. A few of these packages were described in Section 2.10. As of February 1994 the host `harbor.ecn.purdue.edu` provided an archive of freely available extensions in the FTP directory `/pub/tcl`. You can retrieve information from there using anonymous FTP or `ftpmail`. There should be a README file in the top-level archive directory that describes what is available in the archive and how you can contribute your own packages to it. Most of the packages should have a structure similar to the Tcl and Tk distributions and they should follow the conventions described in Section 31.2, but check each individual package to be sure; there should be a README file that tells how to install that package and describes any peculiarities.

A.7 Comp.lang.tcl newsgroup

An Internet newsgroup named `comp.lang.tcl` exists for the exchange of information about Tcl, Tk, and their applications. New releases of Tcl and Tk are announced on this newsgroup, as are releases of other freely available extensions to Tcl and Tk. The newsgroup is also used to answer questions from Tcl/Tk users, to exchange information about bugs and their fixes, and to discuss possible new features in Tcl and Tk.

Index